MACAULAY

MACAULAY

PROSE AND POETRY

SELECTED BY G. M. YOUNG

RUPERT HART-DAVIS

SOHO SQUARE LONDON

1952

PRINTED AND BOUND IN ENGLAND BY
HAZELL WATSON AND VINEY LTD
AYLESBURY AND LONDON

CONTENTS

CONTENTS

INTRODUCTION

THE volumes in this series are designed to give the reader a faithful picture of the range, and the excellences, of each writer's work. As Macaulay is pre-eminently an historian, selections from his *History of England* necessarily take the first, and fill the largest, place. But even if that history had never been written, Macaulay, in virtue of the *Essays* alone, would have a secure standing among our great prose writers; and when to the *Essays* are added the speeches, and to the speeches the *Lays of Ancient Rome*, the breadth of his *œuvre*, and his mastery in each kind, are not easy to parallel in any other author, or in any age of our literature. Nor do these complete the tale, because the *Epitaph on a Jacobite* and *The Last Buccaneer* disclose yet another facet, a glimpse of poetic sensibility and refinement which, without them, we might have thought lacking from the trenchant, emphatic temper of the historian, the critic, the orator. Of that strange piece, *Tirzah and Ahirad*, every reader will judge for himself: to me it sounds as if Macaulay had set himself to write a poem which John Martin might illustrate.

One paper, by the kindness of Dr. G. M. Trevelyan, is now published for the first time—Macaulay's note of the proceedings of the Privy Council on the occasion of an attempt on the life of Queen Victoria. Apart from its historic interest it illustrates Macaulay's habit of putting everything that befell him on to paper at once, a habit which no doubt did much to sharpen his gift for historic narrative.

It is not difficult to understand why Macaulay's writing, so abundant and downright in substance, so highly coloured and so strongly cadenced, should have taken contemporaries captive. Nor is the reaction less comprehensible. When Ruskin, three years before Macaulay's death, spoke of "the beautiful, quiet, English" of Sir Arthur Helps, he anticipated the change of taste that was rapidly setting in. Macaulay is loud. He writes as if his purpose was less to convince than to silence his readers: not to win their agreement but to force their assent. Naturally, the new age rebelled, the more hotly perhaps because the large unlettered public was faithful, not caring whether their favourite was a bad historian, as Seeley said; a bully, as John Morley said; or that his verses sometimes made Matthew Arnold cry out in pain. That revolt has long died away. The last shot was fired by Lytton Strachey when he spoke of the Philistine on Parnassus. On Parnassus, truly. But it was no Philistine who wrote,

> Heard on Lavernia Scargill's whispering trees,
> And pined by Arno for my lovelier Tees;

or who could say of Dante what Dante had said of Virgil:

> Vagliami il lungo studio e il grande amore.

G.M.Y.

CHRONOLOGICAL TABLE

1800	Thomas Babington Macaulay, born at Rothley Temple, Leicestershire, 25 October, eldest son of Zachary Macaulay and Selena Mills.
1812–4	At school in Little Shelford, Cambridgeshire, and Aspenden Hall, near Buntingford, Hertfordshire.
1818	Went up to Trinity College, Cambridge.
1819	His poem, *Pompeii*, won the Chancellor's medal.
1823	First article in *Knight's Quarterly Magazine*, Spring.
1824–31	Fellow of Trinity College, Cambridge.
1825	First article in *Edinburgh Review*, August.
1826	Called to the bar.
1828	Commissioner of Bankruptcy.
1830	Liberal M.P. for Calne. Maiden speech, 5 April.
1831	First speech on Parliamentary Reform, 1 March. Pocket-borough of Calne dissolved by Reform Bill.
1832	Elected M.P. for Leeds. Commissioner, and later Secretary, of the Board of Control.
1834	Sailed for India, 15 February. Member of the Supreme Council for India until 1838.
1835	Minute on Indian Education, 2 February. President of the Commission for Composing a Criminal Code for India.
1837	Indian Criminal Code published (came into force 1862). Embarked for England, December.
1839	Began *History of England*, 9 March. M.P. for Edinburgh, June. Secretary-at-War (until 1841), September.
1840	Edward Oxford's attempt on the life of the Queen and Prince Consort, 10 June.
1841	Fall of Whig Government. General Election. Macaulay re-elected for Edinburgh, August. Resumed work on *History of England*, 5 November.
1842	*Lays of Ancient Rome*.
1843	*Critical and Historical Essays*, January.
1846	Whigs returned to office, Macaulay Paymaster-General, 30 June.
1847	General Election. Macaulay lost his seat, July.
1848	*History of England*, Volumes I and II, December.
1849	Lord Rector of Glasgow University.

1852	M.P. for Edinburgh, 13 July. Breakdown in his health, 22 July.
1854	*Speeches.*
1855	*History of England*, Volumes III and IV.
1857	Created Baron Macaulay of Rothley.
1859	Died, 28 December.
1860	Buried in Westminster Abbey, 9 January.

THE HISTORY OF ENGLAND

The first two volumes of *The History of England from the Accession of James II* were published by Longman in December 1848, though the title-pages are dated 1849. The third and fourth volumes did not appear until 1855. In 1857 Macaulay began revising these first four volumes, adding some new matter, correcting errors which had been pointed out, and taking pains to standardise spelling and typography. Volumes One and Two are especially heavily corrected. "I have no more corrections to make at present," he wrote to Longman. "I am inclined to hope that the book will be as nearly faultless, as to typographical execution, as any work of equal extent that is to be found in the world." This revised edition of Volumes One to Four was printed from the original type, much corrected, and appeared in 1858. When Macaulay died in 1859 the *History* remained unfinished. Three new chapters had been written and were ready for press; he had also left two unrevised fragments. His sister, Lady Trevelyan, edited these remains, and Longman published them as a fifth volume in 1861. The present selection follows the text of the revised edition of 1858, except in the case of the passage on Darien which comes from the fifth volume of 1861. All the original footnotes, most of them references to sources, have been omitted.

MONMOUTH'S CAMPAIGN

On the morning of the eleventh of June [1685] the Helderenbergh, accompanied by two smaller vessels, appeared off the port of Lyme. That town is a small knot of steep and narrow alleys, lying on a coast wild, rocky, and beaten by a stormy sea. The place was then chiefly remarkable for a pier which, in the days of the Plantagenets, had been constructed of stones, unhewn and uncemented. This ancient work, known by the name of the Cob, enclosed the only haven where, in a space of many miles, the fisherman could take refuge from the tempests of the Channel.

The appearance of the three ships, foreign built and without colours, perplexed the inhabitants of Lyme; and the uneasiness increased when it was found that the Customhouse officers, who had gone on board according to usage, did not return. The town's people repaired to the cliffs, and gazed long and anxiously, but could find no solution of the mystery. At length seven boats put off from the largest of the strange vessels, and rowed to the shore. From these boats landed about eighty men, well armed and appointed. Among them were Monmouth, Grey, Fletcher, Ferguson, Wade, and Anthony Buyse, an officer who had been in the service of the Elector of Brandenburg.

Monmouth commanded silence, kneeled down on the shore, thanked God for having preserved the friends of liberty and pure religion from the perils of the sea, and implored the divine blessing on what was yet to be done by land. He then drew his sword and led his men over the cliffs into the town.

As soon as it was known under what leader and for what purpose the expedition came, the enthusiasm of the populace burst through all restraints. The little town was in an uproar with men running to and fro, and shouting "A Monmouth! a Monmouth! the Protestant religion!" Meanwhile the ensign of the adventurers, a blue

13

flag, was set up in the market place. The military stores were deposited in the town hall; and a Declaration setting forth the objects of the expedition was read from the Cross.

This Declaration, the masterpiece of Ferguson's genius, was not a grave manifesto such as ought to be put forth by a leader drawing the sword for a great public cause, but a libel of the lowest class, both in sentiment and language. It contained undoubtedly many just charges against the government. But these charges were set forth in the prolix and inflated style of a bad pamphlet; and the paper contained other charges of which the whole disgrace falls on those who made them. The Duke of York, it was positively affirmed, had burned down London, had strangled Godfrey, had cut the throat of Essex, and had poisoned the late King. On account of those villainous and unnatural crimes, but chiefly of that execrable fact, the late horrible and barbarous parricide,—such was the copiousness and such the felicity of Ferguson's diction,—James was declared a mortal and bloody enemy, a tyrant, a murderer, and an usurper. No treaty should be made with him. The sword should not be sheathed till he had been brought to condign punishment as a traitor. The government should be settled on principles favourable to liberty. All Protestant sects should be tolerated. The forfeited charters should be restored. Parliaments should be held annually, and should no longer be prorogued or dissolved by royal caprice. The only standing force should be the militia: the militia should be commanded by the Sheriffs; and the Sheriffs should be chosen by the freeholders. Finally Monmouth declared that he could prove himself to have been born in lawful wedlock, and to be, by right of blood, King of England, but that, for the present, he waived his claims, that he would leave them to the judgment of a free Parliament, and that, in the meantime, he desired to be considered only as the Captain General of the English Protestants who were in arms against tyranny and Popery.

Disgraceful as this manifesto was to those who put it forth, it was not unskilfully framed for the purpose of stimulating the passions of the vulgar. In the West the effect was great. The gentry and clergy of that part of England were indeed, with few exceptions, Tories. But the yeomen, the traders of the towns, the peasants, and the artisans, were generally animated by the old Roundhead spirit. Many of them were Dissenters, and had been goaded by petty persecution into a temper fit for desperate enterprise. The great mass of the population abhorred Popery and adored Monmouth. He was no stranger to them. His progress through Somersetshire and Devonshire in the summer of 1680 was still fresh in the memory of all men. He was on that occasion sumptuously entertained by Thomas Thynne at Longleat Hall, then, and perhaps still, the most magnificent country house in England. From Longleat to Exeter the hedges were lined with shouting spectators. The roads were strewn with boughs and flowers. The multitude, in their eagerness to see and touch their favourite, broke down the palings of parks, and besieged the mansions where he was feasted. When he reached Chard his escort consisted of five thousand horsemen. At Exeter all Devonshire had been gathered together to welcome him. One striking part of the show was a company of nine hundred young men who, clad in a white uniform, marched before him into the city. The turn of fortune which had alienated the gentry from his cause had produced no effect on the common people. To them he was still the good Duke, the Protestant Duke, the rightful heir whom a vile conspiracy kept out of his own. They came to his standard in crowds. All the clerks whom he could employ were too few to take down the names of the recruits. Before he had been twenty four hours on English ground he was at the head of fifteen hundred men. Dare arrived from Taunton with forty horsemen of no very martial appearance, and brought encouraging intelligence as to the state of public feeling in Somersetshire. As yet all seemed to promise well.

But a force was collecting at Bridport to oppose the insurgents. On the thirteenth of June the red regiment of Dorsetshire militia came pouring into that town. The Somersetshire, or yellow regiment, of which Sir William Portman, a Tory gentleman of great note, was Colonel, was expected to arrive on the following day. The Duke determined to strike an immediate blow. A detachment of his troops was preparing to march to Bridport when a disastrous event threw the whole camp into confusion.

Fletcher of Saltoun had been appointed to command the cavalry under Grey. Fletcher was ill mounted; and indeed there were few chargers in the camp which had not been taken from the plough. When he was ordered to Bridport, he thought that the exigency of the case warranted him in borrowing, without asking permission, a fine horse belonging to Dare. Dare resented this liberty, and assailed Fletcher with gross abuse. Fletcher kept his temper better than any one who knew him expected. At last Dare, presuming on the patience with which his insolence was endured, ventured to shake a switch at the high born and high spirited Scot. Fletcher's blood boiled. He drew a pistol and shot Dare dead. Such sudden and violent revenge would not have been thought strange in Scotland, where the law had always been weak, where he who did not right himself by the strong hand was not likely to be righted at all, and where, consequently, human life was held almost as cheap as in the worst governed provinces of Italy. But the people of the southern part of the island were not accustomed to see deadly weapons used and blood spilled on account of a rude word or gesture, except in duel between gentlemen with equal arms. There was a general cry for vengeance on the foreigner who had murdered an Englishman. Monmouth could not resist the clamour. Fletcher, who, when his first burst of rage had spent itself, was overwhelmed with remorse and sorrow, took refuge on board of the Helderenbergh, escaped to the Continent, and repaired to Hungary, where he fought bravely against the common enemy of Christendom.

Situated as the insurgents were, the loss of a man of parts and energy was not easily to be repaired. Early on the morning of the following day, the fourteenth of June, Grey, accompanied by Wade, marched with about five hundred men to attack Bridport. A confused and indecisive action took place, such as was to be expected when two bands of ploughmen, officered by country gentlemen and barristers, were opposed to each other. For a time Monmouth's men drove the militia before them. Then the militia made a stand, and Monmouth's men retreated in some confusion. Grey and his cavalry never stopped till they were safe at Lyme again: but Wade rallied the infantry, and brought them off in good order.

There was a violent outcry against Grey; and some of the adventurers pressed Monmouth to take a severe course. Monmouth, however, would not listen to this advice. His lenity has been attributed by some writers to his good nature, which undoubtedly often amounted to weakness. Others have supposed that he was unwilling to deal harshly with the only peer who served in his army. It is probable, however, that the Duke, who, though not a general of the highest order, understood war very much better than the preachers and lawyers who were always obtruding their advice on him, made allowances which people altogether inexpert in military affairs never thought of making. In justice to a man who has had few defenders, it must be observed that the task, which, throughout this campaign, was assigned to Grey, was one which, if he had been the boldest and most skilful of soldiers, he could scarcely have performed in such a manner as to gain credit. He was at the head of the cavalry. It is notorious that a horse soldier requires a longer training than a foot soldier, and that the war horse requires a longer training than his rider. Something may be done with a raw infantry which has enthusiasm and animal courage: but nothing can be more helpless than a raw cavalry, consisting of yeomen and tradesmen mounted on cart horses and post horses; and such was the cavalry which Grey commanded. The wonder is, not that his men did not stand fire with resolution, not that they did not use their weapons with vigour, but that they were able to keep their seats.

Still recruits came in by hundreds. Arming and drilling went on all day. Meantime the news of the insurrection had spread fast and wide. On the evening on which the Duke landed, Gregory Alford, Mayor of Lyme, a zealous Tory, and a most bitter persecutor of Nonconformists, sent off his servants to give the alarm to the gentry of Somersetshire and Dorsetshire, and himself took horse for the West. Late at night he stopped at Honiton, and thence despatched a few hurried lines to London with the ill tidings. He then pushed on to Exeter, where he found Christopher Monk, Duke of Albemarle. This nobleman, the son and heir of George Monk, the restorer of the Stuarts, was Lord Lieutenant of Devonshire, and was then holding a muster of militia. Four thousand men of the trainbands were actually assembled under his command. He seems to have thought that, with this force, he should be able at once to crush the rebellion. He therefore marched towards Lyme.

But when, on the afternoon of Monday the fifteenth of June, he reached Axminster, he found the insurgents drawn up there to encounter him. They presented a resolute front. Four field pieces were pointed against the royal troops. The thick hedges, which on each side overhung the narrow lanes, were lined with musketeers. Albemarle, however, was less alarmed by the preparations of the enemy than by the spirit which appeared in his own ranks. Such was Monmouth's popularity among the common people of Devonshire that, if once the trainbands had caught sight of his well known face and figure, they would probably have gone over to him in a body.

Albemarle, therefore, though he had a great superiority of force, thought it advisable to retreat. The retreat soon became a rout. The whole country was strewn with the arms and uniforms which the fugitives had thrown away; and, had Monmouth urged the pursuit with vigour, he would probably have taken Exeter without a blow. But he was satisfied with the advantage which he had gained, and thought it desirable that his recruits should be better trained before they were employed in any hazardous service. He therefore marched towards Taunton, where he arrived on the eighteenth of June, exactly a week after his landing.

The Court and the Parliament had been greatly moved by the news from the West. At five in the morning of Saturday the thirteenth of June, the King had received the letter which the Mayor of Lyme had despatched from Honiton. The Privy Council was instantly called together. Orders were given that the strength of every company of infantry and of every troop of cavalry should be increased. Commissions were issued for the levying of new regiments. Alford's communication was laid before the Lords; and its substance was communicated to the Commons by a message. The Commons examined the couriers who had arrived from the West, and instantly ordered a bill to be brought in for attainting Monmouth of high treason. Addresses were voted assuring the King that both his peers and his people were determined to stand by him with life and fortune against all his enemies. At the next meeting of the Houses they ordered the declaration of the rebels to be burned by the hangman, and passed the bill of attainder through all its stages. That bill received the royal assent on the same day; and a reward of five thousand pounds was promised for the apprehension of Monmouth.

The fact that Monmouth was in arms against the government was so notorious that the bill of attainder became a law with only a faint show of opposition from one or two peers, and has seldom been severely censured even by Whig historians. Yet, when we consider how important it is that legislative and judicial functions should be kept distinct, how important it is that common fame, however strong and general, should not be received as a legal proof of guilt, how important it is to maintain the rule that no man shall be condemned to death without an opportunity of defending himself, and how easily and speedily breaches in great principles, when once made, are widened, we shall probably be disposed to think that the course taken by the Parliament was open to some objection. Neither House had before it any thing which even so corrupt a judge as Jeffreys could have directed a jury to consider as proof of Monmouth's crime. The messengers examined by the Commons were not on oath, and might therefore have related mere fictions without incurring the penalties of perjury. The Lords, who might have administered an oath, appear not to have examined any witness, and to have had no evidence before them except the letter of the Mayor of Lyme, which, in the eye of the law, was no evidence at all. Extreme danger, it is true, justifies extreme remedies. But the Act of Attainder was a remedy which could not operate till all danger was over, and which would become superfluous at the very moment at which it ceased to be null. While Monmouth was in arms it was impossible to execute him. If he should be vanquished and taken, there would be no hazard and no difficulty in trying him.

It was afterwards remembered as a curious circumstance that, among the zealous Tories who went up with the bill from the House of Commons to the bar of the Lords, was Sir John Fenwick, member for Northumberland. This gentleman, a few years later, had occasion to reconsider the whole subject, and then came to the conclusion that acts of attainder are altogether unjustifiable.

The Parliament gave other proofs of loyalty in this hour of peril. The Commons authorised the King to raise an extraordinary sum of four hundred thousand pounds for his present necessities, and, that he might have no difficulty in finding the money, proceeded to devise new imposts. The scheme of taxing houses lately built in the capital was revived and strenuously supported by the country gentlemen. It was resolved not only that such houses should be taxed, but that a bill should be brought in prohibiting the laying of any new foundations within the bills of mortality. The resolution, however, was not carried into effect. Powerful men who had land in the suburbs, and who hoped to see new streets and squares rise on their estates, exerted all their influence against the project. It was found that to adjust the details would be a work of time; and the King's wants were so pressing that he thought it necessary to quicken the movements of the House by a gentle exhortation to speed. The plan of taxing buildings was therefore relinquished; and new duties were imposed for a term of five years on foreign silks, linens, and spirits.

The Tories of the Lower House proceeded to introduce what they called a bill for the preservation of the King's person and government. They proposed that it should be high treason to say that Monmouth was legitimate, to utter any words tending to bring the person or government of the sovereign into hatred or contempt, or to make any motion in Parliament for changing the order of succession. Some of these provisions excited general disgust and alarm. The Whigs, few and weak as they were, attempted to rally, and found themselves reinforced by a considerable number of moderate and sensible Cavaliers. Words, it was said, may easily be misunderstood by a dull man. They may easily be misconstrued by a knave. What was spoken metaphorically may be apprehended literally. What was spoken ludicrously may be apprehended seriously. A particle, a tense, a mood, an emphasis, may make the whole difference between guilt and innocence. The Saviour of mankind himself, in whose blameless life malice could find no act to impeach, had been called in question for words spoken. False witnesses had suppressed a syllable which would have made it clear that those words were figurative, and had thus furnished the

Sanhedrim with a pretext under which the foulest of all judicial murders had been perpetrated. With such an example on record, who could affirm that, if mere talk were made a substantive treason, the most loyal subject would be safe? These arguments produced so great an effect that in the committee amendments were introduced which greatly mitigated the severity of the bill. But the clause which made it high treason in a member of Parliament to propose the exclusion of a prince of the blood seems to have raised no debate, and was retained. The clause was indeed altogether unimportant, except as a proof of the ignorance and inexperience of the hotheaded Royalists who thronged the House of Commons. Had they learned the first rudiments of legislation, they would have known that the enactment to which they attached so much value would be superfluous while the Parliament was disposed to maintain the order of succession, and would be repealed as soon as there was a Parliament bent on changing the order of succession.

The bill, as amended, was passed and carried up to the Lords, but did not become law. The King had obtained from the Parliament all the pecuniary assistance that he could expect; and he conceived that, while rebellion was actually raging, the loyal nobility and gentry would be of more use in their counties than at Westminster. He therefore hurried their deliberations to a close, and, on the second of July, dismissed them. On the same day the royal assent was given to a law reviving that censorship of the press which had terminated in 1679. This object was effected by a few words at the end of a miscellaneous statute which continued several expiring acts. The courtiers did not think that they had gained a triumph. The Whigs did not utter a murmur. Neither in the Lords nor in the Commons was there any division, or even, as far as can now be learned, any debate on a question which would, in our age, convulse the whole frame of society. In truth, the change was slight and almost imperceptible; for, since the detection of the Rye House plot, the liberty of unlicensed printing had existed only in name. During many months scarcely one Whig pamphlet had been published except by stealth; and by stealth such pamphlets might be published still.

The Houses then rose. They were not prorogued, but only adjourned, in order that, when they should reassemble, they might take up their business in the exact state in which they had left it.

While the Parliament was devising sharp laws against Monmouth and his partisans, he found at Taunton a reception which might well encourage him to hope that his enterprise would have a prosperous issue. Taunton, like most other towns in the south of England, was, in that age, more important than at present. Those towns have not indeed declined. On the contrary, they are, with very few exceptions, larger and richer, better built and better peopled, than in the seventeenth century. But, though they have positively advanced, they have relatively gone back. They have been far outstripped in wealth and population by the great manufacturing and commercial cities of the north, cities which, in the time of the Stuarts, were but beginning to be known as seats of industry. When Monmouth marched into Taunton it was an eminently prosperous place. Its markets were plentifully supplied. It was a celebrated seat of the woollen manufacture. The people boasted that they lived in a land flowing with milk and honey. Nor was this language held only by partial natives; for every stranger who climbed the graceful tower of Saint Mary Magdalene owned that he saw beneath him the most fertile of English valleys. It was a country rich with orchards and green pastures, among which were scattered, in gay abundance, manor houses, cottages, and village spires. The townsmen had long leaned towards Presbyterian divinity and Whig politics. In the great civil war Taunton had, through all vicissitudes, adhered to the Parliament, had been twice closely besieged by Goring, and had been twice defended with heroic valour by Robert Blake, afterwards the renowned Admiral of the Commonwealth. Whole streets had been burned down by the mortars and grenades of the Cavaliers. Food had been so scarce that the resolute governor had announced his intention of putting the garrison on rations of horse flesh. But the spirit of the town had never been subdued either by fire or by hunger.

The Restoration had produced no effect on the temper of the Taunton men. They had still continued to celebrate the anniversary of the happy day on which the siege laid to their town by the royal army had been raised; and their stubborn attachment to the old cause had excited so much fear and resentment at Whitehall that, by a royal order, their moat had been filled up, and their wall demolished to the foundation. The puritanical spirit had been kept up to the height among them by the precepts and example of one of the most celebrated of the dissenting clergy, Joseph Alleine. Alleine was the author of a tract, entitled, An Alarm to the Unconverted, which is still popular both in England and in America. From the gaol to which he was consigned by the victorious Cavaliers, he addressed to his loving friends at Taunton many epistles breathing the spirit of a truly heroic piety. His frame soon sank under the effects of study, toil, and persecution: but his memory was long cherished with exceeding love and reverence by those whom he had exhorted and catechised.

The children of the men who, forty years before, had manned the ramparts of Taunton against the Royalists, now welcomed Monmouth with transports of joy and affection. Every door and window was adorned with wreaths of flowers. No man appeared in the streets without wearing in his hat a green bough, the badge of the popular cause. Damsels of the best families in the town wove colours for the insurgents. One flag in particular was embroidered gorgeously with emblems of royal dignity, and was offered to Monmouth by a train of young girls. He received the gift with the winning courtesy which distinguished him. The lady who headed the procession presented him also with a small Bible of great price. He took it with a show of reverence. "I come," he said, "to defend the truths contained in this book, and to seal them, if it must be so, with my blood."

But, while Monmouth enjoyed the applause of the multitude, he could not but perceive, with concern and apprehension, that the higher classes were, with scarcely an exception, hostile to his undertaking, and that no rising had taken place except in the counties where he had himself appeared. He had been assured by agents, who professed to have derived their information from Wildman, that the whole Whig aristocracy was eager to take arms. Nevertheless more than a week had now elapsed since the blue standard had been set up at Lyme. Day labourers, small farmers, shopkeepers, apprentices, dissenting preachers, had flocked to the rebel camp: but not a single peer, baronet, or knight, not a single member of the House of Commons, and scarcely any esquire of sufficient note to have ever been in the commission of the peace, had joined the invaders. Ferguson, who, ever since the death of Charles, had been Monmouth's evil angel, had a suggestion ready. The Duke had put himself into a false position by declining the royal title. Had he declared himself sovereign of England, his cause would have worn a show of legality. At present it was impossible to reconcile his Declaration with the principles of the constitution. It was clear that either Monmouth or his uncle was rightful King. Monmouth did not venture to pronounce himself the rightful King, and yet denied that his uncle was so. Those who fought for James fought for the only person who ventured to claim the throne, and were therefore clearly in their duty, according to the laws of the realm. Those who fought for Monmouth fought for some unknown polity, which was to be set up by a convention not yet in existence. None could wonder that men of high rank and ample fortune stood aloof from an enterprise which threatened with destruction that system in the permanence of which they were deeply interested. If the

Duke would assert his legitimacy and assume the crown, he would at once remove this objection. The question would cease to be a question between the old constitution and a new constitution. It would be merely a question of hereditary right between two princes.

On such grounds as these Ferguson, almost immediately after the landing, had earnestly pressed the Duke to proclaim himself King; and Grey had seconded Ferguson. Monmouth had been very willing to take this advice; but Wade and other republicans had been refractory; and their chief, with his usual pliability, had yielded to their arguments. At Taunton the subject was revived. Monmouth talked in private with the dissentients, assured them that he saw no other way of obtaining the support of any portion of the aristocracy, and succeeded in extorting their reluctant consent. On the morning of the twentieth of June he was proclaimed in the market place of Taunton. His followers repeated his new title with affectionate delight. But, as some confusion might have arisen if he had been called King James the Second, they commonly used the strange appellation of King Monmouth: and by this name their unhappy favourite was often mentioned in the western counties, within the memory of persons still living.

Within twenty four hours after he had assumed the regal title, he put forth several proclamations headed with his sign manual. By one of these he set a price on the head of his rival. Another declared the Parliament then sitting at Westminster an unlawful assembly, and commanded the members to disperse. The third forbade the people to pay taxes to the usurper. The fourth pronounced Albemarle a traitor.

Albemarle transmitted these proclamations to London merely as specimens of folly and impertinence. They produced no effect, except wonder and contempt; nor had Monmouth any reason to think that the assumption of royalty had improved his position. Only a week had elapsed since he had solemnly bound himself not to take the crown till a free Parliament should have acknowledged his rights. By breaking that engagement he had incurred the imputation of levity, if not of perfidy. The class which he had hoped to conciliate still stood aloof. The reasons which prevented the great Whig lords and gentlemen from recognising him as their King were at least as strong as those which had prevented them from rallying round him as their Captain General. They disliked indeed the person, the religion, and the politics of James. But James was no longer young. His eldest daughter was justly popular. She was attached to the reformed faith. She was married to a prince who was the hereditary chief of the Protestants of the Continent, to a prince who had been bred in a republic, and whose sentiments were supposed to be such as became a constitutional King. Was it wise to incur the horrors of civil war, for the mere chance of being able to effect immediately what nature would, without bloodshed, without any violation of law, effect, in all probability, before many years should have expired? Perhaps there might be reasons for pulling down James. But what reason could be given for setting up Monmouth? To exclude a prince from the throne on account of unfitness was a course agreeable to Whig principles. But on no principle could it be proper to exclude rightful heirs, who were admitted to be, not only blameless, but eminently qualified for the highest public trust. That Monmouth was legitimate, nay, that he thought himself legitimate, intelligent men could not believe. He was therefore not merely an usurper, but an usurper of the worst sort, an impostor. If he made out any semblance of a case, he could do so only by means of forgery and perjury. All honest and sensible persons were unwilling to see a fraud which, if practised to obtain an estate, would have been punished with the scourge and the pillory, rewarded with the English crown. To the old nobility of the realm it seemed insupportable that the bastard of Lucy Walters should be set up high above the lawful descendants of the Fitzalans and De Veres. Those who were capable of looking forward must have seen that, if Monmouth should succeed in over-powering the existing government, there would still remain a war between him and the House of Orange, a war which might last longer and produce more misery than the war of the Roses, a war which might probably break up the Protestants of Europe into hostile parties, might arm England and Holland against each other, and might make both those countries an easy prey to France. The opinion, therefore, of almost all the leading Whigs seems to have been that Monmouth's enterprise could not fail to end in some great disaster to the nation, but that, on the whole, his defeat would be a less disaster than his victory.

It was not only by the inaction of the Whig aristocracy that the invaders were disappointed. The wealth and power of London had sufficed in the preceding generation, and might again suffice, to turn the scale in a civil conflict. The Londoners had formerly given many proofs of their hatred of Popery and of their affection for the Protestant Duke. He had too readily believed that, as soon as he landed, there would be a rising in the capital. But, though advices came down to him that many thousands of the citizens had been enrolled as volunteers for the good cause, nothing was done. The plain truth was that the agitators who had encouraged him to invade

England, who had promised to rise on the first signal, and who had perhaps imagined, while the danger was remote, that they should have the courage to keep their promise, lost heart when the critical time drew near. Wildman's fright was such that he seemed to have lost his understanding. The craven Danvers at first excused his inaction by saying that he would not take up arms till Monmouth was proclaimed King, and, when Monmouth had been proclaimed King, turned round and declared that good republicans were absolved from all engagements to a leader who had so shamefully broken faith. In every age the vilest specimens of human nature are to be found among demagogues.

On the day following that on which Monmouth had assumed the regal title he marched from Taunton to Bridgewater. His own spirits, it was remarked, were not high. The acclamations of the devoted thousands who surrounded him wherever he turned could not dispel the gloom which sate on his brow. Those who had seen him during his progress through Somersetshire five years before could not now observe without pity the traces of distress and anxiety on those soft and pleasing features which had won so many hearts.

Ferguson was in a very different temper. With this man's knavery was strangely mingled an eccentric vanity which resembled madness. The thought that he had raised a rebellion and bestowed a crown had turned his head. He swaggered about, brandishing his naked sword, and crying to the crowd of spectators who had assembled to see the army march out of Taunton, "Look at me! You have heard of me. I am Ferguson, the famous Ferguson, the Ferguson for whose head so many hundred pounds have been offered." And this man, at once unprincipled and brainsick, had in his keeping the understanding and the conscience of the unhappy Monmouth.

Bridgewater was one of the few towns which still had some Whig magistrates. The mayor and aldermen came in their robes to welcome the Duke, walked before him in procession to the high cross, and there proclaimed him King. His troops found excellent quarters, and were furnished with necessaries at little or no cost by the people of the town and neighbourhood. He took up his residence in the Castle, a building which had been previously honoured by royal visits. In the Castle Field his army was encamped. It now consisted of about six thousand men, and might easily have been increased to double the number, but for the want of arms. The Duke had brought with him from the Continent but a scanty supply of pikes and muskets. Many of his followers had, therefore, no other weapons than such as could be made out of the tools which they had used in husbandry or mining. Of these rude implements of war the most formidable was made by fastening the blade of a scythe erect on a strong pole. The tithing men of the country round Taunton and Bridgewater received orders to search everywhere for scythes and to bring all that could be found to the camp. It was impossible, however, even with the help of these contrivances, to supply the demand; and great numbers who were desirous to enlist were sent away.

The foot were divided into six regiments. Many of the men had been in the militia, and still wore their uniforms, red and yellow. The cavalry were about a thousand in number; but most of them had only large colts, such as were then bred in great herds on the marshes of Somersetshire for the purpose of supplying London with coach horses and cart horses. These animals were so far from being fit for any military purpose that they had not yet learned to obey the bridle, and became ungovernable as soon as they heard a gun fired or a drum beaten. A small body guard of forty young men, well armed and mounted at their own charge, attended Monmouth. The people of Bridgewater, who were enriched by a thriving coast trade, furnished him with a small sum of money.

All this time the forces of the government were fast assembling. On the west of the rebel army Albemarle still kept together a large body of Devonshire militia. On the east, the trainbands of Wiltshire had mustered under the command of Thomas Herbert, Earl of Pembroke. On the north east, Henry Somerset, Duke of Beaufort, was in arms. The power of Beaufort bore some faint resemblance to that of the great barons of the fifteenth century. He was President of Wales and Lord Lieutenant of four English counties. His official tours through the extensive region in which he represented the majesty of the throne were scarcely inferior in pomp to royal progresses. His household at Badminton was regulated after the fashion of an earlier generation. The land to a great extent round his pleasure grounds was in his own hands; and the labourers who cultivated it formed part of his family. Nine tables were every day spread under his roof for two hundred persons. A crowd of gentlemen and pages were under the orders of his steward. A whole troop of cavalry obeyed the master of the horse. The fame of the kitchen, the cellar, the kennel, and the stables was spread over all England. The gentry, many miles round, were proud of the magnificence of their great neighbour, and were at the same time charmed by his affability and good nature. He was a zealous Cavalier of the old school. At this crisis, therefore, he used his whole influence and authority in support of the crown, and occupied Bristol with the trainbands of Gloucestershire, who seem to have been better disciplined than most other troops of that description.

In the counties more remote from Somersetshire the supporters of the throne were on the alert. The militia of Sussex began to march westward, under the command of Richard, Lord Lumley, who, though he had lately been converted from the Roman Catholic religion, was still firm in his allegiance to a Roman Catholic king. James Bertie, Earl of Abingdon, called out the array of Oxfordshire. John Fell, Bishop of Oxford, who was also Dean of Christchurch, summoned the undergraduates of his University to take arms for the crown. The gownsmen crowded to give in their names. Christchurch alone furnished near a hundred pikemen and musketeers. Young noblemen and gentlemen commoners acted as officers; and the eldest son of the Lord Lieutenant was Colonel.

But it was chiefly on the regular troops that the King relied. Churchill had been sent westward with the Blues; and Feversham was following with all the forces that could be spared from the neighbourhood of London. A courier had started for Holland with a letter directing Skelton instantly to request that the three English regiments in the Dutch service might be sent to the Thames. When the request was made, the party hostile to the House of Orange, headed by the deputies of Amsterdam, again tried to cause delay. But the energy of William, who had almost as much at stake as James, and who saw Monmouth's progress with serious uneasiness, bore down opposition; and in a few days the troops sailed. The three Scotch regiments were already in England. They had arrived at Gravesend in excellent condition, and James had reviewed them on Blackheath. He repeatedly declared to the Dutch Ambassador that he had never in his life seen finer or better disciplined soldiers, and expressed the warmest gratitude to the Prince of Orange and the States for so valuable and seasonable a reinforcement. This satisfaction, however, was not unmixed. Excellently as the men went through their drill, they were not untainted with Dutch politics and Dutch divinity. One of them was shot and another flogged for drinking the Duke of Monmouth's health. It was therefore not thought advisable to place them in the post of danger. They were kept in the neighbourhood of London till the end of the campaign. But their arrival enabled the King to send to the West some infantry which would otherwise have been wanted in the capital.

While the government was thus preparing for a conflict with the rebels in the field, precautions of a different kind were not neglected.

In London alone two hundred of those persons who were thought most likely to be at the head of a Whig movement were arrested. Among the prisoners were some merchants of great note. Every man who was obnoxious to the Court went in fear. A general gloom overhung the capital. Business languished on the Exchange; and the theatres were so generally deserted that a new opera,[1] written by Dryden, and set off by decorations of unprecedented magnificence, was withdrawn, because the receipts would not cover the expenses of the performance. The magistrates and clergy were everywhere active. The Dissenters were everywhere closely observed. In Cheshire and Shropshire a fierce persecution raged: in Northamptonshire arrests were numerous; and the gaol of Oxford was crowded with prisoners. No Puritan divine, however moderate his opinions, however guarded his conduct, could feel any confidence that he should not be torn from his family and flung into a dungeon.

Meanwhile Monmouth advanced from Bridgewater, harassed through the whole march by Churchill, who appears to have done all that, with a handful of men, it was possible for a brave and skilful officer to effect. The rebel army, much annoyed both by the enemy and by a heavy fall of rain, halted in the evening of the twenty-second of June at Glastonbury. The houses of the little town did not afford shelter for so large a force. Some of the troops were therefore quartered in the churches, and others lighted their fires among the venerable ruins of the Abbey, once the wealthiest religious house in our island. From Glastonbury the Duke marched to Wells, and from Wells to Shepton Mallet.

Hitherto he seems to have wandered from place to place with no other object than that of collecting troops. It was now necessary for him to form some plan of military operations. His first scheme was to seize Bristol. Many of the chief inhabitants of that important place were Whigs. One of the ramifications of the Whig plot had extended thither. The garrison consisted only of the Gloucestershire trainbands. If Beaufort and his rustic followers could be overpowered before the regular troops arrived, the rebels would at once find themselves possessed of ample pecuniary resources: the credit of Monmouth's arms would be raised; and his friends throughout the kingdom would be encouraged to declare themselves. Bristol had fortifications which, on the north of the Avon towards Gloucesterhire, were weak, but on the south towards Somersetshire were much stronger. It was therefore determined that the attack should be made on the Gloucestershire side. But for this purpose it was necessary to take a circuitous route, and to cross the Avon at

[1] [Albion and Albanus.]

Keynsham. The bridge at Keynsham had been partly demolished by the militia, and was at present impassable. A detachment was therefore sent forward to make the necessary repairs. The other troops followed more slowly, and on the evening of the twenty-fourth of June halted for repose at Pensford. At Pensford they were only five miles from the Somersetshire side of Bristol; but the Gloucestershire side, which could be reached only by going round through Keynsham, was distant a long day's march.

That night was one of great tumult and expectation in Bristol. The partisans of Monmouth knew that he was almost within sight of their city, and imagined that he would be among them before daybreak. About an hour after sunset a merchantman lying at the quay took fire. Such an occurrence, in a port crowded with shipping, could not but excite great alarm. The whole river was in commotion. The streets were crowded. Seditious cries were heard amidst the darkness and confusion. It was afterwards asserted, both by Whigs and by Tories, that the fire had been kindled by the friends of Monmouth, in the hope that the trainbands would be busied in preventing the conflagration from spreading, and that in the meantime the rebel army would make a bold push, and enter the city on the Somersetshire side. If such was the design of the incendiaries, it completely failed. Beaufort, instead of sending his men to the quay, kept them all night drawn up under arms round the beautiful church of Saint Mary Redcliff, on the south of the Avon. He would see Bristol burned down, he said, nay, he would burn it down himself, rather than that it should be occupied by traitors. He was able, with the help of some regular cavalry which had joined him from Chippenham a few hours before, to prevent an insurrection. It might perhaps have been beyond his power at once to overawe the malecontents within the walls and to repel an attack from without: but no such attack was made. The fire, which caused so much commotion at Bristol, was distinctly seen at Pensford. Monmouth, however, did not think it expedient to change his plan. He remained quiet till sunrise, and then marched to Keynsham. There he found the bridge repaired. He determined to let his army rest during the afternoon, and, as soon as night came, to proceed to Bristol.

But it was too late. The King's forces were now near at hand. Colonel Oglethorpe, at the head of about a hundred men of the Life Guards, dashed into Keynsham, scattered two troops of rebel horse which ventured to oppose him, and retired after inflicting much injury and suffering little. In these circumstances it was thought necessary to relinquish the design on Bristol.

But what was to be done? Several schemes were proposed and discussed. It was suggested that Monmouth might hasten to Gloucester, might cross the Severn there, might break down the bridge behind him, and, with his right flank protected by the river, might march through Worcestershire into Shropshire and Cheshire. He had formerly made a progress through those counties, and had been received there with as much enthusiasm as in Somersetshire and Devonshire. His presence might revive the zeal of his old friends; and his army might in a few days be swollen to double its present numbers.

On full consideration, however, it appeared that this plan, though specious, was impracticable. The rebels were ill shod for such work as they had lately undergone, and were exhausted by toiling, day after day, through deep mud under heavy rain. Harassed and impeded as they would be at every stage by the enemy's cavalry, they could not hope to reach Gloucester without being overtaken by the main body of the royal troops, and forced to a general action under every disadvantage.

Then it was proposed to enter Wiltshire. Persons who professed to know that county well assured the Duke that he would be joined there by such strong reinforcements as would make it safe for him to give battle.

He took this advice, and turned towards Wiltshire. He first summoned Bath. But Bath was strongly garrisoned for the King; and Feversham was fast approaching. The rebels, therefore, made no attempt on the walls, but hastened to Philip's Norton, where they halted on the evening of the twenty-sixth of June.

Feversham followed them thither. Early on the morning of the twenty-seventh they were alarmed by tidings that he was close at hand. They got into order, and lined the hedges leading to the town.

The advanced guard of the royal army soon appeared. It consisted of about five hundred men, commanded by the Duke of Grafton, a youth of bold spirit and rough manners, who was probably eager to show that he had no share in the disloyal schemes of his half brother. Grafton soon found himself in a deep lane with fences on both sides of him, from which a galling fire of musketry was kept up. Still he pushed boldly on till he came to the entrance of Philip's Norton. There his way was crossed by a barricade, from which a third fire met him full in front. His men now lost heart, and made the best of their way back. Before they got out of the lane more than a hundred of them had been killed or wounded. Grafton's retreat was intercepted by some of the rebel cavalry: but he cut his way gallantly through them, and came off safe.

The advanced guard, thus repulsed, fell back on the main body of the royal forces. The two armies were now face to face; and a few shots were exchanged that did little or no execution. Neither side was impatient to come to action. Feversham did not wish to fight till his artillery came up, and fell back to Bradford. Monmouth, as soon as the night closed in, quitted his position, marched southward, and by daybreak arrived at Frome, where he hoped to find reinforcements.

Frome was as zealous in his cause as either Taunton or Bridgewater, but could do nothing to serve him. There had been a rising a few days before; and Monmouth's Declaration had been posted up in the market place. But the news of this movement had been carried to the Earl of Pembroke, who lay at no great distance with the Wiltshire militia. He had instantly marched to Frome, had routed a mob of rustics who, with scythes and pitchforks, attempted to oppose him, had entered the town and had disarmed the inhabitants. No weapons, therefore, were left there; nor was Monmouth able to furnish any.

The rebel army was in evil case. The march of the preceding night had been wearisome. The rain had fallen in torrents; and the roads had become mere quagmires. Nothing was heard of the promised succours from Wiltshire. One messenger brought news that Argyle's forces had been dispersed in Scotland. Another reported that Feversham, having been joined by his artillery, was about to advance. Monmouth understood war too well not to know that his followers, with all their courage and all their zeal, were no match for regular soldiers. He had till lately flattered himself with the hope that some of those regiments which he had formerly commanded would pass over to his standard: but that hope he was now compelled to relinquish. His heart failed him. He could scarcely muster firmness enough to give orders. In his misery he complained bitterly of the evil counsellors who had induced him to quit his happy retreat in Brabant. Against Wildman in particular he broke forth into violent imprecations. And now an ignominious thought rose in his weak and agitated mind. He would leave to the mercy of the government the thousands who had, at his call and for his sake, abandoned their quiet fields and dwellings. He would steal away with his chief officers, would gain some seaport before his flight was suspected, would escape to the Continent, and would forget his ambition and his shame in the arms of Lady Wentworth. He seriously discussed the scheme with his leading advisers. Some of them, trembling for their necks, listened to it with approbation:

but Grey, who, by the admission of his detractors, was intrepid everywhere except where swords were clashing and guns going off around him, opposed the dastardly proposition with great ardour, and implored the Duke to face every danger rather than requite with ingratitude and treachery the devoted attachment of the Western peasantry.

The scheme of flight was abandoned: but it was not now easy to form any plan for a campaign. To advance towards London would have been madness; for the road lay right across Salisbury Plain; and on that vast open space regular troops, and above all regular cavalry, would have acted with every advantage against undisciplined men. At this juncture a report reached the camp that the rustics of the marshes near Axbridge had risen in defence of the Protestant religion, had armed themselves with flails, bludgeons and pitchforks, and were assembling by thousands at Bridgewater. Monmouth determined to return thither, and to strengthen himself with these new allies.

The rebels accordingly proceeded to Wells, and arrived there in no amiable temper. They were, with few exceptions, hostile to Prelacy; and they showed their hostility in a way very little to their honour. They not only tore the lead from the roof of the magnificent Cathedral to make bullets, an act for which they might fairly plead the necessities of war, but wantonly defaced the ornaments of the building. Grey with difficulty preserved the altar from the insults of some ruffians who wished to carouse round it, by taking his stand before it with his sword drawn.

On Thursday, the second of July, Monmouth again entered Bridgewater, in circumstances far less cheering than those in which he had marched thence ten days before. The reinforcement which he found there was inconsiderable. The royal army was close upon him. At one moment he thought of fortifying the town; and hundreds of labourers were summoned to dig trenches and throw up mounds. Then his mind recurred to the plan of marching into Cheshire, a plan which he had rejected as impracticable when he was at Keynsham, and which assuredly was not more practicable now that he was at Bridgewater.

While he was thus wavering between projects equally hopeless, the King's forces came in sight. They consisted of about two thousand five hundred regular troops, and of about fifteen hundred of the Wiltshire militia. Early on the morning of Sunday, the fifth of July, they left Somerton, and pitched their tents that day about three miles from Bridgewater, on the plain of Sedgemoor.

Doctor Peter Mew, Bishop of Winchester, accompanied them.

This prelate had in his youth borne arms for Charles the First against the Parliament. Neither his years nor his profession had wholly extinguished his martial ardour; and he probably thought that the appearance of a father of the Protestant Church in the King's camp might confirm the loyalty of some honest men who were wavering between their horror of Popery and their horror of rebellion.

The steeple of the parish church of Bridgewater is said to be the loftiest in Somersetshire, and commands a wide view over the surrounding country. Monmouth, accompanied by some of his officers, went up to the top of the square tower from which the spire ascends, and observed through a telescope the position of the enemy. Beneath him lay a flat expanse, now rich with cornfields and apple trees, but then, as its name imports, for the most part a dreary morass. When the rains were heavy, and the Parret and its tributary streams rose above their banks, this tract was often flooded. It was indeed anciently part of that great swamp which is renowned in our early chronicles as having arrested the progress of two successive races of invaders, which long protected the Celts against the aggressions of the kings of Wessex, and which sheltered Alfred from the pursuit of the Danes. In those remote times this region could be traversed only in boats. It was a vast pool, wherein were scattered many islets of shifting and treacherous soil, overhung with rank jungle, and swarming with deer and wild swine. Even in the days of the Tudors, the traveller whose journey lay from Ilchester to Bridgewater was forced to make a circuit of several miles in order to avoid the waters. When Monmouth looked upon Sedgemoor, it had been partially reclaimed by art, and was intersected by many deep and wide trenches which, in that country, are called rhines. In the midst of the moor rose, clustering round the towers of churches, a few villages, of which the names seem to indicate that they once were surrounded by waves. In one of these villages, called Weston Zoyland, the royal cavalry lay; and Feversham had fixed his head quarters there. Many persons still liv have seen the daughter of the servant girl who waited on him day at table; and a large dish of Persian ware, which was set him, is still carefully preserved in the neighbourhood. I observed that the population of Somersetshire does not the manufacturing districts, consist of emigrants places. It is by no means unusual to find farmers v same land which their ancestors cultivated whe reigned in England. The Somersetshire tra of no small value to a historian.

At a greater distance from Bridgewater lies the village of Middlezoy. In that village and its neighbourhood, the Wiltshire militia were quartered, under the command of Pembroke.

On the open moor, not far from Chedzoy, were encamped several battalions of regular infantry. Monmouth looked gloomily on them. He could not but remember how, a few years before, he had, at the head of a column composed of some of those very men, driven before him in confusion the fierce enthusiasts who defended Bothwell Bridge. He could distinguish among the hostile ranks that gallant band which was then called, from the name of its Colonel, Dumbarton's regiment, but which has long been known as the first of the line, and which, in all the four quarters of the world, has nobly supported its early reputation. "I know those men," said Monmouth; "they will fight. If I had but them, all would go well!"

Yet the aspect of the enemy was not altogether discouraging. The three divisions of the royal army lay far apart from one another. There was an appearance of negligence and of relaxed discipline in all their movements. It was reported that they were drinking themselves drunk with the Zoyland cider. The incapacity of Feversham, who commanded in chief, was notorious. Even at this momentous crisis he thought only of eating and sleeping. Churchill was indeed a captain equal to tasks far more arduous than that of scattering a crowd of ill armed and ill trained peasants. But the genius, which, at a later period, humbled six Marshals of France, was not now in its proper place. Feversham told Churchill little, and gave him no encouragement to offer any suggestion. The lieutenant, conscious of superior abilities and science, impatient of the control of a chief whom he despised, and trembling for the fate of the army, nevertheless preserved his characteristic self-command, and dissembled his feelings so well that Feversham praised his submissive alacrity, and promised to report it to the King.

Monmouth, having observed the disposition of the royal forces, and having been apprised of the state in which they were, conceived that a night attack might be attended with success. He resolved to run the hazard, and preparations were instantly made.

It was Sunday; and his followers, who had, for the most part, been brought up after the Puritan fashion, passed a great part of the day in religious exercises. The Castle Field, in which the army was encamped, presented a spectacle such as, since the disbanding of Cromwell's soldiers, England had never seen. The dissenting preachers who had taken arms against Popery, and some of whom had probably fought in the great civil war, prayed and preached in

red coats and huge jackboots, with swords by their sides. Ferguson was one of those who harangued. He took for his text the awful imprecation by which the Israelites who dwelt beyond Jordan cleared themselves from the charge ignorantly brought against them by their brethren on the other side of the river. "The Lord God of Gods, the Lord God of Gods, he knoweth; and Israel he shall know. If it be in rebellion, or if in transgression against the Lord, save us not this day."

That an attack was to be made under cover of the night was no secret in Bridgewater. The town was full of women, who had repaired thither by hundreds from the surrounding region, to see their husbands, sons, lovers, and brothers once more. There were many sad partings that day; and many parted never to meet again. The report of the intended attack came to the ears of a young girl who was zealous for the King. Though of modest character, she had the courage to resolve that she would herself bear the intelligence to Feversham. She stole out of Bridgewater, and made her way to the royal camp. But that camp was not a place where female innocence could be safe. Even the officers, despising alike the irregular force to which they were opposed, and the negligent general who commanded them, had indulged largely in wine, and were ready for any excess of licentiousness and cruelty. One of them seized the unhappy maiden, refused to listen to her errand, and brutally outraged her. She fled in agonies of rage and shame, leaving the wicked army to its doom.

And now the time for the great hazard drew near. The night was not ill suited for such an enterprise. The moon was indeed at the full, and the northern streamers were shining brilliantly. But the marsh fog lay so thick on Sedgemoor that no object could be discerned there at the distance of fifty paces.

The clock struck eleven; and the Duke with his body guard rode out of the Castle. He was not in the frame of mind which befits one who is about to strike a decisive blow. The very children who pressed to see him pass observed, and long remembered, that his look was sad and full of evil augury. His army marched by a circuitous path, nearly six miles in length, towards the royal encampment on Sedgemoor. Part of the route is to this day called War Lane. The foot were led by Monmouth himself. The horse were confided to Grey, in spite of the remonstrances of some who remembered the mishap at Bridport. Orders were given that strict silence should be preserved, that no drum should be beaten, and no shot fired. The word by which the insurgents were to recognise one another in the darkness was Soho. It had doubtless been selected in allusion to Soho Fields in London, where their leader's palace stood.

At about one in the morning of Monday the sixth of July, the rebels were on the open moor. But between them and the enemy lay three broad rhines filled with water and soft mud. Two of these, called the Black Ditch and the Langmoor Rhine, Monmouth knew that he must pass. But, strange to say, the existence of a trench, called the Bussex Rhine, which immediately covered the royal encampment, had not been mentioned to him by any of his scouts.

The wains which carried the ammunition remained at the entrance of the moor. The horse and foot, in a long narrow column, passed the Black Ditch by a causeway. There was a similar causeway across the Langmoor Rhine; but the guide, in the fog, missed his way. There was some delay and some tumult before the error could be rectified. At length the passage was effected: but, in the confusion, a pistol went off. Some men of the Horse Guards, who were on watch, heard the report, and perceived that a great multitude was advancing through the mist. They fired their carbines, and galloped off in different directions to give the alarm. Some hastened to Weston Zoyland, where the cavalry lay. One trooper spurred to the encampment of the infantry, and cried out vehemently that the enemy was at hand. The drums of Dumbarton's regiment beat to arms; and the men got fast into their ranks. It was time; for Monmouth was already drawing up his army for action. He ordered Grey to lead the way with the cavalry, and followed himself at the head of the infantry. Grey pushed on till his progress was unexpectedly arrested by the Bussex Rhine. On the opposite side of the ditch the King's foot were hastily forming in order of battle.

"For whom are you?" called out an officer of the Foot Guards. "For the King," replied a voice from the ranks of the rebel cavalry. "For which King?" was then demanded. The answer was a shout of "King Monmouth," mingled with the war cry, which forty years before had been inscribed on the colours of the parliamentary regiments, "God with us." The royal troops instantly fired such a volley of musketry as sent the rebel horse flying in all directions. The world agreed to ascribe this ignominious rout to Grey's pusillanimity. Yet it is by no means clear that Churchill would have succeeded better at the head of men who had never before handled arms on horseback, and whose horses were unused, not only to stand fire, but to obey the rein.

A few minutes after the Duke's horse had dispersed themselves over the moor, his infantry came up running fast, and guided through the gloom by the lighted matches of Dumbarton's regiment.

Monmouth was startled by finding that a broad and profound trench lay between him and the camp which he had hoped to surprise. The insurgents halted on the edge of the rhine, and fired. Part of the royal infantry on the opposite bank returned the fire. During three quarters of an hour the roar of the musketry was incessant. The Somersetshire peasants behaved themselves as if they had been veteran soldiers, save only that they levelled their pieces too high.

But now the other divisions of the royal army were in motion. The Life Guards and Blues came pricking fast from Weston Zoyland, and scattered in an instant some of Grey's horse, who had attempted to rally. The fugitives spread a panic among their comrades in the rear, who had charge of the ammunition. The waggoners drove off at full speed, and never stopped till they were many miles from the field of battle. Monmouth had hitherto done his part like a stout and able warrior. He had been seen on foot, pike in hand, encouraging his infantry by voice and by example. But he was too well acquainted with military affairs not to know that all was over. His men had lost the advantage which surprise and darkness had given them. They were deserted by the horse and by the ammunition waggons. The King's forces were now united and in good order. Feversham had been awakened by the firing, had got out of bed, had adjusted his cravat, had looked at himself well in the glass, and had come to see what his men were doing. Meanwhile, what was of much more importance. Churchill had rapidly made an entirely new disposition of the royal infantry. The day was about to break. The event of a conflict on an open plain, by broad sunlight, could not be doubtful. Yet Monmouth should have felt that it was not for him to fly, while thousands whom affection for him had hurried to destruction were still fighting manfully in his cause. But vain hopes and the intense love of life prevailed. He saw that if he tarried the royal cavalry would soon intercept his retreat. He mounted and rode from the field.

Yet his foot, though deserted, made a gallant stand. The Life Guards attacked them on the right, the Blues on the left: but the Somersetshire clowns, with their scythes and the but ends of their muskets, faced the royal horse like old soldiers. Oglethorpe made a vigorous attempt to break them and was manfully repulsed. Sarsfield, a brave Irish officer, whose name afterwards obtained a melancholy celebrity, charged on the other flank. His men were beaten back. He was himself struck to the ground, and lay for a time as one dead. But the struggle of the hardy rustics could not last. Their powder and ball were spent. Cries were heard of "Ammunition! for God's sake ammunition!" But no ammunition was at hand. And now the King's artillery came up. It had been posted half a mile off, on the high road from Weston Zoyland to Bridgewater. So defective were then the appointments of an English army that there would have been much difficulty in dragging the great guns to the place where the battle was raging, had not the Bishop of Winchester offered his coach horses and traces for the purpose. This interference of a Christian prelate in a matter of blood has, with strange inconsistency, been condemned by some Whig writers who can see nothing criminal in the conduct of the numerous Puritan ministers then in arms against the government. Even when the guns had arrived, there was such a want of gunners that a sergeant of Dumbarton's regiment was forced to take on himself the management of several pieces. The cannon, however, though ill served, brought the engagement to a speedy close. The pikes of the rebel battalions began to shake: the ranks broke; the King's cavalry charged again, and bore down every thing before them; the King's infantry came pouring across the ditch. Even in that extremity the Mendip miners stood bravely to their arms, and sold their lives dearly. But the rout was in a few minutes complete. Three hundred of the soldiers had been killed or wounded. Of the rebels more than a thousand lay dead on the moor.

So ended the last fight, deserving the name of battle, that has been fought on English ground. The impression left on the simple inhabitants of the neighbourhood was deep and lasting. That impression, indeed, has been frequently renewed. For even in our own time the plough and the spade have not seldom turned up ghastly memorials of the slaughter, skulls, and thighbones, and strange weapons made out of implements of husbandry. Old peasants related very recently that, in their childhood, they were accustomed to play on the moor at the fight between King James's men and King Monmouth's men, and that King Monmouth's men always raised the cry of Soho.

What seems most extraordinary in the battle of Sedgemoor is that the event should have been for a moment doubtful, and that the rebels should have resisted so long. That five or six thousand colliers and ploughmen should contend during an hour with half that number of regular cavalry and infantry would now be thought a miracle. Our wonder will, perhaps, be diminished when we remember that, in the time of James the Second, the discipline of the regular army was extremely lax, and that, on the other hand, the peasantry were accustomed to serve in the militia. The difference, therefore, between a regiment of Foot Guards and a regiment of clowns just enrolled, though doubtless considerable, was by no means what it now is. Monmouth did not lead a mere mob to attack good soldiers. For his followers were not altogether without a tincture of soldiership; and Feversham's troops, when compared with English troops of our time, might almost be called a mob.

It was four o'clock: the sun was rising; and the routed army came pouring into the streets of Bridgewater. The uproar, the blood, the gashes, the ghastly figures which sank down and never rose again, spread horror and dismay through the town. The pursuers, too, were close behind. Those inhabitants who had favoured the insurrection expected sack and massacre, and implored the protection of their neighbours who professed the Roman Catholic religion, or had made themselves conspicuous by Tory politics; and it is acknowledged by the bitterest of Whig historians that this protection was kindly and generously given.

During that day the conquerors continued to chase the fugitives. The neighbouring villagers long remembered with what a clatter of horsehoofs and what a storm of curses the whirlwind of cavalry swept by. Before evening five hundred prisoners had been crowded into the parish church of Weston Zoyland. Eighty of them were wounded; and five expired within the consecrated walls. Great numbers of labourers were impressed for the purpose of burying the slain. A few, who were notoriously partial to the vanquished side, were set apart for the hideous office of quartering the captives. The tithing men of the neighbouring parishes were busied in setting up gibbets and providing chains. All this while the bells of Weston Zoyland and Chedzoy rang joyously, and the soldiers sang and rioted on the moor amidst the corpses. For the farmers of the neighbourhood had made haste, as soon as the event of the fight was known, to send hogsheads of their best cider as peace offerings to the victors.

Feversham passed for a goodnatured man: but he was a foreigner, ignorant of the laws and careless of the feelings of the English.[1] He was accustomed to the military license of France, and had learned from his great kinsman, the conqueror and devastator of the Palatinate, not indeed how to conquer, but how to devastate. A considerable number of prisoners were immediately selected for execution. Among them was a youth famous for his speed. Hopes were held out to him that his life would be spared if he could run a

[1] [Louis Duras, Earl of Feversham, was a Frenchman and a nephew of Turenne.]

race with one of the colts of the marsh. The space through which the man kept up with the horse is still marked by well known bounds on the moor, and is about three quarters of a mile. Feversham was not ashamed, after seeing the performance, to send the wretched performer to the gallows. The next day a long line of gibbets appeared on the road leading from Bridgewater to Weston Zoyland. On each gibbet a prisoner was suspended. Four of the sufferers were left to rot in irons.

Meanwhile Monmouth, accompanied by Grey, by Buyse, and by a few other friends, was flying from the field of battle. At Chedzoy he stopped a moment to mount a fresh horse and to hide his blue riband and his George. He then hastened towards the Bristol Channel. From the rising ground on the north of the field of battle he saw the flash and the smoke of the last volley fired by his deserted followers. Before six o'clock he was twenty miles from Sedgemoor. Some of his companions advised him to cross the water, and to seek refuge in Wales; and this would undoubtedly have been his wisest course. He would have been in Wales many hours before the news of his defeat was known there; and, in a country so wild, and so remote from the seat of government, might have remained long undiscovered. He determined, however, to push for Hampshire, in the hope that he might lurk in the cabins of deerstealers among the oaks of the New Forest, till means of conveyance to the Continent could be procured. He therefore, with Grey and the German, turned to the south east. But the way was beset with dangers. The three fugitives had to traverse a country in which every one already knew the event of the battle, and in which no traveller of suspicious appearance could escape a close scrutiny. They rode on all day shunning towns and villages. Nor was this so difficult as it may now appear. For men then living could remember the time when the wild deer ranged freely through a succession of forests from the banks of the Avon in Wiltshire to the southern coast of Hampshire. At length, on Cranbourne Chase, the strength of the horses failed. They were therefore turned loose. The bridles and saddles were concealed. Monmouth and his friends procured rustic attire, disguised themselves, and proceeded on foot towards the New Forest. They passed the night in the open air: but before morning they were surrounded on every side by toils. Lord Lumley, who lay at Ringwood with a strong body of the Sussex militia, had sent forth parties in every direction. Sir William Portman, with the Somerset militia, had formed a chain of posts from the sea to the northern extremity of Dorset. At five in the morning of the seventh, Grey, who had wandered from his friends, was seized by two of the

Sussex scouts. He submitted to his fate with the calmness of one to whom suspense was more intolerable than despair. "Since we landed," he said, "I have not had one comfortable meal or one quiet night." It could hardly be doubted that the chief rebel was not far off. The pursuers redoubled their vigilance and activity. The cottages scattered over the heathy country on the boundaries of Dorsetshire and Hampshire were strictly examined by Lumley; and the clown with whom Monmouth had changed clothes was discovered. Portman came with a strong body of horse and foot to assist in the search. Attention was soon drawn to a place well fitted to shelter fugitives. It was an extensive tract of land separated by an enclosure from the open country, and divided by numerous hedges into small fields. In some of these fields the rye, the pease, and the oats were high enough to conceal a man. Others were overgrown by fern and brambles. A poor woman reported that she had seen two strangers lurking in this covert. The near prospect of reward animated the zeal of the troops. It was agreed that every man who did his duty in the search should have a share of the promised five thousand pounds. The outer fence was strictly guarded: the space within was examined with indefatigable diligence; and several dogs of quick scent were turned out among the bushes. The day closed before the work could be completed: but careful watch was kept all night. Thirty times the fugitives ventured to look through the outer hedge: but everywhere they found a sentinel on the alert: once they were seen and fired at; they then separated and concealed themselves in different hiding places.

At sunrise the next morning the search recommenced, and Buyse was found. He owned that he had parted from the Duke only a few hours before. The corn and copsewood were now beaten with more care than ever. At length a gaunt figure was discovered hidden in a ditch. The pursuers sprang on their prey. Some of them were about to fire: but Portman forbade all violence. The prisoner's dress was that of a shepherd; his beard, prematurely grey, was of several days' growth. He trembled greatly, and was unable to speak. Even those who had often seen him were at first in doubt whether this were truly the brilliant and graceful Monmouth. His pockets were searched by Portman, and in them were found, among some raw pease gathered in the rage of hunger, a watch, a purse of gold, a small treatise on fortification, an album filled with songs, receipts, prayers, and charms, and the George with which, many years before, King Charles the Second had decorated his favourite son. Messengers were instantly despatched to Whitehall with the good news, and with the George as a token that the news was true.

The prisoner was conveyed under a strong guard to Ringwood.

And all was lost; and nothing remained but that he should prepare to meet death as became one who had thought himself not unworthy to wear the crown of William the Conqueror and of Richard the Lionhearted, of the hero of Cressy and of the hero of Agincourt. The captive might easily have called to mind other domestic examples, still better suited to his condition. Within a hundred years, two sovereigns whose blood ran in his veins, one of them a delicate woman, had been placed in the same situation in which he now stood. They had shown, in the prison and on the scaffold, a virtue of which, in the season of prosperity, they had seemed incapable, and had half redeemed great crimes and errors by enduring with Christian meekness and princely dignity all that victorious enemies could inflict. Of cowardice Monmouth had never been accused; and, even had he been wanting in constitutional courage, it might have been expected that the defect would be supplied by pride and by despair. The eyes of the whole world were upon him. The latest generations would know how, in that extremity, he had borne himself. To the brave peasants of the West he owed it to show that they had not poured forth their blood for a leader unworthy of their attachment. To her who had sacrificed every thing for his sake he owed it so to bear himself that, though she might weep for him, she should not blush for him. It was not for him to lament and supplicate. His reason, too, should have told him that lamentation and supplication would be unavailing. He had done that which could never be forgiven. He was in the grasp of one who never forgave.

But the fortitude of Monmouth was not that highest sort of fortitude which is derived from reflection and from selfrespect; nor had nature given him one of those stout hearts from which neither adversity nor peril can extort any sign of weakness. His courage rose and fell with his animal spirits. It was sustained on the field of battle by the excitement of action, by the hope of victory, by the strange influence of sympathy. All such aids were now taken away. The spoiled darling of the court and of the populace, accustomed to be loved and worshipped wherever he appeared, was now surrounded by stern gaolers in whose eyes he read his doom. Yet a few hours of gloomy seclusion, and he must die a violent and shameful death. His heart sank within him. Life seemed worth purchasing by any humiliation; nor could his mind, always feeble, and now distracted by terror, perceive that humiliation must degrade, but could not save him.

As soon as he reached Ringwood he wrote to the King. The

letter was that of a man whom a craven fear had made insensible to shame. He professed in vehement terms his remorse for his treason. He affirmed that, when he promised his cousins at the Hague not to raise troubles in England, he had fully meant to keep his word. Unhappily he had afterwards been seduced from his allegiance by some horrid people who had heated his mind by calumnies and misled him by sophistry: but now he abhorred them: he abhorred himself. He begged in piteous terms that he might be admitted to the royal presence. There was a secret which he could not trust to paper, a secret which lay in a single word, and which, if he spoke that word, would secure the throne against all danger. On the following day he despatched letters, imploring the Queen Dowager and the Lord Treasurer to intercede in his behalf.

When it was known in London how he had abased himself the general surprise was great; and no man was more amazed than Barillon, who had resided in England during two bloody proscriptions, and had seen numerous victims, both of the Opposition and of the Court, submit to their fate without womanish entreaties and lamentations.

Monmouth and Grey remained at Ringwood two days. They were then carried up to London, under the guard of a large body of regular troops and militia. In the coach with the Duke was an officer whose orders were to stab the prisoner if a rescue were attempted. At every town along the road the trainbands of the neighbourhood had been mustered under the command of the principal gentry. The march lasted three days, and terminated at Vauxhall, where a regiment, commanded by George Legge, Lord Dartmouth, was in readiness to receive the prisoners. They were put on board of a state barge, and carried down the river to Whitehall Stairs. Lumley and Portman had alternately watched the Duke day and night till they had brought him within the walls of the palace.

Both the demeanour of Monmouth and that of Grey, during the journey, filled all observers with surprise. Monmouth was altogether unnerved. Grey was not only calm but cheerful, talked pleasantly of horses, dogs, and field sports, and even made jocose allusions to the perilous situation in which he stood.

The King cannot be blamed for determining that Monmouth should suffer death. Every man who heads a rebellion against an established government stakes his life on the event: and rebellion was the smallest part of Monmouth's crime. He had declared against his uncle a war without quarter. In the manifesto put forth at Lyme, James had been held up to execration as an incendiary, as an assassin who had strangled one innocent man and cut the throat of another, and, lastly, as the poisoner of his own brother. To spare an enemy who had not scrupled to resort to such extremities would have been an act of rare, perhaps of blamable generosity. But to see him and not to spare him was an outrage on humanity and decency. This outrage the King resolved to commit. The arms of the prisoner were bound behind him with a silken cord; and, thus secured, he was ushered into the presence of the implacable kinsman whom he had wronged.

Then Monmouth threw himself on the ground, and crawled to the King's feet. He wept. He tried to embrace his uncle's knees with his pinioned arms. He begged for life, only life, life at any price. He owned that he had been guilty of a great crime, but tried to throw the blame on others, particularly on Argyle, who would rather have put his legs into the boots[1] than have saved his own life by such baseness. By the ties of kindred, by the memory of the late King, who had been the best and truest of brothers, the unhappy man adjured James to show some mercy. James gravely replied that this repentance was of the latest, that he was sorry for the misery which the prisoner had brought on himself, but that the case was not one for lenity. A Declaration, filled with atrocious calumnies, had been put forth. The regal title had been assumed. For treasons so aggravated there could be no pardon on this side of the grave. The poor terrified Duke vowed that he had never wished to take the crown, but had been led into that fatal error by others. As to the Declaration, he had not written it: he had not read it: he had signed it without looking at it: it was all the work of Ferguson, that bloody villain Ferguson. "Do you expect me to believe," said James, with contempt but too well merited, "that you set your hand to a paper of such moment without knowing what it contained?" One depth of infamy only remained; and even to that the prisoner descended. He was preeminently the champion of the Protestant religion. The interest of that religion had been his plea for conspiring against the government of his father, and for bringing on his country the miseries of civil war: yet he was not ashamed to hint that he was inclined to be reconciled to the Church of Rome. The King eagerly offered him spiritual assistance, but said nothing of pardon or respite. "Is there then no hope?" asked Monmouth. James turned away in silence. Then Monmouth strove to rally his courage, rose from his knees, and retired with a firmness which he had not shown since his overthrow.

Grey was introduced next. He behaved with a propriety and

[1] [An instrument of torture.]

fortitude which moved even the stern and resentful King, frankly owned himself guilty, made no excuses, and did not once stoop to ask his life. Both the prisoners were sent to the Tower by water. There was no tumult; but many thousands of people, with anxiety and sorrow in their faces, tried to catch a glimpse of the captives. The Duke's resolution failed as soon as he had left the royal presence. On his way to his prison he bemoaned himself, accused his followers, and abjectly implored the intercession of Dartmouth. "I know, my Lord, that you loved my father. For his sake, for God's sake, try if there be any room for mercy." Dartmouth replied that the King had spoken the truth, and that a subject who assumed the regal title excluded himself from all hope of pardon.

Soon after Monmouth had been lodged in the Tower, he was informed that his wife had, by the royal command, been sent to see him. She was accompanied by the Earl of Clarendon, Keeper of the Privy Seal. Her husband received her very coldly, and addressed almost all his discourse to Clarendon, whose intercession he earnestly implored. Clarendon held out no hopes; and that same evening two prelates, Turner, Bishop of Ely, and Ken, Bishop of Bath and Wells, arrived at the Tower with a solemn message from the King. It was Monday night. On Wednesday morning Monmouth was to die.

He was greatly agitated. The blood left his cheeks; and it was some time before he could speak. Most of the short time which remained to him he wasted in vain attempts to obtain, if not a pardon, at least a respite. He wrote piteous letters to the King and to several courtiers, but in vain. Some Roman Catholic divines were sent to him from Whitehall. But they soon discovered that, though he would gladly have purchased his life by renouncing the religion of which he had professed himself in an especial manner the defender, yet, if he was to die, he would as soon die without their absolution as with it.

Nor were Ken and Turner much better pleased with his frame of mind. The doctrine of nonresistance was, in their view, as in the view of most of their brethren, the distinguishing badge of the Anglican Church. The two Bishops insisted on Monmouth's owning that, in drawing the sword against the government, he had committed a great sin; and, on this point, they found him obstinately heterodox. Nor was this his only heresy. He maintained that his connection with Lady Wentworth was blameless in the sight of God. He had been married, he said, when a child. He had never cared for his Duchess. The happiness which he had not found at home he had sought in a round of loose amours, condemned by religion and morality. Henrietta had reclaimed him from a life of vice. To her he had been strictly constant. They had, by common consent, offered up fervent prayers for the divine guidance. After those prayers they had found their affection for each other strengthened; and they could then no longer doubt that, in the sight of God, they were a wedded pair. The Bishops were so much scandalised by this view of the conjugal relation that they refused to administer the sacrament to the prisoner. All that they could obtain from him was a promise that, during the single night which still remained to him, he would pray to be enlightened if he were in error.

On the Wednesday morning, at his particular request, Doctor Thomas Tenison, who then held the vicarage of Saint Martin's, and, in that important cure, had obtained the high esteem of the public, came to the Tower. From Tenison, whose opinions were known to be moderate, the Duke expected more indulgence than Ken and Turner were disposed to show. But Tenison, whatever might be his sentiments concerning nonresistance in the abstract, thought the late rebellion rash and wicked, and considered Monmouth's notion respecting marriage as a most dangerous delusion. Monmouth was obstinate. He had prayed, he said, for the divine direction. His sentiments remained unchanged; and he could not doubt that they were correct. Tenison's exhortations were in a milder tone than those of the Bishops. But he, like them, thought that he should not be justified in administering the Eucharist to one whose penitence was of so unsatisfactory a nature.

The hour drew near: all hope was over; and Monmouth had passed from pusillanimous fear to the apathy of despair. His children were brought to his room that he might take leave of them, and were followed by his wife. He spoke to her kindly, but without emotion. Though she was a woman of great strength of mind, and had little cause to love him, her misery was such that none of the bystanders could refrain from weeping. He alone was unmoved.

It was ten o'clock. The coach of the Lieutenant of the Tower was ready. Monmouth requested his spiritual advisers to accompany him to the place of execution; and they consented: but they told him that, in their judgment, he was about to die in a perilous state of mind, and that, if they attended him, it would be their duty to exhort him to the last. As he passed along the ranks of the guards he saluted them with a smile, and mounted the scaffold with a firm tread. Tower Hill was covered up to the chimney tops with an innumerable multitude of gazers, who, in awful silence, broken only by sighs and the noise of weeping, listened for the last accents of the darling of the people. "I shall say little," he began. "I come here, not to speak, but to die. I die a Protestant of the Church of England." The Bishops interrupted him, and told him that, unless he acknowledged resistance to be sinful, he was no member of their church. He went on to speak of his Henrietta. She was, he said, a young lady of virtue and honour. He loved her to the last, and he could not die without giving utterance to his feelings. The Bishops again interfered and begged him not to use such language. Some altercation followed. The divines have been accused of dealing harshly with the dying man. But they appear to have only discharged what, in their view, was a sacred duty. Monmouth knew their principles, and, if he wished to avoid their importunity, should have dispensed with their attendance. Their general arguments against resistance had no effect on him. But when they reminded him of the ruin which he had brought on his brave and loving followers, of the blood which had been shed, of the souls which had been sent unprepared to the great account, he was touched, and said, in a softened voice, "I do own that. I am sorry that it ever happened." They prayed with him long and fervently; and he joined in their petitions till they invoked a blessing on the King. He remained silent. "Sir," said one of the Bishops, "do you not pray for the King with us?" Monmouth paused some time, and, after an internal struggle, exclaimed "Amen." But it was in vain that the prelates implored him to address to the soldiers and to the people a few words on the duty of obedience to the government. "I will make no speeches," he exclaimed. "Only ten words, my Lord." He turned away, called his servant, and put into the man's hand a toothpick case, the last token of ill starred love. "Give it," he said "to that person." He then accosted John Ketch the executioner, a wretch who had butchered many brave and noble victims, and whose name has, during a century and a half, been vulgarly given to all who have succeeded him in his odious office. "Here," said the Duke, "are six guineas for you. Do not hack me as you did my Lord Russell. I have heard that you struck him three or four times. My servant will give you some more gold if you do the work well." He then undressed, felt the edge of the axe, expressed some fear that it was not sharp enough, and laid his head on the block. The divines in the meantime continued to ejaculate with great energy; "God accept your repentance! God accept your imperfect repentance!"

The hangman addressed himself to his office. But he had been disconcerted by what the Duke had said. The first blow inflicted only a slight wound. The Duke struggled, rose from the block, and looked reproachfully at the executioner. The head sank down once more. The stroke was repeated again and again; but still the neck was not severed, and the body continued to move. Yells of rage and horror rose from the crowd. Ketch flung down the axe with a curse. "I cannot do it," he said; "my heart fails me." "Take up the axe, man," cried the sheriff. "Fling him over the rails," roared the mob. At length the axe was taken up. Two more blows extinguished the last remains of life; but a knife was used to separate the head from the shoulders. The crowd was wrought up to such an ecstasy of rage that the executioner was in danger of being torn in pieces, and was conveyed away under a strong guard.

In the meantime many handkerchiefs were dipped in the Duke's blood; for by a large part of the multitude he was regarded as a martyr who had died for the Protestant religion. The head and body were placed in a coffin covered with black velvet, and were laid privately under the communion table of Saint Peter's Chapel in the Tower. Within four years the pavement of that chancel was again disturbed, and hard by the remains of Monmouth were laid the remains of Jeffreys. In truth there is no sadder spot on the earth than that little cemetery. Death is there associated, not, as in Westminster Abbey and Saint Paul's, with genius and virtue, with public veneration and with imperishable renown; not, as in our humblest churches and churchyards, with every thing that is most endearing in social and domestic charities; but with whatever is darkest in human nature and in human destiny, with the savage triumph of implacable enemies, with the inconstancy, the ingratitude, the cowardice of friends, with all the miseries of fallen greatness and of blighted fame. Thither have been carried, through successive ages, by the rude hands of gaolers, without one mourner following, the bleeding relics of men who had been the captains of armies, the leaders of parties, the oracles of senates, and the ornaments of courts. Thither was borne, before the window where Jane Grey was praying, the mangled corpse of Guilford Dudley. Edward Seymour, Duke of Somerset, and Protector of the realm, reposes there by the brother whom he murdered. There has mouldered away the headless trunk of John Fisher, Bishop of Rochester and Cardinal of Saint Vitalis, a man worthy to have lived in a better age, and to have died in a better cause. There are laid John Dudley, Duke of Northumberland, Lord High Admiral, and Thomas Cromwell, Earl of Essex, Lord High Treasurer. There, too, is another Essex, on whom nature and fortune had lavished all their bounties in vain, and whom valour, grace, genius, royal favour, popular applause, conducted to an early and ignominious doom. Not far off sleep two chiefs of the great house of Howard, Thomas, fourth Duke of Norfolk, and Philip, eleventh Earl of Arundel. Here and there, among the thick graves of unquiet and aspiring statesmen, lie more delicate sufferers; Margaret of Salisbury, the last of the proud name of Plantagenet, and those two fair Queens who perished by the jealous rage of Henry. Such was the dust with which the dust of Monmouth mingled.

Yet a few months, and the quiet village of Toddington, in Bedfordshire, witnessed a still sadder funeral. Near that village stood an ancient and stately hall, the seat of the Wentworths. The transept of the parish church had long been their burial place. To that burial place, in the spring which followed the death of Monmouth, was borne the coffin of the young Baroness Wentworth of Nettlestede. Her family reared a sumptuous mausoleum over her remains: but a less costly memorial of her was long contemplated with far deeper interest. Her name, carved by the hand of him whom she loved too well, was, a few years ago, still discernible on a tree in the adjoining park.

It was not by Lady Wentworth alone that the memory of Monmouth was cherished with idolatrous fondness. His hold on the hearts of the people lasted till the generation which had seen him had passed away. Ribands, buckles, and other trifling articles of apparel which he had worn, were treasured up as precious relics by those who had fought under him at Sedgemoor. Old men who long survived him desired, when they were dying, that these trinkets might be buried with them. One button of gold thread which narrowly escaped this fate may still be seen at a house which overlooks the field of battle. Nay, such was the devotion of the people to their unhappy favourite that, in the face of the strongest evidence by which the fact of a death was ever verified, many continued to cherish a hope that he was still living, and that he would again appear in arms. A person, it was said, who was remarkably like Monmouth, had sacrificed himself to save the Protestant hero. The vulgar long continued, at every important crisis, to whisper that the time was at hand, and that King Monmouth would soon show himself. In 1686, a knave who had pretended to be the Duke, and had levied contributions in several villages of Wiltshire, was apprehended, and whipped from Newgate to Tyburn. In 1698, when England had long enjoyed constitutional freedom under a new dynasty, the son of an innkeeper passed himself on the yeomanry of Sussex as their beloved Monmouth, and defrauded many who were by no means of the lowest class. Five hundred pounds were collected for him. The farmers provided him with a horse. Their wives sent him baskets of chickens and ducks, and were lavish, it was said, of favours of a more tender kind; for, in gallantry at least, the counterfeit was a not unworthy representative of the original. When this impostor was thrown into prison for his fraud, his followers maintained him in luxury. Several of them appeared at the bar to countenance him when he was tried at the Horsham assizes. So long did this delusion last that, when George the Third had been some years on the English throne, Voltaire thought it necessary gravely to confute the hypothesis that the man in the iron mask was the Duke of Monmouth.

THE SEVEN BISHOPS

ON the twenty-seventh of April 1688, the King put forth a second Declaration of Indulgence. In this paper he recited at length the Declaration of the preceding April. His past life, he said, ought to have convinced his people that he was not a man who could easily be induced to depart from any resolution which he had formed. But, as designing men had attempted to persuade the world that he might be prevailed on to give way in this matter, he thought it necessary to proclaim that his purpose was immutably fixed, that he was resolved to employ those only who were prepared to concur in his design, and that he had, in pursuance of that resolution, dismissed many of his disobedient servants from civil and military employments. He announced that he meant to hold a Parliament in November at the latest; and he exhorted his subjects to choose representatives who would assist him in the great work which he had undertaken.

This Declaration at first produced little sensation. It contained nothing new; and men wondered that the King should think it worth while to publish a solemn manifesto merely for the purpose of telling them that he had not changed his mind. Perhaps James was nettled by the indifference with which the announcement of his fixed resolution was received by the public, and thought that his dignity and authority would suffer unless he without delay did something novel and striking. On the fourth of May, accordingly, he made an Order in Council that his Declaration of the preceding week should be read, on two successive Sundays, at the time of divine service, by the officiating ministers of all the churches and chapels of the kingdom. In London and in the suburbs the reading was to take place on the twentieth and twenty-seventh of May, in other parts of England on the third and tenth of June. The

Bishops were directed to distribute copies of the Declaration through their respective dioceses.

When it is considered that the clergy of the Established Church, with scarcely an exception, regarded the Indulgence as a violation of the laws of the realm, as a breach of the plighted faith of the King, and as a fatal blow levelled at the interest and dignity of their own profession, it will scarcely admit of doubt that the Order in Council was intended to be felt by them as a cruel affront. It was popularly believed that Petre had avowed this intention in a coarse metaphor borrowed from the rhetoric of the East. He would, he said, make them eat dirt, the vilest and most loathsome of all dirt. But, tyrannical and malignant as the mandate was, would the Anglican priesthood refuse to obey? The King's temper was arbitrary and severe. The proceedings of the Ecclesiastical Commission were as summary as those of a court martial. Whoever ventured to resist might in a week be ejected from his parsonage, deprived of his whole income, pronounced incapable of holding any other spiritual preferment, and left to beg from door to door. If, indeed, the whole body offered an united opposition to the royal will, it was probable that even James would scarcely venture to punish ten thousand delinquents at once. But there was not time to form an extensive combination. The Order in Council was gazetted on the seventh of May. On the twentieth the Declaration was to be read in all the pulpits of London and the neighbourhood. By no exertion was it possible in that age to ascertain within a fortnight the intentions of one tenth part of the parochial ministers who were scattered over the kingdom. It was not easy to collect in so short a time the sense even of the episcopal order. It might also well be apprehended that, if the clergy refused to read the Declaration, the Protestant Dissenters would misinterpret the refusal, would despair of obtaining any toleration from the members of the Church of England, and would throw their whole weight into the scale of the Court.

The clergy therefore hesitated; and this hesitation may well be excused: for some eminent laymen, who possessed a large share of the public confidence, were disposed to recommend submission. They thought that a general opposition could hardly be expected, and that a partial opposition would be ruinous to individuals, and of little advantage to the Church and to the nation. Such was the opinion given at this time by Halifax and Nottingham. The day drew near; and still there was no concert and no formed resolution.

At this conjuncture the Protestant Dissenters of London won for themselves a title to the lasting gratitude of their country. They had hitherto been reckoned by the government as part of its strength. A few of their most active and noisy preachers, corrupted by the favours of the Court, had got up addresses in favour of the King's policy. Others, estranged by the recollection of many cruel wrongs both from the Church of England and from the House of Stuart, had seen with resentful pleasure the tyrannical prince and the tyrannical hierarchy separated by a bitter enmity, and bidding against each other for the help of sects lately persecuted and despised. But this feeling, however natural, had been indulged long enough. The time had come when it was necessary to make a choice; and the Nonconformists of the City, with a noble spirit, arrayed themselves side by side with the members of the Church in defence of the fundamental laws of the realm. Baxter, Bates, and Howe distinguished themselves by their efforts to bring about this coalition: but the generous enthusiasm which pervaded the whole Puritan body made the task easy. The zeal of the flocks outran that of the pastors. Those Presbyterian and Independent teachers who showed an inclination to take part with the King against the ecclesiastical establishment received distinct notice that, unless they changed their conduct, their congregations would neither hear them nor pay them. Alsop, who had flattered himself that he should be able to bring over a great body of his disciples to the royal side, found himself on a sudden an object of contempt and abhorrence to those who had lately revered him as their spiritual guide, sank into a deep melancholy, and hid himself from the public eye. Deputations waited on several of the London clergy imploring them not to judge of the dissenting body from the servile adulation which had lately filled the London Gazette, and exhorting them, placed as they were in the van of this great fight, to play the men for the liberties of England and for the faith delivered to the Saints. These assurances were received with joy and gratitude. Yet there was still much anxiety and much difference of opinion among those who had to decide whether, on Sunday the twentieth, they would or would not obey the King's command. The London clergy, then universally acknowledged to be the flower of their profession, held a meeting. Fifteen Doctors of Divinity were present. Tillotson, Dean of Canterbury, the most celebrated preacher of the age, came thither from a sick bed. Sherlock, Master of the Temple, Patrick, Dean of Peterborough and Rector of Saint Paul's, Covent Garden, and Stillingfleet, Archdeacon of London and Dean of Saint Paul's Cathedral, attended. The general feeling of the assembly seemed to be that it was, on the whole, advisable to obey the Order in Council. The dispute began to wax warm, and might have produced fatal consequences, if it had not been brought to a close by the firmness and wisdom of Doctor Edward Fowler, Vicar of Saint Giles's, Cripplegate, one of a small but remarkable class of divines who united that love of civil liberty which belonged to the school of Calvin with the theology of the school of Arminius. Standing up, Fowler spoke thus: "I must be plain. The question is so simple that argument can throw no new light on it, and can only beget heat. Let every man say Yes or No. But I cannot consent to be bound by the vote of the majority. I shall be sorry to cause a breach of unity. But this Declaration I cannot in conscience read." Tillotson, Patrick, Sherlock, and Stillingfleet declared that they were of the same mind. The majority yielded to the authority of a minority so respectable. A resolution by which all present pledged themselves to one another not to read the Declaration was then drawn up. Patrick was the first who set his hand to it; Fowler was the second. The paper was sent round the city, and was speedily subscribed by eighty five incumbents.

Meanwhile several of the Bishops were anxiously deliberating as to the course which they should take. On the twelfth of May a grave and learned company was assembled round the table of the Primate at Lambeth. Compton, Bishop of London, Turner, Bishop of Ely, White, Bishop of Peterborough, and Tenison, rector of Saint Martin's Parish, were among the guests. The Earl of Clarendon, a zealous and uncompromising friend of the Church, had been invited. Cartwright, Bishop of Chester, intruded himself on the meeting, probably as a spy. While he remained, no confidential communication could take place; but, after his departure, the great question of which all minds were full was propounded and discussed. The general opinion was that the Declaration ought not to be read. Letters were forthwith written to several of the most respectable prelates of the province of Canterbury, entreating them to come up without delay to London, and to strengthen the hands of their metropolitan at this conjuncture. As there was little doubt that these letters would be opened if they passed through the office in Lombard Street, they were sent by horsemen to the nearest country post towns on the different roads. The Bishop of Winchester, whose loyalty had been so signally proved at Sedgemoor, though suffering from indisposition, resolved to set out in obedience to the summons, but found himself unable to bear the motion of a coach. The letter addressed to William Lloyd, Bishop of Norwich, was, in spite of all precautions, detained by a postmaster; and that prelate, inferior to none of his brethren in courage and in zeal for the common cause of his order, did not reach London in time. His namesake, William Lloyd, Bishop of Saint Asaph, a pious, honest, and learned man, but of slender judgment, and half crazed by his persevering endeavours to extract from the Book of Daniel and from the Revelations some information about the Pope and the King of France, hastened to the capital and arrived on the sixteenth. On the following day came the excellent Ken, Bishop of Bath and Wells, Lake, Bishop of Chichester, and Sir John Trelawney, Bishop of Bristol, a baronet of an old and honourable Cornish family.

On the eighteenth a meeting of prelates and of other eminent divines was held at Lambeth. Tillotson, Tenison, Stillingfleet, Patrick, and Sherlock were present. Prayers were solemnly read before the consultation began. After long deliberation, a petition embodying the general sense was written by the Archbishop with his own hand. It was not drawn up with much felicity of style. Indeed, the cumbrous and inelegant structure of the sentences brought on Sancroft some raillery, which he bore with less patience than he showed under much heavier trials. But in substance nothing could be more skilfully framed than this memorable document. All disloyalty, all intolerance, was earnestly disclaimed. The King was assured that the Church still was, as she had ever been, faithful to the throne. He was assured also that the Bishops would, in proper place and time, as Lords of Parliament and members of the Upper House of Convocation, show that they by no means wanted tenderness for the conscientious scruples of Dissenters. But Parliament had, both in the late and in the present reign, pronounced that the sovereign was not constitutionally competent to dispense with statutes in matters ecclesiastical. The Declaration was therefore illegal; and the petitioners could not, in prudence, honour, or conscience, be parties to the solemn publishing of an illegal Declaration in the house of God, and during the time of divine service.

This paper was signed by the Archbishop and by six of his suffragans, Lloyd of Saint Asaph, Turner of Ely, Lake of Chichester, Ken of Bath and Wells, White of Peterborough, and Trelawney of Bristol. The Bishop of London, being under suspension, did not sign.

It was now late on Friday evening: and on Sunday morning the Declaration was to be read in the churches of London. It was necessary to put the paper into the King's hands without delay. The six Bishops crossed the river to Whitehall. The Archbishop, who had long been forbidden the Court, did not accompany them. Lloyd, leaving his five brethren at the house of Lord Dartmouth in the vicinity of the palace, went to Sunderland, and begged that minister to read the petition, and to ascertain when the King would be willing to receive it. Sunderland, afraid of compromising himself, refused to look at the paper, but went immediately to the royal closet. James directed that the Bishops should be admitted. He had heard from his tool Cartwright that they were disposed to obey the royal mandate, but that they wished for some little modifications in form, and that they meant to present a humble request to that effect. His Majesty was therefore in very good humour. When they knelt before him, he graciously told them to rise, took the paper from Lloyd, and said, "This is my Lord of Canterbury's hand." "Yes, sir, his own hand," was the answer. James read the petition: he folded it up; and his countenance grew dark. "This," he said, "is a great surprise to me. I did not expect this from your Church, especially from some of you. This is a standard of rebellion." The Bishops broke out into passionate professions of loyalty: but the King, as usual, repeated the same words over and over. "I tell you, this is a standard of rebellion." "Rebellion!" cried Trelawney, falling on his knees. "For God's sake, sir, do not say so hard a thing of us. No Trelawney can be a rebel. Remember that my family has fought for the crown. Remember how I served Your Majesty when Monmouth was in the West." "We put down the last rebellion," said Lake: "we shall not raise another." "We rebel!" exclaimed Turner; "we are ready to die at Your Majesty's feet." "Sir," said Ken, in a more manly tone, "I hope that you will grant to us that liberty of conscience which you grant to all mankind." Still James went on. "This is rebellion. This is a standard of rebellion. Did ever a good Church-man question the dispensing power before? Have not some of you preached for it and written for it? It is a standard of rebellion. I will have my Declaration published." "We have two duties to perform," answered Ken, "our duty to God, and our duty to Your Majesty. We honour you: but we fear God." "Have I deserved this?" said the King, more and more angry: "I who have been such a friend to your Church? I did not expect this from some of you. I will be obeyed. My Declaration shall be published. You are trumpeters of sedition. What do you do here? Go to your dioceses; and see that I am obeyed. I will keep this paper. I will not part with it. I will remember you that have signed it." "God's will be done," said Ken. "God has given me the dispensing power," said the King, "and I will maintain it. I tell you that there are still seven thousand of your Church who have not bowed the knee to Baal." The Bishops respectfully retired. That very evening the document which they had put into the hands of the King appeared word for word in print, was laid on the tables of all the coffee-houses, and was cried about the streets. Everywhere the people rose from their beds, and came out to stop the hawkers. It was said that the printer cleared a thousand pounds in a few hours by this penny broadside. This is probably an exaggeration; but it is an exaggeration which proves that the sale was enormous. How the petition got abroad is still a mystery. Sancroft declared that he had taken every precaution against publication, and that he knew of no copy except that which he had himself written, and which James had taken out of Lloyd's hand. The veracity of the Arch-bishop is beyond all suspicion. But it is by no means improbable that some of the divines who assisted in framing the petition may have remembered so short a composition accurately, and may have sent it to the press. The prevailing opinion, however, was that some person about the King had been indiscreet or treacherous. Scarcely less sensation was produced by a short letter which was written with great power of argument and language, printed secretly, and largely circulated on the same day by the post and by the common carriers. A copy was sent to every clergyman in the kingdom. The writer did not attempt to disguise the danger which those who disobeyed the royal mandate would incur: but he set forth in a lively manner the still greater danger of submission. "If we read the Declaration," said he, "we fall to rise no more. We fall unpitied and despised. We fall amidst the curses of a nation whom our compliance will have ruined." Some thought that this paper came from Holland. Others attributed it to Sherlock. But Prideaux, Dean of Norwich, who was a principal agent in dis-tributing it, believed it to be the work of Halifax.

The conduct of the prelates was rapturously extolled by the general voice: but some murmurs were heard. It was said that such grave men, if they thought themselves bound in conscience to remonstrate with the King, ought to have remonstrated earlier. Was it fair to him to leave him in the dark till within thirty six hours of the time fixed for the reading of the Declaration? Even if he wished to revoke the Order in Council, it was too late to do so. The inference seemed to be that the petition was intended, not to move the royal mind, but merely to inflame the discontents of the people. These complaints were uttterly groundless. The King had laid on the Bishops a command new, surprising, and embarrassing. It was their duty to communicate with each other, and to ascertain as far as possible the sense of the profession of which they were the heads before they took any step. They were dispersed over the whole kingdom. Some of them were distant from others a full week's journey. James allowed them only a fortnight to inform themselves, to meet, to deliberate, and to decide; and he surely had no right to think himself aggrieved because that fortnight was drawing to a close before he learned their decision. Nor is it true that they did not leave him time to revoke his order if he had been wise enough to do so. He might have called together his Council on Saturday morning, and before night it might have been known throughout London and the suburbs that he had yielded to the entreaties of the fathers of the Church. The Saturday, however, passed over without any sign of relenting on the part of the government; and the Sunday arrived, a day long remembered.

In the City and liberties of London were about a hundred parish churches. In only four of these was the Order in Council obeyed. At Saint Gregory's the Declaration was read by a divine of the name of Martin. As soon as he uttered the first words, the whole congregation rose and withdrew. At Saint Matthew's, in Friday Street, a wretch named Timothy Hall, who had disgraced his gown by acting as broker for the Duchess of Portsmouth in the sale of pardons, and who now had hopes of obtaining the vacant bishopric of Oxford, was in like manner left alone in his church. At Serjeant's Inn, in Chancery Lane, the clerk pretended that he had forgotten to bring a copy; and the Chief Justice of the King's Bench, who had attended in order to see that the royal mandate was obeyed, was forced to content himself with this excuse. Samuel Wesley, the father of John and Charles Wesley, a curate in London, took for his text that day the noble answer of the three Jews to the Chaldean tyrant; "Be it known unto thee, O King, that we will not serve thy gods, nor worship the golden image which thou hast set up." Even in the chapel of Saint James's Palace the officiating minister had the courage to disobey the order. The Westminster boys long remembered what took place that day in the Abbey. Sprat, Bishop of Rochester, officiated there as Dean. As soon as he began to read the Declaration, murmurs and the noise of people crowding out of the choir drowned his voice. He trembled so violently that men saw the paper shake in his hand. Long before he had finished, the place was deserted by all but those whose situation made it necessary for them to remain.

Never had the Church been so dear to the nation as on the afternoon of that day. The spirit of dissent seemed to be extinct. Baxter from his pulpit pronounced an eulogium on the Bishops and parochial clergy. The Dutch minister, a few hours later, wrote to inform the States General that the Anglican priesthood had risen in the estimation of the public to an incredible degree. The universal cry of the Nonconformists, he said, was that they would rather continue to be under the penal statutes than separate their cause from that of the prelates.

Another week of anxiety and agitation passed away. Sunday came again. Again the churches of the capital were thronged by hundreds of thousands. The Declaration was read nowhere except at the very few places where it had been read the week before. The minister who had officiated at the chapel in Saint James's Palace had been turned out of his situation: and a more obsequious divine appeared with the paper in his hand: but his agitation was so great that he could not articulate. In truth the feeling of the whole nation had now become such as none but the very best and noblest, or the very worst and basest, of mankind could without much discomposure encounter.

Even the King stood aghast for a moment at the violence of the tempest which he had raised. What step was he next to take? He must either advance or recede: and it was impossible to advance without peril, or to recede without humiliation. At one moment he determined to put forth a second order enjoining the clergy in high and angry terms to publish his Declaration, and menacing every one who should be refractory with instant suspension. This order was drawn up and sent to the press, then recalled, then a second time sent to the press, then recalled a second time. A different plan was suggested by some of those who were for rigorous measures. The prelates who had signed the petition might be cited before the Ecclesiastical Commission and deprived of their sees. But to this course strong objections were urged in Council. It had been announced that the Houses would be convoked before the end of the year. The Lords would assuredly treat the sentence of deprivation as a nullity, would insist that Sancroft and his fellow petitioners should be summoned to Parliament, and would refuse to acknowledge a new Archbishop of Canterbury or a new Bishop of Bath and Wells. Thus the session, which at best was likely to be sufficiently stormy, would commence with a deadly quarrel between the crown and the peers. If therefore it were thought necessary to punish the Bishops, the punishment ought to be inflicted according to the known course of English law. Sunderland had from the beginning objected, as far as he dared, to the Order in Council. He now suggested a course which, though not free from inconveniences, was the most prudent and the most dignified that a series of errors had left open to the government. The King might with grace and majesty announce to the world that he was deeply hurt by the undutiful conduct of the Church of England; but that he could not forget all the services rendered by that Church, in trying times, to his father, to his brother, and to himself; that, as a friend to the liberty of conscience, he was unwilling to deal severely by men whom conscience, ill informed indeed, and unreasonably scrupulous, might have prevented from obeying his commands; and that he would therefore leave the offenders to that punishment which their own reflections would inflict whenever they should calmly compare their recent acts with the loyal doctrines of which they had so loudly boasted. Not only Powis and Bellasyse, who had always been for moderate counsels, but Dover and Arundell, leaned towards this proposition. Jeffreys, on the other hand, maintained that the government would be disgraced if such transgressors as the seven Bishops were suffered to escape with a mere reprimand. He did not, however, wish them to be cited before the Ecclesiastical Commission, in which he sate as chief or rather as sole Judge. For the load of public hatred under which he already lay was too much even for his shameless forehead and obdurate heart; and he shrank from the responsibility which he would have incurred by pronouncing an illegal sentence on the rulers of the Church and the favourites of the nation. He therefore recommended a criminal information. It was accordingly resolved that the Archbishop and the six other petitioners should be brought before the Court of King's Bench on a charge of seditious libel. That they would be convicted it was scarcely possible to doubt. The Judges and their officers were tools of the Court. Since the old charter of the City of London had been forfeited, scarcely one prisoner whom the government was bent on bringing to punishment had been absolved by a jury. The refractory prelates would probably be condemned to ruinous fines and to long imprisonment, and would be glad to ransom themselves by serving, both in and out of Parliament, the designs of the Sovereign.

On the twenty-seventh of May it was notified to the Bishops that on the eighth of June they must appear before the King in Council. Why so long an interval was allowed we are not informed. Perhaps James hoped that some of the offenders, terrified by his displeasure, might submit before the day fixed for the reading of the Declaration in their dioceses, and might, in order to make their peace with him, persuade their clergy to obey his order. If such was his hope it was signally disappointed. Sunday the third of June came; and all parts of England followed the example of the capital. Already the Bishops of Norwich, Gloucester, Salisbury, Winchester, and Exeter had signed copies of the petition in token of their approbation. The Bishop of Worcester had refused to distribute the Declaration among his clergy. The Bishop of Hereford had distributed it: but it was generally understood that he was overwhelmed by remorse and shame for having done so. Not one parish priest in fifty complied with the Order in Council. In the great diocese of Chester, including the county of Lancaster, only three clergymen could be prevailed on by Cartwright to obey the King. In the diocese of Norwich are many hundreds of parishes. In only four of these was the Declaration read. The courtly Bishop of Rochester could not overcome the scruples of the minister of the ordinary of Chatham, who depended on the government for bread. There is still extant a pathetic letter which this honest priest sent to the Secretary of the Admiralty. "I cannot," he wrote, "reasonably expect Your Honour's protection. God's will be done. I must choose suffering rather than sin."

On the evening of the eighth of June the seven prelates, furnished by the ablest lawyers in England with full advice, repaired to the palace, and were called into the Council chamber. Their petition was lying on the table. The Chancellor took the paper up, showed it to the Archbishop, and said, "Is this the paper which Your Grace wrote, and which the six Bishops present delivered to His Majesty?" Sancroft looked at the paper, turned to the King, and spoke thus: "Sir, I stand here a culprit. I never was so before. Once I little thought that I ever should be so. Least of all could I think that I should be charged with any offence against my King: but since I am so unhappy as to be in this situation, Your Majesty will not be offended if I avail myself of my lawful right to decline saying anything which may criminate me." "This is mere chicanery," said the King. "I hope that Your Grace will not do so ill a thing as to deny your own hand." "Sir," said Lloyd, whose studies had been much among the casuists, "all divines agree that a person situated as we are may refuse to answer such a question." The King, as slow of understanding as quick of temper, could not comprehend what the prelates meant. He persisted, and was evidently becoming very angry. "Sir," said the Archbishop, "I am not bound to accuse myself. Nevertheless, if Your Majesty positively commands me to answer, I will do so in the confidence that a just and generous prince will not suffer what I say in obedience to his orders to be brought in evidence against me."

"You must not capitulate with your Sovereign," said the Chancellor. "No," said the King; "I will not give any such command. If you choose to deny your own hands, I have nothing more to say to you."

The Bishops were repeatedly sent out into the antechamber, and repeatedly called back into the Council room. At length James positively commanded them to answer the question. He did not expressly engage that their confession should not be used against them. But they, not unnaturally, supposed that, after what had passed, such an engagement was implied in his command. Sancroft acknowledged his handwriting; and his brethren followed his example. They were then interrogated about the meaning of some words in the petition, and about the letter which had been circulated with so much effect all over the kingdom: but their language was so guarded that nothing was gained by the examination. The Chancellor then told them that a criminal information would be exhibited against them in the Court of King's Bench, and called upon them to enter into recognisances. They refused. They were peers of Parliament, they said. They were advised by the best lawyers in Westminster Hall that no peer could be required to enter into a recognisance in a case of libel; and they should not think themselves justified in relinquishing the privilege of their order. The King was so absurd as to think himself personally affronted because they chose, on a legal question, to be guided by legal advice. "You believe every body," he said, "rather than me." He was indeed mortified and alarmed. For he had gone so far that, if they persisted, he had no choice left but to send them to prison; and, though he by no means foresaw all the consequences of such a step, he foresaw probably enough to disturb him. They were resolute. A warrant was therefore made out directing the Lieutenant of the Tower to keep them in safe custody, and a barge was manned to convey them down the river.

It was known all over London that the Bishops were before the Council. The public anxiety was intense. A great multitude filled the courts of Whitehall and all the neighbouring streets. Many people were in the habit of refreshing themselves at the close of a summer day with the cool air of the Thames. But on this evening the whole river was alive with wherries. When the Seven came forth under a guard, the emotions of the people broke through all restraint. Thousands fell on their knees and prayed aloud for the men who had, with the Christian courage of Ridley and Latimer, confronted a tyrant inflamed by all the bigotry of Mary. Many dashed into the stream, and, up to their waists in ooze and water, cried to the holy fathers to bless them. All down the river, from Whitehall to London Bridge, the royal barge passed between lines of boats, from which arose a shout of "God bless Your Lordships." The King, in great alarm, gave orders that the garrison of the Tower should be doubled, that the Guards should be held ready for action, and that two companies should be detached from every regiment in the kingdom, and sent up instantly to London. But the force on which he relied as the means of coercing the people shared all the feelings of the people. The very sentinels who were under arms at the Traitors' Gate reverently asked for a blessing from the martyrs whom they were to guard. Sir Edward Hales was Lieutenant of the Tower. He was little inclined to treat his prisoners with kindness. For he was an apostate from that Church for which they suffered; and he held several lucrative posts by virtue of that dispensing power against which they had protested. He learned with indignation that his soldiers were drinking the health of the Bishops. He ordered his officers to see that it was done no more. But the officers came back with a report that the thing could not be prevented, and that no other health was drunk in the garrison. Nor was it only by carousing that the troops showed their reverence for the fathers of the Church. There was such a show of devotion throughout the Tower that pious divines thanked God for bringing good out of evil, and for making the persecution of His faithful servants the means of saving many souls. All day the coaches and liveries of the first nobles of England were seen round the prison gates. Thousands of humbler spectators constantly covered Tower Hill. But among the marks of public respect and sympathy which the prelates received there was one which more than all the rest enraged and alarmed the King. He learned that a deputation of ten Nonconformist ministers had visited the Tower. He sent for four of these persons, and himself upbraided them. They courageously answered that they thought it their duty to forget past quarrels, and to stand by the men who stood by the Protestant religion.

[Here is omitted an account of the birth of the Pretender.]

The demeanour of the seven prelates meanwhile strengthened the interest which their situation excited. On the evening of the Black Friday, as it was called, on which they were committed, they reached their prison just at the hour of divine service. They instantly hastened to the chapel. It chanced that in the second lesson were these words: "In all things approving ourselves as the ministers of God, in much patience, in afflictions, in distresses, in stripes, in imprisonments." All zealous Churchmen were delighted by this coincidence, and remembered how much comfort a similar coincidence had given, near forty years before, to Charles the First at the time of his death.

On the evening of the next day, Saturday the ninth, a letter came from Sunderland enjoining the chaplain of the Tower to read the Declaration during divine service on the following morning. As the time fixed by the Order in Council for the reading in London had long expired, this proceeding of the government could be considered only as a personal insult of the meanest and most childish kind to the venerable prisoners. The chaplain refused to comply: he was dismissed from his situation; and the chapel was shut up.

The Bishops edified all who approached them by the firmness and cheerfulness with which they endured confinement, by the modesty and meekness with which they received the applauses and blessings of the whole nation, and by the loyal attachment which they professed for the persecutor who sought their destruction. They remained only a week in custody. On Friday the fifteenth of June, the first day of term, they were brought before the King's Bench. An immense throng awaited their coming. From the landing-place to the Court of Requests they passed through a lane of spectators who blessed and applauded them. "Friends," said the prisoners as they passed, "honour the King; and remember us in your prayers." These humble and pious expressions moved the hearers, even to tears. When at length the procession had made its way through the crowd into the presence of the Judges, the Attorney General exhibited the information which he had been commanded to prepare, and moved that the defendants might be ordered to plead. The counsel on the other side objected that the Bishops had been unlawfully committed, and were therefore not regularly before the Court. The question whether a peer could be required to enter into recognisances on a charge of libel was argued at great length, and decided by a majority of the Judges in favour of the crown. The prisoners then pleaded Not Guilty. That day fortnight, the twenty-ninth of June, was fixed for their trial. In the meantime they were allowed to be at large on their own recognisances. The crown lawyers acted prudently in not requiring sureties. For Halifax had arranged that twenty one temporal peers of the highest consideration should be ready to put in bail, three for each defendant; and such a manifestation of the feeling of the nobility would have been no slight blow to the government. It was also known that one of the most opulent

Dissenters of the City had begged that he might have the honour of giving security for Ken.

The Bishops were now permitted to depart to their own homes. The common people, who did not understand the nature of the legal proceedings which had taken place in the King's Bench, and who saw that their favourites had been brought to Westminster Hall in custody and were suffered to go away in freedom, imagined that the good cause was prospering. Loud acclamations were raised. The steeples of the churches sent forth joyous peals. Sprat was amazed to hear the bells of his own Abbey ringing merrily. He promptly silenced them; but his interference caused much angry muttering. The Bishops found it difficult to escape from the importunate crowd of their well-wishers. Lloyd was detained in Palace Yard by admirers who struggled to touch his hands and to kiss the skirt of his robe, till Clarendon, with some difficulty, rescued him and conveyed him home by a bypath. Cartwright, it is said, was so unwise as to mingle with the crowd. A person who saw his episcopal habit asked and received his blessing. A bystander cried out, "Do you know who blessed you?" "Surely," said he who had just been honoured by the benediction, "it was one of the Seven." "No," said the other; "it is the Popish Bishop of Chester." "Popish dog," cried the enraged Protestant; "take your blessing back again."

Such was the concourse, and such the agitation, that the Dutch Ambassador was surprised to see the day close without an insurrection. The King had been anxious and irritable. In order that he might be ready to suppress any disturbance, he had passed the morning in reviewing several battalions of infantry in Hyde Park. It is, however, by no means certain that his troops would have stood by him if he had needed their services. When Sancroft reached Lambeth, in the afternoon, he found the footguards, who were quartered in that suburb, assembled before the gate of his palace. They formed in two lines on his right and left, and asked his benediction as he went through them. He with difficulty prevented them from lighting a bonfire in honour of his return to his dwelling. There were, however, many bonfires that evening in the City. Two Roman Catholics, who were so indiscreet as to beat some boys for joining in these rejoicings, were seized by the mob, stripped naked, and ignominiously branded.

Sir Edward Hales now came to demand fees from those who had lately been his prisoners. They refused to pay anything for a detention which they regarded as illegal to an officer whose commission was, on their principles, a nullity. The Lieutenant hinted very intelligibly that, if they came into his hands again, they should be put into heavy irons and should lie on bare stones. "We are under our King's displeasure," was the answer; "and most deeply do we feel it: but a fellow subject who threatens us does but lose his breath." It is easy to imagine with what indignation the people, excited as they were, must have learned that a renegade from the Protestant faith, who held a command in defiance of the fundamental laws of England, had dared to menace divines of venerable age and dignity with all the barbarities of Lollard's Tower.

Before the day of trial the agitation had spread to the farthest corners of the island. From Scotland the Bishops received letters assuring them of the sympathy of the Presbyterians of that country, so long and so bitterly hostile to prelacy. The people of Cornwall, a fierce, bold, and athletic race, among whom there was a stronger provincial feeling than in any other part of the realm, were greatly moved by the danger of Trelawney, whom they reverenced less as a ruler of the Church than as the head of an honourable house, and the heir through twenty descents of ancestors who had been of great note before the Normans had set foot on English ground. All over the county the peasants chanted a ballad of which the burden is still remembered:

"And shall Trelawney die, and shall Trelawney die?
Then thirty thousand Cornish boys will know the reason why."

The miners from their caverns reechoed the song with a variation:

"Then twenty thousand under ground will know the reason why."

The rustics in many parts of the country loudly expressed a strange hope which had never ceased to live in their hearts. Their Protestant Duke, their beloved Monmouth, would suddenly appear, would lead them to victory, and would tread down the King and the Jesuits under his feet.

The ministers were appalled. Even Jeffreys would gladly have retraced his steps. He charged Clarendon with friendly messages to the Bishops, and threw on others the blame of the prosecution which he had himself recommended. Sunderland again ventured to recommend concession. The late auspicious birth, he said, had furnished the King with an excellent opportunity of withdrawing from a position full of danger and inconvenience without incurring the reproach of timidity or of caprice. On such happy occasions it had been usual for sovereigns to make the hearts of subjects glad by acts of clemency; and nothing could be more advantageous to the Prince of Wales than that he should, while still in his cradle, be the peacemaker between his father and the agitated nation.

M—3

But the King's resolution was fixed. "I will go on," he said. "I have been only too indulgent. Indulgence ruined my father." The artful minister found that his advice had been formerly taken only because it had been shaped to suit the royal temper, and that, from the moment at which he began to counsel well, he began to counsel in vain. He had shown some signs of slackness in the proceeding against Magdalene College. He had recently attempted to convince the King that Tyrconnel's scheme of confiscating the property of the English colonists in Ireland was full of danger, and had, with the help of Powis and Bellasyse, so far succeeded that the execution of the design had been postponed for another year. But this timidity and scrupulosity had excited disgust and suspicion in the royal mind. The day of retribution had arrived. Sunderland was in the same situation in which his rival Rochester had been some months before. Each of the two statesmen in turn experienced the misery of clutching with an agonizing grasp, power which was perceptibly slipping away. Each in turn saw his suggestions scornfully rejected. Both endured the pain of reading displeasure and distrust in the countenance and demeanour of their master; yet both were by their country held responsible for those crimes and errors from which they had vainly endeavoured to dissuade him. While he suspected them of trying to win popularity at the expense of his authority and dignity, the public voice loudly accused them of trying to win his favour at the expense of their own honour and of the general weal. Yet, in spite of mortifications and humiliations, they both clung to office with the gripe of drowning men. Both attempted to propitiate the King by affecting a willingness to be reconciled to his Church. But there was a point at which Rochester was determined to stop. He went to the verge of apostasy: but there he recoiled: and the world, in consideration of the firmness with which he refused to take the final step, granted him a liberal amnesty for all former compliances. Sunderland, less scrupulous and less sensible of shame, resolved to atone for his late moderation, and to recover the royal confidence, by an act which, to a mind impressed with the importance of religious truth, must have appeared to be one of the most flagitious of crimes, and which even men of the world regard as the last excess of baseness. About a week before the day fixed for the great trial, it was publicly announced that he was a Papist. The King talked with delight of this triumph of divine grace. Courtiers and envoys kept their countenances as well as they could while the renegade protested that he had been long convinced of the impossibility of finding salvation out of the communion of Rome, and that his conscience would not let him rest till he had renounced the heresies in which he had been brought up. The news spread fast. At all the coffeehouses it was told how the prime minister of England, his feet bare, and a taper in his hand, had repaired to the royal chapel and knocked humbly for admittance; how a priestly voice from within had demanded who was there; how Sunderland had made answer that a poor sinner who had long wandered from the true Church implored her to receive and to absolve him; how the doors were opened; and how the neophyte partook of the holy mysteries.

This scandalous apostasy could not but heighten the interest with which the nation looked forward to the day when the fate of the seven brave confessors of the English Church was to be decided. To pack a jury was now the great object of the King. The crown lawyers were ordered to make strict inquiry as to the sentiments of the persons who were registered in the freeholders' book. Sir Samuel Astry, Clerk of the Crown, whose duty it was, in cases of this description, to select the names, was summoned to the palace, and had an interview with James in the presence of the Chancellor. Sir Samuel seems to have done his best. For, among the forty eight persons whom he nominated, were said to be several servants of the King, and several Roman Catholics. But as the counsel for the Bishops had a right to strike off twelve, these persons were removed. The crown lawyers also struck off twelve. The list was thus reduced to twenty four. The first twelve who answered to their names were to try the issue.

On the twenty-ninth of June, Westminster Hall, Old and New Palace Yard, and all the neighbouring streets to a great distance were thronged with people. Such an auditory had never before and has never since been assembled in the Court of King's Bench. Thirty five temporal peers of the realm were counted in the crowd.

All the four Judges of the Court were on the bench. Wright, who presided, had been raised to his high place over the heads of many abler and more learned men solely on account of his unscrupulous servility. Allibone was a Papist, and owed his situation to that dispensing power, the legality of which was now in question. Holloway had hitherto been a serviceable tool of the government. Even Powell, whose character for honesty stood high, had borne a part in some proceedings which it is impossible to defend. He had, in the great case of Sir Edward Hales, with some hesitation, it is true, and after some delay, concurred with the majority of the bench, and had thus brought on his character a stain which his honourable conduct on this day completely effaced.

The counsel were by no means fairly matched. The government had required from its law officers services so odious and disgraceful that all the ablest jurists and advocates of the Tory party had, one after another, refused to comply, and had been dismissed from their employments. Sir Thomas Powis, the Attorney General, was scarcely of the third rank in his profession. Sir William Williams, the Solicitor General, had great abilities and dauntless courage: but he wanted discretion; he loved wrangling; he had no command over his temper; and he was hated and despised by all political parties. The most conspicuous assistants of the Attorney and Solicitor were Serjeant Trinder, a Roman Catholic, and Sir Bartholomew Shower, Recorder of London, who had some legal learning, but whose fulsome apologies and endless repetitions were the jest of Westminster Hall. The government had wished to secure the services of Maynard: but he had plainly declared that he could not in conscience do what was asked of him.

On the other side were arrayed almost all the eminent forensic talents of the age. Sawyer and Finch, who, at the time of the accession of James, had been Attorney and Solicitor General, and who, during the persecution of the Whigs in the late reign, had served the crown with but too much vehemence and success, were of counsel for the defendants. With them were joined two persons who, since age had diminished the activity of Maynard, were reputed the two best lawyers that could be found in the Inns of Court; Pemberton, who had, in the time of Charles the Second, been Chief Justice of the King's Bench, who had been removed from his high place on account of his humanity and moderation, and who had resumed his practice at the bar; and Pollexfen, who had long been at the head of the Western circuit, and who, though he had incurred much unpopularity by holding briefs for the crown at the Bloody Assizes, and particularly by appearing against Alice Lisle, was known to be at heart a Whig, if not a republican. Sir Creswell Levinz was also there, a man of great knowledge and experience, but of singularly timid nature. He had been removed from the bench some years before, because he was afraid to serve the purposes of the government. He was now afraid to appear as the advocate of the Bishops, and had at first refused to receive their retainer: but it had been intimated to him by the whole body of attorneys who employed him that, if he declined this brief, he should never have another.

Sir George Treby, an able and zealous Whig, who had been Recorder of London under the old charter, was on the same side. Sir John Holt, a still more eminent Whig lawyer, was not retained for the defence, in consequence, it should seem, of some prejudice conceived against him by Sancroft, but was privately consulted on the case by the Bishop of London. The junior counsel for the Bishops was a young barrister named John Somers. He had no advantages of birth or fortune; nor had he yet had any opportunity of distinguishing himself before the eyes of the public: but his genius, his industry, his great and various accomplishments, were well known to a small circle of friends; and, in spite of his Whig opinions, his pertinent and lucid mode of arguing and the constant propriety of his demeanour had already secured to him the ear of the Court of King's Bench. The importance of obtaining his services had been strongly represented to the Bishops by Johnstone; and Pollexfen, it is said, had declared that no man in Westminster Hall was so well qualified to treat a historical and constitutional question as Somers.

The jury was sworn. It consisted of persons of highly respectable station. The foreman was Sir Roger Langley, a baronet of old and honourable family. With him were joined a knight and ten esquires, several of whom are known to have been men of large possessions. There were some Nonconformists in the number; for the Bishops had wisely resolved not to show any distrust of the Protestant Dissenters. One name excited considerable alarm, that of Michael Arnold. He was brewer to the palace; and it was apprehended that the government counted on his voice. The story goes that he complained bitterly of the position in which he found himself. "Whatever I do," he said, "I am sure to be half ruined. If I say Not Guilty, I shall brew no more for the King; and if I say Guilty, I shall brew no more for anybody else."

The trial then commenced, a trial which, even when coolly perused after the lapse of more than a century and a half, has all the interest of a drama. The advocates contended on both sides with far more than professional keenness and vehemence; the audience listened with as much anxiety as if the fate of every one of them was to be decided by the verdict; and the turns of fortune were so sudden and amazing that the multitude repeatedly passed in a single minute from anxiety to exultation, and back again from exultation to still deeper anxiety.

The information charged the Bishops with having written or published, in the county of Middlesex, a false, malicious, and seditious libel. The Attorney and Solicitor first tried to prove the writing. For this purpose several persons were called to speak to the hands of the Bishops. But the witnesses were so unwilling that hardly a single plain answer could be extracted from any of them. Pemberton, Pollexfen, and Levinz contended that there was no evidence to go to the jury. Two of the Judges, Holloway and Powell, declared themselves of the same opinion; and the hopes of the spectators rose high. All at once the crown lawyers announced their intention to take another line. Powis, with shame and reluctance which he could not dissemble, put into the witness box Blathwayt, a Clerk of the Privy Council, who had been present when the King interrogated the Bishops. Blathwayt swore that he had heard them own their signatures. His testimony was decisive. "Why," said Judge Holloway to the Attorney, "when you had such evidence, did you not produce it at first, without all this waste of time?" It soon appeared why the counsel for the crown had been unwilling, without absolute necessity, to resort to this mode of proof. Pemberton stopped Blathwayt, subjected him to a searching cross examination, and insisted upon having all that had passed between the King and the defendants fully related. "That is a pretty thing indeed," cried Williams. "Do you think," said Powis, "that you are at liberty to ask our witnesses any impertinent question that comes into your heads?" The advocates of the Bishops were not men to be so put down. "He is sworn," said Pollexfen, "to tell the truth and the whole truth; and an answer we must and will have." The witness shuffled, equivocated, pretended to misunderstand the questions, implored the protection of the Court. But he was in hands from which it was not easy to escape. At length the Attorney again interposed. "If," he said, "you persist in asking such a question, tell us, at least, what use you mean to make of it." Pemberton, who, through the whole trial, did his duty manfully and ably, replied without hesitation; "My Lords, I will answer Mr. Attorney. I will deal plainly with the Court. If the Bishops owned this paper under a promise from His Majesty that their confession should not be used against them, I hope that no unfair advantage will be taken of them." "You put on His Majesty what I dare hardly name," said Williams. "Since you will be so pressing, I demand, for the King, that the question may be recorded." "What do you mean, Mr. Solicitor?" said Sawyer, interposing. "I know what I mean," said the apostate: "I desire that the question may be recorded in court." "Record what you will. I am not afraid of you, Mr. Solicitor," said Pemberton. Then came a loud and fierce altercation, which Wright could with difficulty quiet. In other circumstances, he would probably have ordered the question to be recorded, and Pemberton to be committed. But on this great day the unjust Judge was overawed. He often cast a side glance towards the thick rows of Earls and Barons by whom he was watched, and before whom, in the next Parliament he might stand at the bar. He looked, a bystander said, as if all the peers present had halters in their pockets. At length Blathwayt was forced to give a full account of what had passed. It appeared that the King had entered into no express covenant with the Bishops. But it appeared also that the Bishops might not unreasonably think that there was an implied engagement. Indeed, from the unwillingness of the crown lawyers to put the Clerk of the Council into the witness box, and from the vehemence with which they objected to Pemberton's cross examination, it is plain that they were themselves of this opinion.

However, the handwriting was now proved. But a new and serious objection was raised. It was not sufficient to prove that the Bishops had written the alleged libel. It was necessary to prove also that they had written it in the county of Middlesex. And not only was it out of the power of the Attorney and Solicitor to prove this; but it was in the power of the defendants to prove the contrary. For it so happened that Sancroft had never once left the palace at Lambeth from the time when the Order in Council appeared till after the petition was in the King's hands. The whole case for the prosecution had therefore completely broken down; and the audience, with great glee, expected a speedy acquittal.

The crown lawyers then changed their ground again, abandoned altogether the charge of writing a libel, and undertook to prove that the Bishops had published a libel in the county of Middlesex. The difficulties were great. The delivery of the petition to the King was undoubtedly, in the eye of the law, a publication. But how was this delivery to be proved? No person had been present at the audience in the royal closet, except the King and the defendants. The King could not well be sworn. It was therefore only by the admissions of the defendants that the fact of publication could be established. Blathwayt was again examined, but in vain. He well remembered, he said, that the Bishops owned their hands; but he did not remember that they owned the paper which lay on the table of the Privy Council to be the same paper which they had delivered to the King, or that they were even interrogated on that point. Several other official men who had been in attendance on the Council were called, and among them Samuel Pepys, Secretary of the Admiralty; but none of them could remember that anything was said about the delivery. It was to no purpose that Williams put leading questions till the counsel on the other side declared that such twisting, such wiredrawing, was never seen in a court of justice, and till Wright himself was forced to admit that the

Solicitor's mode of examination was contrary to all rule. As witness after witness answered in the negative, roars of laughter and shouts of triumph, which the Judges did not even attempt to silence, shook the hall.

It seemed that at length this hard fight had been won. The case for the crown was closed. Had the counsel for the Bishops remained silent, an acquittal was certain; for nothing which the most corrupt and shameless Judge could venture to call legal evidence of publication had been given. The Chief Justice was beginning to charge the jury, and would undoubtedly have directed them to acquit the defendants; but Finch, too anxious to be perfectly discreet, interfered, and begged to be heard. "If you will be heard," said Wright, "you shall be heard; but you do not understand your own interests." The other counsel for the defence made Finch sit down, and begged the Chief Justice to proceed. He was about to do so, when a messenger came to the Solicitor General with news that Lord Sunderland could prove the publication, and would come down to the court immediately. Wright maliciously told the counsel for the defence that they had only themselves to thank for the turn which things had taken. The countenances of the great multitude fell. Finch was, during some hours, the most unpopular man in the country. Why could he not sit still as his betters, Sawyer, Pemberton, and Pollexfen had done? His love of meddling, his ambition to make a fine speech, had ruined everything.

Meanwhile the Lord President was brought in a sedan chair through the hall. Not a hat moved as he passed; and many voices cried out "Popish dog." He came into court pale and trembling, with eyes fixed on the ground, and gave his evidence in a faltering voice. He swore that the Bishops had informed him of their intention to present a petition to the King, and that they had been admitted into the royal closet for that purpose. This circumstance, coupled with the circumstance that, after they left the closet, there was in the King's hands a petition signed by them, was such proof as might reasonably satisfy a jury of the fact of the publication.

Publication in Middlesex was then proved. But was the paper thus published a false, malicious, and seditious libel? Hitherto the matter in dispute had been whether a fact which everybody well knew to be true could be proved according to technical rules of evidence; but now the contest became one of deeper interest. It was necessary to inquire into the limits of prerogative and liberty, into the right of the King to dispense with statutes, into the right of the subject to petition for the redress of grievances. During three hours the counsel for the petitioners argued with great force in defence of the fundamental principles of the constitution, and proved from the Journals of the House of Commons that the Bishops had affirmed no more than the truth when they represented to the King that the dispensing power which he claimed had been repeatedly declared illegal by Parliament. Somers rose last. He spoke little more than five minutes: but every word was full of weighty matter; and when he sate down his reputation as an orator and a constitutional lawyer was established. He went through the expressions which were used in the information to describe the offence imputed to the Bishops, and showed that every word, whether adjective or substantive, was altogether inappropriate. The offence imputed was a false, a malicious, a seditious libel. False the paper was not; for every fact which it set forth had been proved from the journals of Parliament to be true. Malicious the paper was not; for the defendants had not sought an occasion of strife, but had been placed by the government in such a situation that they must either oppose themselves to the royal will, or violate the most sacred obligations of conscience and honour. Seditious the paper was not; for it had not been scattered by the writers among the rabble, but delivered privately into the hands of the King alone; and a libel it was not, but a decent petition such as, by the laws of England, nay, by the laws of imperial Rome, by the laws of all civilised states, a subject who thinks himself aggrieved may with propriety present to the sovereign.

The Attorney replied shortly and feebly. The Solicitor spoke at great length and with great acrimony, and was often interrupted by the clamours and hisses of the audience. He went so far as to lay it down that no subject or body of subjects, except the Houses of Parliament, had a right to petition the King. The galleries were furious; and the Chief Justice himself stood aghast at the effrontery of this venal turncoat.

At length Wright proceeded to sum up the evidence. His language showed that the awe in which he stood of the government was tempered by the awe with which the audience, so numerous, so splendid, and so strongly excited, had impressed him. He said that he would give no opinion on the question of the dispensing power; that it was not necessary for him to do so; that he could not agree with much of the Solicitor's speech; that it was the right of the subject to petition; but that the particular petition before the Court was improperly worded, and was, in the contemplation of law, a libel. Allibone was of the same mind, but, in giving his opinion, showed such gross ignorance of law and history as brought on him the contempt of all who heard him. Holloway evaded the question of the dispensing power, but said that the petition seemed to him to be such as subjects who think themselves aggrieved are entitled to present, and therefore no libel. Powell took a bolder course. He avowed that, in his judgment, the Declaration of Indulgence was a nullity, and that the dispensing power, as lately exercised, was utterly inconsistent with all law. If these encroachments of prerogative were allowed, there was an end of Parliaments. The whole legislative authority would be in the King. "That issue, gentlemen," he said, "I leave to God and to your consciences."

It was dark before the jury retired to consider of their verdict. The night was a night of intense anxiety. Some letters are extant which were despatched during that period of suspense, and which have therefore an interest of a peculiar kind. "It is very late," wrote the Papal Nuncio; "and the decision is not yet known. The Judges and the culprits have gone to their own homes. The jury remain together. Tomorrow we shall learn the event of this great struggle."

The solicitor for the Bishops sate up all night with a body of servants on the stairs leading to the room where the jury was consulting. It was absolutely necessary to watch the officers who watched the doors; for those officers were supposed to be in the interest of the crown, and might, if not carefully observed, have furnished a courtly juryman with food, which would have enabled him to starve out the other eleven. Strict guard was therefore kept. Not even a candle to light a pipe was permitted to enter. Some basins of water for washing were suffered to pass at about four in the morning. The jurymen, raging with thirst, soon lapped up the whole. Great numbers of people walked the neighbouring streets till dawn. Every hour a messenger came from Whitehall to know what was passing. Voices, high in altercation, were repeatedly heard within the room: but nothing certain was known.

At first nine were for acquitting and three for convicting. Two of the minority soon gave way: but Arnold was obstinate. Thomas Austin, a country gentleman of great estate, who had paid close attention to the evidence and speeches, and had taken full notes, wished to argue the question. Arnold declined. He was not used, he doggedly said, to reasoning and debating. His conscience was not satisfied; and he should not acquit the Bishops. "If you come to that," said Austin, "look at me. I am the largest and strongest of the twelve; and before I find such a petition as this a libel, here I will stay till I am no bigger than a tobacco pipe." It was six in the morning before Arnold yielded. It was soon known that the jury were agreed: but what the verdict would be was still a secret.

At ten the Court again met. The crowd was greater than ever.

The jury appeared in their box; and there was a breathless stillness.

Sir Samuel Astry spoke. "Do you find the defendants, or any of them, guilty of the misdemeanour whereof they are impeached, or not guilty?" Sir Roger Langley answered, "Not Guilty." As the words were uttered, Halifax sprang up and waved his hat. At that signal, benches and galleries raised a shout. In a moment ten thousand persons, who crowded the great hall, replied with a still louder shout, which made the old oaken roof crack; and in another moment the innumerable throng without set up a third huzza, which was heard at Temple Bar. The boats which covered the Thames gave an answering cheer. A peal of gunpowder was heard on the water, and another, and another; and so, in few moments, the glad tidings went flying past the Savoy and the Friars to London Bridge, and to the forest of masts below. As the news spread, streets and squares, marketplaces and coffeehouses, broke forth into acclamations. Yet were the acclamations less strange than the weeping. For the feelings of men had been wound up to such a point that at length the stern English nature, so little used to outward signs of emotion, gave way, and thousands sobbed aloud for very joy. Meanwhile, from the outskirts of the multitude, horsemen were spurring off to bear along all the great roads intelligence of the victory of our Church and nation. Yet not even that astounding explosion could awe the bitter and intrepid spirit of the Solicitor. Striving to make himself heard above the din, he called on the Judges to commit those who had violated, by clamour, the dignity of a court of justice. One of the rejoicing populace was seized. But the tribunal felt that it would be absurd to punish a single individual for an offence common to hundreds of thousands, and dismissed him with a gentle reprimand.

It was vain to think of passing at that moment to any other business. Indeed the roar of the multitude was such that, during half an hour, scarcely a word could be heard in court. Williams got to his coach amidst a tempest of hisses and curses. Cartwright, whose curiosity was ungovernable, had been guilty of the folly and indecency of coming to Westminster in order to hear the decision. He was recognised by his sacerdotal garb and by his corpulent figure, and was hooted through the hall. "Take care," said one, "of the wolf in sheep's clothing." "Make room," cried another, "for the man with the Pope in his belly."

The acquitted prelates took refuge in the nearest chapel from the crowd which implored their blessing. Many churches were open on that morning throughout the capital; and many pious persons repaired thither. The bells of all the parishes of the City and liberties were ringing. The jury meanwhile could scarcely make their way out of the hall. They were forced to shake hands with hundreds. "God bless you!" cried the people; "God prosper your families! you have done like honest goodnatured gentlemen: you have saved us all today." As the noblemen who had appeared to support the good cause drove off, they flung from their carriage windows handfuls of money, and bade the crowd drink to the health of the King, the Bishops, and the jury.

The Attorney went with the tidings to Sunderland, who happened to be conversing with the Nuncio. "Never," said Powis, "within man's memory, have there been such shouts and such tears of joy as today." The King had that morning visited the camp on Hounslow Heath. Sunderland instantly sent a courier thither with the news. James was in Lord Feversham's tent when the express arrived. He was greatly disturbed, and exclaimed in French, "So much the worse for them." He soon set out for London. While he was present, respect prevented the soldiers from giving a loose to their feelings; but he had scarcely quitted the camp when he heard a great shouting behind him. He was surprised, and asked what that uproar meant. "Nothing," was the answer: "the soldiers are glad that the Bishops are acquitted." "Do you call that nothing?" said James. And then he repeated, "So much the worse for them."

He might well be out of temper. His defeat had been complete and most humiliating. Had the prelates escaped on account of some technical defect in the case for the crown, had they escaped because they had not written the petition in Middlesex, or because it was impossible to prove, according to the strict rules of law, that they had delivered to the King the paper for which they were called in question, the prerogative would have suffered no shock. Happily for the country, the fact of publication had been fully established. The counsel for the defence had therefore been forced to attack the dispensing power. They had attacked it with great learning, eloquence, and boldness. The advocates of the government had been by universal acknowledgment overmatched in the contest. Not a single Judge had ventured to declare that the Declaration of Indulgence was legal. One Judge had in the strongest terms pronounced it illegal. The language of the whole town was that the dispensing power had received a fatal blow. Finch, who had the day before been universally reviled, was now universally applauded. He had been unwilling, it was said, to let the case be decided in a way which would have left the great constitutional question still doubtful. He had felt that a verdict which should acquit his clients, without condemning the Declaration of Indulgence, would be but half a victory. It is certain that Finch deserved neither the reproaches which had been cast on him while the event was doubtful, nor the praises which he received when it had proved happy. It was absurd to blame him because, during the short delay which he occasioned, the crown lawyers unexpectedly discovered new evidence. It was equally absurd to suppose that he deliberately exposed his clients to risk, in order to establish a general principle; and still more absurd was it to praise him for what would have been a gross violation of professional duty.

That joyful day was followed by a not less joyful night. The Bishops, and some of their most respectable friends, in vain exerted themselves to prevent tumultuous demonstrations of public feeling. Never within the memory of the oldest, not even on that evening on which it was known through London that the army of Scotland had declared for a free Parliament, had the streets been in such a glare with bonfires. Round every bonfire crowds were drinking good health to the Bishops and confusion to the Papists. The windows were lighted with rows of candles. Each row consisted of seven; and the taper in the centre, which was taller than the rest, represented the Primate. The noise of rockets, squibs, and firearms, was incessant. One huge pile of faggots blazed right in front of the great gate of Whitehall. Others were lighted before the doors of Roman Catholic peers. Lord Arundell of Wardour wisely quieted the mob with a little money: but at Salisbury House in the Strand an attempt at resistance was made. Lord Salisbury's servants sallied out and fired: but they killed only the unfortunate beadle of the parish, who had come thither to put out the fire; and they were soon routed and driven back into the house. None of the spectacles of that night interested the common people so much as one with which they had, a few years before, been familiar, and which they now, after a long interval, enjoyed once more, the burning of the Pope. This once familiar pageant is known to our generation only by descriptions and engravings. A figure, by no means resembling those rude representations of Guy Fawkes which are still paraded on the fifth of November, but made of wax with some skill, and adorned at no small expense with robes and a tiara, was mounted on a chair resembling that in which the Bishops of Rome are still, on some great festivals, borne through Saint Peter's Church to the high altar. His Holiness was generally accompanied by a train of Cardinals and Jesuits. At his ear stood a buffoon disguised as a devil with horns and tail. No rich and zealous Protestant grudged his guinea on such an occasion, and, if rumour could be trusted, the cost of the procession was sometimes not less than a thousand pounds. After the Pope had been borne some time in state over the heads of the multitude, he was committed to the flames with loud acclamations. In the time of the popularity of Oates and Shaftesbury, this show was exhibited annually in Fleet Street before the windows of the Whig Club on the anniversary of the birth of Queen Elizabeth. Such was the celebrity of these grotesque rites, that Barillon once risked his life in order to peep at them from a hiding place. But, from the day when the Rye House Plot was discovered, till the day of the acquittal of the Bishops, the ceremony had been disused. Now, however, several Popes made their appearance in different parts of London. The Nuncio was much shocked; and the King was more hurt by this insult to his Church than by all the other affronts which he had received. The magistrates, however, could do nothing. The Sunday had dawned, and the bells of the parish churches were ringing for early prayers, before the fires began to languish and the crowds to disperse. A proclamation was speedily put forth against the rioters. Many of them, mostly young apprentices, were apprehended; but the bills were thrown out at the Middlesex sessions. The Justices, many of whom were Roman Catholics, expostulated with the grand jury and sent them three or four times back, but to no purpose.

Meanwhile the glad tidings were flying to every part of the kingdom, and were everywhere received with rapture. Gloucester, Bedford, and Lichfield, were among the places which were distinguished by peculiar zeal: but Bristol and Norwich, which stood nearest to London in population and wealth, approached nearest to London in enthusiasm on this joyful occasion.

The prosecution of the Bishops is an event which stands by itself in our history. It was the first and the last occasion on which two feelings of tremendous potency, two feelings which have generally been opposed to each other, and either of which, when strongly excited, has sufficed to convulse the state, were united in perfect harmony. Those feelings were love of the Church and love of freedom. During many generations every violent outbreak of High Church feeling, with one exception, has been unfavourable to civil liberty; every violent outbreak of zeal for liberty, with one exception, has been unfavourable to the authority and influence of the prelacy and the priesthood. In 1688 the cause of the hierarchy was for a moment that of the popular party. More than nine thousand clergymen, with the Primate and his most respectable suffragans at their head, offered themselves to endure bonds and the spoiling of their goods for the great fundamental principle of our free constitution. The effect was a coalition which included the most zealous Cavaliers, the most zealous republicans, and all the intermediate sections of the community. The spirit which had supported Hampden in the preceding generation, the spirit which, in the succeeding generation, supported Sacheverell, combined to support the Archbishop who was Hampden and Sacheverell in one. Those classes of society which are most deeply interested in the preservation of order, which in troubled times are generally most ready to strengthen the hands of government, and which have a natural antipathy to agitators, followed, without scruple, the guidance of a venerable man, the first peer of Parliament, the first minister of the Church, a Tory in politics, a saint in manners, whom tyranny had in his own despite turned into a demagogue. Many, on the other hand, who had always abhorred episcopacy, as a relic of Popery, and as an instrument of arbitrary power, now asked on bended knees the blessing of a prelate who was ready to wear fetters and to lay his aged limbs on bare stones rather than betray the interests of the Protestant religion and set the prerogative above the laws. With love of the Church and with love of freedom was mingled, at this great crisis, a third feeling which is among the most honourable peculiarities of our national character. An individual oppressed by power, even when destitute of all claim to public respect and gratitude, generally finds strong sympathy among us. Thus, in the time of our grandfathers, society was thrown into confusion by the persecution of Wilkes. We have ourselves seen the nation roused almost to madness by the wrongs of Queen Caroline. It is probable, therefore, that, even if no great political and religious interest had been staked on the event of the proceeding against the Bishops, England would not have seen, without strong emotions of pity and anger, old men of stainless virtue pursued by the vengeance of a harsh and inexorable prince who owed to their fidelity the crown which he wore.

Actuated by these sentiments our ancestors arrayed themselves against the government in one huge and compact mass. All ranks, all parties, all Protestant sects, made up that vast phalanx. In the van were the Lords Spiritual and Temporal. Then came the landed gentry and the clergy, both the Universities, all the Inns of Court, merchants, shopkeepers, farmers, the porters who plied in the streets of the great towns, the peasants who ploughed the fields. The league against the King included the very foremast[1]

[1] [Thus, in the first edition. The revised edition reads *foremost*, but *foremast* makes the better sense.]

men who manned his ships, the very sentinels who guarded his palace. The names of Whig and Tory were for a moment forgotten. The old Exclusionist took the old Abhorrer by the hand. Episcopalians, Presbyterians, Independents, Baptists, forgot their long feud and remembered only their common Protestantism and their common danger. Divines bred in the school of Laud talked loudly, not only of toleration, but of comprehension. The Archbishop soon after his acquittal put forth a pastoral letter which is one of the most remarkable compositions of that age. He had, from his youth up, been at war with the Nonconformists, and had repeatedly assailed them with unjust and unchristian asperity. His principal work was a hideous caricature of the Calvinistic theology. He had drawn up for the thirtieth of January and for the twenty-ninth of May forms of prayer which reflected on the Puritans in language so strong that the government had thought fit to soften it down. But now his heart was melted and opened. He solemnly enjoined the Bishops and clergy to have a very tender regard to their brethren the Protestant Dissenters, to visit them often, to entertain them hospitably, to discourse with them civilly, to persuade them, if it might be, to conform to the Church, but, if that were found impossible, to join them heartily and affectionately in exertions for the blessed cause of the Reformation.

Many pious persons in subsequent years remembered that time with bitter regret. They described it as a short glimpse of a golden age between two iron ages. Such lamentation, though natural, was not reasonable. The coalition of 1688 was produced, and could be produced, only by tyranny which approached to insanity, and by danger which threatened at once all the great institutions of the country. If there has never since been similar union, the reason is that there has never since been similar misgovernment. It must be remembered that, though concord is in itself better than discord, discord may indicate a better state of things than is indicated by concord. Calamity and peril often force men to combine. Prosperity and security often encourage them to separate.

THE ARRIVAL OF WILLIAM
AND THE FLIGHT OF JAMES

ON the sixteenth of October [1688], according to the English reckoning, was held a solemn sitting of the States of Holland. The Prince came to bid them farewell. He thanked them for the kindness with which they had watched over him when he was left an orphan child, for the confidence which they had reposed in him during his administration, and for the assistance which they had granted to him at this momentous crisis. He entreated them to believe that he had always meant and endeavoured to promote the interest of his country. He was now quitting them, perhaps never to return. If he should fall in defence of the reformed religion and of the independence of Europe, he commended his beloved wife to their care. The Grand Pensionary answered in a faltering voice; and in all that grave senate there was none who could refrain from shedding tears. But the iron stoicism of William never gave way; and he stood among his weeping friends calm and austere as if he had been about to leave them only for a short visit to his hunting grounds at Loo.

The deputies of the principal towns accompanied him to his yacht. Even the representatives of Amsterdam, so long the chief seat of opposition to his administration, joined in paying him this compliment. Public prayers were offered for him on that day in all the churches of the Hague.

In the evening he arrived at Helvoetsluys and went on board of a frigate called the Brill. His flag was immediately hoisted. It displayed the arms of Nassau quartered with those of England. The motto, embroidered in letters three feet long, was happily chosen. The House of Orange had long used the elliptical device, "I will maintain." The ellipsis was now filled up with words of high import, "The liberties of England and the Protestant religion."

The Prince had not been many hours on board when the wind became fair. On the nineteenth the armament put out to sea, and traversed, before a strong breeze, about half the distance between the Dutch and English coasts. Then the wind changed, blew hard from the west, and swelled into a violent tempest. The ships, scattered and in great distress, regained the shore of Holland as they best might. The Brill reached Helvoetsluys on the twenty-first. The Prince's fellow passengers had observed with admiration that neither peril nor mortification had for one moment disturbed his composure. He now, though suffering from sea sickness, refused to go on shore: for he conceived that, by remaining on board, he should in the most effectual manner notify to Europe that the late misfortune had only delayed for a very short time the execution of his purpose. In two or three days the fleet reassembled. One vessel only had been cast away. Not a single soldier or sailor was missing. Some horses had perished: but this loss the Prince with great expedition repaired; and, before the London Gazette had spread the news of his mishap, he was again ready to sail.

His Declaration preceded him only by a few hours. On the

first of November it began to be mentioned in mysterious whispers by the politicians of London, was passed secretly from man to man, and was slipped into the boxes of the post office. One of the agents was arrested, and the packets of which he was in charge were carried to Whitehall. The King read, and was greatly troubled. His first impulse was to hide the paper from all human eyes. He threw into the fire every copy which had been brought to him, except one; and that one he would scarcely trust out of his own hands.

The paragraph in the manifesto which disturbed him most was that in which it was said that some of the Peers, Spiritual and Temporal, had invited the Prince of Orange to invade England. Halifax, Clarendon, and Nottingham were then in London. They were immediately summoned to the palace and interrogated. Halifax, though conscious of innocence, refused at first to make any answer. "Your Majesty asks me," said he, "whether I have committed high treason. If I am suspected, let me be brought before my peers. And how can Your Majesty place any dependence on the answer of a culprit whose life is at stake? Even if I had invited His Highness over, I should without scruple plead Not Guilty." The King declared that he did not at all consider Halifax as a culprit, and that he had asked the question as one gentleman asks another who has been calumniated whether there be the least foundation for the calumny. "In that case," said Halifax, "I have no objection to aver, as a gentleman speaking to a gentleman, on my honour, which is as sacred as my oath, that I have not invited the Prince of Orange over." Clarendon and Nottingham said the same. The King was still more anxious to ascertain the temper of the Prelates. If they were hostile to him, his throne was indeed in danger. But it could not be. There was something monstrous in the supposition that any Bishop of the Church of England could rebel against his Sovereign. Compton was called into the royal closet, and asked whether he believed that there was the slightest ground for the Prince's assertion. The Bishop was in a strait; for he was himself one of the seven who had signed the invitation; and his conscience, not a very enlightened conscience, would not suffer him, it seems, to utter a direct falsehood. "Sir," he said, "I am quite confident that there is not one of my brethren who is not as guiltless as myself in this matter." The equivocation was ingenious: but whether the difference between the sin of such an equivocation and the sin of a lie be worth any expense of ingenuity may perhaps be doubted. The King was satisfied. "I fully acquit you all," he said. "But I think it necessary that you should publicly contradict the slanderous charge brought against you in the Prince's Declaration." The Bishop very naturally begged that he might be allowed to read the paper which he was required to contradict: but the King would not suffer him to look at it.

On the following day appeared a proclamation threatening with the severest punishment all who should circulate, or who should even dare to read, William's manifesto. The Primate and the few Spiritual Peers who happened to be then in London had orders to wait upon the King. Preston was in attendance with the Prince's Declaration in his hand. "My Lords," said James, "listen to this passage. It concerns you." Preston then read the sentence in which the Spiritual Peers were mentioned. The King proceeded: "I do not believe one word of this: I am satisfied of your innocence: but I think it fit to let you know of what you are accused."

The Primate, with many dutiful expressions, protested that the King did him no more than justice. "I was born in Your Majesty's allegiance. I have repeatedly confirmed that allegiance by my oath. I can have but one King at one time. I have not invited the Prince over; and I do not believe that a single one of my brethren has done so." "I am sure I have not," said Crewe of Durham. "Nor I," said Cartwright of Chester. Crewe and Cartwright might well be believed; for both had sate in the Ecclesiastical Commission. When Compton's turn came, he parried the question with an adroitness which a Jesuit might have envied. "I gave Your Majesty my answer yesterday."

James repeated again and again that he fully acquitted them all. Nevertheless it would, in his judgment, be for his service and for their own honour that they should publicly vindicate themselves. He therefore required them to draw up a paper setting forth their abhorrence of the Prince's design. They remained silent: their silence was supposed to imply consent; and they were suffered to withdraw.

Meanwhile the fleet of William was on the German Ocean. It was on the evening of Thursday the first of November that he put to sea the second time. The wind blew fresh from the east. The armament, during twelve hours, held a course towards the north-west. The light vessels sent out by the English Admiral for the purpose of obtaining intelligence brought back news which confirmed the prevailing opinion that the enemy would try to land in Yorkshire. All at once, on a signal from the Prince's ship, the whole fleet tacked, and made sail for the British Channel. The same breeze which favoured the voyage of the invaders prevented Dartmouth from coming out of the Thames. His ships were forced to strike yards and topmasts; and two of his frigates, which had gained the open sea, were shattered by the violence of the weather and driven back into the river.

Meanwhile the Dutch fleet ran fast before the gale, and reached the Straits at about ten in the morning of Saturday the third of November. William himself, in the Brill, led the way. More than six hundred vessels, with canvass spread to a favourable wind, followed in his train. The transports were in the centre. The men of war, more than fifty in number, formed an outer rampart. Herbert, with the title of Lieutenant Admiral General, commanded the whole fleet. His post was in the rear, and many English sailors, inflamed against Popery, and attracted by high pay, served under him. It was not without great difficulty that the Prince had prevailed on some Dutch officers of high reputation to submit to the authority of a stranger. But the arrangement was eminently judicious. There was, in the King's fleet, much discontent and an ardent zeal for the Protestant faith. But within the memory of old mariners the Dutch and English navies had thrice, with heroic spirit and various fortune, contended for the empire of the sea. Our sailors had not forgotten the broom with which Tromp had threatened to sweep the Channel, or the fire which De Ruyter had lighted in the dockyards of the Medway. Had the rival nations been once more brought face to face on the element of which both claimed the sovereignty, all other thoughts might have given place to mutual animosity. A bloody and obstinate battle might have been fought. Defeat would have been fatal to William's enterprise. Even victory would have deranged all his deeply meditated schemes of policy. He therefore wisely determined that the pursuers, if they overtook him, should be hailed in their own mother tongue, and adjured, by an admiral under whom they had served, and whom they esteemed, not to fight against old messmates for Popish tyranny. Such an appeal might possibly avert a conflict. If a conflict took place, one English commander would be opposed to another: nor would the pride of the islanders be wounded by learning that Dartmouth had been compelled to strike to Herbert.

Happily William's precautions were not necessary. Soon after midday he passed the Straits. His fleet spread to within a league of Dover on the north and of Calais on the south. The men of war on the extreme right and left saluted both fortresses at once. The troops appeared under arms on the decks. The flourish of trumpets, the clash of cymbals, and the rolling of drums were distinctly heard at once on the English and French shores. An innumerable company of gazers blackened the white beach of Kent. Another mighty multitude covered the coast of Picardy. Rapin de Thoyras, who, driven by persecution from his country, had taken service in the Dutch army, and now went with the Prince to England, described the spectacle, many years later, as the most magnificent and affecting that was ever seen by human eyes. At sunset the armament was off Beachy Head. Then the lights were kindled. The sea was in a blaze for many miles. But the eyes of all the steersmen were directed throughout the night to three huge lanterns which flamed on the stern of the Brill.

Meanwhile a courier had been riding post from Dover Castle to Whitehall with news that the Dutch had passed the Straits and were steering westward. It was necessary to make an immediate change in all the military arrangements. Messengers were despatched in every direction. Officers were roused from their beds at dead of night. At three on the Sunday morning there was a great muster by torchlight in Hyde Park. The King had sent several regiments northward in the expectation that William would land in Yorkshire. Expresses were despatched to recall them. All the forces except those which were necessary to keep the peace of the capital were ordered to move to the West. Salisbury was appointed as the place of rendezvous; but, as it was thought possible that Portsmouth might be the first point of attack, three battalions of guards and a strong body of cavalry set out for that fortress. In a few hours it was known that Portsmouth was safe; and these troops received orders to change their route and to hasten to Salisbury.

When Sunday the fourth of November dawned, the cliffs of the Isle of Wight were full in view of the Dutch armament. That day was the anniversary both of William's birth and of his marriage. Sail was slackened during part of the morning; and divine service was performed on board of the ships. In the afternoon and through the night the fleet held on its course. Torbay was the place where the Prince intended to land. But the morning of Monday the fifth of November was hazy. The pilot of the Brill could not discern the sea marks, and carried the fleet too far to the west. The danger was great. To return in the face of the wind was impossible. Plymouth was the next port. But at Plymouth a garrison had been posted under the command of the Earl of Bath. The landing might be opposed; and a check might produce serious consequences. There could be little doubt, moreover, that by this time the royal fleet had got out of the Thames and was hastening full sail down the Channel. Russell saw the whole extent of the peril, and exclaimed to Burnet,

"You may go to prayers, Doctor. All is over." At that moment the wind changed: a soft breeze sprang up from the south: the mist dispersed: the sun shone forth; and under the mild light of an autumnal noon, the fleet turned back, passed round the lofty cape of Berry Head, and rode safe in the harbour of Torbay.

Since William looked on that harbour its aspect has greatly changed. The amphitheatre which surrounds the spacious basin now exhibits everywhere the signs of prosperity and civilisation. At the northeastern extremity has sprung up a great watering place, to which strangers are attracted from the most remote parts of our island by the Italian softness of the air: for in that climate the myrtle flourishes unsheltered; and even the winter is milder than the Northumbrian April. The inhabitants are about ten thousand in number. The newly built churches and chapels, the baths and libraries, the hotels and public gardens, the infirmary and the museum, the white streets, rising terrace above terrace, the gay villas peeping from the midst of shrubberies and flower beds, present a spectacle widely different from any that in the seventeenth century England could show. At the opposite end of the bay lies, sheltered by Berry Head, the stirring market town of Brixham, the wealthiest seat of our fishing trade. A pier and a haven were formed there at the beginning of the present century, but have been found insufficient for the increasing traffic. The population is about six thousand souls. The shipping amounts to more than two hundred sail. The tonnage exceeds many times the tonnage of the port of Liverpool under the kings of the House of Stuart. But Torbay, when the Dutch fleet cast anchor there, was known only as a haven where ships sometimes took refuge from the tempests of the Atlantic. Its quiet shores were undisturbed by the bustle either of commerce or of pleasure; and the huts of ploughmen and fishermen were thinly scattered over what is now the site of crowded marts and of luxurious pavilions.

The peasantry of the coast of Devonshire remembered the name of Monmouth with affection, and held Popery in detestation. They therefore crowded down to the seaside with provisions and offers of service. The disembarkation instantly commenced. Sixty boats conveyed the troops to the coast. Mackay was sent on shore first with the British regiments. The Prince soon followed. He landed where the quay of Brixham now stands. The whole aspect of the place has been altered. Where we now see a port crowded with shipping, and a marketplace swarming with buyers and sellers, the waves then broke on a desolate beach; but a fragment of the rock on which the deliverer stepped from his boat has been carefully preserved, and is set up as an object of public veneration in the centre of that busy wharf.

As soon as the Prince had planted his foot on dry ground he called for horses. Two beasts, such as the small yeomen of that time were in the habit of riding, were procured from the neighbouring village. William and Schomberg mounted and proceeded to examine the country.

As soon as Burnet was on shore he hastened to the Prince. An amusing dialogue took place between them. Burnet poured forth his congratulations with genuine delight, and then eagerly asked what were his Highness's plans. Military men are seldom disposed to take counsel with gownsmen on military matters; and William regarded the interference of unprofessional advisers, in questions relating to war, with even more than the disgust ordinarily felt by soldiers on such occasions. But he was at that moment in an excellent humour, and, instead of signifying his displeasure by a short and cutting reprimand, graciously extended his hand, and answered his chaplain's question by another question: "Well, Doctor, what do you think of predestination now?" The reproof was so delicate that Burnet, whose perceptions were not very fine, did not perceive it. He answered with great fervour that he should never forget the signal manner in which Providence had favoured their undertaking.

During the first day the troops who had gone on shore had many discomforts to endure. The earth was soaked with rain. The baggage was still on board of the ships. Officers of high rank were compelled to sleep in wet clothes on the wet ground: the Prince himself had no better quarters than a hut afforded. His banner was displayed on the thatched roof; and some bedding brought from his ship was spread for him on the floor. There was some difficulty about landing the horses; and it seemed probable that this operation would occupy several days. But on the following morning the prospect cleared. The wind was gentle. The water in the bay was as even as glass. Some fishermen pointed out a place where the ships could be brought within sixty feet of the beach. This was done; and in three hours many hundreds of horses swam safely to shore.

The disembarkation had hardly been effected when the wind rose again, and swelled into a fierce gale from the west. The enemy coming in pursuit down the Channel had been stopped by the same change of weather which enabled William to land. During two days the King's fleet lay on an unruffled sea in sight of Beachy Head. At length Dartmouth was able to proceed. He passed the Isle of

Wight, and one of his ships came in sight of the Dutch topmasts in Torbay. Just at this moment he was encountered by the tempest, and compelled to take shelter in the harbour of Portsmouth. At that time James, who was not incompetent to form a judgment on a question of seamanship, declared himself perfectly satisfied that the Admiral had done all that man could do, and had yielded only to the irresistible hostility of the winds and waves. At a later period the unfortunate prince began, with little reason, to suspect Dartmouth of treachery, or at least of slackness.

The weather had indeed served the Protestant cause so well that some men of more piety than judgment fully believed the ordinary laws of nature to have been suspended for the preservation of the liberty and religion of England. Exactly a hundred years before, they said, the Armada, invincible by man, had been scattered by the wrath of God. Civil freedom and divine truth were again in jeopardy; and again the obedient elements had fought for the good cause. The wind had blown strong from the east while the Prince wished to sail down the Channel, had turned to the south when he wished to enter Torbay, had sunk to a calm during the disembarkation, and, as soon as the disembarkation was completed, had risen to a storm, and had met the pursuers in the face. Nor did men omit to remark that, by an extraordinary coincidence, the Prince had reached our shores on a day on which the Church of England commemorated, by prayer and thanksgiving, the wonderful escape of the royal House and of the three Estates from the blackest plot ever devised by Papists. Carstairs, whose suggestions were sure to meet with attention from the Prince, recommended that, as soon as the landing had been effected, public thanks should be offered to God for the protection so conspicuously accorded to the great enterprise. This advice was taken, and with excellent effect. The troops, taught to regard themselves as favourites of heaven, were inspired with new courage; and the English people formed the most favourable opinion of a general and an army so attentive to the duties of religion.

On Tuesday, the sixth of November, William's army began to march up the country. Some regiments advanced as far as Newton Abbot. A stone, set up in the midst of that little town, still marks the spot where the Prince's Declaration was solemnly read to the people. The movements of the troops were slow: for the rain fell in torrents; and the roads of England were then in a state which seemed frightful to persons accustomed to the excellent communications of Holland. William took up his quarters, during two days, at Ford, a seat of the ancient and illustrious family of Courtenay, in the neighbourhood of Newton Abbot. He was magnificently lodged and feasted there: but it is remarkable that the owner of the house, though a strong Whig, did not choose to be the first to put life and fortune in peril, and cautiously abstained from doing anything which, if the King should prevail, could be treated as a crime.

Exeter, in the meantime, was greatly agitated. Lamplugh, the Bishop, as soon as he heard that the Dutch were at Torbay, set off in terror for London. The Dean fled from the deanery. The magistrates were for the King, the body of the inhabitants for the Prince. Everything was in confusion when, on the morning of Thursday, the eighth of November, a body of troops, under the command of Mordaunt, appeared before the city. With Mordaunt came Burnet, to whom William had entrusted the duty of protecting the clergy of the Cathedral from injury and insult. The Mayor and Aldermen had ordered the gates to be closed, but yielded on the first summons. The deanery was prepared for the reception of the Prince. On the following day, Friday the ninth, he arrived. The magistrates had been pressed to receive him in state at the entrance of the city, but had steadfastly refused. The pomp of that day, however, could well spare them. Such a sight had never been seen in Devonshire. Many of the citizens went forth half a day's journey to meet the champion of their religion. All the neighbouring villages poured forth their inhabitants. A great crowd, consisting chiefly of young peasants, brandishing their cudgels, had assembled on the top of Haldon Hill, whence the army, marching from Chudleigh, first descried the rich valley of the Exe, and the two massive towers rising from the cloud of smoke which overhung the capital of the West. The road, all down the long descent and through the plain to the banks of the river, was lined, mile after mile, with spectators. From the West Gate to the Cathedral Close, the pressing and shouting on each side was such as reminded Londoners of the crowds on the Lord Mayor's day. The houses were gaily decorated. Doors, windows, balconies, and roofs were thronged with gazers. An eye accustomed to the pomp of war would have found much to criticise in the spectacle. For several toilsome marches in the rain, through roads where one who travelled on foot sank at every step up to the ankles in clay, had not improved the appearance either of the men or of their accoutrements. But the people of Devonshire, altogether unused to the splendour of well ordered camps, were overwhelmed with delight and awe. Descriptions of the martial pageant were circulated all over the kingdom. They contained much that was well fitted to gratify the vulgar appetite for the marvellous. For the Dutch army, composed of men who had been born in various climates and had served under various standards, presented an aspect at once grotesque, gorgeous, and terrible to islanders who had, in general, a very indistinct notion of foreign countries. First rode Macclesfield at the head of two hundred gentlemen, mostly of English blood, glittering in helmets and cuirasses, and mounted on Flemish war horses. Each was attended by a negro, brought from the sugar plantations on the coast of Guiana. The citizens of Exeter, who had never seen so many specimens of the African race, gazed with wonder on those black faces set off by embroidered turbans and white feathers. Then, with drawn broadswords came a squadron of Swedish horsemen in black armour and fur cloaks. They were regarded with a strange interest; for it was rumoured that they were natives of a land where the ocean was frozen and where the night lasted through half the year, and that they had themselves slain the huge bears whose skins they wore. Next, surrounded by a goodly company of gentlemen and pages, was borne aloft the Prince's banner. On its broad folds the crowd which covered the roofs and filled the windows read with delight that memorable inscription, "The Protestant religion and the liberties of England." But the acclamations redoubled when, attended by forty running footmen, the Prince himself appeared, armed on back and breast, wearing a white plume and mounted on a white charger. With how martial an air he curbed his horse, how thoughtful and commanding was the expression of his ample forehead and falcon eye, may still be seen on the canvass of Kneller. Once his grave features relaxed into a smile. It was when an ancient woman, perhaps one of those zealous Puritans who, through twenty eight years of persecution, had waited with firm faith for the consolation of Israel, perhaps the mother of some rebel who had perished in the carnage of Sedgemoor, or in the more fearful carnage of the Bloody Circuit, broke from the crowd, rushed through the drawn swords and curvetting horses, touched the hand of the deliverer, and cried out that now she was happy. Near to the Prince was one who divided with him the gaze of the multitude. That, men said, was the great Count Schomberg, the first soldier in Europe, since Turenne and Condé were gone, the man whose genius and valour had saved the Portuguese monarchy on the field of Montes Claros, the man who had earned a still higher glory by resigning the truncheon of a Marshal of France for the sake of his religion. It was not forgotten that the two heroes who, indissolubly united by their common Protestantism, were entering Exeter together, had twelve years before been opposed to each other under the walls of Maestricht, and that the energy of the young Prince had not then been found a match for the cool science of the veteran who now rode in friendship by his side. Then came a long column of the whiskered infantry of Switzerland, distinguished in all the Continental wars of two centuries by preeminent valour and discipline, but never till that week seen on English ground. And then marched a succession of bands designated, as was the fashion of that age, after their leaders, Bentinck, Solmes, and Ginkell, Talmash and Mackay. With peculiar pleasure Englishmen might look on one gallant regiment which still bore the name of the honoured and lamented Ossory. The effect of the spectacle was heightened by the recollection of more than one renowned event in which the warriors now pouring through the West Gate had borne a share. For they had seen service very different from that of the Devonshire militia or of the camp at Hounslow. Some of them had repelled the fiery onset of the French on the field of Seneff; and others had crossed swords with the infidels in the cause of Christendom on that great day when the siege of Vienna was raised. The very senses of the multitude were fooled by imagination. Newsletters conveyed to every part of the kingdom fabulous accounts of the size and strength of the invaders. It was affirmed that they were, with scarcely an exception, above six feet high, and that they wielded such huge pikes, swords, and muskets, as had never before been seen in England. Nor did the wonder of the population diminish when the artillery arrived, twenty one huge pieces of brass cannon, which were with difficulty lugged along by sixteen cart horses to each. Much curiosity was excited by a strange structure mounted on wheels. It proved to be a movable smithy, furnished with all tools and materials necessary for repairing arms and carriages. But nothing caused so much admiration as the bridge of boats, which was laid with great speed on the Exe for the conveyance of waggons and afterwards as speedily taken to pieces and carried away. It was made, if report said true, after a pattern contrived by the Christians who were warring against the Great Turk on the Danube. The foreigners inspired as much good will as admiration. Their politic leader took care to distribute the quarters in such a manner as to cause the smallest possible inconvenience to the inhabitants of Exeter and of the neighbouring villages. The most rigid discipline was maintained. Not only were pillage and outrage effectually prevented, but the troops were required to demean themselves with civility towards all classes. Those who had formed their notions of an army from the conduct of Kirke and his Lambs were amazed to see soldiers who never swore at a landlady or took an egg without paying for it. In return for this moderation the people furnished the troops with provisions in great abundance and at reasonable prices.

Much depended on the course which, at this great crisis, the clergy of the Church of England might take; and the members of the Chapter of Exeter were the first who were called upon to declare their sentiments. Burnet informed the Canons, now left without a head by the flight of the Dean, that they could not be permitted to use the prayer for the Prince of Wales, and that a solemn service must be performed in honour of the safe arrival of the Prince. The Canons did not choose to appear in their stalls; but some of the choristers and prebendaries attended. William repaired in military state to the Cathedral. As he passed under the gorgeous screen, that renowned organ, scarcely surpassed by any of those which are the boast of his native Holland, gave out a peal of triumph. He mounted the Bishop's seat, a stately throne rich with the carving of the fifteenth century. Burnet stood below; and a crowd of warriors and nobles appeared on the right hand and on the left. The singers, robed in white, sang the Te Deum. When the chaunt was over, Burnet read the Prince's Declaration: but as soon as the first words were uttered, prebendaries and singers crowded in all haste out of the choir. At the close Burnet cried in a loud voice, "God save the Prince of Orange!" and many fervent voices answered, "Amen."

On Sunday, the eleventh of November, Burnet preached before the Prince in the Cathedral, and dilated on the signal mercy vouchsafed by God to the English Church and nation. At the same time a singular event happened in a humbler place of worship. Ferguson resolved to preach at the Presbyterian meeting house. The minister and elders would not consent: but the turbulent and halfwitted knave, fancying that the times of Fleetwood and Harrison were come again, forced the door, went through the congregation sword in hand, mounted the pulpit, and there poured forth a fiery invective against the King. The time for such follies had gone by; and this exhibition excited nothing but derision and disgust.

While these things were passing in Devonshire the ferment was great in London. The Prince's Declaration, in spite of all precautions, was now in every man's hands. On the sixth of November James, still uncertain on what part of the coast the invaders had landed, summoned the Primate and three other Bishops, Compton of London, White of Peterborough, and Sprat of Rochester, to a conference in the closet. The King listened graciously while the prelates made warm professions of loyalty, and assured them that he did not suspect them. "But where," said he, "is the paper that you were to bring me?" "Sir," answered Sancroft, "we have brought no paper. We are not solicitous to clear our fame to the world. It is no new thing to us to be reviled and falsely accused. Our consciences acquit us: Your Majesty acquits us; and we are satisfied." "Yes," said the King; "but a declaration from you is necessary to my service." He then produced a copy of the Prince's manifesto. "See," he said, "how you are mentioned here." "Sir," answered one of the Bishops, "not one person in five hundred believes this manifesto to be genuine." "No!" cried the King fiercely: "then those five hundred would bring the Prince of Orange to cut my throat." "God forbid," exclaimed the prelates in concert. But the King's understanding, never very clear, was now quite bewildered. One of his peculiarities was that, whenever his opinion was not adopted, he fancied that his veracity was questioned. "This paper not genuine!" he exclaimed, turning over the leaves with his hands. "Am I not worthy to be believed? Is my word not to be taken?" "At all events, sir," said one of the Bishops, "this is not an ecclesiastical matter. It lies within the sphere of the civil power. God has entrusted Your Majesty with the sword: and it is not for us to invade your functions." Then the Archbishop, with that gentle and temperate malice which inflicts the deepest wounds, declared that he must be excused from setting his hand to any political document. "I and my brethren, sir," he said, "have already smarted severely for meddling with affairs of state; and we shall be very cautious how we do so again. We once subscribed a petition of the most harmless kind: we presented it in the most respectful manner; and we found that we had committed a high offence. We were saved from ruin only by the merciful protection of God. And, sir, the ground then taken by Your Majesty's Attorney and Solicitor was that, out of Parliament, we were private men, and that it was criminal presumption in private men to meddle with politics. They attacked us so fiercely that for my part I gave myself over for lost." "I thank you for that, my Lord of Canterbury," said the King: "I should have hoped that you would not have thought yourself lost by falling into my hands." Such a speech might have become the mouth of a merciful sovereign, but it came with bad grace from a prince who had burned a woman alive for harbouring one of his flying enemies, from a prince round whose knees his own nephew had clung in vain agonies of supplication. The Archbishop was not to be so silenced. He resumed his story, and recounted the insults which the creatures of the Court had offered to the Church of England, among which some ridicule thrown on his own style occupied a conspicuous place. The King had nothing to say but that there was no use in repeating old grievances, and that he had hoped that these things had been quite forgotten. He, who never forgot the smallest injury that he had suffered, could not understand how others should remember for a few weeks the most deadly injuries that he had inflicted.

At length the conversation came back to the point from which it had wandered. The King insisted on having from the Bishops a paper declaring their abhorrence of the Prince's enterprise. They, with many professions of the most submissive loyalty, pertinaciously refused. The Prince, they said, asserted that he had been invited by temporal as well as by spiritual peers. The imputation was common. Why should not the purgation be common also? "I see how it is," said the King. "Some of the temporal peers have been with you, and have persuaded you to cross me in this matter." The Bishops solemnly averred that it was not so. But it would, they said, seem strange that, on a question involving grave political and military considerations, the temporal peers should be entirely passed over, and the prelates alone should be required to take a prominent part. "But this," said James, "is my method. I am your King. It is for me to judge what is best. I will go my own way; and I call on you to assist me." The Bishops assured him that they would assist him in their proper department, as Christian ministers with their prayers, and as peers of the realm with their advice in his Parliament. James, who wanted neither the prayers of heretics nor the advice of Parliaments, was bitterly disappointed. After a long altercation, "I have done," he said; "I will urge you no further. Since you will not help me, I must trust to myself and to my own arms."

The Bishops had hardly left the royal presence, when a courier arrived with the news that on the preceding day the Prince of Orange had landed in Devonshire. During the following week London was violently agitated. On Sunday, the eleventh of November, a rumour was circulated that knives, gridirons, and caldrons, intended for the torturing of heretics, were concealed in the monastery which had been established under the King's protection at Clerkenwell. Great multitudes assembled round the building, and were about to demolish it, when a military force arrived. The crowd was dispersed and several of the rioters were slain. An inquest sate on the bodies, and came to a decision which strongly indicated the temper of the public mind. The jury found that certain loyal and well disposed persons, who had gone to put down the meetings of traitors and public enemies at a mass house, had been wilfully murdered by the soldiers; and this strange verdict was signed by all the jurors. The ecclesiastics at Clerkenwell, naturally alarmed by these symptoms of popular feeling, were desirous to place their property in safety. They succeeded in removing most of their furniture before any report of their intentions got abroad. But at length the suspicions of the rabble were excited. The two last carts were stopped in Holborn, and all that they contained was publicly burned in the middle of the street. So great was the alarm among the Catholics that all their places of worship were closed, except those which belonged to the royal family and to foreign Ambassadors.

On the whole, however, things as yet looked not unfavourably for James. The invaders had been more than a week on English ground. Yet no man of note had joined them. No rebellion had broken out in the north or the east. No servant of the crown appeared to have betrayed his trust. The royal army was assembling fast at Salisbury, and, though inferior in discipline to that of William, was superior in numbers.

The Prince was undoubtedly surprised and mortified by the slackness of those who had invited him to England. By the common people of Devonshire, indeed, he had been received with every sign of good will: but no nobleman, no gentleman of high consideration, had yet repaired to his quarters. The explanation of this singular fact is probably to be found in the circumstance that he had landed in a part of the island where he had not been expected. His friends in the north had made their arrangements for a rising, on the supposition that he would be among them with an army. His friends in the west had made no arrangements at all, and were naturally disconcerted at finding themselves suddenly called upon to take the lead in a movement so important and perilous. They had also fresh in their recollection, and indeed full in their sight, the disastrous consequences of rebellion, gibbets, heads, mangled quarters, families still in deep mourning for brave sufferers who had loved their country well but not wisely. After a warning so terrible and so recent, some hesitation was natural. It was equally natural, however, that William, who, trusting to promises from England, had put to hazard, not only his own fame and fortunes, but also the prosperity and independence of his native land, should feel deeply mortified. He was, indeed, so indignant, that he talked of falling back to Torbay, reembarking his troops, returning to Holland, and leaving those who had betrayed him to the fate which they deserved. At length, on Monday, the twelfth of November, a gentleman named Burrington, who resided in the neighbourhood of Crediton, joined the Prince's standard, and his example was followed by several of his neighbours.

Men of higher consequence had already set out from different parts of the country for Exeter. The first of these was John Lord Lovelace, distinguished by his taste, by his magnificence, and by the audacious and intemperate vehemence of his Whiggism. He had been five or six times arrested for political offences. The last crime laid to his charge was, that he had contemptuously denied the validity of a warrant, signed by a Roman Catholic Justice of the Peace. He had been brought before the Privy Council and strictly examined, but to little purpose. He resolutely refused to criminate himself; and the evidence against him was insufficient. He was dismissed; but, before he retired, James exclaimed in great heat, "My Lord, this is not the first trick that you have played me." "Sir," answered Lovelace, with undaunted spirit, "I never played any trick to Your Majesty, or to any other person. Whoever has accused me to Your Majesty of playing tricks is a liar." Lovelace had subsequently been admitted into the confidence of those who planned the Revolution. His mansion, built by his ancestors out of the spoils of Spanish galleons from the Indies, rose on the ruins of a house of Our Lady in that beautiful valley through which the Thames, not yet defiled by the precincts of a great capital, nor rising and falling with the flow and ebb of the sea, rolls under woods of beech round the gentle hills of Berkshire. Beneath the stately saloon, adorned by Italian pencils, was a subterraneous vault, in which the bones of ancient monks had sometimes been found. In this dark chamber some zealous and daring opponents of the government had held many midnight conferences during that anxious time when England was impatiently expecting the Protestant wind. The season for action had now arrived. Lovelace, with seventy followers, well armed and mounted, quitted his dwelling, and directed his course westward. He reached Gloucestershire without difficulty. But Beaufort, who governed that county, was exerting all his great authority and influence in support of the crown. The militia had been called out. A strong party had been posted at Cirencester. When Lovelace arrived there he was informed that he could not be suffered to pass. It was necessary for him either to relinquish his undertaking or to fight his way through. He resolved to force a passage; and his friends and tenants stood gallantly by him. A sharp conflict took place. The militia lost an officer and six or seven men; but at length the followers of Lovelace were overpowered: he was made a prisoner, and sent to Gloucester Castle.

Others were more fortunate. On the day on which the skirmish took place at Cirencester, Richard Savage, Lord Colchester, son and heir of the Earl Rivers, and father, by a lawless amour, of that unhappy poet whose misdeeds and misfortunes form one of the darkest portions of literary history, came with between sixty and seventy horse to Exeter. With him arrived the bold and turbulent Thomas Wharton. A few hours later came Edward Russell, son of the Earl of Bedford, and brother of the virtuous nobleman whose blood had been shed on the scaffold. Another arrival still more important was speedily announced. Colchester, Wharton, and Russell belonged to that party which had been constantly opposed to the Court. James Bertie, Earl of Abingdon, had, on the contrary, been regarded as a supporter of arbitrary government. He had been true to James in the days of the Exclusion Bill. He had, as Lord Lieutenant of Oxfordshire, acted with vigour and severity against the adherents of Monmouth, and had lighted bonfires to celebrate the defeat of Argyle. But dread of Popery had driven him into opposition and rebellion. He was the first peer of the realm who made his appearance at the quarters of the Prince of Orange.

But the King had less to fear from those who openly arrayed themselves against his authority, than from the dark conspiracy which had spread its ramifications through his army and his family. Of that conspiracy Churchill, unrivalled in sagacity and address, endowed by nature with a certain cool intrepidity which never failed him either in fighting or lying, high in military rank, and high in the favour of the Princess Anne, must be regarded as the soul. It was not yet time for him to strike the decisive blow. But even thus early he inflicted, by the instrumentality of a subordinate agent, a wound, serious if not deadly, on the royal cause.

Edward, Viscount Cornbury, eldest son of the Earl of Clarendon, was a young man of slender abilities, loose principles, and violent temper. He had been early taught to consider his relationship to the Princess Anne as the groundwork of his fortunes, and had been exhorted to pay her assiduous court. It had never occurred to his father that the hereditary loyalty of the Hydes could run any risk of contamination in the household of the King's favourite daughter: but in that household the Churchills held absolute sway; and Cornbury became their tool. He commanded one of the regiments of dragoons which had been sent westward. Such dispositions had been made that, on the fourteenth of November, he was, during a few hours, the senior officer at Salisbury, and all the troops assembled there were subject to his authority. It seems extraordinary that, at such a crisis, the army on which everything depended should have been left, even for a moment, under the command of a young Colonel, who had neither abilities nor experience. There can be little doubt that so strange an arrangement was the result of deep design, and as little doubt to what head and to what heart the design is to be imputed.

Suddenly three of the regiments of cavalry which had assembled at Salisbury were ordered to march westward. Cornbury put himself at their head, and conducted them first to Blandford and thence to Dorchester. From Dorchester, after a halt of an hour or two, they set out for Axminster. Some of the officers began to be uneasy, and demanded an explanation of these strange movements. Cornbury replied that he had instructions to make a night attack on some troops whom the Prince of Orange had posted at Honiton. But suspicion was awake. Searching questions were put, and were evasively answered. At last Cornbury was pressed to produce his orders. He perceived, not only that it would be impossible for him to carry over all the three regiments, as he had hoped, but that he was himself in a situation of considerable peril. He accordingly stole away with a few followers to the Dutch quarters. Most of his troops returned to Salisbury: but some who had been detached from the main body, and who had no suspicion of the designs of their commander, proceeded to Honiton. There they found themselves in the midst of a large force which was fully prepared to receive them. Resistance was impossible. Their leader pressed them to take service under William. A gratuity of a month's pay was offered to them, and was by most of them accepted.

The news of these events reached London on the fifteenth. James had been on the morning of that day in high good humour. Bishop Lamplugh had just presented himself at court on his arrival from Exeter, and had been most graciously received. "My Lord," said the King, "you are a genuine old Cavalier." The archbishopric of York, which had now been vacant more than two years and a half, was immediately bestowed on Lamplugh as the reward of loyalty. That afternoon, just as the King was sitting down to dinner, arrived an express with the tidings of Cornbury's defection. James turned away from his untasted meal, swallowed a crust of bread and a glass of wine, and retired to his closet. He afterwards learned that, as he was rising from table, several of the Lords in whom he reposed the greatest confidence were shaking hands and congratulating each other in the adjoining gallery. When the news was carried to the Queen's apartments she and her ladies broke out into tears and loud cries of sorrow.

The blow was indeed a heavy one. It was true that the direct loss to the crown and the direct gain to the invaders hardly amounted to two hundred men and as many horses. But where could the King henceforth expect to find those sentiments in which consists the strength of states and of armies? Cornbury was the heir of a house conspicuous for its attachment to monarchy. His father Clarendon, his uncle Rochester, were men whose loyalty was supposed to be proof to all temptation. What must be the strength of that feeling against which the most deeply rooted hereditary prejudices were of no avail, of that feeling which could reconcile a young officer of high birth to desertion, aggravated by breach of trust and by gross falsehood? That Cornbury was not a man of brilliant parts or enterprising temper made the event more alarming. It was impossible to doubt that he had in some quarter a powerful and artful prompter. Who that prompter was soon became evident. In the meantime no man in the royal camp could feel assured that he was not surrounded by traitors. Political rank, military rank, the honour of a nobleman, the honour of a soldier, the strongest professions, the purest Cavalier blood, could no longer afford security. Every man might reasonably doubt whether every order which he received from his superior was not meant to serve the purposes of the enemy. That prompt obedience without which an army is merely a rabble was necessarily at an end. What discipline could there be among soldiers who had just been saved from a snare by refusing to follow their commanding officer on a secret expedition, and by insisting on a sight of his orders?

Cornbury was soon kept in countenance by a crowd of deserters superior to him in rank and capacity: but during a few days he stood alone in his shame, and was bitterly reviled by many who afterwards imitated his example and envied his dishonourable precedence. Among these was his own father. The first outbreak of Clarendon's rage and sorrow was highly pathetic. "Oh God!" he ejaculated, "that a son of mine should be a rebel!" A fortnight later he made up his mind to be a rebel himself. Yet it would be unjust to pronounce him a mere hypocrite. In revolutions men live fast: the experience of years is crowded into hours: old habits of thought and action are violently broken; and novelties, which at first sight inspire dread and disgust become in a few days familiar, endurable, attractive. Many men of far purer virtue and higher spirit than Clarendon were prepared, before that memorable year ended, to do what they would have pronounced wicked and infamous when it began.

The unhappy father composed himself as well as he could, and sent to ask a private audience of the King. It was granted. James said, with more than his usual graciousness, that he from his heart pitied Cornbury's relations, and should not hold them at all accountable for the crime of their unworthy kinsman. Clarendon went home, scarcely daring to look his friends in the face. Soon, however, he learned with surprise that the act which had, as he at first thought, for ever dishonoured his family was applauded by some persons of high station. His niece, the Princess of Denmark, asked him why he shut himself up. He answered that he had been overwhelmed with confusion by his son's villany. Anne seemed not at all to understand this feeling. "People," she said, "are very uneasy about Popery. I believe that many of the army will do the same."

And now the King, greatly disturbed, called together the principal officers who were still in London. Churchill, who was about this time promoted to the rank of Lieutenant General, made his appearance with that bland serenity which neither peril nor infamy could ever disturb. The meeting was attended by Henry Fitzroy, Duke of Grafton, whose audacity and activity made him conspicuous among the natural children of Charles the Second. Grafton was colonel of the first regiment of Foot Guards. He seems to have been at this time completely under Churchill's influence, and was prepared to desert the royal standard as soon as the favourable moment should arrive. Two other traitors were in the circle, Kirke and Trelawney, who commanded those two fierce and lawless bands then known as the Tangier regiments. Both of them had, like the other Protestant officers of the army, long seen with extreme displeasure the partiality which the King had shown to members of his own Church; and Trelawney remembered with bitter resentment the persecution of his brother the Bishop of Bristol. James addressed the assembly in language worthy of a better man and of a better cause. It might be, he said, that some of the officers had conscientious scruples about fighting for him. If so, he was willing to receive back their commissions. But he adjured them as gentlemen and soldiers not to imitate the shameful example of Cornbury. All seemed moved; and none more than Churchill. He was the first to vow with well feigned enthusiasm that he would shed the last drop of his blood in the service of his gracious master: Grafton was loud and forward in similar protestations; and the example was followed by Kirke and Trelawney.

Deceived by these professions, the King prepared to set out for Salisbury. Before his departure he was informed that a considerable number of peers, temporal and spiritual, desired to be admitted to an audience. They came, with Sancroft at their head, to present a petition, praying that a free and legal Parliament might be called, and that a negotiation might be opened with the Prince of Orange.

The history of this petition is curious. The thought seems to have occurred at once to two great chiefs of parties who had long been rivals and enemies, Rochester and Halifax. They both, independently of one another, consulted the Bishops. The Bishops warmly approved of the suggestion. It was then proposed that a general meeting of peers should be called to deliberate on the form of an address to the King. It was term time; and in term time men of rank and fashion then lounged every day in Westminster Hall as they now lounge in the clubs of Pall Mall and Saint James's Street. Nothing could be easier than for the Lords who assembled there to step aside into some adjoining room and to hold a consultation. But unexpected difficulties arose. Halifax became first cold and then adverse. It was his nature to discover objections to everything; and on this occasion his sagacity was quickened by rivalry. The scheme, which he had approved while he regarded it as his own, began to displease him as soon as he found that it was also the scheme of Rochester, by whom he had been long thwarted and at length supplanted, and whom he disliked as much as it was in his easy nature to dislike anybody. Nottingham was at that time much under the influence of Halifax. They both declared that they would not join in the address if Rochester signed it. Clarendon expostulated in vain. "I mean no disrespect," said Halifax, "to my Lord Rochester: but he has been a member of the Ecclesiastical Commission: the proceedings of that Court must soon be the subject of a very serious inquiry; and it is not fit that one who has sate there should take any part in our proceedings." Nottingham, with strong expressions of personal esteem for Rochester, avowed the same opinion. The authority of the two dissentient Lords prevented several other noblemen from subscribing the address; but the Hydes and the Bishops persisted. Nineteen signatures were procured; and the petitioners waited in a body on the King.

He received their address ungraciously. He assured them, indeed, that he passionately desired the meeting of a free Parliament; and he promised them, on the faith of a King, that he would call one as soon as the Prince of Orange should have left the island. "But how," said he, "can a Parliament be free when an enemy is in the kingdom, and can return near a hundred votes?" To the prelates he spoke with peculiar acrimony. "I could not," he said, "prevail on you the other day to declare against this invasion: but you are ready enough to declare against me. Then you would not meddle with politics. You have no scruple about meddling now. You have excited this rebellious temper among your flocks; and now you foment it. You would be better employed in teaching them how to obey than in teaching me how to govern." He was much incensed against his nephew Grafton, whose signature stood next to that of Sancroft, and said to the young man, with great asperity, "You know nothing about religion: you care nothing about it; and yet, forsooth, you must pretend to have a conscience." "It is true, sir," answered Grafton, with impudent frankness, "that I have very little conscience: but I belong to a party which has a great deal."

Bitter as was the King's language to the petitioners, it was far less bitter than that which he held after they had withdrawn. He had done, he said, far too much already in the hope of satisfying an undutiful and ungrateful people. He had always hated the thought of concession: but he had suffered himself to be talked over; and now he, like his father before him, had found that concession only made subjects more encroaching. He would yield nothing more, not an atom; and, after his fashion, he vehemently repeated many times, "Not an atom." Not only would he make no overtures to the invaders, but he would receive none. If the Dutch sent flags of truce, the first messenger should be dismissed without an answer; the second should be hanged. In such a mood James set out for Salisbury. His last act before his departure was to appoint a Council of five Lords to represent him in London during his absence. Of the five, two were Papists, and by law incapable of office. Joined with them was Jeffreys, a Protestant indeed, but more detested by the nation than any Papist. To the other two members of this board, Preston and Godolphin, no serious objection could be made. On the day on which the King left London the Prince of Wales was sent to Portsmouth. That fortress was strongly garrisoned, and was under the government of Berwick. The fleet commanded by Dartmouth lay close at hand: and it was supposed that, if things went ill, the royal infant would, without difficulty, be conveyed from Portsmouth to France.

On the nineteenth James reached Salisbury, and took up his quarters in the episcopal palace. Evil news was now fast pouring in upon him from all sides. The western counties had at length risen. As soon as the news of Cornbury's desertion was known, many wealthy landowners took heart and hastened to Exeter. Among them was Sir William Portman of Bryanstone, one of the greatest men in Dorsetshire, and Sir Francis Warre of Hestercombe, whose interest was great in Somersetshire. But the most important of the new comers was Seymour, who had recently inherited a baronetcy which added nothing to his dignity, and who, in birth, in politica influence, and in parliamentary abilities, was beyond comparison the foremost among the Tory gentlemen of England. At his first audience he is said to have exhibited his characteristic pride in a way which surprised and amused the Prince. "I think, Sir Edward," said William, meaning to be very civil, "that you are of the family of the Duke of Somerset." "Pardon me, sir," said Sir Edward, who never forgot that he was the head of the elder branch of the Seymours: "the Duke of Somerset is of my family."

The quarters of William now began to present the appearance of a court. More than sixty men of rank and fortune were lodged at Exeter; and the daily display of rich liveries, and of coaches drawn by six horses in the Cathedral Close, gave to that quiet precinct something of the splendour and gaiety of Whitehall. The common people were eager to take arms; and it would have been easy to form many battalions of infantry. But Schomberg, who thought little of soldiers fresh from the plough, maintained that, if the expedition could not succeed without such help, it would not succeed at all; and William, who had as much professional feeling as Schomberg, concurred in this opinion. Commissions therefore for raising new regiments were very sparingly given; and none but picked recruits were enlisted.

It was now thought desirable that the Prince should give a public reception to the whole body of noblemen and gentlemen who had assembled at Exeter. He addressed them in a short but dignified and well considered speech. He was not, he said, acquainted with the faces of all whom he saw. But he had a list of their names, and knew how high they stood in the estimation of their country. He gently chid their tardiness, but expressed a confident hope that it was not yet too late to save the kingdom. "Therefore," he said, "gentlemen, friends, and fellow Protestants, we bid you and all your followers most heartily welcome to our court and camp."

Seymour, a keen politician, long accustomed to the tactics of faction, saw in a moment that the party which had begun to rally round the Prince stood in need of organisation. It was as yet, he said, a mere rope of sand: no common object had been publicly and formally avowed: nobody was pledged to anything. As soon as the assembly at the deanery broke up, he sent for Burnet, and suggested that an association should be formed, and that all the English adherents of the Prince should put their hands to an instrument binding them to be true to their leader and to each other. Burnet carried the suggestion to the Prince and to Shrewsbury, by both of whom it was approved. A meeting was held in the Cathedral. A short paper drawn up by Burnet was produced, approved, and eagerly signed. The subscribers engaged to pursue in concert the objects set forth in the Prince's Declaration; to stand by him and by each other; to take signal vengeance on all who should make any attempt on his person; and, even if such an attempt should unhappily succeed, to persist in their undertaking till the liberties and the religion of the nation should be effectually secured.

About the same time a messenger arrived at Exeter from the Earl of Bath, who commanded at Plymouth. Bath declared that he placed himself, his troops, and the fortress which he governed at the Prince's disposal. The invaders therefore had now not a single enemy in their rear.

While the West was thus rising to confront the King, the North was all in a flame behind him. On the sixteenth Delamere took arms in Cheshire. He convoked his tenants, called upon them to stand by him, promised that, if they fell in the cause, their leases should be renewed to their children, and exhorted every one who had a good horse either to take the field, or to provide a substitute. He appeared at Manchester with fifty men armed and mounted, and his force had trebled before he reached Boaden Downs.

The neighbouring counties were violently agitated. It had been arranged that Danby should seize York, and that Devonshire should appear at Nottingham. At Nottingham no resistance was anticipated. But at York there was a small garrison under the command of Sir John Reresby. Danby acted with rare dexterity. A meeting of the gentry and freeholders of Yorkshire had been summoned for the twenty-second of November to address the King on the state of affairs. All the Deputy Lieutenants of the three Ridings, several noblemen, and a multitude of opulent esquires and substantial yeomen had been attracted to the provincial capital. Four troops of militia had been drawn out under arms to preserve the public peace. The Common Hall was crowded with freeholders, and the discussion had begun, when a cry was suddenly raised that the Papists were up, and were slaying the Protestants. The Papists of York were much more likely to be employed in seeking for hiding places than in attacking enemies who outnumbered them in the proportion of a hundred to one. But at that time no story of Popish atrocity could be so wild and marvellous as not to find ready belief. The meeting separated in dismay. The whole city was in confusion. At this moment Danby at the head of about a hundred horsemen rode up to the militia, and raised the cry "No Popery! A free Parliament! The Protestant religion!" The militia echoed the shout. The garrison was instantly surprised and disarmed. The governor was placed under arrest. The gates were closed. Sentinels were placed everywhere. The populace was suffered to pull down a Roman Catholic chapel; but no other harm appears to have been done. On the following morning the Guildhall was crowded with the first gentlemen of the shire, and with the principal magistrates of the city. The Lord Mayor was placed in the chair. Danby proposed a Declaration setting forth the reasons which had induced the friends of the constitution and of the Protestant religion to rise in arms. This Declaration was eagerly adopted, and received in a few hours the signatures of six peers, of five baronets, of six knights, and of many gentlemen of high consideration.

Devonshire meantime, at the head of a great body of friends and dependents, quitted the palace which he was rearing at Chatsworth, and appeared in arms at Derby. There he formally delivered to the municipal authorities a paper stating the reasons which had moved him to this enterprise. He then proceeded to Nottingham, which soon became the head quarters of the Northern insurrection. Here a proclamation was put forth couched in bold and severe terms. The name of rebellion, it was said, was a bugbear which could frighten no reasonable man. Was it rebellion to defend those laws and that religion which every king of England bound himself by oath to maintain? How that oath had lately been observed was a question on which, it was to be hoped, a free Parliament would soon pronounce. In the meantime, the insurgents declared that they held it to be not rebellion, but legitimate self defence, to resist a tyrant who knew no law but his own will. The Northern rising became every day more formidable. Four powerful and wealthy Earls, Manchester, Stamford, Rutland, and Chesterfield, repaired to Nottingham, and were joined there by Lord Cholmondeley and by Lord Grey de Ruthyn.

All this time the hostile armies in the south were approaching each other. The Prince of Orange, when he learned that the King had arrived at Salisbury, thought it time to leave Exeter. He placed that city and the surrounding country under the government of Sir Edward Seymour, and set out on Wednesday the twenty-first of November, escorted by many of the most considerable gentlemen of the western counties, for Axminster, where he remained several days.

The King was eager to fight; and it was obviously his interest to

M—4*

do so. Every hour took away something from his own strength, and added something to the strength of his enemies. It was most important, too, that his troops should be blooded. A great battle, however it might terminate, could not but injure the Prince's popularity. All this William perfectly understood, and determined to avoid an action as long as possible. It is said that, when Schomberg was told that the enemy were advancing and were determined to fight, he answered, with the composure of a tactician confident in his skill, "That will be just as we may choose." It was, however, impossible to prevent all skirmishing between the advanced guards of the armies. William was desirous that in such skirmishing nothing might happen which could wound the pride or rouse the vindictive feelings of the nation which he meant to deliver. He therefore, with admirable prudence, placed his British regiments in the situations where there was most risk of collision. The outposts of the royal army were Irish. The consequence was that, in the little combats of this short campaign, the invaders had on their side the hearty sympathy of all Englishmen.

The first of these encounters took place at Wincanton. Mackay's regiment, composed of British soldiers, lay near a body of the King's Irish troops, commanded by their countryman, the gallant Sarsfield. Mackay sent out a small party under a lieutenant named Campbell, to procure horses for the baggage. Campbell found what he wanted at Wincanton, and was just leaving that town on his return, when a strong detachment of Sarsfield's troops approached. The Irish were four to one: but Campbell resolved to fight it out to the last. With a handful of resolute men he took his stand in the road. The rest of his soldiers lined the hedges which overhung the highway on the right and on the left. The enemy came up. "Stand," cried Campbell; "for whom are you?" "I am for King James," answered the leader of the other party. "And I for the Prince of Orange," cried Campbell. "We will prince you," answered the Irishman with a curse. "Fire!" exclaimed Campbell; and a sharp fire was instantly poured in from both the hedges. The King's troops received three well aimed volleys before they could make any return. At length they succeeded in carrying one of the hedges; and would have overpowered the little band which was opposed to them, had not the country people, who mortally hated the Irish, given a false alarm that more of the Prince's troops were coming up. Sarsfield recalled his men and fell back; and Campbell proceeded on his march unmolested with the baggage horses. This affair, creditable undoubtedly to the valour and discipline of the Prince's army, was magnified by report into a victory won against great odds by British Protestants over Popish barbarians who had been brought from Connaught to oppress our island.

A few hours after this skirmish an event took place which put an end to all risk of a more serious struggle between the armies. Churchill and some of his principal accomplices were assembled at Salisbury. Two of the conspirators, Kirke and Trelawney, had proceeded to Warminster, where their regiments were posted. All was ripe for the execution of the long meditated treason.

Churchill advised the King to visit Warminster, and to inspect the troops stationed there. James assented; and his coach was at the door of the episcopal palace when his nose began to bleed violently. He was forced to postpone his expedition and to put himself under medical treatment. Three days elapsed before the hemorrhage was entirely subdued; and during those three days alarming rumours reached his ears.

It was impossible that a conspiracy so widely spread as that of which Churchill was the head could be kept altogether secret. There was no evidence which could be laid before a jury or a court martial; but strange whispers wandered about the camp. Feversham, who held the chief command, reported that there was a bad spirit in the army. It was hinted to the King that some who were near his person were not his friends, and that it would be a wise precaution to send Churchill and Grafton under a guard to Portsmouth. James rejected this counsel. A propensity to suspicion was not among his vices. Indeed the confidence which he reposed in professions of fidelity and attachment was such as might rather have been expected from a goodhearted and inexperienced stripling than from a politician who was far advanced in life, who had seen much of the world, who had suffered much from villanous arts, and whose own character was by no means a favourable specimen of human nature. It would be difficult to mention any other man who, having himself so little scruple about breaking faith with his neighbours, was so slow to believe that his neighbours could break faith with him. Nevertheless the reports which he had received of the state of his army disturbed him greatly. He was now no longer impatient for a battle. He even began to think of retreating. On the evening of Saturday, the twenty-fourth of November, he called a council of war. The meeting was attended by those officers against whom he had been most earnestly cautioned. Feversham expressed an opinion that it was desirable to fall back. Churchill argued on the other side. The consultation lasted till midnight. At length the King declared that he had decided for a retreat. Churchill saw or imagined that he was distrusted, and, though gifted with a rare self command, could not conceal his uneasiness. Before the day broke he fled to the Prince's quarters, accompanied by Grafton.

Churchill left behind him a letter of explanation. It was written with that decorum which he never failed to preserve in the midst of guilt and dishonour. He acknowledged that he owed everything to the royal favour. Interest, he said, and gratitude impelled him in the same direction. Under no other government could he hope to be so great and prosperous as he had been: but all such considerations must yield to a paramount duty. He was a Protestant; and he could not conscientiously draw his sword against the Protestant cause. As to the rest he would ever be ready to hazard life and fortune in defence of the sacred person and of the lawful rights of his gracious master.

Next morning all was confusion in the royal camp. The King's friends were in dismay. His enemies could not conceal their exultation. The consternation of James was increased by news which arrived on the same day from Warminster. Kirke, who commanded at that post, had refused to obey orders which he had received from Salisbury. There could no longer be any doubt that he too was in league with the Prince of Orange. It was rumoured that he had actually gone over with all his troops to the enemy: and the rumour, though false, was, during some hours, fully believed. A new light flashed on the mind of the unhappy King. He thought that he understood why he had been pressed, a few days before, to visit Warminster. There he would have found himself helpless, at the mercy of the conspirators, and in the vicinity of the hostile outposts. Those who might have attempted to defend him would have been easily overpowered. He would have been carried a prisoner to the head quarters of the invading army. Perhaps some still blacker treason might have been committed; for men who have once engaged in a wicked and perilous enterprise are no longer their own masters, and are often impelled, by a fatality which is part of their just punishment, to crimes such as they would at first have shuddered to contemplate. Surely it was not without the special intervention of some guardian Saint that a King devoted to the Catholic Church had, at the very moment when he was blindly hastening to captivity, perhaps to death, been suddenly arrested by what he had then thought a disastrous malady.

All these things confirmed James in the resolution which he had taken on the preceding evening. Orders were given for an immediate retreat. Salisbury was in an uproar. The camp broke up with the confusion of a flight. No man knew whom to trust or whom to obey. The material strength of the army was little diminished: but its moral strength had been destroyed. Many whom shame would have restrained from leading the way to the Prince's quarters were eager to imitate an example which they never would have set; and many, who would have stood by their King while he appeared to be resolutely advancing against the invaders, felt no inclination to follow a receding standard.

James went that day as far as Andover. He was attended by his son in law Prince George, and by the Duke of Ormond. Both were among the conspirators, and would probably have accompanied Churchill, had he not, in consequence of what had passed at the council of war, thought it expedient to take his departure suddenly. The impenetrable stupidity of Prince George served his turn on this occasion better than cunning would have done. It was his habit, when any news was told him, to exclaim in French, "Est-il-possible?" "Is it possible?" This catchword was now of great use to him. "Est-il-possible?" he cried, when he had been made to understand that Churchill and Grafton were missing. And when the ill tidings came from Warminster he again ejaculated, "Est-il-possible?"

Prince George and Ormond were invited to sup with the King at Andover. The meal must have been a sad one. The King was overwhelmed by his misfortunes. His son in law was the dullest of companions. "I have tried Prince George sober," said Charles the Second; "and I have tried him drunk; and, drunk or sober, there is nothing in him." Ormond, who was through life taciturn and bashful, was not likely to be in high spirits at such a moment. At length the repast terminated. The King retired to rest. Horses were in waiting for the Prince and Ormond, who, as soon as they left the table, mounted and rode off. They were accompanied by the Earl of Drumlanrig, eldest son of the Duke of Queensberry. The defection of this young nobleman was no insignificant event. For Queensberry was the head of the Protestant Episcopalians of Scotland, a class compared with whom the bitterest English Tories might be called Whiggish; and Drumlanrig himself was Lieutenant Colonel of Dundee's regiment of horse, a band more detested by the Whigs than even Kirke's Lambs. This fresh calamity was announced to the King on the following morning. He was less disturbed by the news than might have been expected. The shock which he had undergone twenty four hours before had prepared him for almost any disaster; and it was impossible to be seriously angry with Prince George, who was hardly an accountable being, for having yielded to the arts of such a tempter as Churchill. "What!" said James, "Is Est-il-possible gone too? After all, a good trooper would have been a greater loss." In truth the King's whole anger seems, at this time, to have been concentrated, and not without cause, on one object. He set off for London, breathing vengeance against Churchill, and learned, on arriving, a new crime of the archdeceiver. The Princess Anne had been some hours missing.

Anne, who had no will but that of the Churchills, had been induced by them to notify under her own hand to William, a week before, her approbation of his enterprise. She assured him that she was entirely in the hands of her friends, and that she would remain in the palace, or take refuge in the City, as they might determine. On Sunday the twenty-fifth of November, she, and those who thought for her, were under the necessity of coming to a sudden resolution. That afternoon a courier from Salisbury brought tidings that Churchill had disappeared, that he had been accompanied by Grafton, that Kirke had proved false, and that the royal forces were in full retreat. There was, as usually happened when great news, good or bad, arrived in town, a great crowd that evening in the galleries of Whitehall. Curiosity and anxiety sate on every face. The Queen broke forth into natural expressions of indignation against the chief traitor, and did not altogether spare his too partial mistress. The sentinels were doubled round that part of the palace which Anne occupied. The Princess was in dismay. In a few hours her father would be at Westminster. It was not likely that he would treat her personally with severity; but that he would permit her any longer to enjoy the society of her friend was not to be hoped. It could hardly be doubted that Sarah would be placed under arrest, and would be subjected to a strict examination by shrewd and rigorous inquisitors. Her papers would be seized. Perhaps evidence affecting her life might be discovered. If so, the worst might well be dreaded. The vengeance of the implacable King knew no distinction of sex. For offences much smaller than those which might probably be brought home to Lady Churchill he had sent women to the scaffold and the stake. Strong affection braced the feeble mind of the Princess. There was no tie which she would not break, no risk which she would not run, for the object of her idolatrous affection. "I will jump out of the window," she cried, "rather than be found here by my father." The favourite undertook to manage an escape. She communicated in all haste with some of the chiefs of the conspiracy. In a few hours everything was arranged. That evening Anne retired to her chamber as usual. At dead of night she rose, and, accompanied by her friend Sarah and two other female attendants, stole down the back stairs in a dressing gown and slippers. The fugitives gained the open street unchallenged. A hackney coach was in waiting for them there. Two men guarded the humble vehicle. One of them was Compton, Bishop of London, the Princess's old tutor: the other was the magnificent and accomplished Dorset, whom the extremity of the public danger had roused from his luxurious repose. The coach drove instantly to Aldersgate Street, where the town residence of the Bishops of London then stood, within the shadow of their Cathedral. There the Princess passed the night. On the following morning she set out for Epping Forest. In that wild tract Dorset possessed a venerable mansion, which has long since been destroyed. In his hospitable dwelling, the favourite resort, during many years, of wits and poets, the fugitives made a short stay. They could not safely attempt to reach William's quarters; for the road thither lay through a country occupied by the royal forces. It was therefore determined that Anne should take refuge with the northern insurgents. Compton wholly laid aside, for the time, his sacerdotal character. Danger and conflict had rekindled in him all the military ardour which he had felt twenty eight years before, when he rode in the Life Guards. He preceded the Princess's carriage in a buff coat and jackboots, with a sword at his side and pistols in his holsters. Long before she reached Nottingham, she was surrounded by a body guard of gentlemen who volunteered to escort her. They invited the Bishop to act as their colonel; and he consented with an alacrity which gave great scandal to rigid Churchmen, and did not much raise his character even in the opinion of Whigs.

When, on the morning of the twenty-sixth, Anne's apartment was found empty, the consternation was great in Whitehall. While the Ladies of her Bedchamber ran up and down the courts of the palace, screaming and wringing their hands, while Lord Craven, who commanded the Foot Guards, was questioning the sentinels in the gallery, while the Chancellor was sealing up the papers of the Churchills, the Princess's nurse broke into the royal apartments crying out that the dear lady had been murdered by the Papists. The news flew to Westminster Hall. There the story was that Her Highness had been hurried away by force to a place of confinement. When it could no longer be denied that her flight had been voluntary, numerous fictions were invented to account for it. She had been grossly insulted: she had been threatened: nay, though she was in that situation in which woman is entitled to peculiar tenderness, she had been beaten by her cruel stepmother. The populace, which years of misrule had made suspicious and irritable, was so much excited by these calumnies that the Queen was scarcely safe. Many Roman Catholics, and some Protestant Tories whose loyalty was proof to all trials, repaired to the palace that they might be in readiness to defend her in the event of an outbreak. In the midst of this distress and terror arrived the news of Prince George's flight. The courier who brought these evil tidings was fast followed by the King himself. The evening was closing in when James arrived, and was informed that his daughter had disappeared. After all that he had suffered this affliction forced a cry of misery from his lips. "God help me!" he said; "my own children have forsaken me."

That evening he sate in Council with his principal ministers till a late hour. It was determined that he should summon all the Lords Spiritual and Temporal who were then in London to attend him on the following day, and that he should solemnly ask their advice. Accordingly, on the afternoon of Tuesday the twenty-seventh, the Lords met in the diningroom of the palace. The assembly consisted of nine prelates and between thirty and forty noblemen, all Protestants. The two Secretaries of State, Middleton and Preston, though not peers of England, were in attendance. The King himself presided. The traces of severe bodily and mental suffering were discernible in his countenance and deportment. He opened the proceedings by referring to the petition which had been put into his hands just before he set out for Salisbury. The prayer of that petition was that he would convoke a free Parliament. Situated as he then was, he had not, he said, thought it right to comply. But, during his absence from London, great changes had taken place. He had also observed that his people everywhere seemed anxious that the Houses should meet. He had therefore commanded the attendance of his faithful Peers, in order to ask their counsel.

For a time there was silence. Then Oxford, whose pedigree, unrivalled in antiquity and splendour, gave him a kind of primacy in the meeting, said that, in his opinion those Lords who had signed the petition to which His Majesty had referred ought now to explain their views.

These words called up Rochester. He defended the petition, and declared that he still saw no hope for the throne or the country, but in a Parliament. He would not, he said, venture to affirm that, in so disastrous an extremity, even that remedy would be efficacious: but he had no other remedy to propose. He added that it might be advisable to open a negotiation with the Prince of Orange. Jeffreys and Godolphin followed; and both declared that they agreed with Rochester.

Then Clarendon rose, and, to the astonishment of all who remembered his loud professions of loyalty, and the agony of shame and sorrow into which he had been thrown, only a few days before, by the news of his son's defection, broke forth into a vehement invective against tyranny and Popery. "Even now," he said, "His Majesty is raising in London a regiment into which no Protestant is admitted." "That is not true," cried James in great agitation from the head of the board. Clarendon persisted, and left this offensive topic only to pass to a topic still more offensive. He accused the unfortunate King of pusillanimity. Why retreat from Salisbury? Why not try the event of a battle? Could people be blamed for submitting to the invader when they saw their sovereign run away at the head of his army? James felt these insults keenly, and remembered them long. Indeed even Whigs thought the language of Clarendon indecent and ungenerous. Halifax spoke in a very different tone. During several years of peril he had defended with admirable ability the civil and ecclesiastical constitution of his country against the prerogative. But his serene intellect, singularly unsusceptible of enthusiasm, and singularly averse to extremes, began to lean towards the cause of royalty at the very moment at which those noisy Royalists who had lately execrated the Trimmers as little better than rebels were everywhere rising in rebellion. It was his ambition to be, at this conjuncture, the peacemaker between the throne and the nation. His talents and character fitted him for that office; and, if he failed, the failure is to be ascribed to causes against which no human skill could contend, and chiefly to the folly, faithlessness, and obstinacy of the Prince whom he tried to save.

Halifax now gave utterance to much unpalatable truth, but with a delicacy which brought on him the reproach of flattery from spirits too abject to understand that what would justly be called flattery when offered to the powerful is a debt of humanity to the fallen. With many expressions of sympathy and deference, he declared it to be his opinion that the King must make up his mind to great sacrifices. It was not enough to convoke a Parliament or to open a negotiation with the Prince of Orange. Some at least of the grievances of which the nation complained should be instantly redressed without waiting till redress was demanded by the Houses or by the captain of the hostile army. Nottingham, in language equally respectful, declared that he agreed with Halifax. The chief concessions which these Lords pressed the King to make were three. He ought, they said, forthwith to dismiss all Roman Catholics from office, to separate himself wholly from France, and to grant an unlimited amnesty to those who were in arms against him. The last of these propositions, it should seem, admitted of no dispute. For, though some of those who were banded together against the King had acted towards him in a manner which might not unreasonably excite his bitter resentment, it was more likely that he would soon be at their mercy than that they would ever be at his. It would have been childish to open a negotiation with William, and yet to denounce vengeance against men whom William could not without infamy abandon. But the clouded understanding and implacable temper of James held out long against the arguments of those who laboured to convince him that it would be wise to pardon offences which he could not punish. "I cannot do it," he exclaimed: "I must make examples, Churchill above all; Churchill whom I raised so high. He and he alone has done all this. He has corrupted my army. He has corrupted my child. He would have put me into the hands of the Prince of Orange, but for God's special providence. My Lords, you are strangely anxious for the safety of traitors. None of you troubles himself about my safety." In answer to this burst of impotent anger, those who had recommended the amnesty represented with profound respect, but with firmness, that a prince attacked by powerful enemies can be safe only by conquering or by conciliating. "If Your Majesty, after all that has happened, has still any hope of safety in arms, we have done: but if not, you can be safe only by regaining the affections of your people." After long and animated debate the King broke up the meeting. "My Lords," he said, "you have used great freedom: but I do not take it ill of you. I have made up my mind on one point. I shall call a Parliament. The other suggestions which have been offered are of grave importance; and you will not be surprised that I take a night to reflect on them before I decide."

At first James seemed disposed to make excellent use of the time which he had taken for consideration. The Chancellor was directed to issue writs convoking a Parliament for the thirteenth of January. Halifax was sent for to the closet, had a long audience, and spoke with much more freedom than he had thought it decorous to use in the presence of a large assembly. He was informed that he had been appointed a Commissioner to treat with the Prince of Orange. With him were joined Nottingham and Godolphin. The King declared that he was prepared to make great sacrifices for the sake of peace. Halifax answered that great sacrifices would doubtless be required. "Your Majesty," he said, "must not expect that those who have the power in their hands will consent to any terms which would leave the laws at the mercy of the prerogative." With this distinct explanation of his views, he accepted the Commission which the King wished him to undertake. The concessions which a few hours before had been so obstinately refused were now made in the most liberal manner. A proclamation was put forth by which the King not only granted a free pardon to all who were in rebellion against him, but declared them eligible to be members of the approaching Parliament. It was not even required as a condition of eligibility that they should lay down their arms. The same Gazette which announced that the Houses were about to meet contained a notification that Sir Edward Hales, who, as a Papist, as a renegade, as the foremost champion of the dispensing power, and as the harsh gaoler of the Bishops, was one of the most unpopular men in the realm, had ceased to be Lieutenant of the Tower, and had been succeeded by his late prisoner, Bevil Skelton, who, though he held no high place in the esteem of his countrymen, was at least not disqualified by law for public trust.

But these concessions were meant only to blind the Lords and the nation to the King's real designs. He had secretly determined that, even in this extremity, he would yield nothing. On the very day on which he issued the proclamation of amnesty, he fully explained his intentions to Barillon. "This negotiation," said James, "is a mere feint. I must send Commissioners to my nephew, that I may gain time to ship off my wife and the Prince of Wales. You know the temper of my troops. None but the Irish will stand by me; and the Irish are not in sufficient force to resist the enemy. A Parliament would impose on me conditions which I could not endure. I should be forced to undo all that I have done for the Catholics, and to break with the King of France. As soon, therefore, as the Queen and my child are safe, I will leave England and take refuge in Ireland, in Scotland, or with your master."

Already James had made preparations for carrying this scheme into effect. Dover had been sent to Portsmouth with instructions to take charge of the Prince of Wales; and Dartmouth, who commanded the fleet there, had been ordered to obey Dover's directions in all things concerning the royal infant, and to have a yacht manned by trusty sailors in readiness to sail for France at a moment's notice. The King now sent positive orders that the child should instantly be conveyed to the nearest Continental port. Next to the Prince of Wales the chief object of anxiety was the Great Seal. To that symbol of kingly authority our jurists have always ascribed a peculiar and almost mysterious importance. It is held that, if the Keeper of the Seal should affix it, without taking the royal pleasure, to a patent of peerage or to a pardon, though he may be guilty of a high offence, the instrument cannot be questioned by any court of law, and can be annulled only by an Act of Parliament. James seems to have been afraid that his enemies might get this organ of his will into their hands, and might thus give a legal validity to acts which might affect him injuriously. Nor will his apprehensions be thought unreasonable when it is remembered that, exactly a hundred years later, the Great Seal of a King was used, with the assent of Lords and Commons, and with the approbation of many great statesmen and lawyers, for the purpose of transferring his prerogatives to his son. Lest the talisman which possessed such formidable powers should be abused, James determined that it should be kept within a few yards of his own closet. Jeffreys was therefore ordered to quit the costly mansion which he had lately built in Duke Street, and to take up his residence in a small apartment at Whitehall.

The King had made all his preparations for flight, when an unexpected impediment compelled him to postpone the execution of his design. His agents at Portsmouth began to entertain scruples. Even Dover, though a member of the Jesuitical cabal, showed signs of hesitation. Dartmouth was still less disposed to comply with the royal wishes. He was zealous for the crown, and had done all that he could do, with a disaffected fleet, and in the face of an adverse wind, to prevent the Dutch from landing in England: but he was also zealous for the Established Church, and was by no means friendly to the policy of that government of which he was the defender. The mutinous temper of the officers and men under his command had caused him much anxiety; and he had been greatly relieved by the news that a free Parliament had been convoked, and that Commissioners had been named to treat with the Prince of Orange. The joy was clamorous throughout the fleet. An address, warmly thanking the King for these gracious concessions to public feeling, was drawn up on board of the flag ship. The Admiral signed first. Thirty eight Captains wrote their names under his. This paper on its way to Whitehall crossed the messenger who brought to Portsmouth the order that the Prince of Wales should instantly be conveyed to France. Dartmouth learned, with bitter grief and resentment, that the free Parliament, the general amnesty, the negotiation, were all parts of a great fraud on the nation, and that in this fraud he was expected to be an accomplice. His conduct on this occasion was the most honourable part of a not very honourable life. In a sensible and spirited letter he declared that he had already carried his obedience to the furthest point to which a Protestant and an Englishman could go. To put the heir apparent of the British crown into the hands of Lewis would be nothing less than treason against the monarchy. The nation, already too much alienated from the Sovereign, would be roused to madness. The Prince of Wales would either not return at all, or would return attended by a French army. If His Royal Highness remained in the island, the worst that could be apprehended was that he would be brought up a member of the national Church; and that he might be so brought up ought to be the prayer of every loyal subject. Dartmouth concluded by declaring that he would risk his life in defence of the throne, but that he would be no party to the transporting of the Prince into France.

This letter deranged all the projects of James. He learned too that he could not on this occasion expect from his admiral even passive obedience. For Dartmouth had gone so far as to station several sloops at the mouth of the harbour of Portsmouth with orders to suffer no vessel to pass out unexamined. A change of plan was necessary. The child must be brought back to London, and sent thence to France. An interval of some days must elapse before this could be done. During that interval the public mind must be amused by the hope of a Parliament and the semblance of a negotiation. Writs were sent out for the elections. Trumpeters went backward and forward between the capital and the Dutch head quarters. At length passes for the King's Commissioners arrived; and the three Lords set out on their embassy.

They left the capital in a state of fearful distraction. The passions which, during three troubled years, had been gradually gathering force, now, emancipated from the restraint of fear, and stimulated by victory and sympathy, showed themselves without disguise, even in the precincts of the royal dwelling. The Grand Jury of Middlesex found a bill against the Earl of Salisbury for turning Papist. The Lord Mayor ordered the houses of the Roman Catholics of the city to be searched for arms. The mob broke into the house of one respectable merchant who held the unpopular faith, in order to ascertain whether he had not run a mine from his cellars under the neighbouring parish church, for the purpose of blowing up parson and congregation. The hawkers bawled about the streets a hue and cry after Father Petre, who had withdrawn himself, and not before it was time, from his apartments in Whitehall. Wharton's celebrated song, with many additional verses, was chaunted more loudly than ever in all the streets of the capital. The very sentinels who guarded the palace hummed, as they paced their rounds,

> " The English confusion to Popery drink,
> Lillibullero bullen a la."

The secret presses of London worked without ceasing. Many papers daily came into circulation by means which the magistracy could not discover, or would not check. One of these has been preserved from oblivion by the skilful audacity with which it was written, and by the immense effect which it produced. It purported to be a supplemental declaration under the hand and seal of the Prince of Orange: but it was written in a style very different from that of his genuine manifesto. Vengeance alien from the usages of Christian and civilised nations was denounced against all Papists who should dare to espouse the royal cause. They should be treated, not as soldiers or gentlemen, but as freebooters. The ferocity and licentiousness of the invading army, which had hitherto been restrained with a strong hand, should be let loose on them. Good Protestants, and especially those who inhabited the capital, were adjured, as they valued all that was dear to them, and commanded, on peril of the Prince's highest displeasure, to seize, disarm, and imprison their Roman Catholic neighbours. This document, it is said, was found by a Whig bookseller one morning under his shop door. He made haste to print it. Many copies were dispersed by the post, and passed rapidly from hand to hand. Discerning readers had no difficulty in pronouncing it a forgery devised by some unquiet and unprincipled adventurer, such as, in troubled times, are always busy in the foulest and darkest offices of faction. But the multitude was completely duped. Indeed to such a height had national and religious feeling been excited against the Irish Papists that most of those who believed the spurious proclamation to be genuine were inclined to applaud it as a seasonable exhibition of vigour. When it was known that no such document had really proceeded from William, men asked anxiously what impostor had so daringly and so successfully personated His Highness. Some suspected Ferguson, others Johnson. At length, after the lapse of twenty seven years, Hugh Speke avowed the forgery, and demanded from the House of Brunswick a reward for so eminent a service rendered to the Protestant religion. He asserted, in the tone of a man who conceives himself to have done something eminently virtuous and honourable, that, when the Dutch invasion had thrown Whitehall into consternation, he had offered his services to the Court, had pretended to be estranged from the Whigs, and had promised to act as a spy upon them; that he had thus obtained admittance to the royal closet, had vowed fidelity, had been promised large pecuniary rewards, and had procured blank passes which enabled him to travel backwards and forwards across the hostile outposts. All these things he protested that he had done solely in order that he might, unsuspected, aim a deadly blow at the government, and produce a violent outbreak of popular feeling against the Roman Catholics. The forged proclamation he claimed as one of his contrivances: but whether his claim were well founded may be doubted. He delayed to make it so long that we may reasonably suspect him of having waited for the death of those who could confute him; and he produced no evidence but his own.

While these things happened in London, every post from every part of the country brought tidings of some new insurrection. Lumley had seized Newcastle. The inhabitants had welcomed him with transport. The statue of the King, which stood on a lofty pedestal of marble, had been pulled down and hurled into the Tyne. The third of December was long remembered at Hull as the Town-taking day. That place had a garrison commanded by Lord Langdale, a Roman Catholic. The Protestant officers concerted with the magistracy a plan of revolt: Langdale and his adherents were arrested; and soldiers and citizens united in declaring for the Protestant religion and a free Parliament.

The Eastern counties were up. The Duke of Norfolk, attended by three hundred gentlemen armed and mounted, appeared in the stately marketplace of Norwich. The Mayor and Aldermen met him there, and engaged to stand by him against Popery and arbitrary power. Lord Herbert of Cherbury and Sir Edward Harley took up arms in Worcestershire. Bristol, the second city of the realm, opened its gates to Shrewsbury. Trelawney, the Bishop, who had entirely unlearned in the Tower the doctrine of nonresistance, was the first to welcome the Prince's troops. Such was the temper of the inhabitants that it was thought unnecessary to leave any garrison among them. The people of Gloucester rose and delivered Lovelace from confinement. An irregular army soon gathered round him. Some of his horsemen had only halters for bridles. Many of his infantry had only clubs for weapons. But this force, such as it was, marched unopposed through counties once devoted to the House of Stuart, and at length entered Oxford in triumph. The magistrates came in state to welcome the insurgents. The University itself, exasperated by recent injuries, was little disposed to pass censures on rebellion. Already some of the Heads of Houses had despatched one of their number to assure the Prince of Orange that they were cordially with him, and that they would gladly coin their plate for his service. The Whig chief, therefore, rode through the capital of Toryism amidst general acclamation. Before him the drums beat Lillibullero. Behind him came a long stream of horse and foot. The whole High Street was gay with orange ribands. For already the orange riband had the double signification which, after the lapse of one hundred and sixty years, it still retains. Already it was the emblem to the Protestant Englishman of civil and religious freedom, to the Roman Catholic Celt of subjugation and persecution.

While foes were thus rising up all round the King, friends were fast shrinking from his side. The idea of resistance had become familiar to every mind. Many, who had been struck with horror when they heard of the first defections now blamed themselves for having been so slow to discern the signs of the times. There was no longer any difficulty or danger in repairing to William. The King, in calling on the nation to elect representatives, had, by implication, authorised all men to repair to the places where they had votes or interest; and many of those places were already occupied by invaders or insurgents. Clarendon eagerly caught at this opportunity of deserting the falling cause. He knew that his speech in the Council of Peers had given deadly offence; and he was mortified by finding that he was not to be one of the royal Commissioners. He had estates in Wiltshire; and he determined that his son, the son of whom he had lately spoken with grief and horror, should be a candidate for that county. Under pretence of looking after the election, Clarendon set out for the West. He was speedily followed by the Earl of Oxford, and by others who had hitherto disclaimed all connection with the Prince's enterprise.

By this time the invaders, steadily though slowly advancing, were within seventy miles of London. Though midwinter was approaching the weather was fine: the way was pleasant; and the turf of Salisbury Plain seemed luxuriously smooth to men who had been toiling through the miry ruts of the Devonshire and Somersetshire highways. The route of the army lay close by Stonehenge; and regiment after regiment halted to examine that mysterious ruin, celebrated all over the Continent as the greatest wonder of our island. William entered Salisbury with the same military pomp which he had displayed at Exeter, and was lodged there in the palace which the King had occupied a few days before.

The Prince's train was now swelled by the Earls of Clarendon and Oxford, and by other men of high rank, who had, till within a few days, been considered as zealous Royalists. Van Citters also made his appearance at the Dutch head quarters. He had been during some weeks almost a prisoner in his house near Whitehall, under the constant observation of relays of spies. Yet, in spite of those spies, or perhaps by their help, he had succeeded in obtaining full and accurate intelligence of all that passed in the palace; and now, full fraught with valuable information about men and things, he came to assist the deliberations of William.

Thus far the Prince's enterprise had prospered beyond the anticipations of the most sanguine. And now, according to the general law which governs human affairs, prosperity began to produce disunion. The Englishmen assembled at Salisbury were divided into two parties. One party consisted of Whigs who had always regarded the doctrines of passive obedience and of indefeasible hereditary right as slavish superstitions. Many of them had passed years in exile. All had been long shut out from participation in the favours of the crown. They now exulted in the near prospect of greatness and of vengeance. Burning with resentment, flushed with victory and hope, they would hear of no compromise. Nothing less than the deposition of the tyrant would content them; nor can it be disputed that herein they were perfectly consistent. They had exerted themselves, nine years earlier, to exclude him from the throne, because they thought it likely that he would be a bad King. It could therefore scarcely be expected that they would willingly leave him on the throne, now that he had turned out a far worse King than any reasonable man could have anticipated.

On the other hand, not a few of William's followers were zealous Tories, who had, till very recently, held the doctrine of non-resistance in the most absolute form, but whose faith in that doctrine had, for a moment, given way to the strong passions excited by the ingratitude of the King and by the peril of the Church. No situation could be more painful or perplexing than that of the old Cavalier who found himself in arms against the throne. The scruples which had not prevented him from repairing to the Dutch camp began to torment him cruelly as soon as he was there. His mind misgave him that he had committed a crime. At all events he had exposed himself to reproach, by acting in diametrical opposition to the professions of his whole life. He felt insurmountable disgust for his new allies. They were people whom, ever since he could remember, he had been reviling and persecuting, Presbyterians, Independents, Anabaptists, old soldiers of Cromwell, brisk boys of Shaftesbury, accomplices in the Rye House plot, captains of the Western insurrection. He naturally wished to find out some salvo which might sooth his conscience, which might vindicate his consistency, and which might put a distinction between him and the crew of schismatical rebels whom he had always despised and abhorred, but with whom he was now in danger of being confounded. He therefore disclaimed, with vehemence, all thought of taking the crown from that anointed head which the ordinance of heaven and the fundamental laws of the realm had made sacred. His dearest wish was to see a reconciliation effected on terms which would not lower the royal dignity. He was no traitor. He was not, in truth, resisting the kingly authority. He was in arms only because he was convinced that the best service which could be rendered to the throne was to rescue His Majesty, by a little gentle coercion, from the hands of wicked counsellors.

The evils which the mutual animosity of these factions tended to produce were, to a great extent, averted by the ascendency and by the wisdom of the Prince. Surrounded by eager disputants, officious advisers, abject flatterers, vigilant spies, malicious talebearers, he remained serene and inscrutable. He preserved silence while silence was possible. When he was forced to speak, the earnest and peremptory tone in which he uttered his well weighed opinions soon silenced everybody else. Whatever some of his too zealous adherents might say, he uttered not a word indicating any design on the English crown. He was doubtless well aware that between him and that crown were still interposed obstacles which no prudence might be able to surmount, and which a single false step would make insurmountable. His only chance of obtaining the splendid prize was not to seize it rudely, but to wait till, without any appearance of exertion or stratagem on his part, his secret wish should be accomplished by the force of circumstances, by the blunders of his opponents, and by the free choice of the Estates of the Realm. Those who ventured to interrogate him learned nothing, and yet could not accuse him of shuffling. He quietly referred them to his Declaration, and assured them that his views had undergone no change since that instrument had been drawn up. So skilfully did he manage his followers that their discord seems rather to have strengthened than to have weakened his hands: but it broke forth with violence when his control was withdrawn, interrupted the harmony of convivial meetings, and did not respect even the sanctity of the house of God. Clarendon, who tried to hide from others and from himself, by an ostentatious display of loyal sentiments, the plain fact that he was a rebel, was shocked to hear some of his new associates laughing over their wine at the royal amnesty which had just been graciously offered to them. They wanted no pardon, they said. They would make the King ask pardon before they had done with him. Still more alarming and disgusting to every good Tory was an incident which happened at Salisbury Cathedral. As soon as the officiating minister began to read the collect for the King, Burnet, among whose many good qualities selfcommand and a fine sense of the becoming cannot be reckoned, rose from his knees, sate down in his stall, and uttered some contemptuous noises which disturbed the devotions of the whole congregation.

In a short time the factions which divided the Prince's camp had an opportunity of measuring their strength. The royal Commissioners were on their way to him. Several days had elapsed since they had been appointed; and it was thought strange that, in a case of such urgency, there should be such delay. But in truth neither James nor William was desirous that negotiations should speedily commence; for James wished only to gain time sufficient for sending his wife and son into France; and the position of William became every day more commanding. At length the Prince caused it to be notified to the Commissioners that he would meet them at Hungerford. He probably selected this place because, lying at an equal distance from Salisbury and from Oxford, it was well situated for a rendezvous of his most important adherents. At Salisbury were those noblemen and gentlemen who had accompanied him from Holland or had joined him in the West; and at Oxford were many chiefs of the Northern insurrection.

Late on Thursday, the sixth of December, he reached Hungerford. The little town was soon crowded with men of rank and note who came thither from opposite quarters. The Prince was escorted by a strong body of troops. The northern Lords brought with them hundreds of irregular cavalry, whose accoutrements and horsemanship moved the mirth of men accustomed to the splendid aspect and exact movements of regular armies.

While the Prince lay at Hungerford a sharp encounter took place between two hundred and fifty of his troops and six hundred Irish who were posted at Reading. The superior discipline of the invaders was signally proved on this occasion. Though greatly outnumbered, they, at one onset, drove the King's forces in confusion through the streets of the town into the marketplace. There the Irish attempted to rally; but being vigorously attacked in front and fired upon at the same time by the inhabitants from the windows of the neighbouring houses, they soon lost heart, and fled with the loss of their colours and of fifty men. Of the conquerors only five fell. The satisfaction which this news gave to the Lords and gentlemen who had joined William was unmixed. There was nothing in what had happened to gall their national feelings. The Dutch had not beaten the English, but had assisted an English town to free itself from the insupportable dominion of the Irish.

On the morning of Saturday, the eighth of December, the King's Commissioners reached Hungerford. The Prince's body guard was drawn up to receive them with military respect. Bentinck welcomed them, and proposed to conduct them immediately to his master. They expressed a hope that the Prince would favour them with a private audience; but they were informed that he had resolved to hear them and answer them in public. They were ushered into his bedchamber, where they found him surrounded by a crowd of noblemen and gentlemen. Halifax, whose rank, age, and abilities entitled him to precedence, was spokesman. The proposition which the Commissioners had been instructed to make was that the points in dispute should be referred to the Parliament for which the writs were already sealing, and that in the mean time the Prince's army would not come within thirty or forty miles of London. Halifax, having explained that this was the basis on which he and his colleagues were prepared to treat, put into William's hands a letter from the King, and retired. William opened the letter and seemed unusually moved. It was the first letter which he had received from his father in law since they had become avowed enemies. Once they had been on good terms and had written to each other familiarly; nor had they, even when they had begun to regard each other with suspicion and aversion, banished from their correspondence those forms of kindness which persons nearly related by blood and marriage commonly use. The letter which the Commissioners had brought was drawn up by a secretary in diplomatic form and in the French language. "I have had many letters from the King," said William, "but they were all in English, and in his own hand." He spoke with a sensibility which he was little in the habit of displaying. Perhaps he thought at that moment how much reproach his enterprise, just, beneficent, and necessary as it was, must bring on him and on the wife who was devoted to him. Perhaps he repined at the hard fate which had placed him in such a situation that he could fulfil his public duties only by breaking through domestic ties, and envied the happier condition of those who are not responsible for the welfare of nations and Churches. But such thoughts, if they rose in his mind, were firmly suppressed. He requested the Lords and gentlemen whom he had convoked on this occasion to consult together, unrestrained by his presence, as to the answer which ought to be returned. To himself, however, he reserved the power of deciding in the last resort, after hearing their opinion. He then left them and retired to Littlecote Hall, a manor house situated about two miles off, and renowned down to our own times, not more on account of its venerable architecture and furniture than on account of a horrible and mysterious crime which was perpetrated there in the days of the Tudors.

Before he left Hungerford he was told that Halifax had expressed a great desire to see Burnet. In this desire there was nothing strange; for Halifax and Burnet had long been on terms of friendship. No two men, indeed, could resemble each other less. Burnet was utterly destitute of delicacy and tact. Halifax's taste was fastidious, and his sense of the ludicrous morbidly quick. Burnet viewed every act and every character through a medium distorted and coloured by party spirit. The tendency of Halifax's mind was always to see the faults of his allies more strongly than the faults of his opponents. Burnet was, with all his infirmities, and through all the vicissitudes of a life passed in circumstances not very favourable to piety, a sincerely pious man. The sceptical and sarcastic Halifax lay under the imputation of infidelity. Halifax therefore often incurred Burnet's indignant censure; and Burnet was often the butt of Halifax's keen and polished pleasantry. Yet they were drawn to each other by a mutual attraction, liked each other's conversation, appreciated each other's abilities, interchanged opinions freely, and interchanged also good offices in perilous times. It was not, however, merely from personal regard that Halifax now wished to see his old acquaintance. The Commissioners must have been anxious to know what was the Prince's real aim. He had refused to see them in private; and little could be learned from what he might say in a formal and public interview. Almost all those who were admitted to his confidence were men taciturn and impenetrable as himself. Burnet was the only exception. He was notoriously garrulous and indiscreet. Yet circumstances had made it necessary to trust him; and he would doubtless, under the dexterous management of Halifax, have poured out secrets as fast as words. William knew this well, and, when he was informed that Halifax was asking for the Doctor, could not refrain from exclaiming, "If they get together there will be fine tattling." Burnet was forbidden to see the Commissioners in private; but he was assured in very courteous terms that his fidelity was regarded by the Prince as above all suspicion; and, that there might be no ground for complaint, the prohibition was made general.

That afternoon the noblemen and gentlemen whose advice William had asked met in the great room of the principal inn at Hungerford. Oxford was placed in the chair; and the King's overtures were taken into consideration. It soon appeared that the assembly was divided into two parties, a party anxious to come to terms with the King, and a party bent on his destruction. The latter party had the numerical superiority: but it was observed that Shrewsbury, who of all the English nobles was supposed to enjoy the largest share of William's confidence, though a Whig, sided on this occasion with the Tories. After much altercation the question was put. The majority was for rejecting the proposition which the royal Commissioners had been instructed to make. The resolution of the assembly was reported to the Prince at Littlecote. On no occasion during the whole course of his eventful life did he show more prudence and selfcommand. He could not wish the negotiation to succeed. But he was far too wise a man not to know that, if unreasonable demands made by him should cause it to fail, public feeling would no longer be on his side. He therefore overruled the opinion of his too eager followers, and declared his determination to treat on the basis proposed by the King. Many of the Lords and gentlemen assembled at Hungerford remonstrated: a whole day was spent in bickering: but William's purpose was immovable. He declared himself willing to refer all the questions in dispute to the Parliament which had just been summoned, and not to advance within forty miles of London. On his side he made some demands which even those who were least disposed to commend him allowed to be moderate. He insisted that the existing statutes should be obeyed till they should be altered by competent authority, and that all persons who held offices without a legal qualification should be forthwith dismissed. The deliberations of the Parliament, he justly conceived, could not be free if it was to sit surrounded by Irish regiments while he and his army lay at a distance of several marches. He therefore thought it reasonable that, since his troops were not to advance within forty miles of London on the west, the King's troops should fall back as far to the east. There would thus be, round the spot where the Houses were to meet, a wide circle of neutral ground. Within that circle, indeed, there were two fastnesses of great importance to the people of the capital, the Tower, which commanded their dwellings, and Tilbury Fort, which commanded their maritime trade. It was impossible to leave these places ungarrisoned. William therefore proposed that they should be temporarily entrusted to the care of the City of London. It might possibly be convenient that, when the Parliament assembled, the King should repair to Westminster with a body guard. The Prince announced that, in that case, he should claim the right of repairing thither also with an equal number of soldiers. It seemed to him just that, while military operations were suspended, both the armies should be considered as alike engaged in the service of the English nation, and should be alike maintained out of the

English revenue. Lastly, he required some guarantee that the King would not take advantage of the armistice for the purpose of introducing a French force into England. The point where there was most danger was Portsmouth. The Prince did not insist that this important fortress should be delivered up to him, but proposed that it should, during the truce, be under the government of an officer in whom both himself and James could confide.

The propositions of William were framed with a punctilious fairness, such as might have been expected rather from a disinterested umpire pronouncing an award than from a victorious prince dictating to a helpless enemy. No fault could be found with them by the partisans of the King. But among the Whigs there was much murmuring. They wanted no reconciliation with their old master. They thought themselves absolved from all allegiance to him. They were not disposed to recognise the authority of a Parliament convoked by his writ. They were averse to an armistice; and they could not conceive why, if there was to be an armistice, it should be an armistice on equal terms. By all the laws of war the stronger party had a right to take advantage of his strength; and what was there in the character of James to justify any extraordinary indulgence? Those who reasoned thus little knew from how elevated a point of view, and with how discerning an eye, the leader whom they censured contemplated the whole situation of England and Europe. They were eager to ruin James, and would therefore either have refused to treat with him on any conditions, or have imposed on him conditions insupportably hard. To the success of William's vast and profound scheme of policy it was necessary that James should ruin himself by rejecting conditions ostentatiously liberal. The event proved the wisdom of the course which the majority of the Englishmen at Hungerford were inclined to condemn.

On Sunday, the ninth of December, the Prince's demands were put in writing, and delivered to Halifax. The Commissioners dined at Littlecote. A splendid assemblage had been invited to meet them. The old hall, hung with coats of mail which had seen the wars of the Roses, and with portraits of gallants who had adorned the court of Philip and Mary, was now crowded with Peers and Generals. In such a throng a short question and answer might be exchanged without attracting notice. Halifax seized this opportunity, the first which had presented itself, of extracting all that Burnet knew or thought. "What is it that you want?" said the dexterous diplomatist: "do you wish to get the King into your power?" "Not at all," said Burnet: "we would not do the least harm to his person." "And if he were to go away?" said Halifax. "There is nothing," said Burnet, "so much to be wished." There can be no doubt that Burnet expressed the general sentiment of the Whigs in the Prince's camp. They were all desirous that James should fly from the country: but only a few of the wisest among them understood how important it was that his flight should be ascribed by the nation to his own folly and perverseness, and not to harsh usage and well grounded apprehension. It seems probable that, even in the extremity to which he was now reduced, all his enemies united would have been unable to effect his complete overthrow had he not been his own worst enemy: but, while his Commissioners were labouring to save him, he was labouring as earnestly to make all their efforts useless.

His plans were at length ripe for execution. The pretended negotiation had answered its purpose. On the same day on which the three Lords reached Hungerford the Prince of Wales arrived at Westminster. It had been intended that he should come over London Bridge; and some Irish troops were sent to Southwark to meet him. But they were received by a great multitude with such hooting and execration that they thought it advisable to retire with all speed. The poor child crossed the Thames at Kingston, and was brought into Whitehall so privately that many believed him to be still at Portsmouth.

To send him and the Queen out of the country without delay was now the first object of James. But who could be trusted to manage the escape? Dartmouth was the most loyal of Protestant Tories; and Dartmouth had refused. Dover was a creature of the Jesuits; and even Dover had hesitated. It was not very easy to find an Englishman of rank and honour who would undertake to place the heir apparent of the English crown in the hands of the King of France. In these circumstances, James bethought him of a French nobleman who then resided in London, Antonine Count of Lauzun. Of this man it has been said that his life was stranger than the dreams of other people. At an early age he had been the intimate associate of Lewis, and had been encouraged to expect the highest employments under the French crown. Then his fortunes had undergone an eclipse. Lewis had driven from him the friend of his youth with bitter reproaches, and had, it was said, scarcely refrained from adding blows. The fallen favourite had been sent prisoner to a fortress: but he had emerged from his confinement, had again enjoyed the smiles of his master, and had gained the heart of one of the greatest ladies in Europe, Anna Maria, daughter of Gaston Duke of Orleans, granddaughter of King Henry the

Fourth, and heiress of the immense domains of the house of Mont-pensier. The lovers were bent on marriage. The royal consent was obtained. During a few hours Lauzun was regarded by the court as an adopted member of the house of Bourbon. The portion which the princess brought with her might well have been an object of competition to sovereigns; three great dukedoms, an independent principality with its own mint and with its own tribunals, and an income greatly exceeding the whole revenue of the kingdom of Scotland. But this splendid prospect had been overcast. The match had been broken off. The aspiring suitor had been, during many years, shut up in a remote castle. At length Lewis relented. Lauzun was forbidden to appear in the royal presence, but was allowed to enjoy liberty at a distance from the court. He visited England, and was well received at the palace of James and in the fashionable circles of London; for in that age the gentlemen of France were regarded throughout Europe as models of grace; and many Chevaliers and Viscounts, who had never been admitted to the interior circle at Versailles, found themselves objects of general curiosity and admiration at Whitehall. Lauzun was in every respect the man for the present emergency. He had courage and a sense of honour, had been accustomed to eccentric adventures, and, with the keen observation and ironical pleasantry of a finished man of the world, had a strong propensity to knight errantry. All his national feelings and all his personal interests impelled him to undertake the adventure from which the most devoted subjects of the English crown seemed to shrink. As the guardian, at a perilous crisis, of the Queen of Great Britain and of the Prince of Wales, he might return with honour to his native land: he might once more be admitted to see Lewis dress and dine, and might, after so many vicissitudes, recommence, in the decline of life, the strangely fascinating chase of royal favour.

Animated by such feelings, Lauzun eagerly accepted the high trust which was offered to him. The arrangements for the flight were promptly made: a vessel was ordered to be in readiness at Gravesend: but to reach Gravesend was not easy. The City was in a state of extreme agitation. The slightest cause sufficed to bring a crowd together. No foreigner could appear in the streets without risk of being stopped, questioned, and carried before a magistrate as a Jesuit in disguise. It was, therefore, necessary to take the road on the south of the Thames. No precaution which could quiet suspicion was omitted. The King and Queen retired to rest as usual. When the palace had been some time profoundly quiet, James rose and called a servant who was in attendance. "You will find," said the King, "a man at the door of the antechamber: bring him hither." The servant obeyed, and Lauzun was ushered into the royal bedchamber. "I confide to you," said James, "my Queen and my son; everything must be risked to carry them into France." Lauzun, with a truly chivalrous spirit, returned thanks for the dangerous honour which had been conferred on him, and begged permission to avail himself of the assistance of his friend Saint Victor, a gentleman of Provence, whose courage and faith had been often tried. The services of so valuable an assistant were readily accepted. Lauzun gave his hand to Mary. Saint Victor wrapped up in his warm cloak the ill fated heir of so many Kings. The party stole down the back stairs, and embarked in an open skiff. It was a miserable voyage. The night was bleak: the rain fell: the wind roared: the water was rough: at length the boat reached Lambeth; and the fugitives landed near an inn, where a coach and horses were in waiting. Some time elapsed before the horses could be harnessed. Mary, afraid that her face might be known, would not enter the house. She remained with her child, cowering for shelter from the storm under the tower of Lambeth Church, and distracted by terror whenever the ostler approached her with his lantern. Two of her women attended her, one who gave suck to the Prince, and one whose office was to rock his cradle; but they could be of little use to their mistress; for both were foreigners who could hardly speak the English language, and who shuddered at the rigour of the English climate. The only consolatory circumstance was that the little boy was well, and uttered not a single cry. At length the coach was ready. Saint Victor followed it on horseback. The fugitives reached Gravesend safely, and embarked in the yacht which waited for them. They found there Lord Powis and his wife. Three Irish officers were also on board. These men had been sent thither in order that they might assist Lauzun in any desperate emergency; for it was thought not impossible that the captain of the ship might prove false; and it was fully determined that, on the first suspicion of treachery, he should be stabbed to the heart. There was, however, no necessity for violence. The yacht proceeded down the river with a fair wind; and Saint Victor, having seen her under sail, spurred back with the good news to Whitehall.

On the morning of Monday the tenth of December, the King learned that his wife and son had begun their voyage with a fair prospect of reaching their destination. About the same time a courier arrived at the palace with despatches from Hungerford. Had James been a little more discerning, or a little less obstinate, those despatches would have induced him to reconsider all his plans. The Commissioners wrote hopefully. The conditions proposed by the conqueror were strangely liberal. The King himself could not refrain from exclaiming that they were more favourable than he could have expected. He might indeed not unreasonably suspect that they had been framed with no friendly design: but this mattered nothing; for, whether they were offered in the hope that, by closing with them, he would lay the ground for a happy reconciliation, or, as is more likely, in the hope that, by rejecting them, he would exhibit himself to the whole nation as utterly unreasonable and incorrigible, his course was equally clear. In either case his policy was to accept them promptly and to observe them faithfully.

But it soon appeared that William had perfectly understood the character with which he had to deal, and, in offering those terms which the Whigs at Hungerford had censured as too indulgent, had risked nothing. The solemn farce by which the public had been amused since the retreat of the royal army from Salisbury was prolonged during a few hours. All the Lords who were still in the capital were invited to the palace that they might be informed of the progress of the negotiation which had been opened by their advice. Another meeting of Peers was appointed for the following day. The Lord Mayor and the Sheriffs of London were also summoned to attend the King. He exhorted them to perform their duties vigorously, and owned that he had thought it expedient to send his wife and child out of the country, but assured them that he would himself remain at his post. While he uttered this unkingly and unmanly falsehood, his fixed purpose was to depart before daybreak. Already he had entrusted his most valuable movables to the care of several foreign Ambassadors. His most important papers had been deposited with the Tuscan minister. But before the flight there was still something to be done. The tyrant pleased himself with the thought that he might avenge himself on a people who had been impatient of his despotism by inflicting on them at parting all the evils of anarchy. He ordered the Great Seal and the writs for the new Parliament to be brought to his apartment. The writs he threw into the fire. Some which had been already sent out he annulled by an instrument drawn up in legal form. To Feversham he wrote a letter which could be understood only as a command to disband the army. Still, however, he concealed, even from his chief ministers, his intention of absconding. Just before he retired he directed Jeffreys to be in the closet early on the morrow, and, while stepping into bed, whispered to Mulgrave that the news from Hungerford was highly satisfactory. Everybody withdrew except the Duke of Northumberland. This young man, a natural son of Charles the Second by the Duchess of Cleveland, commanded a troop of Life Guards, and was a Lord of the Bedchamber. It seems to have been then the custom of the court that, in the Queen's absence, a Lord of the Bedchamber should sleep on a pallet in the King's room; and it was Northumberland's turn to perform this duty.

At three in the morning of Tuesday the eleventh of December, James rose, took the Great Seal in his hand, laid his commands on Northumberland not to open the door of the bedchamber till the usual hour, and disappeared through a secret passage, the same passage probably through which Huddleston had been brought to the bedside of the late King. Sir Edward Hales was in attendance with a hackney coach. James was conveyed to Millbank where he crossed the Thames in a small wherry. As he passed Lambeth he flung the Great Seal into the midst of the stream, where, after many months, it was accidentally caught by a fishing net and dragged up.

At Vauxhall he landed. A carriage and horses had been stationed there for him; and he immediately took the road towards Sheerness, where a hoy belonging to the Custom House had been ordered to await his arrival.

LONDONDERRY

THE other great fastness of Protestantism was a place of more importance. Eighty years before, during the troubles caused by the last struggle of the houses of O'Neil and O'Donnel against the authority of James the First, the ancient city of Derry had been surprised by one of the native chiefs: the inhabitants had been slaughtered, and the houses reduced to ashes. The insurgents were speedily put down and punished: the government resolved to restore the ruined town: the Lord Mayor, Aldermen, and Common Council of London were invited to assist in the work; and King James the First made over to them in their corporate capacity the ground covered by the ruins of the old Derry, and about six thousand acres in the neighbourhood.

This country, then uncultivated and uninhabited, is now enriched by industry, embellished by taste, and pleasing even to eyes accustomed to the well tilled fields and stately manor houses of England. A new city soon arose which, on account of its connection with the capital of the empire, was called Londonderry. The buildings covered the summit and slope of a hill which overlooked the broad stream of the Foyle, then whitened by vast flocks of wild swans. On the highest ground stood the Cathedral, a church which, though erected when the secret of Gothic architecture was lost, and though ill qualified to sustain a comparison with the awful temples of the middle ages, is not without grace and dignity. Near the Cathedral rose the Palace of the Bishop, whose see was one of the most valuable in Ireland. The city was in form nearly an ellipse; and the principal streets formed a cross, the arms of which met in a square called the Diamond. The original houses have been either rebuilt or so much repaired that their ancient character can no longer be traced; but many of them were standing within living memory. They were in general two stories in height; and some of them had stone staircases on the outside. The dwellings were encompassed by a wall of which the whole circumference was little less than a mile. On the bastions were planted culverins and sakers presented by the wealthy guilds of London to the colony. On some of these ancient guns, which have done memorable service to a great cause, the devices of the Fishmongers' Company, of the Vintners' Company, and of the Merchant Tailors' Company are still discernible.

The inhabitants were Protestants of Anglosaxon blood. They were indeed not all of one country or of one church: but Englishmen and Scotchmen, Episcopalians and Presbyterians, seem to have generally lived together in friendship, a friendship which is sufficiently explained by their common antipathy to the Irish race and to the Popish religion. During the rebellion of 1641, Londonderry had resolutely held out against the native chieftains, and had been repeatedly besieged in vain. Since the Restoration the city had prospered. The Foyle, when the tide was high, brought up ships of large burden to the quay. The fisheries throve greatly. The nets, it was said, were sometimes so full that it was necessary to fling back multitudes of fish into the waves. The quantity of salmon caught annually was estimated at eleven hundred thousand pounds' weight.

The people of Londonderry shared in the alarm which, towards the close of the year 1688, was general among the Protestants settled in Ireland. It was known that the aboriginal peasantry of the neighbourhood were laying in pikes and knives. Priests had been haranguing in a style of which, it must be owned, the Puritan part of the Anglosaxon colony had little right to complain, about the slaughter of the Amalekites, and the judgments which Saul had brought on himself by sparing one of the proscribed race. Rumours from various quarters and anonymous letters in various hands agreed in naming the ninth of December as the day fixed for the extirpation of the strangers. While the minds of the citizens were agitated by these reports, news came that a regiment of twelve hundred Papists, commanded by a Papist, Alexander Macdonnell, Earl of Antrim, had received orders from the Lord Deputy to occupy Londonderry, and was already on the march from Coleraine. The consternation was extreme. Some were for closing the gates and resisting; some for submitting; some for temporising. The corporation had, like the other corporations of Ireland, been remodelled. The magistrates were men of low station and character. Among them was only one person of Anglosaxon extraction; and he had turned Papist. In such rulers the inhabitants could place no confidence. The Bishop, Ezekiel Hopkins, resolutely adhered to the political doctrines which he had preached during many years, and exhorted his flock to go patiently to the slaughter rather than incur the guilt of disobeying the Lord's Anointed. Antrim was meanwhile drawing nearer and nearer. At length the citizens saw from the walls his troops arrayed on the opposite shore of the Foyle. There was then no bridge: but there was a ferry which kept up a constant communication between the two banks of the river; and by this ferry a detachment from Antrim's regiment crossed. The officers presented themselves at the gate, produced a warrant directed to the Mayor and Sheriffs, and demanded admittance and quarters for his Majesty's soldiers.

Just at this moment thirteen young apprentices, most of whom appear, from their names, to have been of Scottish birth or descent, flew to the guard room, armed themselves, seized the keys of the city, rushed to the Ferry Gate, closed it in the face of the King's officers, and let down the portcullis. James Morison, a citizen more advanced in years, addressed the intruders from the top of the wall and advised them to be gone. They stood in consultation before the gate till they heard him cry, "Bring a great gun this way." They then thought it time to get beyond the range of shot. They retreated, reembarked, and rejoined their comrades on the other side of the river. The flame had already spread. The whole city was up. The other gates were secured. Sentinels paced the ramparts everywhere. The magazines were opened. Muskets and gunpowder were distributed. Messengers were sent, under cover of the following night, to the Protestant gentlemen of the neighbouring counties. The bishop expostulated in vain. It is indeed probable that the vehement and daring young Scotchmen who had taken the lead on this occasion had little respect for his office. One of them broke in on a discourse with which he interrupted the military preparations by exclaiming, "A good sermon, my lord; a very good sermon; but we have not time to hear it just now."

The Protestants of the neighbourhood promptly obeyed the summons of Londonderry. Within forty eight hours hundreds of horse and foot came by various roads to the city. Antrim, not thinking himself strong enough to risk an attack, or not disposed to take on himself the responsibility of commencing a civil war without further orders, retired with his troops to Coleraine.

[A passage is here omitted: Tyrconnel called the Irish peasantry to arms to defend the Catholic Church from King William, and there was a violent insurrection against the Protestants in Ireland.]

In Leinster, Munster and Connaught, it was utterly impossible for the English settlers, few as they were and dispersed, to offer any effectual resistance to this terrible outbreak of the aboriginal population. Charleville, Mallow, Sligo, fell into the hands of the natives. Bandon, where the Protestants had mustered in considerable force, was reduced by Lieutenant General Macarthy, an Irish officer who was descended from one of the most illustrious Celtic houses, and who had long served, under a feigned name, in the French army. The people of Kenmare held out in their little fastness till they were attacked by three thousand regular soldiers, and till it was known that several pieces of ordnance were coming to batter down the turf wall which surrounded the agent's house. Then at length a capitulation was concluded. The colonists were suffered to embark in a small vessel scantily supplied with food and water. They had no experienced navigator on board: but after a voyage of a fortnight, during which they were crowded together like slaves in a Guinea ship, and suffered the extremity of thirst and hunger, they reached Bristol in safety. When such was the fate of the towns, it was evident that the country seats which the Protestant landowners had recently fortified in the three southern provinces could no longer be defended. Many families submitted, delivered up their arms, and thought themselves happy in escaping with life. But many resolute and highspirited gentlemen and yeomen were determined to perish rather than yield. They packed up such valuable property as could easily be carried away, burned whatever they could not remove, and, well armed and mounted, set out for those spots in Ulster which were the strongholds of their race and of their faith. The flower of the Protestant population of Munster and Connaught found shelter at Enniskillen. Whatever was bravest and most truehearted in Leinster took the road to Londonderry.

.   .   .   .   .

In the camp[1] it was generally expected that Londonderry would fall without a blow. Rosen confidently predicted that the mere sight of the Irish army would terrify the garrison into submission. But Richard Hamilton, who knew the temper of the colonists better, had misgivings. The assailants were sure of one important ally within the walls. Lundy, the Governor, professed the Protestant religion, and had joined in proclaiming William and Mary; but he was in secret communication with the enemies of his Church and of the Sovereigns to whom he had sworn fealty. Some have suspected that he was a concealed Jacobite, and that he had affected to acquiesce in the Revolution only in order that he might be better able to assist in bringing about a Restoration: but it is probable that his conduct is rather to be attributed to faintheartedness and poverty of spirit than to zeal for any public cause. He seems to have thought resistance hopeless; and in truth, to a military eye, the defences of Londonderry appeared contemptible. The fortifications consisted of a simple wall overgrown with grass and weeds: there was no ditch even before the gates: the drawbridges had long been neglected: the chains were rusty and could scarcely be used: the parapets and towers were built after a fashion which might well move disciples of Vauban to laughter; and these feeble defences were on almost every side commanded by heights. Indeed those who laid out the city had never meant that it should be able to stand a regular siege, and had contented themselves with throwing up works sufficient to protect the inhabitants against a tumultuary attack of the Celtic peasantry. Avaux assured Louvois that a single French battalion would easily storm such a fastness. Even if the place should, notwithstanding all disadvantages, be able to repel a large army directed by the science and experience of generals who had served under Condé and Turenne, hunger must soon bring the contest to an end. The stock of provisions was small; and the population had been swollen to seven or eight times the ordinary number by a multitude of colonists flying from the rage of the natives.

Lundy, therefore, from the time when the Irish army entered Ulster, seems to have given up all thought of serious resistance. He talked so despondingly that the citizens and his own soldiers murmured against him. He seemed, they said, to be bent on discouraging them. Meanwhile the enemy drew daily nearer and nearer; and it was known that James himself was coming to take the command of his forces.

[1] [The Jacobite camp besieging Londonderry. It had been commanded by Richard Hamilton, but James had just arrived and had placed two French generals, Rosen and Maumont, over him.]

Just at this moment a glimpse of hope appeared. On the fourteenth of April ships from England anchored in the bay. They had on board two regiments which had been sent, under the command of a Colonel named Cunningham, to reinforce the garrison. Cunningham and several of his officers went on shore and conferred with Lundy. Lundy dissuaded them from landing their men. The place, he said, could not hold out. To throw more troops into it would therefore be worse than useless: for the more numerous the garrison, the more prisoners would fall into the hands of the enemy. The best thing that the two regiments could do would be to sail back to England. He meant, he said, to withdraw himself privately; and the inhabitants must then try to make good terms for themselves.

He went through the form of holding a council of war: but from this council he excluded all those officers of the garrison whose sentiments he knew to be different from his own. Some who had ordinarily been summoned on such occasions, and who now came uninvited, were thrust out of the room. Whatever the Governor said was echoed by his creatures. Cunningham and Cunningham's companions could scarcely venture to oppose their opinion to that of a person whose local knowledge was necessarily far superior to theirs, and whom they were by their instructions directed to obey. One brave soldier murmured. "Understand this," he said: "to give up Londonderry is to give up Ireland." But his objections were contemptuously overruled. The meeting broke up. Cunningham and his officers returned to the ships, and made preparations for departing. Meanwhile Lundy privately sent a messenger to the head quarters of the enemy, with assurances that the city should be peaceably surrendered on the first summons.

But as soon as what had passed in the council of war was whispered about the streets, the spirit of the soldiers and citizens swelled up high and fierce against the dastardly and perfidious chief who had betrayed them. Many of his own officers declared that they no longer thought themselves bound to obey him. Voices were heard threatening, some that his brains should be blown out, some that he should be hanged on the walls. A deputation was sent to Cunningham imploring him to assume the command. He excused himself on the plausible ground that his orders were to take directions in all things from the Governor. Meanwhile it was rumoured that the persons most in Lundy's confidence were stealing out of the town one by one. Long after dusk on the evening of the seventeenth it was found that the gates were open and that the keys had disappeared. The officers who made the discovery

M—5*

took on themselves to change the passwords and to double the guards. The night, however, passed over without any assault.

After some anxious hours the day broke. The Irish, with James at their head, were now within four miles of the city. A tumultuous council of the chief inhabitants was called. Some of them vehemently reproached the Governor to his face with his treachery. He had sold them, they cried, to their deadliest enemy: he had refused admission to the force which good King William had sent to defend them. While the altercation was at the height, the sentinels who paced the ramparts announced that the vanguard of the hostile army was in sight. Lundy had given orders that there should be no firing: but his authority was at an end. Two gallant soldiers, Major Henry Baker and Captain Adam Murray, called the people to arms. They were assisted by the eloquence of an aged clergyman, George Walker, rector of the parish of Donaghmore, who had, with many of his neighbours, taken refuge in Londonderry. The whole crowded city was moved by one impulse. Soldiers, gentlemen, yeomen, artisans, rushed to the walls and manned the guns. James, who, confident of success, had approached within a hundred yards of the southern gate, was received with a shout of "No surrender," and with a fire from the nearest bastion. An officer of his staff fell dead by his side. The King and his attendants made all haste to get out of reach of the cannon balls. Lundy, who was now in imminent danger of being torn limb from limb by those whom he had betrayed, hid himself in an inner chamber. There he lay during the day, and at night, with the generous and politic connivance of Murray and Walker, made his escape in the disguise of a porter. The part of the wall from which he let himself down is still pointed out; and people still living talk of having tasted the fruit of a pear tree which assisted him in his descent. His name is, to this day, held in execration by the Protestants of the North of Ireland; and his effigy is still annually hung and burned by them with marks of abhorrence similar to those which in England are appropriated to Guy Fawkes.

And now Londonderry was left destitute of all military and of all civil government. No man in the town had a right to command any other: the defences were weak: the provisions were scanty: an incensed tyrant and a great army were at the gates. But within was that which has often, in desperate extremities, retrieved the fallen fortunes of nations. Betrayed, deserted, disorganised, unprovided with resources, begirt with enemies, the noble city was still no easy conquest. Whatever an engineer might think of the strength of the ramparts, all that was most intelligent, most courageous, most highspirited among the Englishry of Leinster and of Northern Ulster was crowded behind them. The number of men capable of bearing arms within the walls was seven thousand; and the whole world could not have furnished seven thousand men better qualified to meet a terrible emergency with clear judgment, dauntless valour, and stubborn patience. They were all zealous Protestants; and the Protestantism of the majority was tinged with Puritanism. They had much in common with that sober, resolute, and Godfearing class out of which Cromwell had formed his unconquerable army. But the peculiar situation in which they had been placed had developed in them some qualities which, in the mother country, might possibly have remained latent. The English inhabitants of Ireland were an aristocratic caste, which had been enabled, by superior civilisation, by close union, by sleepless vigilance, by cool intrepidity, to keep in subjection a numerous and hostile population. Almost every one of them had been in some measure trained both to military and to political functions. Almost every one was familiar with the use of arms, and was accustomed to bear a part in the administration of justice. It was remarked by contemporary writers that the colonists had something of the Castilian haughtiness of manner, though none of the Castilian indolence, that they spoke English with remarkable purity and correctness, and that they were, both as militiamen and as jurymen, superior to their kindred in the mother country. In all ages, men situated as the Anglosaxons in Ireland were situated have had peculiar vices and peculiar virtues, the vices and virtues of masters, as opposed to the vices and virtues of slaves. The member of a dominant race is, in his dealings with the subject race, seldom indeed fraudulent,—for fraud is the resource of the weak,—but imperious, insolent, and cruel. Towards his brethren, on the other hand, his conduct is generally just, kind, and even noble. His selfrespect leads him to respect all who belong to his own order. His interest impels him to cultivate a good understanding with those whose prompt, strenuous, and courageous assistance may at any moment be necessary to preserve his property and life. It is a truth ever present to his mind that his own wellbeing depends on the ascendency of the class to which he belongs. His very selfishness therefore is sublimed into public spirit: and this public spirit is stimulated to fierce enthusiasm by sympathy, by the desire of applause, and by the dread of infamy. For the only opinion which he values is the opinion of his fellows; and in their opinion devotion to the common cause is the most sacred of duties. The character, thus formed, has two aspects. Seen on one side, it must be regarded by every well constituted mind with disapprobation. Seen on the other, it irresistibly extorts applause. The Spartan, smiting and spurning the wretched Helot, moves our disgust. But the same Spartan, calmly dressing his hair, and uttering his concise jests, on what he well knows to be his last day, in the pass of Thermopylæ, is not to be contemplated without admiration. To a superficial observer it may seem strange that so much evil and so much good should be found together. But in truth the good and the evil, which at first sight appear almost incompatible, are closely connected, and have a common origin. It was because the Spartan had been taught to revere himself as one of a race of sovereigns, and to look down on all that was not Spartan as of an inferior species, that he had no fellow feeling for the miserable serfs who crouched before him, and that the thought of submitting to a foreign master, or of turning his back before an enemy, never, even in the last extremity, crossed his mind. Something of the same character, compounded of tyrant and hero, has been found in all nations which have domineered over more numerous nations. But it has nowhere in modern Europe shown itself so conspicuously as in Ireland. With what contempt, with what antipathy, the ruling minority in that country long regarded the subject majority may be best learned from the hateful laws which, within the memory of men still living, disgraced the Irish statute book. Those laws were at length annulled: but the spirit which had dictated them survived them, and even at this day sometimes breaks out in excesses pernicious to the commonwealth and dishonourable to the Protestant religion. Nevertheless it is impossible to deny that the English colonists have had, with too many of the faults, all the noblest virtues of a sovereign caste. The faults have, as was natural, been most offensively exhibited in times of prosperity and security: the virtues have been most resplendent in times of distress and peril; and never were those virtues more signally displayed than by the defenders of Londonderry, when their Governor had abandoned them, and when the camp of their mortal enemy was pitched before their walls.

No sooner had the first burst of the rage excited by the perfidy of Lundy spent itself than those whom he had betrayed proceeded, with a gravity and prudence worthy of the most renowned senates, to provide for the order and defence of the city. Two governors were elected, Baker and Walker. Baker took the chief military command. Walker's especial business was to preserve internal tranquillity, and to dole out supplies from the magazines. The inhabitants capable of bearing arms were distributed into eight regiments. Colonels, captains, and subordinate officers were appointed. In a few hours every man knew his post, and was ready to repair to it as soon as the beat of the drum was heard. That machinery, by which Oliver had, in the preceding generation, kept up among his soldiers so stern and so pertinacious an enthusiasm, was again employed with not less success. Preaching and praying occupied a large part of every day. Eighteen clergymen of the Established Church and seven or eight nonconformist ministers were within the walls. They all exerted themselves indefatigably to rouse and sustain the spirit of the people. Among themselves there was for the time entire harmony. All disputes about church government, postures, ceremonies, were forgotten. The Bishop, having found that his lectures on passive obedience were derided even by the Episcopalians, had withdrawn himself, first to Raphoe, and then to England, and was preaching in a chapel in London. On the other hand, a Scotch fanatic named Hewson, who had exhorted the Presbyterians not to ally themselves with such as refused to subscribe the Covenant, had sunk under the well merited disgust and scorn of the whole Protestant community. The aspect of the Cathedral was remarkable. Cannon were planted on the summit of the broad tower which has since given place to a tower of different proportions. Ammunition was stored in the vaults. In the choir the liturgy of the Anglican Church was read every morning. Every afternoon the Dissenters crowded to a simpler worship.

James had waited twenty four hours, expecting, as it should seem, the performance of Lundy's promises; and in twenty four hours the arrangements for the defence of Londonderry were complete. On the evening of the nineteenth of April, a trumpeter came to the southern gate, and asked whether the engagements into which the Governor had entered would be fulfilled. The answer was that the men who guarded these walls had nothing to do with the Governor's engagements, and were determined to resist to the last.

On the following day a messenger of higher rank was sent, Claude Hamilton, Lord Strabane, one of the few Roman Catholic peers of Ireland. Murray, who had been appointed to the command of one of the eight regiments into which the garrison was distributed, advanced from the gate to meet the flag of truce; and a short conference was held. Strabane had been authorised to make large promises. The citizens should have a free pardon for all that was past if they would submit to their lawful Sovereign. Murray himself should have a colonel's commission, and a thousand pounds in money. "The men of Londonderry," answered Murray, "have done nothing that requires a pardon, and own no Sovereign but King William and Queen Mary. It will not be safe for your Lordship to stay longer, or to return on the same errand. Let me have the honour of seeing you through the lines."

James had been assured, and had fully expected, that the city would yield as soon as it was known that he was before the walls. Finding himself mistaken, he broke loose from the control of Melfort, and determined to return instantly to Dublin. Rosen accompanied the King. The direction of the siege was entrusted to Maumont. Richard Hamilton was second, and Pusignan third, in command.

The operations now commenced in earnest. The besiegers began by battering the town. It was soon on fire in several places. Roofs and upper stories of houses fell in, and crushed the inmates. During a short time the garrison, many of whom had never before seen the effect of a cannonade, seemed to be discomposed by the crash of chimneys, and by the heaps of ruin mingled with disfigured corpses. But familiarity with danger and horror produced in a few hours the natural effect. The spirit of the people rose so high that their chiefs thought it safe to act on the offensive. On the twenty-first of April a sally was made under the command of Murray. The Irish stood their ground resolutely; and a furious and bloody contest took place. Maumont, at the head of a body of cavalry, flew to the place where the fight was raging. He was struck in the head by a musket ball, and fell a corpse. The besiegers lost several other officers, and about two hundred men, before the colonists could be driven in. Murray escaped with difficulty. His horse was killed under him; and he was beset by enemies: but he was able to defend himself till some of his friends made a rush from the gate to his rescue, with old Walker at their head.

In consequence of the death of Maumont, Richard Hamilton was once more commander of the Irish army. His exploits in that post did not raise his reputation. He was a fine gentleman and a brave soldier; but he had no pretensions to the character of a great general, and had never, in his life, seen a siege. Pusignan had more science and energy. But Pusignan survived Maumont little more than a fortnight. At four in the morning of the sixth of May, the garrison made another sally, took several flags, and killed many of the besiegers. Pusignan, fighting gallantly, was shot through the body. The wound was one which a skilful surgeon might have cured: but there was no such surgeon in the Irish camp; and the communication with Dublin was slow and irregular. The poor Frenchman died, complaining bitterly of the barbarous ignorance and negligence which had shortened his days. A medical man, who had been sent down express from the capital, arrived after the funeral. James, in consequence, as it should seem, of this disaster, established a daily post between Dublin Castle and Hamilton's head quarters. Even by this conveyance letters did not travel very expeditiously: for the couriers went on foot; and, from fear probably of the Enniskilleners, took a circuitous route from military post to military post.

May passed away: June arrived; and still Londonderry held out. There had been many sallies and skirmishes with various success: but, on the whole, the advantage had been with the garrison. Several officers of note had been carried prisoners into the city; and two French banners, torn after hard fighting from the besiegers, had been hung as trophies in the chancel of the Cathedral. It seemed that the siege must be turned into a blockade. But before the hope of reducing the town by main force was relinquished, it was determined to make a great effort. The point selected for assault was an outwork called Windmill Hill, which was not far from the southern gate. Religious stimulants were employed to animate the courage of the forlorn hope. Many volunteers bound themselves by oath to make their way into the works or to perish in the attempt. Captain Butler, son of the Lord Mountgarret, undertook to lead the sworn men to the attack. On the walls the colonists were drawn up in three ranks. The office of those who were behind was to load the muskets of those who were in front. The Irish came on boldly and with a fearful uproar, but after long and hard fighting were driven back. The women of Londonderry were seen amidst the thickest fire serving out water and ammunition to their husbands and brothers. In one place, where the wall was only seven feet high, Butler and some of his sworn men succeeded in reaching the top; but they were all killed or made prisoners. At length, after four hundred of the Irish had fallen, their chiefs ordered a retreat to be sounded.

Nothing was left but to try the effect of hunger. It was known that the stock of food in the city was but slender. Indeed it was thought strange that the supplies should have held out so long. Every precaution was now taken against the introduction of provisions. All the avenues leading to the city by land were closely guarded. On the south were encamped, along the left bank of the Foyle, the horsemen who had followed Lord Galmoy from the valley of the Barrow. Their chief was of all the Irish captains the most dreaded and the most abhorred by the Protestants. For he had disciplined his men with rare skill and care; and many frightful stories were told of his barbarity and perfidy. Long lines of tents, occupied by the infantry of Butler and O'Neil, of Lord Slane and Lord Gormanstown, by Nugent's Westmeath men, by Eustace's Kildare men, and by Cavanagh's Kerry men, extended northward till they again approached the water side. The river was fringed with forts and batteries, which no vessel could pass without great peril. After some time it was determined to make the security still more complete by throwing a barricade across the stream, about a mile and a half below the city. Several boats full of stones were sunk. A row of stakes was driven into the bottom of the river. Large pieces of fir wood, strongly bound together, formed a boom which was more than a quarter of a mile in length, and which was firmly fastened to both shores, by cables a foot thick. A huge stone, to which the cable on the left bank was attached, was removed many years later, for the purpose of being polished and shaped into a column. But the intention was abandoned, and the rugged mass still lies, not many yards from its original site, amidst the shades which surround a pleasant country house named Boom Hall. Hard by is the well from which the besiegers drank. A little further off is the burial ground where they laid their slain, and where even in our own time the spade of the gardener has struck upon many skulls and thighbones at a short distance beneath the turf and flowers.

[A passage is here omitted. It concludes with an account of the successful partisan war waged by the Enniskillen Protestants against the native population.]

Yet, in the midst of success and plenty, the Enniskilleners were tortured by a cruel anxiety for Londonderry. They were bound to the defenders of that city, not only by religious and national sympathy, but by common interest. For there could be no doubt that, if Londonderry fell, the whole Irish army would instantly march in irresistible force upon Lough Erne. Yet what could be done? Some brave men were for making a desperate attempt to relieve the besieged city; but the odds were too great. Detachments however were sent which infested the rear of the blockading army, cut off supplies, and, on one occasion, carried away the horses of three entire troops of cavalry. Still the line of posts which surrounded Londonderry by land remained unbroken. The river was still strictly closed and guarded. Within the walls the distress had become extreme. So early as the eighth of June horseflesh was almost the only meat which could be purchased; and of horseflesh the supply was scanty. It was necessary to make up the deficiency with tallow; and even tallow was doled out with a parsimonious hand.

On the fifteenth of June a gleam of hope appeared. The sentinels on the top of the Cathedral saw sails nine miles off in the bay of Lough Foyle. Thirty vessels of different sizes were counted. Signals were made from the steeples and returned from the mast heads, but were imperfectly understood on both sides. At last a messenger from the fleet eluded the Irish sentinels, dived under the boom, and informed the garrison that Kirke had arrived from England with troops, arms, ammunition, and provisions, to relieve the city.

In Londonderry expectation was at the height: but a few hours of feverish joy were followed by weeks of misery. Kirke thought it unsafe to make any attempt, either by land or by water, on the lines of the besiegers, and retired to the entrance of Lough Foyle, where, during several weeks, he lay inactive.

And now the pressure of famine became every day more severe. A strict search was made in all the recesses of all the houses of the city; and some provisions, which had been concealed in cellars by people who had since died or made their escape, were discovered and carried to the magazines. The stock of cannon balls was almost exhausted; and their place was supplied by brickbats coated with lead. Pestilence began, as usual, to make its appearance in the train of hunger. Fifteen officers died of fever in one day. The Governor Baker was among those who sank under the disease. His place was supplied by Colonel John Mitchelburne.

Meanwhile it was known at Dublin that Kirke and his squadron were on the coast of Ulster. The alarm was great at the Castle. Even before this news arrived, Avaux had given it as his opinion that Richard Hamilton was unequal to the difficulties of the situation. It had therefore been resolved that Rosen should take the chief command. He was now sent down with all speed.

On the nineteenth of June he arrived at the head quarters of the besieging army. At first he attempted to undermine the walls; but his plan was discovered; and he was compelled to abandon it after a sharp fight, in which more than a hundred of his men were slain. Then his fury rose to a strange pitch. He, an old soldier, a Marshal of France in expectancy, trained in the school of the greatest generals, accustomed, during many years, to scientific war, to be baffled by a mob of country gentlemen, farmers, shopkeepers, who were protected only by a wall which any good engineer would at once have pronounced untenable! He raved, he blasphemed, in a language of his own, made up of all the dialects spoken from the Baltic to the Atlantic. He would raze the city to the ground: he would spare no living thing; no, not the young girls; not the babies at the breast. As to the leaders, death was too light a punishment for them: he would rack them: he would roast them alive. In his rage he ordered a shell to be flung into the town with a letter containing a horrible menace. He would, he said, gather into one body all the Protestants who had remained at their homes between Charlemont and the sea, old men, women, children, many of them near in blood and affection to the defenders of Londonderry. No protection, whatever might be the authority by which it had been given, should be respected. The multitude thus brought together should be driven under the walls of Londonderry, and should there be starved to death in the sight of their countrymen, their friends, their kinsmen. This was no idle threat. Parties were instantly sent out in all directions to collect victims. At dawn, on the morning of the second of July, hundreds of Protestants, who were charged with no crime, who were incapable of bearing arms, and many of whom had protections granted by James, were dragged to the gates of the city. It was imagined that the piteous sight would quell the spirit of the colonists. But the only effect was to rouse that spirit to still greater energy. An order was immediately put forth that no man should utter the word Surrender on pain of death; and no man uttered that word. Several prisoners of high rank were in the town. Hitherto they had been well treated, and had received as good rations as were measured out to the garrison. They were now closely confined. A gallows was erected on one of the bastions; and a message was conveyed to Rosen, requesting him to send a confessor instantly to prepare his friends for death. The prisoners in great dismay wrote to the savage Livonian, but received no answer. They then addressed themselves to their countryman, Richard Hamilton. They were willing, they said, to shed their blood for their King; but they thought it hard to die the ignominious death of thieves in consequence of the barbarity of their own companions in arms. Hamilton, though a man of lax principles, was not cruel. He had been disgusted by the inhumanity of Rosen, but, being only second in command, could not venture to express publicly all that he thought. He however remonstrated strongly. Some Irish officers felt on this occasion as it was natural that brave men should feel, and declared, weeping with pity and indignation, that they should never cease to have in their ears the cries of the poor women and children who had been driven at the point of the pike to die of famine between the camp and the city. Rosen persisted during forty eight hours. In that time many unhappy creatures perished: but Londonderry held out as resolutely as ever; and he saw that his crime was likely to produce nothing but hatred and obloquy. He at length gave way, and suffered the survivors to withdraw. The garrison then took down the gallows which had been erected on the bastion.

When the tidings of these events reached Dublin, James, though by no means prone to compassion, was startled by an atrocity of which the civil wars of England had furnished no example, and was displeased by learning that protections, given by his authority, and guaranteed by his honour, had been publicly declared to be nullities. He complained to the French ambassador, and said, with a warmth which the occasion fully justified, that Rosen was a barbarous Muscovite. Melfort could not refrain from adding that, if Rosen had been an Englishman, he would have been hanged. Avaux was utterly unable to understand this effeminate sensibility. In his opinion, nothing had been done that was at all reprehensible; and he had some difficulty in commanding himself when he heard the King and the secretary blame, in strong language, an act of wholesome severity. In truth the French ambassador and the French general were well paired. There was a great difference doubtless, in appearance and manner, between the handsome, graceful, and refined diplomatist, whose dexterity and suavity had been renowned at the most polite courts of Europe, and the military adventurer, whose look and voice reminded all who came near him that he had been born in a half savage country, that he had risen from the ranks, and that he had once been sentenced to death for marauding. But the heart of the diplomatist was really even more callous than that of the soldier.

Rosen was recalled to Dublin; and Richard Hamilton was again left in the chief command. He tried gentler means than those which had brought so much reproach on his predecessor. No trick, no lie, which was thought likely to discourage the starving garrison was spared. One day a great shout was raised by the whole Irish camp. The defenders of Londonderry were soon informed that the army of James was rejoicing on account of the fall of Enniskillen. They were told that they had now no chance of being relieved, and were exhorted to save their lives by capitulating. They consented to negotiate. But what they asked was, that they should be permitted to depart armed and in military array, by land or by water at their choice. They demanded hostages for the exact fulfilment of these conditions, and insisted that the hostages should be sent on board of the fleet which lay in Lough Foyle. Such terms Hamilton durst not grant: the Governors would abate nothing: the treaty was broken off; and the conflict recommenced.

By this time July was far advanced; and the state of the city was, hour by hour, becoming more frightful. The number of the inhabitants had been thinned more by famine and disease than by the fire of the enemy. Yet that fire was sharper and more constant than ever. One of the gates was beaten in: one of the bastions was laid in ruins; but the breaches made by day were repaired by night with indefatigable activity. Every attack was still repelled. But the fighting men of the garrison were so much exhausted that they could scarcely keep their legs. Several of them, in the act of striking at the enemy, fell down from mere weakness. A very small quantity of grain remained, and was doled out by mouthfuls. The stock of salted hides was considerable, and by gnawing them the garrison appeased the rage of hunger. Dogs, fattened on the blood of the slain who lay unburied round the town, were luxuries which few could afford to purchase. The price of a whelp's paw was five shillings and sixpence. Nine horses were still alive, and but barely alive. They were so lean that little meat was likely to be found upon them. It was, however, determined to slaughter them for food. The people perished so fast that it was impossible for the survivors to perform the rites of sepulture. There was scarcely a cellar in which some corpse was not decaying. Such was the extremity of distress, that the rats who came to feast in those hideous dens were eagerly hunted and greedily devoured. A small fish, caught in the river, was not to be purchased with money. The only price for which such a treasure could be obtained was some handfuls of oatmeal. Leprosies, such as strange and unwholesome diet engenders, made existence a constant torment. The whole city was poisoned by the stench exhaled from the bodies of the dead and of the half dead. That there should be fits of discontent and insubordination among men enduring such misery was inevitable. At one moment it was suspected that Walker had laid up somewhere a secret store of food, and was revelling in private, while he exhorted others to suffer resolutely for the good cause. His house was strictly examined: his innocence was fully proved: he regained his popularity; and the garrison, with death in near prospect, thronged to the cathedral to hear him preach, drank in his earnest eloquence with delight, and went forth from the house of God with haggard faces and tottering steps, but with spirit still unsubdued. There were, indeed, some secret plottings. A very few obscure traitors opened communications with the enemy. But it was necessary that all such dealings should be carefully concealed. None dared to utter publicly any words save words of defiance and stubborn resolution. Even in that extremity the general cry was "No surrender." And there were not wanting voices which, in low tones, added, "First the horses and hides; and then the prisoners; and then each other." It was afterwards related, half in jest, yet not without a horrible mixture of earnest, that a corpulent citizen, whose bulk presented a strange contrast to the skeletons which surrounded him, thought it expedient to conceal himself from the numerous eyes which followed him with cannibal looks whenever he appeared in the streets.

It was no slight aggravation of the sufferings of the garrison that all this time the English ships were seen far off in Lough Foyle. Communication between the fleet and the city was almost impossible. One diver who had attempted to pass the boom was drowned. Another was hanged. The language of signals was hardly intelligible. On the thirteenth of July, however, a piece of paper sewed up in a cloth button came to Walker's hands. It was a letter from Kirke, and contained assurances of speedy relief. But more than a fortnight of intense misery had since elapsed; and the hearts of the most sanguine were sick with deferred hope. By no art could the provisions which were left be made to hold out two days more.

Just at this time Kirke received from England a despatch, which contained positive orders that Londonderry should be relieved. He accordingly determined to make an attempt which, as far as appears, he might have made, with at least an equally fair prospect of success, six weeks earlier.

Among the merchant ships which had come to Lough Foyle under his convoy was one called the Mountjoy. The master, Micaiah Browning, a native of Londonderry, had brought from England a large cargo of provisions. He had, it is said, repeatedly remonstrated against the inaction of the armament. He now eagerly volunteered to take the first risk of succouring his fellow citizens; and his offer was accepted. Andrew Douglas, master of the Phœnix, who had on board a great quantity of meal from Scotland, was willing to share the danger and the honour. The two merchantmen were to be escorted by the Dartmouth, a frigate of thirty six guns, commanded by Captain John Leake, afterwards an admiral of great fame.

It was the twenty-eighth of July. The sun had just set: the evening sermon in the cathedral was over; and the heartbroken congregation had separated; when the sentinels on the tower saw the sails of three vessels coming up the Foyle. Soon there was a stir in the Irish camp. The besiegers were on the alert for miles along both shores. The ships were in extreme peril: for the river was low; and the only navigable channel ran very near to the left bank, where the head quarters of the enemy had been fixed, and where the batteries were most numerous. Leake performed his duty with a skill and spirit worthy of his noble profession, exposed his frigate to cover the merchantmen, and used his guns with great effect. At length the little squadron came to the place of peril. Then the Mountjoy took the lead, and went right at the boom. The huge barricade cracked and gave way: but the shock was such that the Mountjoy rebounded, and stuck in the mud. A yell of triumph rose from the banks: the Irish rushed to their boats, and were preparing to board; but the Dartmouth poured on them a well directed broadside, which threw them into disorder. Just then the Phœnix dashed at the breach which the Mountjoy had made, and was in a moment within the fence. Meantime the tide was rising fast. The Mountjoy began to move, and soon passed safe through the broken stakes and floating spars. But her brave master was no more. A shot from one of the batteries had struck him; and he died by the most enviable of all deaths, in sight of the city which was his birthplace, which was his home, and which had just been saved by his courage and selfdevotion from the most frightful form of destruction. The night had closed in before the conflict at the boom began: but the flash of the guns was seen, and the noise heard, by the lean and ghastly multitude which covered the walls of the city. When the Mountjoy grounded, and when the shout of triumph rose from the Irish on both sides of the river, the hearts of the besieged died within them. One who endured the unutterable anguish of that moment has told us that they looked fearfully livid in each other's eyes. Even after the barricade had been passed, there was a terrible half hour of suspense. It was ten o'clock before the ships arrived at the quay. The whole population was there to welcome them. A screen made of casks filled with earth was hastily thrown up to protect the landing place from the batteries on the other side of the river; and then the work of unloading began. First were rolled on shore barrels containing six thousand bushels of meal. Then came great cheeses, casks of beef, flitches of bacon, kegs of butter, sacks of pease and biscuit, ankers of brandy. Not many hours before, half a pound of tallow and three quarters of a pound of salted hide had been weighed out with niggardly care to every fighting man. The ration which each now received was three pounds of flour, two pounds of beef, and a pint of pease. It is easy to imagine with what tears grace was said over the suppers of that evening. There was little sleep on either side of the wall. The bonfires shone bright along the whole circuit of the ramparts. The Irish guns continued to roar all night; and all night the bells of the rescued city made answer to the Irish guns with a peal of joyous defiance. Through the three following days the batteries of the enemy continued to play. But, on the third night, flames were seen arising from the camp; and, when the first of August dawned, a line of smoking ruins marked the site lately occupied by the huts of the besiegers; and the citizens saw far off the long column of pikes and standards retreating up the left bank of the Foyle towards Strabane.

So ended this great siege, the most memorable in the annals of the British Isles. It had lasted a hundred and five days. The garrison had been reduced from about seven thousand effective men to about three thousand. The loss of the besiegers cannot be precisely ascertained. Walker estimated it at eight thousand men. It is certain from the despatches of Avaux that the regiments which returned from the blockade had been so much thinned that many of them were not more than two hundred strong. Of thirty six French gunners who had superintended the cannonading, thirty one had been killed or disabled. The means both of attack and of defence had undoubtedly been such as would have moved the great warriors of the Continent to laughter; and this is the very circumstance which gives so peculiar an interest to the history of the contest. It was a contest, not between engineers, but between nations; and the victory remained with the nation which, though inferior in number, was superior in civilisation, in capacity for self-government, and in stubbornness of resolution.

As soon as it was known that the Irish army had retired, a deputation from the city hastened to Lough Foyle, and invited Kirke to take the command. He came accompanied by a long train of officers, and was received in state by the two Governors, who delivered up to him the authority which, under the pressure of necessity, they had assumed. He remained only a few days; but he had time to show enough of the incurable vices of his character to disgust a population distinguished by austere morals and ardent public spirit. There was, however, no outbreak. The city was in the highest good humour. Such quantities of provisions had been landed from the fleet, that there was in every house a plenty never before known. A few days earlier a man had been glad to obtain for twenty pence a mouthful of carrion scraped from the bones of a starved horse. A pound of good beef was now sold for three half-pence. Meanwhile all hands were busied in removing corpses which had been thinly covered with earth, in filling up the holes which the shells had ploughed in the ground, and in repairing the battered roofs of the houses. The recollection of past dangers and privations, and the consciousness of having deserved well of the English nation and of all Protestant Churches, swelled the hearts of the townspeople with honest pride. That pride grew stronger when they received from William a letter acknowledging, in the most affectionate language, the debt which he owed to the brave and trusty citizens of his good city. The whole population crowded to the Diamond to hear the royal epistle read. At the close all the guns on the ramparts sent forth a voice of joy: all the ships in the river made answer: barrels of ale were broken up; and the health of Their Majesties was drunk with shouts and volleys of musketry.

Five generations have since passed away; and still the wall of Londonderry is to the Protestants of Ulster what the trophy of Marathon was to the Athenians. A lofty pillar, rising from a bastion which bore during many weeks the heaviest fire of the enemy, is seen far up and far down the Foyle. On the summit is the statue of Walker, such as when, in the last and most terrible emergency, his eloquence roused the fainting courage of his brethren. In one hand he grasps a Bible. The other, pointing down the river, seems to direct the eyes of his famished audience to the English topmasts in the distant bay. Such a monument was well deserved: yet it was scarcely needed: for in truth the whole city is to this day a monument of the great deliverance. The wall is carefully preserved; nor would any plea of health or convenience be held by the inhabitants sufficient to justify the demolition of that sacred enclosure which, in the evil time, gave shelter to their race and their religion. The summit of the ramparts forms a pleasant walk. The bastions have been turned into little gardens. Here and there, among the shrubs and flowers, may be seen the old culverins which scattered bricks, cased with lead, among the Irish ranks. One antique gun, the gift of the Fishmongers of London, was distinguished, during the hundred and five memorable days, by the loudness of its report, and still bears the name of Roaring Meg. The cathedral is filled with relics and trophies. In the vestibule is a huge shell, one of many hundreds of shells which were thrown into the city. Over the altar are still seen the French flagstaves, taken by the garrison in a desperate sally. The white ensigns of the House of Bourbon have long been dust: but their place has been supplied by new banners, the work of the fairest hands of Ulster. The anniversary of the day on which the gates were closed, and the anniversary of the day on which the siege was raised, have been down to our own time celebrated by salutes, processions, banquets, and sermons: Lundy has been executed in effigy; and the sword, said by tradition to be that of Maumont, has, on great occasions, been carried in triumph. There is still a Walker Club and a Murray Club. The humble tombs of the Protestant captains have been carefully sought out, repaired, and embellished. It is impossible not to respect the sentiment which indicates itself by these tokens. It is a sentiment which belongs to the higher and purer part of human nature, and which adds not a little to the strength of states. A people which takes no pride in the noble achievements of remote ancestors will never achieve any thing worthy to be remembered with pride by remote descendants. Yet it is impossible for the moralist or the statesman to look with unmixed complacency on the solemnities with which Londonderry commemorates her deliverance, and on the honours which she pays to those who saved her. Unhappily the animosities of her brave champions have descended with their glory. The faults which are ordinarily found in dominant castes and dominant sects have not seldom shown themselves without disguise at her festivities; and even with the expressions of pious gratitude which have resounded from her pulpits have too often been mingled words of wrath and defiance.

BOYNE

WHEN William caught sight of the valley of the Boyne, he could not suppress an exclamation and a gesture of delight. He had been apprehensive that the enemy would avoid a decisive action, and would protract the war till the autumnal rains should return with pestilence in their train. He was now at ease. It was plain that the contest would be sharp and short. The pavilion of James was pitched on the eminence of Donore. The flags of the House of Stuart and of the House of Bourbon waved together in defiance on the walls of Drogheda. All the southern bank of the river was lined by the camp and batteries of the hostile army. Thousands of armed men were moving about among the tents; and every one, horse soldier or foot soldier, French or Irish, had a white badge in his hat. That colour had been chosen in compliment to the House of Bourbon. "I am glad to see you, gentlemen," said the King, as his keen eye surveyed the Irish lines. "If you escape me now, the fault will be mine."

Each of the contending princes had some advantages over his rival. James, standing on the defensive, behind entrenchments, with a river before him, had the stronger position: but his troops were inferior both in number and in quality to those which were opposed to him. He probably had thirty thousand men. About a third part of this force consisted of excellent French infantry and excellent Irish cavalry. But the rest of his army was the scoff of all Europe. The Irish dragoons were bad; the Irish foot worse. It was said that their ordinary way of fighting was to discharge their pieces once, and then to run away bawling "Quarter," and "Murder." Their inefficiency was, in that age, commonly imputed, both by their enemies and by their allies, to natural poltroonery. How little ground there was for such an imputation has since been signally proved by many brave achievements in every part of the globe. It ought indeed, even in the seventeenth century, to have occurred to reasonable men, that a race which furnished some of the best horse soldiers in the world, would certainly, with judicious training, furnish good foot soldiers. But the Irish foot soldiers had not merely not been well trained: they had been elaborately ill trained. The greatest of our generals repeatedly and emphatically declared that even the admirable army which fought its way, under his command, from Torres Vedras to Toulouse, would, if he had suffered it to contract habits of pillage, have become, in a few weeks, unfit for all military purposes. What then was likely to be the character of troops who, from the day on which they enlisted, were not merely permitted, but invited, to supply the deficiencies of pay by marauding? They were, as might have been expected, a mere mob, furious indeed and clamorous in their zeal for the cause which they had espoused, but incapable of opposing a stedfast resistance to a well ordered force. In truth, all that the discipline, if it is to be so called, of James's army had done for the Celtic kerne had been to debase and enervate him. After eighteen months of nominal soldiership, he was positively farther from being a soldier than on the day on which he quitted his hovel for the camp.

William had under his command near thirty six thousand men, born in many lands, and speaking many tongues. Scarcely one Protestant Church, scarcely one Protestant nation, was unrepresented in the army which a strange series of events had brought to fight for the Protestant religion in the remotest island of the west. About half the troops were natives of England. Ormond was there with the Life Guards, and Oxford with the Blues. Sir John Lanier, an officer who had acquired military experience on the Continent, and whose prudence was held in high esteem, was at the head of the Queen's regiment of horse, now the First Dragoon Guards. There were Beaumont's foot, who had, in defiance of the mandate of James, refused to admit Irish papists among them, and Hastings's foot, who had, on the disastrous day of Killiecrankie, maintained the military reputation of the Saxon race. There were the two Tangier battalions, hitherto known only by deeds of violence and rapine, but destined to begin on the following morning a long career of glory. Two fine English regiments, which had been in the service of the States General, and had often looked death in the face under William's leading, followed him in this campaign, not only as their general, but as their native King. They now rank as the fifth and sixth of the line. The former was led by an officer who had no skill in the higher parts of military science, but whom the whole army allowed to be the bravest of all the brave, John Cutts. The Scotch footguards marched under the command of their countryman James Douglas. Conspicuous among the Dutch troops were Portland's and Ginkell's Horse, and Solmes's Blue regiment, consisting of two thousand of the finest infantry in Europe. Germany had sent to the field some warriors, sprung from her noblest houses. Prince George of Hesse Darmstadt, a gallant youth, who was serving his apprenticeship in the military art, rode near the King. A strong brigade of Danish mercenaries was commanded by Duke Charles Frederic of Wurtemberg. It was reported that of all the soldiers of William these were most dreaded by the Irish. For centuries of Saxon domination had not effaced the recollection of the violence and cruelty of the Scandinavian sea kings; and an ancient prophecy that the Danes would one day destroy the children of the soil was still repeated with superstitious horror. Among the foreign auxiliaries were a Brandenburg regiment and a Finland regiment. But in that great array, so variously composed, were two bodies of men animated by a spirit peculiarly fierce and implacable, the Huguenots of France thirsting for the blood of the French, and the Englishry of Ireland impatient to trample down the Irish. The ranks of the refugees had been effectually purged of spies and traitors, and were made up of men such as had contended in the preceding century against the power of the House of Valois and the genius of the House of Lorraine. All the boldest spirits of the unconquerable colony had repaired to William's camp. Mitchelburne was there with the stubborn defenders of Londonderry, and Wolseley with the warriors who had raised the unanimous shout of "Advance" on the day of Newton Butler. Sir Albert Conyngham, the ancester of the noble family whose seat now overlooks the field of battle, had brought from the neighbourhood of Lough Erne a gallant regiment of dragoons which still glories in the name of Enniskillen, and which has proved on the shores of the Euxine that it has not degenerated since the day of the Boyne.

Walker, notwithstanding his advanced age and his peaceful profession, accompanied the men of Londonderry, and tried to animate their zeal by exhortation and by example. He was now a great prelate. Ezekiel Hopkins had taken refuge from Popish persecutors and Presbyterian rebels in the city of London, had brought himself to swear allegiance to the government, had obtained a cure, and had died in the performance of the humble duties of a parish priest. William, on his march through Louth, learned that the rich see of Derry was at his disposal. He instantly made choice of Walker to be the new Bishop. The brave old man, during the few hours of life which remained to him, was overwhelmed with salutations and congratulations. Unhappily he had, during the siege in which he had so highly distinguished himself, contracted a passion for war; and he easily persuaded himself that, in indulging this passion, he was discharging a duty to his country and his religion. He ought to have remembered that the peculiar circumstances which had justified him in becoming a combatant had ceased to exist, and that, in a disciplined army led by generals of long experience and great fame, a fighting divine was likely to give less help than scandal. The Bishop elect was determined to be wherever danger was; and the way in which he exposed himself excited the extreme disgust of his royal patron, who hated a meddler almost as much as a coward. A soldier who ran away from a battle and a gownsman who pushed himself into a battle were the two objects which most strongly excited William's spleen.

It was still early in the day. The King rode slowly along the northern bank of the river, and closely examined the position of the Irish, from whom he was sometimes separated by an interval of little more than two hundred feet. He was accompanied by Schomberg, Ormond, Sidney, Solmes, Prince George of Hesse, Coningsby, and others. "Their army is but small," said one of the Dutch officers. Indeed it did not appear to consist of more than sixteen thousand men. But it was well known, from the reports brought by deserters, that many regiments were concealed from view by the undulations of the ground. "They may be stronger than they look," said William; "but, weak or strong, I will soon know all about them."

At length he alighted at a spot nearly opposite to Oldbridge, sate down on the turf to rest himself, and called for breakfast. The sumpter horses were unloaded: the canteens were opened; and a tablecloth was spread on the grass. The place is marked by an obelisk, built while many veterans who could well remember the events of that day were still living.

While William was at his repast, a group of horsemen appeared close to the water on the opposite shore. Among them his attendants could discern some who had once been conspicuous at reviews in Hyde Park and at balls in the gallery of Whitehall, the youthful Berwick, the small, fairhaired Lauzun, Tyrconnel, once admired by maids of honour as the model of manly vigour and beauty, but now bent down by years and crippled by gout, and, overtopping all, the stately head of Sarsfield.

The chiefs of the Irish army soon discovered that the person who, surrounded by a splendid circle, was breakfasting on the opposite bank, was the Prince of Orange. They sent for artillery. Two field pieces, screened from view by a troop of cavalry, were brought down almost to the brink of the river, and placed behind a hedge. William, who had just risen from his meal, and was again in the saddle, was the mark of both guns. The first shot struck one of the holsters of Prince George of Hesse, and brought his horse to the ground. "Ah!" cried the King; "the poor Prince is killed." As the words passed his lips, he was himself hit by a second ball, a sixpounder. It merely tore his coat, grazed his shoulder, and drew two or three ounces of blood. Both armies saw that the shot had taken effect; for the King sank down for a moment on his horse's neck. A yell of exultation rose from the Irish camp. The English and their allies were in dismay. Solmes flung himself prostrate on the earth, and burst into tears. But William's deportment soon reassured his friends. "There is no harm done," he said: "but the bullet came quite near enough." Coningsby put his handkerchief to the wound: a surgeon was sent for: a plaster was applied; and the King, as soon as the dressing was finished, rode round all the posts of his army amidst loud acclamations. Such was the energy of his spirit that, in spite of his feeble health, in spite of his recent hurt, he was that day nineteen hours on horseback.

A cannonade was kept up on both sides till the evening. William observed with especial attention the effect produced by the Irish shots on the English regiments which had never been in action, and declared himself satisfied with the result. "All is right," he said: "they stand fire well." Long after sunset he made a final inspection of his forces by torchlight, and gave orders that every thing should be ready for forcing a passage across the river on the morrow. Every soldier was to put a green bough in his hat. The baggage and great coats were to be left under a guard. The word was Westminster.

The King's resolution to attack the Irish was not approved by all his lieutenants. Schomberg, in particular, pronounced the experiment too hazardous, and, when his opinion was overruled, retired to his tent in no very good humour. When the order of battle was delivered to him, he muttered that he had been more used to give such orders than to receive them. For this little fit of sullenness, very pardonable in a general who had won great victories when his master was still a child, the brave veteran made, on the following morning, a noble atonement.

The first of July [1690] dawned, a day which has never since returned without exciting strong emotions of very different kinds in the two populations which divide Ireland. The sun rose bright and cloudless. Soon after four both armies were in motion. William ordered his right wing, under the command of Meinhart Schomberg, one of the Duke's sons, to march to the bridge of Slane, some miles up the river, to cross there, and to turn the left flank of the Irish army. Meinhart Schomberg was assisted by Portland and Douglas. James, anticipating some such design, had already sent to the bridge a regiment of dragoons, commanded by Sir Neil O'Neil. O'Neil behaved himself like a brave gentleman: but he soon received a mortal wound: his men fled; and the English right wing passed the river.

This move made Lauzun uneasy. What if the English right wing should get into the rear of the army of James? About four miles south of the Boyne was a place called Duleek, where the road to Dublin was so narrow, that two cars could not pass each other, and where on both sides of the road lay a morass which afforded no firm footing. If Meinhart Schomberg should occupy this spot, it would be impossible for the Irish to retreat. They must either conquer, or be cut off to a man. Disturbed by this apprehension, the French general marched with his countrymen and with Sarsfield's horse in the direction of Slane Bridge. Thus the fords near Oldbridge were left to be defended by the Irish alone.

It was now near ten o'clock. William put himself at the head of his left wing, which was composed exclusively of cavalry, and prepared to pass the river not far above Drogheda. The centre of his army, which consisted almost exclusively of foot, was entrusted to the command of Schomberg, and was marshalled opposite to Oldbridge. At Oldbridge had been collected the whole Irish army, foot, dragoons, and horse, Sarsfield's regiment alone excepted. The Meath bank bristled with pikes and bayonets. A fortification had been made by French engineers out of the hedges and buildings; and a breast work had been thrown up close to the water side. Tyrconnel was there; and under him were Richard Hamilton and Antrim.

Schomberg gave the word. Solmes's Blues were the first to move. They marched gallantly, with drums beating, to the brink of the Boyne. Then the drums stopped; and the men, ten abreast, descended into the water. Next plunged Londonderry and Enniskillen. A little to the left of Londonderry and Enniskillen, Caillemot crossed, at the head of a long column of French refugees. A little to the left of Caillemot and his refugees, the main body of the English infantry struggled through the river, up to their armpits in water. Still further down the stream the Danes found another ford. In a few minutes the Boyne, for a quarter of a mile, was alive with muskets and green boughs.

It was not till the assailants had reached the middle of the channel that they became aware of the whole difficulty and danger of the service in which they were engaged. They had as yet seen little more than half the hostile army. Now whole regiments of foot and horse seemed to start out of the earth. A wild shout of defiance rose from the whole shore: during one moment the event seemed doubtful: but the Protestants pressed resolutely forward; and in another moment the whole Irish line gave way. Tyrconnel looked on in helpless despair. He did not want personal courage: but his military skill was so small that he hardly ever reviewed his regiment in the Phœnix Park without committing some blunder; and to rally the ranks which were breaking all round him was no task for a general who had survived the energy of his body and of his mind, and yet had still the rudiments of his profession to learn. Several of his best officers fell while vainly endeavouring to prevail on their soldiers to look the Dutch Blues in the face. Richard Hamilton ordered a body of foot to fall on the French refugees, who were still deep in water. He led the way, and, accompanied by some courageous gentlemen, advanced, sword in hand, into the river. But neither his commands nor his example could infuse valour into that mob of cowstealers. He was left almost alone, and retired from the bank in despair. Further down the river, Antrim's division ran like sheep at the approach of the English column. Whole regiments flung away arms, colours and cloaks, and scampered off to the hills without striking a blow or firing a shot.

It required many years and many heroic exploits to take away the reproach which that ignominious rout left on the Irish name. Yet, even before the day closed, it was abundantly proved that the reproach was unjust. Richard Hamilton put himself at the head of the cavalry, and, under his command, they made a gallant, though an unsuccessful attempt to retrieve the day. They maintained a desperate fight in the bed of the river with Solmes's Blues. They drove the Danish brigade back into the stream. They fell impetuously on the Huguenot regiments, which, not being provided with pikes, then ordinarily used by foot to repel horse, began to give ground. Caillemot, while encouraging his fellow exiles, received a mortal wound in the thigh. Four of his men carried him back across the ford to his tent. As he passed, he continued to urge forward the rear ranks which were still up to the breast in the water. "On; on; my lads! to glory! to glory!" Schomberg, who had remained on the northern bank, and who had thence watched the progress of his troops with the eye of a general, now thought that the emergency required from him the personal exertion of a soldier. Those who stood about him besought him in vain to put on his cuirass. Without defensive armour he rode through the river, and rallied the refugees whom the fall of Caillemot had dismayed. "Come on," he cried in French, pointing to the Popish squadrons; "come on, gentlemen: there are your persecutors." Those were his last words. As he spoke, a band of Irish horsemen rushed upon him and encircled him for a moment. When they retired, he was on the ground. His friends raised him; but he was already a corpse. Two sabre wounds were on his head; and a bullet from a carbine was lodged in his neck. Almost at the same moment Walker, while exhorting the colonists of Ulster to play the men, was shot dead. During near half an hour the battle continued to rage along the southern shore of the river. All was smoke, dust and din. Old soldiers were heard to say that they had seldom seen sharper work in the Low Countries. But, just at this conjuncture, William came up with the left wing. He had found much difficulty in crossing. The tide was running fast. His charger had been forced to swim, and had been almost lost in the mud. As soon as the King was on firm ground he took his sword in his left hand,—for his right arm was stiff with his wound and his bandage,—and led his men to the place where the fight was the hottest. His arrival decided the fate of the day. Yet the Irish horse retired fighting obstinately. It was long remembered among the Protestants of Ulster that, in the midst of the tumult, William rode to the head of the Enniskilleners. "What will you do for me?" he cried. He was not immediately recognised; and one trooper, taking him for an enemy, was about to fire. William gently put aside the carbine. "What," said he, "do you not know your friends?" "It is His Majesty," said the Colonel. The ranks of sturdy Protestant yeomen set up a shout of joy. "Gentlemen," said William, "you shall be my guards to day. I have heard much of you. Let me see something of you." One of the most remarkable peculiarities of this man, ordinarily so saturnine and reserved, was that danger acted on him like wine, opened his heart, loosened his tongue, and took away all appearance of constraint from his manner. On this memorable day he was seen wherever the peril was greatest. One ball struck the cap of his pistol: another carried off the heel of his jackboot: but his lieutenants in vain implored him to retire to some station from which he could give his orders without exposing a life so valuable to Europe. His troops, animated by his example, gained ground fast. The Irish cavalry made their last stand at a house called Plottin Castle, about a mile and a half south of Old-bridge. There the Enniskilleners were repelled with the loss of fifty men, and were hotly pursued, till William rallied them and turned the chase back. In this encounter Richard Hamilton, who had done all that could be done by valour to retrieve a reputation forfeited by perfidy,[1] was severely wounded, taken prisoner, and instantly brought, through the smoke and over the carnage, before the prince whom he had foully wronged. On no occasion did the character of William show itself in a more striking manner. "Is this business over?" he said; "or will your horse make more fight?" "On my honour, Sir," answered Hamilton, "I believe that they will." "Your honour!" muttered William; "your honour!" That half suppressed exclamation was the only revenge which he condescended to take for an injury for which many sovereigns, far more affable and gracious in their ordinary deportment, would have exacted a terrible retribution. Then, restraining himself, he ordered his own surgeon to look to the hurts of the captive.

And now the battle was over. Hamilton was mistaken in thinking that his horse would continue to fight. Whole troops had been cut to pieces. One fine regiment had only thirty unwounded men left. It was enough that these gallant soldiers had disputed the field till they were left without support, or hope, or guidance, till their bravest leader was a captive, and till their King had fled.

GLENCOE

Mac Ian dwelt in the mouth of a ravine situated not far from the southern shore of Lochleven, an arm of the sea which deeply indents the western coast of Scotland, and separates Argyleshire from Invernesshire. Near his house were two or three small hamlets inhabited by his tribe. The whole population which he governed

---

[1] [Richard Hamilton had been sent over to Ireland on parole by William. But he had broken his word and become one of James's generals.]

was not supposed to exceed two hundred souls. In the neighbourhood of the little cluster of villages was some copsewood and some pasture land: but a little further up the defile no sign of population or of fruitfulness was to be seen. In the Gaelic tongue Glencoe signifies the Glen of Weeping: and in truth that pass is the most dreary and melancholy of all the Scottish passes, the very Valley of the Shadow of Death. Mists and storms brood over it through the greater part of the finest summer; and even on those rare days when the sun is bright, and when there is no cloud in the sky, the impression made by the landscape is sad and awful. The path lies along a stream which issues from the most sullen and gloomy of mountain pools. Huge precipices of naked stone frown on both sides. Even in July the streaks of snow may often be discerned in the rifts near the summits. All down the sides of the crags heaps of ruin mark the headlong paths of the torrents. Mile after mile the traveller looks in vain for the smoke of one hut, for one human form wrapped in a plaid, and listens in vain for the bark of a shepherd's dog, or the bleat of a lamb. Mile after mile the only sound that indicates life is the faint cry of a bird of prey from some stormbeaten pinnacle of rock. The progress of civilisation, which has turned so many wastes into fields yellow with harvests or gay with apple blossoms, has only made Glencoe more desolate. All the science and industry of a peaceful age can extract nothing valuable from that wilderness: but, in an age of violence and rapine, the wilderness itself was valued on account of the shelter which it afforded to the plunderer and his plunder. Nothing could be more natural than that the clan to which this rugged desert belonged should have been noted for predatory habits. For, among the Highlanders generally, to rob was thought at least as honourable an employment as to cultivate the soil; and, of all the Highlanders, the Macdonalds of Glencoe had the least productive soil, and the most convenient and secure den of robbers. Successive governments had tried to punish this wild race: but no large force had ever been employed for that purpose; and a small force was easily resisted or eluded by men familiar with every recess and every outlet of the natural fortress in which they had been born and bred. The people of Glencoe would probably have been less troublesome neighbours if they had lived among their own kindred. But they were an outpost of the Clan Donald, separated from every other branch of their own family, and almost surrounded by the domains of the hostile race of Diarmid. They were impelled by hereditary enmity, as well as by want, to live at the expense of the tribe of Campbell. Breadalbane's property had suffered greatly from their depredations; and he was not of a temper to forgive such injuries. When, therefore, the Chief of Glencoe made his appearance at the congress in Glenorchy, he was ungraciously received. The Earl, who ordinarily bore himself with the solemn dignity of a Castilian grandee, forgot, in his resentment, his wonted gravity, forgot his public character, forgot the laws of hospitality, and, with angry reproaches and menaces, demanded reparation for the herds which had been driven from his lands by Mac Ian's followers. Mac Ian was seriously apprehensive of some personal outrage, and was glad to get safe back to his own glen. His pride had been wounded; and the promptings of interest concurred with those of pride. As the head of a people who lived by pillage, he had strong reasons for wishing that the country might continue to be in a perturbed state. He had little chance of receiving one guinea of the money which was to be distributed among the malecontents. For his share of that money would scarcely meet Breadalbane's demands for compensation; and there could be little doubt that, whoever might be unpaid, Breadalbane would take care to pay himself. Mac Ian therefore did his best to dissuade his allies from accepting terms from which he could himself expect no benefit; and his influence was not small. His own vassals, indeed, were few in number: but he came of the best blood of the Highlands: he had kept up a close connection with his more powerful kinsmen; nor did they like him the less because he was a robber; for he never robbed them; and that robbery, merely as robbery, was a wicked and disgraceful act, had never entered into the mind of any Celtic chief. Mac Ian was therefore held in high esteem by the confederates. His age was venerable: his aspect was majestic; and he possessed in large measure those intellectual qualities which, in rude societies, give men an ascendency over their fellows. Breadalbane found himself, at every step of the negotiation, thwarted by the arts of his old enemy, and abhorred the name of Glencoe more and more every day.

But the government did not trust solely to Breadalbane's diplomatic skill. The authorities at Edinburgh put forth a proclamation exhorting the clans to submit to King William and Queen Mary, and offering pardon to every rebel who, on or before the thirty-first of December 1691, should swear to live peaceably under the government of their Majesties. It was announced that those who should hold out after that day would be treated as enemies and traitors. Warlike preparations were made, which showed that the threat was meant in earnest. The Highlanders were alarmed, and, though the pecuniary terms had not been satisfactorily settled, thought it prudent to give the pledge which was demanded of them.

No chief, indeed, was willing to set the example of submission. Glengarry blustered, and pretended to fortify his house. "I will not," said Lochiel, "break the ice. That is a point of honour with me. But my tacksmen and people may use their freedom." His tacksmen and people understood him, and repaired by hundreds to the Sheriff to take the oaths. The Macdonalds of Sleat, Clanronald, Keppoch, and even Glengarry, imitated the Camerons; and the chiefs, after trying to outstay each other as long as they durst, imitated their vassals.

The thirty-first of December arrived; and still the Macdonalds of Glencoe had not come in. The punctilious pride of Mac Ian was doubtless gratified by the thought that he had continued to defy the government after the boastful Glengarry, the ferocious Keppoch, the magnanimous Lochiel had yielded: but he bought his gratification dear.

At length, on the thirty-first of December, he repaired to Fort William, accompanied by his principal vassals, and offered to take the oaths. To his dismay he found that there was in the fort no person competent to administer them. Colonel Hill, the Governor, was not a magistrate; nor was there any magistrate nearer than Inverary. Mac Ian, now fully sensible of the folly of which he had been guilty in postponing to the very last moment an act on which his life and his estate depended, set off for Inverary in great distress. He carried with him a letter from Hill to the Sheriff of Argyleshire, Sir Colin Campbell of Ardkinglass, a respectable gentleman, who, in the late reign, had suffered severely for his Whig principles. In this letter the Colonel expressed a goodnatured hope that, even out of season, a lost sheep, and so fine a lost sheep, would be gladly received. Mac Ian made all the haste in his power, and did not stop even at his own house, though it lay nigh to the road. But at that time a journey through Argyleshire in the depth of winter was necessarily slow. The old man's progress up steep mountains and along boggy valleys was obstructed by snow storms; and it was not till the sixth of January that he presented himself before the Sheriff at Inverary. The Sheriff hesitated. His power, he said, was limited by the terms of the proclamation; and he did not see how he could swear a rebel who had not submitted within the prescribed time. Mac Ian begged earnestly and with tears that he might be sworn. His people, he said, would follow his example. If any of them proved refractory, he would himself send the recusant to prison, or ship him off for Flanders. His entreaties and Hill's letter overcame Sir Colin's scruples. The oath was administered; and a certificate was transmitted to the Council at Edinburgh, setting forth the special circumstances which had induced the Sheriff to do what he knew not to be strictly regular.

The news that Mac Ian had not submitted within the prescribed time was received with cruel joy by three powerful Scotchmen who were then at the English Court. Breadalbane had gone up to London at Christmas in order to give an account of his stewardship. There he met his kinsman Argyle. Argyle was, in personal qualities, one of the most insignificant of the long line of nobles who have borne that great name. He was the descendant of eminent men, and the parent of eminent men. He was the grandson of one of the ablest of Scottish politicians; the son of one of the bravest and most truehearted of Scottish patriots; the father of one Mac Callum More renowned as a warrior and as an orator, as the model of every courtly grace, and as the judicious patron of arts and letters, and of another Mac Callum More distinguished by talents for business and command, and by skill in the exact sciences. Both of such an ancestry and of such a progeny Argyle was unworthy. He had even been guilty of the crime, common enough among Scottish politicians, but in him singularly disgraceful, of tampering with the agents of James while professing loyalty to William. Still Argyle had the importance inseparable from high rank, vast domains, extensive feudal rights, and almost boundless patriarchal authority. To him, as to his cousin Breadalbane, the intelligence that the tribe of Glencoe was out of the protection of the law was most gratifying; and the Master of Stair more than sympathised with them both.

The feeling of Argyle and Breadalbane is perfectly intelligible. They were the heads of a great clan; and they had an opportunity of destroying a neighbouring clan with which they were at deadly feud. Breadalbane had received peculiar provocation. His estate had been repeatedly devastated; and he had just been thwarted in a negotiation of high moment. Unhappily there was scarcely any excess of ferocity for which a precedent could not be found in Celtic tradition. Among all warlike barbarians revenge is esteemed the most sacred of duties and the most exquisite of pleasures; and so it had long been esteemed among the Highlanders. The history of the clans abounds with frightful tales, some perhaps fabulous or exaggerated, some certainly true, of vindictive massacres and assassinations. The Macdonalds of Glengarry, for example, having been affronted by the people of a parish near Inverness, surrounded the parish church on a Sunday, shut the doors, and burned the whole congregation alive. While the flames were raging, the hereditary musician of the murderers mocked the shrieks of the perishing crowd with the notes of his bagpipe. A band of Macgregors, having cut off the head of an enemy, laid it, the mouth filled with bread and cheese, on his sister's table, and had the satisfaction of seeing her go mad with horror at the sight. They then carried the ghastly trophy in triumph to their chief. The whole clan met under the roof of an ancient church. Every one in turn laid his hand on the dead man's scalp, and vowed to defend the slayers. The inhabitants of Eigg seized some Macleods, bound them hand and foot, and turned them adrift in a boat to be swallowed up by the waves, or to perish of hunger. The Macleods retaliated by driving the population of Eigg into a cavern, lighting a fire at the entrance, and suffocating the whole race, men, women and children. It is much less strange that the two great Earls of the house of Campbell, animated by the passions of Highland chieftains, should have planned a Highland revenge, than that they should have found an accomplice, and something more than an accomplice, in the Master of Stair.

The Master of Stair was one of the first men of his time, a jurist, a statesman, a fine scholar, an eloquent orator. His polished manners and lively conversation were the delight of aristocratical societies; and none who met him in such societies would have thought it possible that he could bear the chief part in any atrocious crime. His political principles were lax, yet not more lax than those of most Scotch politicians of that age. Cruelty had never been imputed to him. Those who most disliked him did him the justice to own that, where his schemes of policy were not concerned, he was a very goodnatured man. There is not the slightest reason to believe that he gained a single pound Scots by the act which has covered his name with infamy. He had no personal reason to wish the Glencoe men any ill. There had been no feud between them and his family. His property lay in a district where their tartan was never seen. Yet he hated them with a hatred as fierce and implacable as if they had laid waste his fields, burned his mansion, murdered his child in the cradle.

To what cause are we to ascribe so strange an antipathy? This question perplexed the Master's contemporaries; and any answer which may now be offered ought to be offered with diffidence. The most probable conjecture is that he was actuated by an inordinate, an unscrupulous, a remorseless zeal for what seemed to him to be the interest of the state. This explanation may startle those who have not considered how large a proportion of the blackest crimes recorded in history is to be ascribed to ill regulated public spirit. We daily see men do for their party, for their sect, for their country, for their favourite schemes of political and social reform, what they would not do to enrich or to avenge themselves. At a temptation directly addressed to our private cupidity or to our private animosity, whatever virtue we have takes the alarm. But virtue itself may contribute to the fall of him who imagines that it is in his power, by violating some general rule of morality, to confer an important benefit on a church, on a commonwealth, on mankind. He silences the remonstrances of conscience, and hardens his heart against the most touching spectacles of misery, by repeating to himself that his intentions are pure, that his objects are noble, that he is doing a little evil for the sake of a great good. By degrees he comes altogether to forget the turpitude of the means in the excellence of the end, and at length perpetrates without one internal twinge acts which would shock a buccaneer. There is no reason to believe that Dominic would, for the best archbishopric in Christendom, have incited ferocious marauders to plunder and slaughter a peaceful and industrious population, that Everard Digby would, for a dukedom, have blown a large assembly of people into the air, or that Robespierre would have murdered for hire one of the thousands whom he murdered from philanthropy.

The Master of Stair seems to have proposed to himself a truly great and good end, the pacification and civilisation of the Highlands. He was, by the acknowledgment of those who most hated him, a man of large views. He justly thought it monstrous that a third part of Scotland should be in a state scarcely less savage than New Guinea, that letters of fire and sword should, through a third part of Scotland, be, century after century, a species of legal process, and that no attempt should be made to apply a radical remedy to such evils. The independence affected by a crowd of petty sovereigns, the contumacious resistance which they were in the habit of offering to the authority of the Crown and of the Court of Session, their wars, their robberies, their fireraisings, their practice of exacting black mail from people more peaceable and more useful than themselves, naturally excited the disgust and indignation of an enlightened and politic gownsman, who was, both by the constitution of his mind and by the habits of his profession, a lover of law and order. His object was no less than a complete dissolution and reconstruction of society in the Highlands, such a dissolution and reconstruction as, two generations later, followed the battle of Culloden. In his view the clans, as they existed, were the plagues of the kingdom; and of all the clans the worst was that which inhabited Glencoe. He had, it is said, been particularly struck by a frightful instance of the lawlessness and ferocity of those marauders. One of them, who had been concerned in some act of violence or rapine, had given information against his companions. He had been bound to a tree and murdered. The old chief had given the first stab; and scores of dirks had then been plunged into the wretch's body. By the mountaineers such an act was probably regarded as a legitimate exercise of patriarchal jurisdiction. To the Master of Stair it seemed that people among whom such things were done and were approved ought to be treated like a pack of wolves, snared by any device, and slaughtered without mercy. He was well read in history, and doubtless knew how great rulers had, in his own and other countries, dealt with such banditti. He doubtless knew with what energy and what severity James the Fifth had put down the mosstroopers of the border, how the chief of Henderland had been hung over the gate of the castle in which he had prepared a banquet for the King; how John Armstrong and his thirty six horsemen, when they came forth to welcome their sovereign, had scarcely been allowed time to say a single prayer before they were all tied up and turned off. Nor probably was the Secretary ignorant of the means by which Sixtus the Fifth had cleared the ecclesiastical state of outlaws. The eulogists of that great pontiff tell us that there was one formidable gang which could not be dislodged from a stronghold among the Apennines. Beasts of burden were therefore loaded with poisoned food and wine, and sent by a road which ran close to the fastness. The robbers sallied forth, seized the prey, feasted and died; and the pious old Pope exulted greatly when he heard that the corpses of thirty ruffians, who had been the terror of many peaceful villages, had been found lying among the mules and packages. The plans of the Master of Stair were conceived in the spirit of James and of Sixtus; and the rebellion of the mountaineers furnished what seemed to be an excellent opportunity for carrying those plans into effect. Mere rebellion, indeed, he could have easily pardoned. On Jacobites, as Jacobites, he never showed any inclination to bear hard. He hated the Highlanders, not as enemies of this or that dynasty, but as enemies of law, of industry, and of trade. In his private correspondence he applied to them the short and terrible form of words in which the implacable Roman pronounced the doom of Carthage. His project was no less than this, that the whole hill country from sea to sea, and the neighbouring islands, should be wasted with fire and sword, that the Camerons, the Macleans, and all the branches of the race of Macdonald, should be rooted out. He therefore looked with no friendly eye on schemes of reconciliation, and, while others were hoping that a little money would set everything right, hinted very intelligibly his opinion that whatever money was to be laid out on the clans would be best laid out in the form of bullets and bayonets. To the last moment he continued to flatter himself that the rebels would be obstinate, and would thus furnish him with a plea for accomplishing that great social revolution on which his heart was set. The letter is still extant in which he directed the commander of the forces in Scotland how to act if the Jacobite chiefs should not come in before the end of December. There is something strangely terrible in the calmness and conciseness with which the instructions are given. "Your troops will destroy entirely the country of Lochaber, Lochiel's lands, Keppoch's, Glengarry's and Glencoe's. Your power shall be large enough. I hope the soldiers will not trouble the government with prisoners."

This despatch had scarcely been sent off when news arrived in London that the rebel chiefs, after holding out long, had at last appeared before the Sheriffs and taken the oaths. Lochiel, the most eminent man among them, had not only declared that he would live and die a true subject to King William, but had announced his intention of visiting England, in the hope of being permitted to kiss His Majesty's hand. In London it was announced exultingly that all the clans had submitted; and the announcement was generally thought most satisfactory. But the Master of Stair was bitterly disappointed. The Highlands were then to continue to be what they had been, the shame and curse of Scotland. A golden opportunity of subjecting them to the law had been suffered to escape, and might never return. If only the Macdonalds would have stood out, nay, if an example could but have been made of the two worst Macdonalds, Keppoch and Glencoe, it would have been something. But it seemed that even Keppoch and Glencoe, marauders who in any well governed country would have been hanged thirty years before, were safe. While the Master was brooding over thoughts like these, Argyle brought him some comfort. The report that Mac Ian had taken the oaths within the prescribed time was erroneous. The Secretary was consoled. One clan, then, was at the mercy of the government, and that clan the most lawless of all. One great act of justice, nay of charity, might be performed. One terrible and memorable example might be made.

Yet there was a difficulty. Mac Ian had taken the oaths. He had taken them, indeed, too late to be entitled to plead the letter of the royal promise: but the fact that he had taken them was one which evidently ought to have been brought under consideration before his fate was decided. By a dark intrigue, of which the history is but imperfectly known, but which was, in all probability, directed by the Master of Stair, the evidence of Mac Ian's tardy submission

M—6*

was suppressed. The certificate which the Sheriff of Argyleshire had transmitted to the Council at Edinburgh, was never laid before the Board, but was privately submitted to some persons high in office, and particularly to Lord President Stair, the father of the Secretary. These persons pronounced the certificate irregular, and, indeed, absolutely null; and it was cancelled.

Meanwhile the Master of Stair was forming, in concert with Breadalbane and Argyle, a plan for the destruction of the people of Glencoe. It was necessary to take the King's pleasure, not, indeed, as to the details of what was to be done, but as to the question whether Mac Ian and his people should or should not be treated as rebels out of the pale of the ordinary law. The Master of Stair found no difficulty in the royal closet. William had, in all probability, never heard the Glencoe men mentioned except as banditti. He knew that they had not come in by the prescribed day. That they had come in after that day he did not know. If he paid any attention to the matter, he must have thought that so fair an opportunity of putting an end to the devastations and depredations from which a quiet and industrious population had suffered so much ought not to be lost.

An order was laid before him for signature. He signed it, but, if Burnet may be trusted, did not read it. Whoever has seen anything of public business knows that princes and ministers daily sign, and indeed must sign, documents which they have not read; and of all documents a document relating to a small tribe of mountaineers, living in a wilderness not set down in any map, was least likely to interest a Sovereign whose mind was full of schemes on which the fate of Europe might depend. But, even on the supposition that he read the order to which he affixed his name, there seems to be no reason for blaming him. That order, directed to the Commander of the Forces in Scotland, runs thus: "As for Mac Ian of Glencoe and that tribe, if they can be well distinguished from the other Highlanders, it will be proper, for the vindication of public justice, to extirpate that set of thieves." These words naturally bear a sense perfectly innocent, and would, but for the horrible event which followed, have been universally understood in that sense. It is undoubtedly one of the first duties of every government to extirpate gangs of thieves. This does not mean that every thief ought to be treacherously assassinated in his sleep, or even that every thief ought to be put to death after a fair trial, but that every gang, as a gang, ought to be completely broken up, and that whatever severity is indispensably necessary for that end ought to be used. It is in this sense that we praise the Marquess of Hastings for extirpating the Pindarees, and Lord William Bentinck for extirpating the Thugs. If William had read and weighed the words which were submitted to him by his Secretary, he would probably have understood them to mean that Glencoe was to be occupied by troops, that resistance, if resistance were attempted, was to be put down with a strong hand, that severe punishment was to be inflicted on those leading members of the clan who could be proved to have been guilty of great crimes, that some active young freebooters, who were more used to handle the broad sword than the plough, and who did not seem likely to settle down into quiet labourers, were to be sent to the army in the Low Countries, that others were to be transported to the American plantations, and that those Macdonalds who were suffered to remain in their native valley were to be disarmed and required to give hostages for good behaviour. A plan very nearly resembling this had, we know, actually been the subject of much discussion in the political circles of Edinburgh. There can be little doubt that William would have deserved well of his people if he had, in this manner, extirpated not only the tribe of Mac Ian, but every Highland tribe whose calling was to steal cattle and burn houses.

The extirpation planned by the Master of Stair was of a different kind. His design was to butcher the whole race of thieves, the whole damnable race. Such was the language in which his hatred vented itself. He studied the geography of the wild country which surrounded Glencoe, and made his arrangements with infernal skill. If possible, the blow must be quick, and crushing, and altogether unexpected. But if Mac Ian should apprehend danger and should attempt to take refuge in the territories of his neighbours, he must find every road barred. The pass of Rannoch must be secured. The Laird of Weems, who was powerful in Strath Tay, must be told that, if he harbours the outlaws, he does so at his peril. Breadalbane promised to cut off the retreat of the fugitives on one side, Mac Callum More on another. It was fortunate, the Secretary wrote, that it was winter. This was the time to maul the wretches. The nights were so long, the mountain tops so cold and stormy, that even the hardiest men could not long bear exposure to the open air without a roof or a spark of fire. That the women and the children could find shelter in the desert was quite impossible. While he wrote thus, no thought that he was committing a great wickedness crossed his mind. He was happy in the approbation of his own conscience. Duty, justice, nay charity and mercy, were the names under which he disguised his cruelty; nor is it by any means improbable that the disguise imposed upon himself.

Hill, who commanded the forces assembled at Fort William, was not entrusted with the execution of the design. He seems to have been a humane man; he was much distressed when he learned that the government was determined on severity; and it was probably thought that his heart might fail him in the most critical moment. He was directed to put a strong detachment under the orders of his second in command, Lieutenant Colonel Hamilton. To Hamilton a significant hint was conveyed that he had now an excellent opportunity of establishing his character in the estimation of those who were at the head of affairs. Of the troops entrusted to him a large proportion were Campbells, and belonged to a regiment lately raised by Argyle, and called by Argyle's name. It was probably thought that, on such an occasion, humanity might prove too strong for the mere habit of military obedience, and that little reliance could be placed on hearts which had not been ulcerated by a feud such as had long raged between the people of Mac Ian and the people of Mac Callum More.

Had Hamilton marched openly against the Glencoe men and put them to the edge of the sword, the act would probably not have wanted apologists, and most certainly would not have wanted precedents. But the Master of Stair had strongly recommended a different mode of proceeding. If the least alarm were given, the nest of robbers would be found empty; and to hunt them down in so wild a region would, even with all the help that Breadalbane and Argyle could give, be a long and difficult business. "Better," he wrote, "not meddle with them than meddle to no purpose. When the thing is resolved, let it be secret and sudden." He was obeyed; and it was determined that the Glencoe men should perish, not by military execution, but by the most dastardly and perfidious form of assassination.

On the first of February a hundred and twenty soldiers of Argyle's regiment, commanded by a captain named Campbell and a lieutenant named Lindsay, marched to Glencoe. Captain Campbell was commonly called in Scotland Glenlyon, from the pass in which his property lay. He had every qualification for the service on which he was employed, an unblushing forehead, a smooth lying tongue, and a heart of adamant. He was also one of the few Campbells who were likely to be trusted and welcomed by the Macdonalds: for his niece was married to Alexander, the second son of Mac Ian.

The sight of the red coats approaching caused some anxiety among the population of the valley. John, the eldest son of the Chief, came, accompanied by twenty clansmen, to meet the strangers, and asked what this visit meant. Lieutenant Lindsay answered that the soldiers came as friends, and wanted nothing but quarters. They were kindly received, and were lodged under the thatched roofs of the little community. Glenlyon and several of his men were taken into the house of a tacksman who was named, from the cluster of cabins over which he exercised authority, Inverriggen. Lindsay was accommodated nearer to the abode of the old chief. Auchintriater, one of the principal men of the clan, who governed the small hamlet of Auchnaion, found room there for a party commanded by a serjeant named Barbour. Provisions were liberally supplied. There was no want of beef, which had probably fattened in distant pastures; nor was any payment demanded: for in hospitality, as in thievery, the Gaelic marauders rivalled the Bedouins. During twelve days the soldiers lived familiarly with the people of the glen. Old Mac Ian, who had before felt many misgivings as to the relation in which he stood to the government, seems to have been pleased with the visit. The officers passed much of their time with him and his family. The long evenings were cheerfully spent by the peat fire with the help of some packs of cards which had found their way to that remote corner of the world, and of some French brandy which was probably part of James's farewell gift to his Highland supporters. Glenlyon appeared to be warmly attached to his niece and her husband Alexander. Every day he came to their house to take his morning draught. Meanwhile he observed with minute attention all the avenues by which, when the signal for the slaughter should be given, the Macdonalds might attempt to escape to the hills; and he reported the result of his observations to Hamilton.

Hamilton fixed five o'clock in the morning of the thirteenth of February for the deed. He hoped that, before that time, he should reach Glencoe with four hundred men, and should have stopped all the earths in which the old fox and his two cubs,—so Mac Ian and his sons were nicknamed by the murderers,—could take refuge. But, at five precisely, whether Hamilton had arrived or not, Glenlyon was to fall on, and to slay every Macdonald under seventy.

The night was rough. Hamilton and his troops made slow progress, and were long after their time. While they were contending with the wind and snow, Glenlyon was supping and playing at cards with those whom he meant to butcher before daybreak. He and Lieutenant Lindsay had engaged themselves to dine with the old Chief on the morrow.

Late in the evening a vague suspicion that some evil was intended crossed the mind of the Chief's eldest son. The soldiers were evidently in a restless state; and some of them uttered strange exclamations. Two men, it is said, were overheard whispering. "I do not like this job," one of them muttered: "I should be glad to fight the Macdonalds. But to kill men in their beds—" "We must do as we are bid," answered another voice. "If there is any thing wrong, our officers must answer for it." John Macdonald was so uneasy that, soon after midnight, he went to Glenlyon's quarters. Glenlyon and his men were all up, and seemed to be getting their arms ready for action. John, much alarmed, asked what these preparations meant. Glenlyon was profuse of friendly assurances. "Some of Glengarry's people have been harrying the country. We are getting ready to march against them. You are quite safe. Do you think that, if you were in any danger, I should not have given a hint to your brother Sandy and his wife?" John's suspicions were quieted. He returned to his house, and lay down to rest.

It was five in the morning. Hamilton and his men were still some miles off; and the avenues which they were to have secured were open. But the orders which Glenlyon had received were precise; and he began to execute them at the little village where he was himself quartered. His host Inverrigen and nine other Macdonalds were dragged out of their beds, bound hand and foot, and murdered. A boy twelve years old clung round the Captain's legs, and begged hard for life. He would do any thing: he would go any where: he would follow Glenlyon round the world. Even Glenlyon, it is said, showed signs of relenting: but a ruffian named Drummond shot the child dead.

At Auchnaion the tacksman Auchintriater was up early that morning, and was sitting with eight of his family round the fire, when a volley of musketry laid him and seven of his companions dead or dying on the floor. His brother, who alone had escaped unhurt, called to Serjeant Barbour, who commanded the slayers, and asked as a favour to be allowed to die in the open air. "Well," said the Serjeant, "I will do you that favour for the sake of your meat which I have eaten." The mountaineer, bold, athletic, and favoured by the darkness, came forth, rushed on the soldiers who were about to level their pieces at him, flung his plaid over their faces, and was gone in a moment.

Meanwhile Lindsay had knocked at the door of the old Chief and had asked for admission in friendly language. The door was opened. Mac Ian, while putting on his clothes and calling to his servants to bring some refreshment for his visitors, was shot through the head. Two of his attendants were slain with him. His wife was already up and dressed in such finery as the princesses of the rude Highland glens were accustomed to wear. The assassins pulled off her clothes and trinkets. The rings were not easily taken from her fingers: but a soldier tore them away with his teeth. She died on the following day.

The statesman, to whom chiefly this great crime is to be ascribed, had planned it with consummate ability: but the execution was complete in nothing but in guilt and infamy. A succession of blunders saved three fourths of the Glencoe men from the fate of their chief. All the moral qualities which fit men to bear a part in a massacre Hamilton and Glenlyon possessed in perfection. But neither seems to have had much professional skill. Hamilton had arranged his plan without making allowance for bad weather, and this at a season when, in the Highlands, the weather was very likely to be bad. The consequence was that the fox earths, as he called them, were not stopped in time. Glenlyon and his men committed the error of despatching their hosts with firearms instead of using the cold steel. The peal and flash of gun after gun gave notice, from three different parts of the valley at once, that murder was doing. From fifty cottages the half naked peasantry fled under cover of the night to the recesses of their pathless glen. Even the sons of Mac Ian, who had been especially marked out for destruction, contrived to escape. They were roused from sleep by faithful servants. John, who, by the death of his father, had become the patriarch of the tribe, quitted his dwelling just as twenty soldiers with fixed bayonets marched up to it. It was broad day long before Hamilton arrived. He found the work not even half performed. About thirty corpses lay wallowing in blood on the dunghills before the doors. One or two women were seen among the number, and a yet more fearful and piteous sight, a little hand, which had been lopped in the tumult of the butchery from some infant. One aged Macdonald was found alive. He was probably too infirm to fly, and, as he was above seventy, was not included in the orders under which Glenlyon had acted. Hamilton murdered the old man in cold blood. The deserted hamlets were then set on fire; and the troops departed, driving away with them many sheep and goats, nine hundred kine, and two hundred of the small shaggy ponies of the Highlands.

It is said, and may but too easily be believed, that the sufferings of the fugitives were terrible. How many old men, how many women with babes in their arms, sank down and slept their last sleep in the snow; how many, having crawled, spent with toil and hunger, into nooks among the precipices, died in those dark holes, and were picked to the bone by the mountain ravens, can never be known. But it is probable that those who perished by cold, weariness and want were not less numerous than those who were slain by the assassins. When the troops had retired, the Macdonalds crept out of the caverns of Glencoe, ventured back to the spot where the huts had formerly stood, collected the scorched corpses from among the smoking ruins, and performed some rude rites of sepulture. The tradition runs that the hereditary bard of the tribe took his seat on a rock which overhung the place of slaughter, and poured forth a long lament over his murdered brethren and his desolate home. Eighty years later that sad dirge was still repeated by the population of the valley.

The survivors might well apprehend that they had escaped the shot and the sword only to perish by famine. The whole domain was a waste. Houses, barns, furniture, implements of husbandry, herds, flocks, horses, were gone. Many months must elapse before the clan would be able to raise on its own ground the means of supporting even the most miserable existence.

It may be thought strange that these events should not have been instantly followed by a burst of execration from every part of the civilised world. The fact, however, is that years elapsed before the public indignation was thoroughly awakened, and that months elapsed before the blackest part of the story found credit even among the enemies of the government. That the massacre should not have been mentioned in the London Gazettes, in the Monthly Mercuries, which were scarcely less courtly than the Gazettes, or in pamphlets licensed by official censors, is perfectly intelligible. But that no allusion to it should be found in private journals and letters, writen by persons free from all restraint, may seem extraordinary. There is not a word on the subject in Evelyn's Diary. In Narcissus Luttrell's Diary is a remarkable entry made five weeks after the butchery. The letters from Scotland, he says, described that kingdom as perfectly tranquil, except that there was still some grumbling about ecclesiastical questions. The Dutch ministers regularly reported all the Scotch news to their government. They thought it worth while, about this time, to mention that a collier had been taken by a privateer near Berwick, that the Edinburgh mail had been robbed, that a whale, with a tongue seventeen feet long and seven feet broad, had been stranded near Aberdeen. But it is not hinted in any of their despatches that there was any rumour of any extraordinary occurrence in the Highlands. Reports that some of the Macdonalds had been slain did indeed, in about three weeks, travel through Edinburgh up to London. But these reports were vague and contradictory; and the very worst of them was far from coming up to the horrible truth. The Whig version of the story was that the old robber Mac Ian had laid an ambuscade for the soldiers, that he had been caught in his own snare, and that he and some of his clan had fallen sword in hand. The Jacobite version, written at Edinburgh on the twenty-third of March, appeared in the Paris Gazette of the seventh of April. Glenlyon, it was said, had been sent with a detachment from Argyle's regiment, under cover of darkness, to surprise the inhabitants of Glencoe, and had killed thirty six men and boys and four women. In this there was nothing very strange or shocking. A night attack on a gang of free-booters occupying a strong natural fortress may be a perfectly legitimate military operation; and, in the obscurity and confusion of such an attack, the most humane man may be so unfortunate as to shoot a woman or a child. The circumstances which give a peculiar character to the slaughter of Glencoe, the breach of faith, the breach of hospitality, the twelve days of feigned friendship and conviviality, of morning calls, of social meals, of healthdrinking, of cardplaying, were not mentioned by the Edinburgh correspondent of the Paris Gazette; and we may therefore confidently infer that those circumstances were as yet unknown even to inquisitive and busy malecontents residing in the Scottish capital within a hundred miles of the spot where the deed had been done. In the south of the island the matter produced, as far as can now be judged, scarcely any sensation. To the Londoner of those days Appin was what Caffraria or Borneo is to us. He was not more moved by hearing that some Highland thieves had been surprised and killed than we are by hearing that a band of Amakosah cattle stealers has been cut off, or that a bark full of Malay pirates has been sunk. He took it for granted that nothing had been done in Glencoe beyond what was doing in many other glens. There might have been violence; but it had been in a land of violence. There had been a night brawl, one of a hundred night brawls, between the Macdonalds and the Campbells; and the Campbells had knocked the Macdonalds on the head.

By slow degrees the whole came out. From a letter written at Edinburgh before the end of April, it appears that the horrible story was already current among the Jacobites of that city. In the summer Argyle's regiment was quartered in the south of England, and some of the men made strange confessions, over their ale, about what they had been forced to do in the preceding winter. The non-jurors soon got hold of the clue, and followed it resolutely: their secret presses went to work; and at length, near a year after the crime had been committed, it was published to the world. But the world was long incredulous. The habitual mendacity of the Jacobite libellers had brought on them an appropriate punishment. Now, when, for the first time, they told the truth, they were supposed to be romancing. They complained bitterly that the story, though perfectly authentic, was regarded by the public as a factious lie. So late as the year 1695, Hickes, in a tract in which he endeavoured to defend his darling tale of the Theban legion against the unanswerable argument drawn from the silence of historians, remarked that it might well be doubted whether any historian would make mention of the massacre of Glencoe. There were in England, he said, many thousands of well educated men who had never heard of that massacre, or who regarded it as a mere fable.

Nevertheless the punishment of some of the guilty began very early. Hill, who indeed can hardly be called guilty, was much disturbed. Breadalbane, hardened as he was, felt the stings of conscience or the dread of retribution. A few days after the Macdonalds had returned to their old dwellingplace, his steward visited the ruins of the house of Glencoe, and endeavoured to persuade the sons of the murdered chief to sign a paper declaring that they held the Earl guiltless of the blood which had been shed. They were assured that, if they would do this, all His Lordship's great influence should be employed to obtain for them from the Crown a free pardon and a remission of all forfeitures. Glenlyon did his best to assume an air of unconcern. He made his appearance in the most fashionable coffeehouse at Edinburgh, and talked loudly and self-complacently about the important service in which he had been engaged among the mountains. Some of his soldiers, however, who observed him closely, whispered that all this bravery was put on. He was not the man that he had been before that night. The form of his countenance was changed. In all places, at all hours, whether he waked or slept, Glencoe was for ever before him.

But, whatever apprehensions might disturb Breadalbane, whatever spectres might haunt Glenlyon, the Master of Stair had neither fear nor remorse. He was indeed mortified: but he was mortified only by the blunders of Hamilton and by the escape of so many of the damnable breed. "Do right, and fear nobody;" such is the language of his letters. "Can there be a more sacred duty than to rid the country of thieving? The only thing that I regret is that any got away."

LA HOGUE

TOURVILLE had with him only his own squadron, consisting of forty four ships of the line. But he had received positive orders to protect the descent on England, and not to decline a battle. Though these orders had been given before it was known at Versailles that the Dutch and English fleets had joined, he was not disposed to take on himself the responsibility of disobedience. He still remembered with bitterness the reprimand which his extreme caution had drawn upon him after the fight of Beachy Head. He would not again be told that he was a timid and unenterprising commander, that he had no courage but the vulgar courage of a common sailor. He was also persuaded that the odds against him were rather apparent than real. He believed, on the authority of James and Melfort, that the English seamen, from the flag officers down to the cabin boys, were Jacobites. Those who fought would fight with half a heart; and there would probably be numerous desertions at the most critical moment. Animated by such hopes he sailed from Brest, steered first towards the north east, came in sight of the coast of Dorsetshire, and then struck across the Channel towards La Hogue, where the army which he was to convoy to England had already begun to embark on board of the transports. He was within a few leagues of Barfleur when, before sunrise, on the morning of the nineteenth of May [1692], he saw the great armament of the allies stretching along the eastern horizon. He determined to bear down on them. By eight the two lines of battle were formed; but it was eleven before the firing began. It soon became plain that the English, from the Admiral downwards, were resolved to do their duty. Russell had visited all his ships, and exhorted all his crews. "If your commanders play false," he said, "overboard with them, and with myself the first." There was no defection. There was no slackness. Carter was the first who broke the French line. He was struck by a splinter of one of his own yard arms, and fell dying on the deck. He would not be carried below. He would not let go his sword. "Fight the ship," were his last words: "fight the ship as long as she can swim." The battle lasted till four in the afternoon. The roar of the guns was distinctly heard more than twenty miles off by the army which was encamped on the coast of Normandy. During the earlier part of the day the wind was favourable to the French: they were opposed to only half of the allied fleet; and against that half they maintained the conflict with their usual courage and with more than their usual seamanship. After a hard and doubtful fight of five hours, Tourville thought that enough had been done to maintain the honour of the white flag, and began to draw off. But by this time the wind had veered, and was with the allies. They were now able to avail themselves of their great superiority of force. They came on fast. The retreat of the French became a flight. Tourville fought his own ship desperately. She was named, in allusion to Lewis's favourite emblem, the Royal Sun, and was widely renowned as the finest vessel in the world. It was reported among the English sailors that she was adorned with an image of the Great King, and that he appeared there, as he appeared in the Place of Victories, with vanquished nations in chains beneath his feet. The gallant ship, surrounded by enemies, lay like a great fortress on the sea, scattering death on every side from her hundred and four portholes. She was so formidably manned that all attempts to board her failed. Long after sunset, she got clear of her assailants, and, with all her scuppers spouting blood, made for the coast of Normandy. She had suffered so much that Tourville hastily removed his flag to a ship of ninety guns which was named the Ambitious. By this time his fleet was scattered far over the sea. About twenty of his smallest ships made their escape by a road which was too perilous for any courage but the courage of despair. In the double darkness of night and of a thick sea fog, they ran, with all their sails spread, through the boiling waves and treacherous rocks of the Race of Alderney, and, by a strange good fortune, arrived without a single disaster at Saint Maloes. The pursuers did not venture to follow the fugitives into that terrible strait, the place of innumerable shipwrecks.

Those French vessels which were too bulky to venture into the Race of Alderney fled to the havens of the Cotentin. The Royal Sun and two other three-deckers reached Cherburg in safety. The Ambitious, with twelve other ships, all first rates or second rates, took refuge in the Bay of La Hogue, close to the headquarters of the army of James.

The three ships which had fled to Cherburg were closely chased by an English squadron under the command of Delaval. He found them hauled up into shoal water where no large man of war could get at them. He therefore determined to attack them with his fire-ships and boats. The service was gallantly and successfully performed. In a short time the Royal Sun and her two consorts were burned to ashes. Part of the crews escaped to the shore; and part fell into the hands of the English.

Meanwhile Russell with the greater part of his victorious fleet had blockaded the Bay of La Hogue. Here, as at Cherburg, the French men of war had been drawn up into shallow water. They lay close to the camp of the army which was destined for the invasion of England. Six of them were moored under a fort named Lisset. The rest lay under the guns of another fort named Saint Vaast, where James had fixed his headquarters, and where the British flag, variegated by the crosses of Saint George and Saint Andrew, hung by the side of the white flag of France. Marshal Bellefonds had planted several batteries which, it was thought, would deter the boldest enemy from approaching either Fort Lisset or Fort Saint Vaast. James, however, who knew something of English seamen, was not perfectly at ease, and proposed to send strong bodies of soldiers on board of the ships. But Tourville would not consent to put such a slur on his profession.

Russell meanwhile was preparing for an attack. On the afternoon of the twenty-third of May all was ready. A flotilla consisting of sloops, of fireships, and of two hundred boats, was entrusted to the command of Rooke. The whole armament was in the highest spirits. The rowers, flushed by success, and animated by the thought that they were going to fight under the eyes of the French and Irish troops who had been assembled for the purpose of subjugating England, pulled manfully and with loud huzzas towards the six huge wooden castles which lay close to Fort Lisset. The French, though an eminently brave people, have always been more liable to sudden panics than their phlegmatic neighbours the English and Germans. On this day there was a panic both in the fleet and in the army. Tourville ordered his sailors to man their boats, and would have led them to encounter the enemy in the bay. But his example and his exhortations were vain. His boats turned round and fled in confusion. The ships were abandoned. The cannonade from Fort Lisset was so feeble and ill directed that it did no execution. The regiments on the beach, after wasting a few musket shots, drew off. The English boarded the men of war, set them on fire, and having performed this great service without the loss of a single life, retreated at a late hour with the retreating tide. The bay was in a blaze during the night; and now and then a loud explosion announced that the flames had reached a powder room or a tier of loaded guns. At eight the next morning the tide came back strong; and with the tide came back Rooke and his two hundred boats. The enemy made a faint attempt to defend the vessels which were near Fort Saint Vaast. During a few minutes the batteries did some execution among the crews of our skiffs: but the struggle was soon over. The French poured fast out of their ships on one side: the English poured in as fast on the other, and, with loud shouts, turned the captured guns against the shore. The batteries were speedily silenced. James and Melfort, Bellefonds and Tourville, looked on in helpless despondency while the second conflagration proceeded. The conquerors, leaving the ships of war in flames, made their way into an inner basin where many transports lay. Eight of these vessels were set on fire. Several were taken in tow. The rest would have been either destroyed or carried off, had not the sea again begun to ebb. It was impossible to do more; and the victorious flotilla slowly retired, insulting the hostile camp with a thundering chant of "God save the King."

Thus ended, at noon on the twenty-fourth of May, the great conflict which had raged during five days over a wide extent of sea and shore. One English fireship had perished in its calling. Sixteen French men of war, all noble vessels, and eight of them three-deckers, had been sunk or burned down to the water-edge. The battle is called, from the place where it terminated, the battle of La Hogue.

STEINKIRK

IN the month of July [1692] William's headquarters were at Lambeque. About six miles off, at Steinkirk, Luxemburg had encamped with the main body of his army; and about six miles further off lay a considerable force commanded by the Marquess of Boufflers, one of the best officers in the service of Lewis.

The country between Lambeque and Steinkirk was intersected by innumerable hedges and ditches; and neither army could approach the other without passing through several long and narrow defiles. Luxemburg had therefore little reason to apprehend that he should be attacked in his entrenchments; and he felt assured that he should have ample notice before any attack was made: for he had succeeded in corrupting an adventurer named Millevoix, who was chief musician and private secretary of the Elector of Bavaria. This man regularly sent to the French headquarters authentic information touching the designs of the allies.

The Marshal, confident in the strength of his position and in the accuracy of his intelligence, lived in his tent as he was accustomed to live in his hotel at Paris. He was at once a valetudinarian and a voluptuary; and, in both characters, he loved his ease. He scarcely ever mounted his horse. Light conversation and cards occupied most of his hours. His table was luxurious; and, when he had sate down to supper, it was a service of danger to disturb him. Some scoffers remarked that in his military dispositions he was not guided exclusively by military reasons, that he generally contrived to entrench himself in some place where the veal and the poultry were remarkably good, and that he was always solicitous to keep open such communications with the sea as might ensure him, from September to April, a regular supply of Sandwich oysters. If there were any agreeable women in the neighbourhood of his camp, they were generally to be found at his banquets. It may easily be supposed that, under such a commander, the young princes and nobles of France vied with one another in splendour and gallantry.

While he was amusing himself after his wonted fashion, the confederate princes discovered that their counsels were betrayed. A peasant picked up a letter which had been dropped, and carried it to the Elector of Bavaria. It contained full proofs of the guilt of Millevoix. William conceived a hope that he might be able to take his enemies in the snare which they had laid for him. The perfidious secretary was summoned to the royal presence and taxed with his crime. A pen was put into his hand: a pistol was held to his breast; and he was commanded to write on pain of instant death. His letter, dictated by William, was conveyed to the French camp. It apprised Luxemburg that the allies meant to send out a strong foraging party on the next day. In order to protect this party from molestation, some battalions of infantry, accompanied by artillery, would march by night to occupy the defiles which lay between the armies. The Marshal read, believed, and went to rest, while William urged forward the preparations for a general assault on the French lines.

The whole allied army was under arms while it was still dark. In the grey of the morning, Luxemburg was awakened by scouts, who brought tidings that the enemy was advancing in great force. He at first treated the news very lightly. His correspondent, it seemed, had been, as usual, diligent and exact. The Prince of Orange had sent out a detachment to protect his foragers, and this detachment had been magnified by fear into a great host. But one alarming report followed another fast. All the passes, it was said, were choked with multitudes of foot, horse, and artillery, under the banners of England and of Spain, of the United Provinces and of the Empire; and every column was moving towards Steinkirk. At length the Marshal rose, got on horseback, and rode out to see what was doing.

By this time the vanguard of the allies was close to his outposts. About half a mile in advance of his army was encamped a brigade named from the province of Bourbonnais. These troops had to bear the first brunt of the onset. Amazed and panickstricken, they were swept away in a moment, and ran for their lives, leaving their tents and seven pieces of cannon to the assailants.

Thus far William's plans had been completely successful: but now fortune began to turn against him. He had been misinformed as to the nature of the ground which lay between the station of the brigade of Bourbonnais and the main encampment of the enemy. He had expected that he should be able to push forward without a moment's pause, that he should find the French army in a state of wild disorder, and that his victory would be easy and complete. But his progress was obstructed by several fences and ditches: there was a short delay; and a short delay sufficed to frustrate his design. Luxemburg was the very man for such a conjuncture. He had committed great faults: he had kept careless guard: he had trusted implicitly to information which had proved false: he had neglected information which had proved true: one of his divisions was flying in confusion: the other divisions were unprepared for action. That crisis would have paralysed the faculties of an ordinary captain: it only braced and stimulated those of Luxemburg. His mind, nay his sickly and distorted body, seemed to derive health and vigour from disaster and dismay. In a short time he had disposed every thing. The French army was in battle order. Conspicuous in that great array were the household troops of Lewis, the most renowned body of fighting men in Europe; and at their head appeared, glittering in lace and embroidery hastily thrown on and half fastened, a crowd of young princes and lords who had just been roused by the trumpet from their couches or their revels, and who had hastened to look death in the face with the gay and festive intrepidity characteristic of French gentlemen. Highest in rank among these highborn warriors was a lad of sixteen, Philip Duke of Chartres, son of the Duke of Orleans, and nephew of the King of France. It was with difficulty and by importunate solicitation that the gallant boy had extorted Luxemburg's permission to be where the fire was hottest. Two other youths of royal blood, Lewis Duke of Bourbon, and Armand Prince of Conti, showed a spirit worthy of their descent. With them was a descendant of one of the bastards of Henry the Fourth, Lewis Duke of Vendome, a man sunk in indolence and in the foulest vice, yet capable of exhibiting on a great occasion the qualities of a great soldier. Berwick, who was beginning to earn for himself an honourable name in arms, was there; and at his side rode Sarsfield, whose courage and ability earned, on that day, the esteem of the whole French army. Meanwhile Luxemburg had sent off a pressing message to summon Boufflers. But the message was needless. Boufflers had heard the firing, and, like a brave and intelligent captain, was already hastening towards the point from which the sound came.

Though the assailants had lost all the advantage which belongs to a surprise, they came on manfully. In the front of the battle were the British commanded by Count Solmes. The division which was to lead the way was Mackay's. He was to have been supported, according to William's plan, by a strong body of foot and horse. Though most of Mackay's men had never before been under fire, their behaviour gave promise of Blenheim and Ramilies. They first encountered the Swiss, who held a distinguished place in the French army. The fight was so close and desperate that the muzzles of the muskets crossed. The Swiss were driven back with fearful slaughter. More than eighteen hundred of them appear from the French returns to have been killed or wounded. Luxemburg afterwards said that he had never in his life seen so furious a struggle. He collected in haste the opinion of the generals who surrounded him. All thought that the emergency was one which could be met by no common means. The King's household must charge the English. The Marshal gave the word; and the household, headed by the princes of the blood, came on, flinging their muskets back on their shoulders. "Sword in hand," was the cry through all the ranks of that terrible brigade: "sword in hand. No firing. Do it with the cold steel." After a long and bloody contest, the English were borne down. They never ceased to repeat that, if Solmes had done his duty by them, they would have beaten even the household. But Solmes gave them no effective support. He pushed forward some cavalry which, from the nature of the ground, could do little or nothing. His infantry he would not suffer to stir. They could do no good, he said; and he would not send them to be slaughtered. Ormond was eager to hasten to the assistance of his countrymen, but was not permitted. Mackay sent a pressing message to represent that he and his men were left to certain destruction: but all was vain. "God's will be done," said the brave veteran. He died as he had lived, like a good Christian and a good soldier. With him fell Douglas and Lanier, two generals distinguished among the conquerors of Ireland. Mountjoy too was among the slain. After languishing three years in the Bastille, he had just been exchanged for Richard Hamilton, and, having been converted to Whiggism by wrongs more powerful than all the arguments of Locke and Sidney, had instantly hastened to join William's camp as a volunteer. Five fine regiments were entirely cut to pieces. No part of this devoted band would have escaped but for the courage and conduct of Auverquerque, who came to the rescue in the moment of extremity with two fresh battalions. The gallant manner in which he brought off the remains of Mackay's division was long remembered and talked of with grateful admiration by the British camp fires. The ground where the conflict had raged was piled with corpses; and those who buried the slain remarked that almost all the wounds had been given in close fighting by the sword or the bayonet.

It was said that William so far forgot his wonted stoicism as to utter a passionate exclamation at the way in which the English regiments had been sacrificed. Soon, however, he recovered his equanimity, and determined to fall back. It was high time: for the French army was every moment becoming stronger, as the regiments commanded by Boufflers came up in rapid succession. The allied army returned to Lambeque unpursued and in unbroken order.

The French owned that they had about seven thousand men killed and wounded. The loss of the allies had been little, if at all, greater. The relative strength of the armies was what it had been on the preceding day; and they continued to occupy their old positions. But the moral effect of the battle was great. The splendour of William's fame grew pale. Even his admirers were forced to own that, in the field, he was not a match for Luxemburg. In France the news was received with transports of joy and pride. The Court, the Capital, even the peasantry of the remotest provinces, gloried in the impetuous valour which had been displayed by so many youths, the heirs of illustrious names. It was exultingly and fondly repeated all over the kingdom that the young Duke of Chartres could not by any remonstrances be kept out of danger, that a ball had passed through his coat, that he had been wounded in the shoulder. The people lined the roads to see the princes and nobles who returned from Steinkirk. The jewellers devised Steinkirk buckles: the perfumers sold Steinkirk powder. But the name of the field of battle was peculiarly given to a new species of collar. Lace neckcloths were then worn by men of fashion; and it had been usual to arrange them with great care. But at the terrible moment when the brigade of Bourbonnais was flying before the onset of the allies, there was no time for foppery; and the finest gentlemen of the Court came spurring to the front of the line of battle with their rich cravats in disorder. It therefore became a fashion among the beauties of Paris to wear round their necks kerchiefs of the finest lace studiously disarranged; and these kerchiefs were called Steinkirks.

LANDEN

THOUGH the French army in the Netherlands had been weakened by the departure of the forces commanded by the Dauphin and Boufflers, and though the allied army was daily strengthened by the arrival of fresh troops, Luxemburg still had a superiority of force; and that superiority he increased by an adroit stratagem. He marched towards Liege, and made as if he were about to form the siege of that city. William was uneasy, and the more uneasy because he knew that there was a French party among the inhabitants. He quitted his position near Louvain, advanced to Nether Hespen, and encamped there with the river Gette in his rear. On his march he learned that Huy had opened its gates to the French. The news increased his anxiety about Liege, and determined him to send thither a force sufficient to overawe malecontents within the city, and to repel any attack from without. This was exactly what Luxemburg had expected and desired. His feint had served its purpose. He turned his back on the fortress which had hitherto seemed to be his object, and hastened towards the Gette. William, who had detached more than twenty thousand men, and who had but fifty thousand left in his camp, was alarmed by learning from his scouts, on the eighteenth of July [1693], that the French General, with near eighty thousand, was close at hand.

It was still in the King's power, by a hasty retreat, to put between his army and the enemy the narrow, but deep, waters of the Gette, which had lately been swollen by rains. But the site which he occupied was strong; and it could easily be made still stronger. He set all his troops to work. Ditches were dug, mounds thrown up, palisades fixed in the earth. In a few hours the ground wore a new aspect; and the King trusted that he should be able to repel the attack even of a force greatly outnumbering his own. Nor was it without much appearance of reason that he felt this confidence. When the morning of the nineteenth of July broke, the bravest men of Lewis's army looked gravely and anxiously on the fortress which had suddenly sprung up to arrest their progress. The allies were protected by a breastwork. Here and there along the entrenchments were formed little redoubts and half moons. A hundred pieces of cannon were disposed along the ramparts. On the left flank, the village of Romsdorff rose close to the little stream of Landen, from which the English have named the disastrous day. On the right was the village of Neerwinden. Both villages were, after the fashion of the Low Countries, surrounded by moats and fences; and, within these enclosures, the little plots of ground occupied by different families were separated by mud walls five feet in height and a foot in thickness. All these barricades William had repaired and strengthened. Saint Simon, who, after the battle, surveyed the ground, could hardly, he tells us, believe that defences so extensive and so formidable could have been created with such rapidity.

Luxemburg, however, was determined to try whether even this position could be maintained against the superior numbers and the impetuous valour of his soldiers. Soon after sunrise the roar of the cannon began to be heard. William's batteries did much execution before the French artillery could be so placed as to return the fire. It was eight o'clock before the close fighting began. The village of Neerwinden was regarded by both commanders as the point on which every thing depended. There an attack was made by the French left wing commanded by Montchevreuil, a veteran officer of high reputation, and by Berwick, who, though young, was fast rising to an eminent place among the captains of his time. Berwick led the onset, and forced his way into the village, but was soon driven out again with a terrible carnage. His followers fled or perished: he, while trying to rally them, and cursing them for not doing their duty better, was surrounded by foes. He concealed his white cockade, and hoped to be able, by the help of his native tongue, to pass himself off as an officer of the English army. But his face was recognised by one of his mother's brothers, George Churchill, who held on that day the command of a brigade. A hurried embrace was exchanged between the kinsmen; and the uncle conducted the nephew to William, who, as long as every thing seemed to be going well, remained in the rear. The meeting of the King and the captive, united by such close domestic ties, and divided by such inexpiable injuries, was a strange sight. Both behaved as became them. William uncovered, and addressed to his prisoner a few words of courteous greeting. Berwick's only reply was a solemn bow. The King put on his hat: the Duke put on his hat; and the cousins parted for ever.

By this time the French, who had been driven in confusion out of Neerwinden, had been reinforced by a division under the command of the Duke of Bourbon, and came gallantly back to the attack. William, well aware of the importance of this post, gave orders that troops should move thither from other parts of his line. The second conflict was long and bloody. The assailants again forced an entrance into the village. They were again driven out with immense slaughter, and showed little inclination to return to the charge.

Meanwhile the battle had been raging all along the entrenchments of the allied army. Again and again Luxemburg brought up
his troops within pistolshot of the breastwork: but he could bring
them no nearer. Again and again they recoiled from the heavy fire
which was poured on their front and on their flanks. It seemed that
all was over. Luxemburg retired to a spot which was out of gun-
shot, and summoned a few of his chief officers to a consultation.
They talked together during some time; and their animated gestures
were observed with deep interest by all who were within sight.

At length Luxemburg formed his decision. A last attempt must
be made to carry Neerwinden; and the invincible household troops,
the conquerors of Steinkirk, must lead the way.

The household troops came on in a manner worthy of their long
and terrible renown. A third time Neerwinden was taken. A third
time William tried to retake it. At the head of some English regiments he charged the guards of Lewis with such fury that, for the
first time in the memory of the oldest warrior, that far famed band
was driven back. It was only by the strenuous exertions of
Luxemburg, of the Duke of Chartres, and of the Duke of Bourbon,
that the broken ranks were rallied. But by this time the centre and
left of the allied army had been so much thinned for the purpose
of supporting the conflict at Neerwinden that the entrenchments
could no longer be defended on other points. A little after four in
the afternoon the whole line gave way. All was havoc and confusion. Solmes had received a mortal wound, and fell, still alive,
into the hands of the enemy. The English soldiers, to whom his
name was hateful, accused him of having in his sufferings shown
pusillanimity unworthy of a soldier. The Duke of Ormond was
struck down in the press; and in another moment he would have
been a corpse, had not a rich diamond on his finger caught the eye
of one of the French guards, who justly thought that the owner of
such a jewel would be a valuable prisoner. The Duke's life was
saved; and he was speedily exchanged for Berwick. Ruvigny,
animated by the true refugee hatred of the country which had cast
him out, was taken fighting in the thickest of the battle. Those into
whose hands he had fallen knew him well, and knew that, if they
carried him to their camp, his head would pay for that treason to
which persecution had driven him. With admirable generosity
they pretended not to recognise him, and suffered him to make his
escape in the tumult.

It was only on such occasions as this that the whole greatness of
William's character appeared. Amidst the rout and uproar, while
arms and standards were flung away, while multitudes of fugitives

were choking up the bridges and fords of the Gette or perishing in its waters, the King, having directed Talmash to superintend the retreat, put himself at the head of a few brave regiments, and by desperate efforts arrested the progress of the enemy. His risk was greater than that which others ran. For he could not be persuaded either to encumber his feeble frame with a cuirass, or to hide the ensigns of the garter. He thought his star a good rallying point for his own troops, and only smiled when he was told that it was a good mark for the enemy. Many fell on his right hand and on his left. Two led horses, which in the field always closely followed his person, were struck dead by cannon shots. One musket ball passed through the curls of his wig, another through his coat: a third bruised his side and tore his blue riband to tatters. Many years later greyheaded old pensioners who crept about the arcades and alleys of Chelsea Hospital used to relate how he charged at the head of Galway's horse, how he dismounted four times to put heart into the infantry, how he rallied one corps which seemed to be shrinking: "That is not the way to fight, gentlemen. You must stand close up to them. Thus, gentlemen, thus." "You might have seen him,"—thus an eye witness wrote, only four days after the battle,—"with his sword in his hand, throwing himself upon the enemy. It is certain that one time among the rest, he was seen at the head of two English regiments, and that he fought seven with these two in sight of the whole army, driving them before him above a quarter of an hour. Thanks be to God that preserved him." The enemy pressed on him so close that it was with difficulty that he at length made his way over the Gette. A small body of brave men, who shared his peril to the last, could hardly keep off the pursuers as he crossed the bridge.

Never, perhaps, was the change which the progress of civilisation has produced in the art of war more strikingly illustrated than on that day. Ajax beating down the Trojan leader with a rock which two ordinary men could scarcely lift, Horatius defending the bridge against an army, Richard the Lionhearted spurring along the whole Saracen line without finding an enemy to stand his assault, Robert Bruce crushing with one blow the helmet and head of Sir Henry Bohun in sight of the whole array of England and Scotland, such are the heroes of a dark age. In such an age bodily vigour is the most indispensable qualification of a warrior. At Landen two poor sickly beings, who, in a rude state of society, would have been regarded as too puny to bear any part in combats, were the souls of two great armies. In some heathen countries they would have been exposed while infants. In Christendom they would, six hundred years earlier, have been sent to some quiet cloister. But their lot had fallen on a time when men had discovered that the strength of the muscles is far inferior in value to the strength of the mind. It is probable that, among the hundred and twenty thousand soldiers who were marshalled round Neerwinden under all the standards of Western Europe, the two feeblest in body were the hunchbacked dwarf who urged forward the fiery onset of France, and the asthmatic skeleton who covered the slow retreat of England.

The French were victorious: but they had bought their victory dear. More than ten thousand of the best troops of Lewis had fallen. Neerwinden was a spectacle at which the oldest soldiers stood aghast. The streets were piled breast high with corpses. Among the slain were some great lords and some renowned warriors. Montchevreuil was there, and the mutilated trunk of the Duke of Uzes, first in order of precedence among the whole aristocracy of France. Thence too Sarsfield was borne desperately wounded to a pallet from which he never rose again. The Court of Saint Germains had conferred on him the empty title of Earl of Lucan; but history knows him by the name which is still dear to the most unfortunate of nations. The region, renowned as the battle-field, through many ages, of the greatest powers of Europe, has seen only two more terrible days, the day of Malplaquet and the day of Waterloo. During many months the ground was strewn with skulls and bones of men and horses, and with fragments of hats and shoes, saddles and holsters. The next summer the soil, fertilised by twenty thousand corpses, broke forth into millions of poppies. The traveller who, on the road from Saint Tron to Tirlemont, saw that vast sheet of rich scarlet spreading from Landen to Neerwinden, could hardly help fancying that the figurative prediction of the Hebrew prophet was literally accomplished, that the earth was disclosing her blood, and refusing to cover the slain.

There was no pursuit, though the sun was still high in the heaven when William crossed the Gette. The conquerors were so much exhausted by marching and fighting that they could scarcely move; and the horses were in even worse condition than the men. The Marshal thought it necessary to allow some time for rest and refreshment. The French nobles unloaded their sumpter horses, supped gaily, and pledged one another in Champagne amidst the heaps of dead; and, when night fell, whole brigades gladly lay down to sleep in their ranks on the field of battle. The inactivity of Luxemburg did not escape censure. None could deny that he had in the action shown great skill and energy. But some complained that he wanted patience and perseverance. Others whispered that he had no wish to bring to an end a war which made him necessary to a Court where he had never, in time of peace, found favour or even justice. Lewis, who on this occasion was perhaps not altogether free from some emotions of jealousy, contrived, it was reported, to mingle with the praise which he bestowed on his lieutenant blame which, though delicately expressed, was perfectly intelligible. "In the battle," he said, "the Duke of Luxemburg behaved like Condé; and since the battle the Prince of Orange has behaved like Turenne."

In truth the ability and vigour with which William repaired his terrible defeat might well excite admiration. "In one respect," said the Admiral Coligni, "I may claim superiority over Alexander, over Scipio, over Cæsar. They won great battles, it is true. I have lost four great battles; and yet I show to the enemy a more formidable front than ever." The blood of Coligni ran in the veins of William; and with the blood had descended the unconquerable spirit which could derive from failure as much glory as happier commanders owed to success. The defeat of Landen was indeed a heavy blow. The King had a few days of cruel anxiety. If Luxemburg pushed on, all was lost. Louvain must fall, and Mechlin, and Nieuport, and Ostend. The Batavian frontier would be in danger. The cry for peace throughout Holland might be such as neither States General nor Stadtholder would be able to resist. But there was delay; and a very short delay was enough for William. From the field of battle he made his way through the multitude of fugitives to the neighbourhood of Louvain, and there began to collect his scattered forces. His character is not lowered by the anxiety which, at that moment, the most disastrous of his life, he felt for the two persons who were dearest to him. As soon as he was safe, he wrote to assure his wife of his safety. In the confusion of the flight he had lost sight of Portland, who was then in very feeble health, and had therefore run more than the ordinary risks of war. A short note which the King sent to his friend a few hours later is still extant. "Though I hope to see you this evening, I cannot help writing to tell you how rejoiced I am that you got off so well. God grant that your health may soon be quite restored. These are great trials, which he has been pleased to send me in quick succession. I must try to submit to his pleasure without murmuring, and to deserve his anger less."

William's forces rallied fast. Large bodies of troops which he had, perhaps imprudently, detached from his army while he supposed that Liege was the object of the enemy, rejoined him by forced marches. Three weeks after his defeat he held a review a few miles from Brussels. The number of men under arms was greater than on the morning of the bloody day of Landen: their appearance was soldierlike; and their spirit seemed unbroken. William now wrote to Heinsius that the worst was over. "The crisis," he said, "has been a terrible one. Thank God that it has ended thus." He did not, however, think it prudent to try at that time the event of another pitched field. He therefore suffered the French to besiege and take Charleroy; and this was the only advantage which they derived from the most sanguinary battle fought in Europe during the seventeenth century.

RECOINAGE

TILL the reign of Charles the Second our coin had been struck by a process as old as the thirteenth century. Edward the First had invited hither skilful artists from Florence, which, in his time, was to London what London, in the time of William the Third, was to Moscow. During many generations, the instruments which were then introduced into our mint continued to be employed with little alteration. The metal was divided with shears, and afterwards shaped and stamped by the hammer. In these operations much was left to the hand and eye of the workman. It necessarily happened that some pieces contained a little more and some a little less than the just quantity of silver: few pieces were exactly round; and the rims were not marked. It was therefore in the course of years discovered that to clip the coin was one of the easiest and most profitable kinds of fraud. In the reign of Elizabeth it had been thought necessary to enact that the clipper should be, as the coiner had long been, liable to the penalties of high treason. The practice of paring down money, however, was far too lucrative to be so checked; and, about the time of the Restoration, people began to observe that a large proportion of the crowns, halfcrowns and shillings which were passing from hand to hand had undergone some slight mutilation.

That was a time fruitful of experiments and inventions in all the departments of science. A great improvement in the mode of shaping and striking the coin was suggested. A mill, which to a great extent superseded the human hand, was set up in the Tower of London. This mill was worked by horses, and would doubtless be considered by modern engineers as a rude and feeble machine. The pieces which it produced, however, were among the best in Europe. It was not easy to counterfeit them; and, as their shape was exactly circular, and their edges were inscribed with a legend, clipping was not to be apprehended. The hammered coins and the milled coins were current together. They were received without distinction in public, and consequently in private, payments. The financiers of that age seem to have expected that the new money, which was excellent, would soon displace the old money which was much impaired. Yet any man of plain understanding might have known that, when the State treats perfect coin and light coin as of equal value, the perfect coin will not drive the light coin out of circulation, but will itself be driven out. A clipped crown, on English ground, went as far in the payment of a tax or a debt as a milled crown. But the milled crown, as soon as it had been flung into the crucible or carried across the Channel, became much more valuable than the clipped crown. It might therefore have been predicted, as confidently as any thing can be predicted which depends on the human will, that the inferior pieces would remain in the only market in which they could fetch the same price as the superior pieces, and that the superior pieces would take some form or fly to some place in which some advantage could be derived from their superiority.

The politicians of that age, however, generally overlooked these very obvious considerations. They marvelled exceedingly that every body should be so perverse as to use light money in preference to good money. In other words, they marvelled that nobody chose to pay twelve ounces of silver when ten would serve the turn. The horse in the Tower still paced his rounds. Fresh waggon loads of choice money still came forth from the mill; and still they vanished as fast as they appeared. Great masses were melted down; great masses exported; great masses hoarded: but scarcely one new piece was to be found in the till of a shop, or in the leathern bag which the farmer carried home from the cattle fair. In the receipts and payments of the Exchequer the milled money did not exceed ten shillings in a hundred pounds. A writer of that age mentions the case of a merchant who, in a sum of thirty five pounds, received only a single halfcrown in milled silver. Meanwhile the shears of the clippers were constantly at work. The coiners too multiplied and prospered: for the worse the current money became the more easily it was imitated. During many years this evil went on increasing. At first it was disregarded: but it at length became an insupportable curse to the country. It was to no purpose that the rigorous laws against coining and clipping were rigorously executed. At every session that was held at the Old Bailey terrible examples were made. Hurdles, with four, five, six wretches convicted of counterfeiting or mutilating the money of the realm, were dragged month after month up Holborn Hill. One morning seven men were hanged and a woman burned for clipping. But all was vain. The gains were such as to lawless spirits seemed more than proportioned to the risks. Some clippers were said to have made great fortunes. One in particular offered six thousand pounds for a pardon. His bribe was indeed rejected; but the fame of his riches did much to counteract the effect which the spectacle of his death was designed to produce. Nay the severity of the punishment gave encouragement to the crime. For the practice of clipping, pernicious as it was, did not excite in the common mind a detestation resembling that with which men regard murder, arson, robbery, even theft. The injury done by the whole body of clippers to the whole society was indeed immense: but each particular act of clipping was a trifle. To pass a halfcrown, after paring a pennyworth of silver from it, seemed a minute, an almost imperceptible, fault. Even while the nation was crying out most loudly under the distress which the state of the currency had produced, every individual who was capitally punished for contributing to bring the currency into that state had the general sympathy on his side. Constables were unwilling to arrest the offenders. Justices were unwilling to commit. Witnesses were unwilling to tell the whole truth. Juries were unwilling to pronounce the word Guilty. The convictions, therefore, numerous as they might seem, were few indeed when compared with the offences; and the offenders who were convicted looked on themselves as murdered men, and were firm in the belief that their sin, if sin it were, was as venial as that of a schoolboy who goes nutting in the wood of a neighbour. All the eloquence of the ordinary could seldom induce them to conform to the wholesome usage of acknowledging in their dying speeches the enormity of their wickedness.

The evil proceeded with constantly accelerating velocity. At length in the autumn of 1695 it could hardly be said that the country possessed, for practical purposes, any measure of the value of commodities. It was a mere chance whether what was called a shilling was really tenpence, sixpence or a groat. The results of some experiments which were tried at that time deserve to be mentioned. The officers of the Exchequer weighed fifty seven thousand two hundred pounds of hammered money which had recently been paid in. The weight ought to have been above two hundred and twenty thousand ounces. It proved to be under one hundred and fourteen thousand ounces. Three eminent London goldsmiths were invited to send a hundred pounds each in current silver to be tried by the balance. Three hundred pounds ought to have weighed about twelve hundred ounces. The actual weight proved to be six hundred and twenty four ounces. The same test was applied in various parts of the kingdom. It was found that a hundred pounds, which should have weighed about four hundred ounces, did actually weigh at Bristol two hundred and forty ounces, at Cambridge two hundred and three, at Exeter one hundred and eighty, and at Oxford only one hundred and sixteen. There were, indeed, some northern districts into which the clipped money had only begun to find its way. An honest Quaker, who lived in one of these districts, recorded, in some notes which are still extant, the amazement with which, when he travelled southward, shopkeepers and innkeepers stared at the broad and heavy halfcrowns with which he paid his way. They asked whence he came, and where such money was to be found. The guinea which he purchased for twenty two shillings at Lancaster bore a different value at every stage of his journey. When he reached London it was worth thirty shillings, and would indeed have been worth more had not the government fixed that rate as the highest at which gold should be received in the payment of taxes.

The evils produced by this state of the currency were not such as have generally been thought worthy to occupy a prominent place in history. Yet it may well be doubted whether all the misery which had been inflicted on the English nation in a quarter of a century by bad Kings, bad Ministers, bad Parliaments and bad Judges, was equal to the misery caused in a single year by bad crowns and bad shillings. Those events which furnish the best themes for pathetic or indignant eloquence are not always those which most affect the happiness of the great body of the people. The misgovernment of Charles and James, gross as it had been, had not prevented the common business of life from going steadily and prosperously on. While the honour and independence of the State were sold to a foreign power, while chartered rights were invaded, while fundamental laws were violated, hundreds of thousands of quiet, honest and industrious families laboured and traded, ate their meals and lay down to rest, in comfort and security. Whether Whigs or Tories, Protestants or Jesuits were uppermost, the grazier drove his beasts to market: the grocer weighed out his currants: the draper measured out his broadcloth: the hum of buyers and sellers was as loud as ever in the towns: the harvest home was celebrated as joyously as ever in the hamlets: the cream overflowed the pails of Cheshire: the apple juice foamed in the presses of Herefordshire: the piles of crockery glowed in the furnaces of the Trent; and the barrows of coal rolled fast along the timber railways of the Tyne. But when the great instrument of exchange became thoroughly deranged, all trade, all industry, were smitten as with a palsy. The evil was felt daily and hourly in almost every place and by almost every class, in the dairy and on the threshing floor, by the anvil and by the loom, on the billows of the ocean and in the depths of the mine. Nothing could be purchased without a dispute. Over every counter there was wrangling from morning to night. The workman and his employer had a quarrel as regularly as the Saturday came round. On a fair day or a market day the clamours, the reproaches, the taunts, the curses, were incessant; and it was well if no booth was overturned and no head broken. No merchant would contract to deliver goods without making some stipulation about the quality of the coin in which he was to be paid. Even men of business were often bewildered by the confusion into which all pecuniary transactions were thrown. The simple and the careless were pillaged without mercy by extortioners whose demands grew even more rapidly than the money shrank. The price of the necessaries of life, of shoes, of ale, of oatmeal, rose fast. The labourer found that the bit of metal, which, when he received it, was called a shilling, would hardly, when he wanted to purchase a pot of beer or a loaf of rye bread, go as far as sixpence. Where artisans of more than usual intelligence were collected together in great numbers, as in the dockyard at Chatham, they were able to make their complaints heard and to obtain some redress. But the ignorant and helpless peasant was cruelly ground between one class which would give money only by tale and another which would take it only by weight. Yet his sufferings hardly exceeded those of the unfortunate race of authors. Of the way in which obscure writers were treated we may easily form a judgment from the letters, still extant, of Dryden to his bookseller Tonson. One day Tonson sends forty brass shillings, to say nothing of clipped money. Another day he pays a debt with pieces so bad that none of them will go. The great poet sends them all back, and demands in their place guineas at twenty nine shillings each. "I expect," he says in one letter, "good silver, not such as I have had formerly." "If you have any silver that will go," he says in another letter, "my wife will be glad of it. I lost thirty shillings or more by the last payment of fifty pounds." These complaints and demands, which have been preserved from destruction only by the eminence of the writer, are doubtless merely a fair sample of the correspondence which filled all the mail bags of England during several months.

In the midst of the public distress one class prospered greatly, the bankers; and among the bankers none could in skill or in luck bear a comparison with Charles Duncombe. He had been, not many years before, a goldsmith of very moderate wealth. He had probably, after the fashion of his craft, plied for customers under the arcades of the Royal Exchange, had saluted merchants with profound bows, and had begged to be allowed the honour of keeping their cash. But so dexterously did he now avail himself of the opportunities of profit which the general confusion of prices gave to a moneychanger, that, at the moment when the trade of the kingdom was depressed to the lowest point, he laid down near ninety thousand pounds for the estate of Helmsley in the North Riding of Yorkshire. That great property had, in a troubled time, been bestowed by the Commons of England on their victorious general Fairfax, and had been part of the dower which Fairfax's daughter had brought to the brilliant and dissolute Buckingham. Thither Buckingham, having wasted in mad intemperance, sensual and intellectual, all the choicest bounties of nature and of fortune, had carried the feeble ruins of his fine person and of his fine mind; and there he had closed his chequered life under that humble roof and on that coarse pallet which the great satirist of the succeeding generation described in immortal verse. The spacious domain passed to a new race; and in a few years a palace more splendid and costly than had ever been inhabited by the magnificent Villiers rose amidst the beautiful woods and waters which had been his, and was called by the once humble name of Duncombe.

Since the Revolution the state of the currency had been repeatedly discussed in Parliament. In 1689 a committee of the Commons had been appointed to investigate the subject, but had made no report. In 1690 another committee had reported that immense quantities of silver were carried out of the country by Jews, who, it was said, would do anything for profit. Schemes were formed for encouraging the importation and discouraging the exportation of the precious metals. One foolish bill after another was brought in and dropped. At length, in the beginning of the year 1695, the question assumed so serious an aspect that the Houses applied themselves to it in earnest. The only practical result of their deliberations, however, was a new penal law which, it was hoped, would prevent the clipping of the hammered coin and the melting and exporting of the milled coin. It was enacted that every person who informed against a clipper should be entitled to a reward of forty pounds, that every clipper who informed against two clippers should be entitled to a pardon, and that whoever should be found in possession of silver filings or parings should be burned in the cheek with a redhot iron. Certain officers were empowered to search for bullion. If bullion were found in a house or on board of a ship, the burden of proving that it had never been part of the money of the realm was thrown on the owner. If he failed in making out a satisfactory history of every ingot he was liable to severe penalties. This Act was, as might have been expected, altogether ineffective. During the following summer and autumn, the coins went on dwindling, and the cry of distress from every county in the realm became louder and more piercing.

But happily for England there were among her rulers some who clearly perceived that it was not by halters and branding irons that her decaying industry and commerce could be restored to health. The state of the currency had during some time occupied the serious attention of four eminent men closely connected by public and private ties. Two of them were politicians who had never, in the midst of official and parliamentary business, ceased to love and honour philosophy; and two were philosophers, in whom habits of abstruse meditation had not impaired the homely good sense without which even genius is mischievous in politics. Never had there been an occasion which more urgently required both practical and speculative abilities; and never had the world seen the highest practical and the highest speculative abilities united in an alliance so close, so harmonious, and so honourable as that which bound Somers and Montague to Locke and Newton.

It is much to be lamented that we have not a minute history of the conferences of the men to whom England owed the restoration of her currency and the long series of prosperous years which dates from that restoration. It would be interesting to see how the pure gold of scientific truth found by the two philosophers was mingled by the two statesmen with just that quantity of alloy which was necessary for the working. It would be curious to study the many plans which were propounded, discussed and rejected, some as inefficacious, some as unjust, some as too costly, some as too hazardous, till at length a plan was devised of which the wisdom was proved by the best evidence, complete success.

Newton has left to posterity no exposition of his opinions touching the currency. But the tracts of Locke on this subject are happily still extant; and it may be doubted whether in any of his writings, even in those ingenious and deeply meditated chapters on language which form perhaps the most valuable part of the Essay on the Human Understanding, the force of his mind appears more conspicuously. Whether he had ever been acquainted with Dudley North is not known. In moral character the two men bore little resemblance to each other. They belonged to different parties. Indeed, had not Locke taken shelter from tyranny in Holland, it is by no means impossible that he might have been sent to Tyburn by a jury which Dudley North had packed. Intellectually, however, there was much in common between the Tory and the Whig. They had laboriously thought out, each for himself, a theory of political economy, substantially the same with that which Adam Smith afterwards expounded. Nay, in some respects the theory of Locke and North was more complete and symmetrical than that of their illustrious successor. Adam Smith has often been justly blamed for maintaining, in direct opposition to all his own principles, that the rate of interest ought to be regulated by the State; and he is the more blamable because, long before he was born, both Locke and North had taught that it was as absurd to make laws fixing the price of money as to make laws fixing the price of cutlery or of broad-cloth.

Dudley North died in 1693. A short time before his death he published, without his name, a small tract which contains a concise sketch of a plan for the restoration of the currency. This plan appears to have been substantially the same with that which was afterwards fully developed and ably defended by Locke.

One question, which was doubtless the subject of many anxious deliberations, was whether any thing should be done while the war lasted. In whatever way the restoration of the coin might be effected, great sacrifices must be made, either by the whole community or by a part of the community. And to call for such sacrifices at a time when the nation was already paying taxes such as, ten years before, no financier would have thought it possible to raise, was undoubtedly a course full of danger. Timorous politicians were for delay: but the deliberate conviction of the great Whig leaders was that something must be hazarded, or that every thing was lost. Montague, in particular, is said to have expressed in strong language his determination to kill or cure. If indeed there had been any hope that the evil would merely continue to be what it was, it might have been wise to defer till the return of peace an experiment which must severely try the strength of the body politic. But the evil was one which daily made progress almost visible to the eye. There might have been a recoinage in 1694 with half the risk which must be run in 1696; and, great as would be the risk in 1696, that risk would be doubled if the recoinage were postponed till 1698.

Those politicians whose voice was for delay gave less trouble than another set of politicians, who were for a general and immediate recoinage, but who insisted that the new shilling should be worth only ninepence or ninepence halfpenny. At the head of this party was William Lowndes, Secretary of the Treasury, and member of Parliament for the borough of Seaford, a most respectable and industrious public servant, but much more versed in the details of his office than in the higher parts of political philosophy. He was not in the least aware that a piece of metal with the King's head on it was a commodity of which the price was governed by the same laws which govern the price of a piece of metal fashioned into a spoon or a buckle, and that it was no more in the power of Parliament to make the kingdom richer by calling a crown a pound than to make the kingdom larger by calling a furlong a mile. He seriously believed, incredible as it may seem, that, if the ounce of silver were divided into seven shillings instead of five, foreign nations would sell us their wines and their silks for a smaller number of ounces. He had a considerable following, composed partly of dull men who really believed what he told them, and partly of shrewd men who were perfectly willing to be authorised by law to pay a hundred pounds with eighty. Had his arguments prevailed, the evils of a vast confiscation would have been added to all the other evils which afflicted the nation: public credit, still in its tender and sickly infancy, would have been destroyed; and there would have been much risk of a general mutiny of the fleet and army. Happily Lowndes was completely refuted by Locke in a paper drawn up for the use of Somers. Somers was delighted with this little treatise, and desired that it might be printed. It speedily became the text book of all the most enlightened politicians in the kingdom, and may still be read with pleasure and profit. The effect of Locke's forcible and perspicuous reasoning is greatly heightened by his evident anxiety to get at the truth, and by the singularly generous and grateful courtesy with which he treats an antagonist of powers far inferior to his own. Flamsteed, the Astronomer Royal, described the controversy well by saying that the point in dispute was whether five was six or only five.

Thus far Somers and Montague entirely agreed with Locke: but as to the manner in which the restoration of the currency ought to be effected there was some difference of opinion. Locke recommended, as Dudley North had recommended, that the King should by proclamation fix a near day after which the hammered money should in all payments pass only by weight. The advantages of this plan were doubtless great and obvious. It was most simple, and, at the same time, most efficient. What searching, fining, branding, hanging, burning, had failed to do would be done in an instant. The clipping of the hammered pieces, the melting of the milled pieces would cease. Great quantities of good coin would come

M—7*

forth from secret drawers and from behind the panels of wainscots. The mutilated silver would gradually flow into the mint, and would come forth again in a form which would make mutilation impossible. In a short time the whole currency of the realm would be in a sound state; and, during the progress of this great change, there would never at any moment be any scarcity of money.

These were weighty considerations; and to the joint authority of North and Locke on such a question great respect is due. Yet it must be owned that their plan was open to one serious objection, which did not indeed altogether escape their notice, but of which they seem to have thought too lightly. The restoration of the currency was a benefit to the whole community. On what principle then was the expense of restoring the currency to be borne by a part of the community? It was most desirable doubtless that the words pound and shilling should again have a fixed signification, that every man should know what his contracts meant and what his property was worth. But was it just to attain this excellent end by means of which the effect would be that every farmer who had put by a hundred pounds to pay his rent, every trader who had scraped together a hundred pounds to meet his acceptances, would find his hundred pounds reduced in a moment to fifty or sixty? It was not the fault of such a farmer or of such a trader that his crowns and halfcrowns were not of full weight. The government itself was to blame. The evil which the State had caused the State was bound to repair; and it would evidently have been wrong to throw the charge of the reparation on a particular class, merely because that class was so situated that it could conveniently be pillaged. It would have been as reasonable to require the timber merchants to bear the whole cost of fitting out the Channel fleet, or the gun-smiths to bear the whole cost of supplying arms to the regiments in Flanders, as to restore the currency of the kingdom at the expense of those individuals in whose hands the clipped silver happened at a particular moment to be.

Locke declared that he regretted the loss which, if his advice were taken, would fall on the holders of the short money. But it appeared to him that the nation must make a choice between evils. And in truth it was much easier to lay down the general proposition that the expenses of restoring the currency ought to be borne by the public than to devise any mode in which they could without extreme inconvenience and danger be so borne. Was it to be announced that every person who should within a term of a year or half a year carry to the mint a clipped crown should receive in ex-change for it a milled crown, and that the difference between the value of the two pieces should be made good out of the public purse? That would be to offer a premium for clipping. The shears would be more busy than ever. The short money would every day become shorter. The difference which the taxpayers would have to make good would probably be greater by a million at the end of the term than at the beginning: and the whole of this million would go to reward malefactors. If only a very short time were allowed for the bringing in of the hammered coin, the danger of further clipping would be reduced to little or nothing; but another danger would be incurred. The silver would flow into the mint so much faster than it could possibly flow out, that there must during some months be a grievous scarcity of money.

A singularly bold and ingenious expedient occurred to Somers and was approved by William. It was that a proclamation should be prepared with great secresy, and published at once in all parts of the kingdom. This proclamation was to announce that hammered coins would thenceforth pass only by weight. But every possessor of such coins was to be invited to deliver them up within three days, in a sealed packet, to the public authorities. The coins were to be examined, numbered, weighed, and returned to the owner with a promissory note entitling him to receive from the Treasury at a future time the difference between the actual quantity of silver in his pieces and the quantity of silver which, according to the standard, those pieces ought to have contained. Had this plan been adopted an immediate stop would have been put to the clipping, the melting and the exporting; and the expense of the restoration of the currency would have been borne, as was right, by the public. The inconvenience arising from a scarcity of money would have been of very short duration: for the mutilated pieces would have been detained only till they could be told and weighed: they would then have been sent back into circulation; and the recoinage would have taken place gradually and without any perceptible suspension or disturbance of trade. But against these great advantages were to be set off hazards, which Somers was prepared to brave, but from which it is not strange that politicians of less elevated character should have shrunk. The course which he recommended to his colleagues was indeed the safest for the country, but was by no means the safest for themselves. His plan could not be successful unless the execution was sudden: the execution could not be sudden if the previous sanction of Parliament were asked and obtained; and to take a step of such fearful importance without the previous sanction of Parliament was to run the risk of censure, impeachment, imprisonment, ruin. The King and the Lord Keeper were alone in the Council. Even Montague quailed; and it was determined to do nothing without the authority of the legislature. Montague undertook to submit to the Commons a scheme, which was not indeed without dangers and inconveniences, but which was probably the best which he could hope to carry.

On the twenty-second of November the Houses met. Foley was on that day again chosen Speaker. On the following day he was presented and approved. The King opened the session with a speech very skilfully framed. He congratulated his hearers on the success of the campaign on the Continent. That success he attributed, in language which must have gratified their feelings, to the bravery of the English army. He spoke of the evils which had arisen from the deplorable state of the coin, and of the necessity of applying a speedy remedy. He intimated very plainly his opinion that the expense of restoring the currency ought to be borne by the State: but he declared that he referred the whole matter to the wisdom of his Great Council. Before he concluded he addressed himself particularly to the newly elected House of Commons, and warmly expressed his approbation of the excellent choice which his people had made. The speech was received with a low but very significant hum of assent both from above and from below the bar, and was as favourably received by the public as by the Parliament. In the Commons an address of thanks was moved by Wharton, faintly opposed by Musgrave, adopted without a division, and carried up by the whole House to Kensington. At the palace the loyalty of the crowd of gentlemen showed itself in a way which would now be thought hardly consistent with senatorial gravity. When refreshments were handed round in the antechamber, the Speaker filled his glass, and proposed two toasts, the health of King William, and confusion to King Lewis; and both were drunk with loud acclamations. Yet near observers could perceive that, though the representatives of the nation were as a body zealous for civil liberty and for the Protestant religion, and though they were prepared to endure every thing rather than see their country again reduced to vassalage, they were anxious and dispirited. All were thinking of the state of the coin: all were saying that something must be done; and all acknowledged that they did not know what could be done. "I am afraid," said a member who expressed what many felt, "that the nation can bear neither the disease nor the cure."

There was indeed a minority by which the difficulties and dangers of that crisis were seen with malignant delight; and of that minority the keenest, boldest and most factious leader was Howe, whom poverty had made more acrimonious than ever. He moved that the

House should resolve itself into a Committee on the State of the Nation; and the Ministry,—for that word may now with propriety be used,—readily consented. Indeed the great question touching the currency could not be brought forward more conveniently than in such a Committee. When the Speaker had left the chair, Howe harangued against the war as vehemently as he had in former years harangued for it. He called for peace, peace on any terms. The nation, he said, resembled a wounded man, fighting desperately on, with blood flowing in torrents. During a short time the spirit might bear up the frame: but faintness must soon come on. No moral energy could long hold out against physical exhaustion. He found very little support. The great majority of his hearers were fully determined to put every thing to hazard rather than submit to France. It was sneeringly remarked that the state of his own finances had suggested to him the image of a man bleeding to death, and that, if a cordial were administered to him in the form of a salary, he would trouble himself little about the drained veins of the commonwealth. "We did not," said the Whig orators, "degrade ourselves by suing for peace when our flag was chased out of our own Channel, when Tourville's fleet lay at anchor in Torbay, when the Irish nation was in arms against us, when every post from the Netherlands brought news of some disaster, when we had to contend against the genius of Louvois in the Cabinet and of Luxemburg in the field. And are we to turn suppliants now, when no hostile squadron dares to show itself even in the Mediterranean, when our arms are victorious on the Continent, when God has removed the great statesman and the great soldier whose abilities long frustrated our efforts, and when the weakness of the French administration indicates, in a manner not to be mistaken, the ascendency of a female favourite?" Howe's suggestion was contemptuously rejected; and the Committee proceeded to take into consideration the state of the currency.

Meanwhile the newly liberated presses of the capital never rested a moment. Innumerable pamphlets and broadsides about the coin lay on the counters of the booksellers, and were thrust into the hands of members of Parliament in the lobby. In one of the most curious and amusing of these pieces Lewis and his ministers are introduced, expressing the greatest alarm lest England should make herself the richest country in the world by the simple expedient of calling ninepence a shilling, and confidently predicting that, if the old standard were maintained, there would be another revolution. Some writers vehemently objected to the proposition that the public should bear the expense of restoring the currency: some urged the government to take this opportunity of assimilating the money of England to the money of neighbouring nations: one projector was for coining guilders; another for coining dollars.

Within the walls of Parliament the debates continued during several anxious days. At length Montague, after defeating, first those who were for letting things remain unaltered till the peace, and then those who were for the little shilling, carried eleven resolutions in which the outlines of his own plan were set forth. It was resolved that the money of the kingdom should be recoined according to the old standard both of weight and of fineness; that all the new pieces should be milled; that the loss on the clipped pieces should be borne by the public; that a time should be fixed after which no clipped money should pass, except in payments to the government; and that a later time should be fixed, after which no clipped money should pass at all. What divisions took place in the Committee cannot be ascertained. When the resolutions were reported there was one division. It was on the question whether the old standard of weight should be maintained. The Noes were a hundred and fourteen; the Ayes two hundred and twenty five.

It was ordered that a bill founded on the resolutions should be brought in. A few days later the Chancellor of the Exchequer explained to the Commons, in a Committee of Ways and Means, the plan by which he proposed to meet the expense of the recoinage. It was impossible to estimate with precision the charge of making good the deficiencies of the clipped money. But it was certain that at least twelve hundred thousand pounds would be required. Twelve hundred thousand pounds the Bank of England undertook to advance on good security. It was a maxim received among financiers that no security which the government could offer was so good as the old hearth money had been. That tax, odious as it was to the great majority of those who paid it, was remembered with regret at the Treasury and in the City. It occurred to the Chancellor of the Exchequer that it might be possible to devise an impost on houses, which might be not less productive nor less certain than the hearth money, but which might press less heavily on the poor, and might be collected by a less vexatious process. The number of hearths in a house could not be ascertained without domiciliary visits. The windows a collector might count without passing the threshold. Montague proposed that the inhabitants of cottages, who had been cruelly harassed by the chimney men, should be altogether exempted from the new duty. His plan was approved by the Committee of Ways and Means, and was sanctioned by the House without a division. Such was the origin of the window tax, a tax which, though doubtless a great evil, must be considered as a blessing when compared with the curse from which it was the means of rescuing the nation.

Thus far things had gone smoothly. But now came a crisis which required the most skilful steering. The news that the Parliament and the government were determined on a reform of the currency produced an ignorant panic among the common people. Every man wished to get rid of his clipped crowns and halfcrowns. No man liked to take them. There were brawls approaching to riots in half the streets of London. The Jacobites, always full of joy and hope in a day of adversity and public danger, ran about with eager looks and noisy tongues. The health of King James was publicly drunk in taverns and on ale benches. Many members of Parliament, who had hitherto supported the government, began to waver; and, that nothing might be wanting to the difficulties of the conjuncture, a dispute on a point of privilege arose between the Houses. The Recoinage Bill, framed in conformity with Montague's resolutions, had gone up to the Peers and had come back with amendments, some of which, in the opinion of the Commons, their Lordships had no right to make. The emergency was too serious to admit of delay. Montague brought in a new bill, which was in fact his former bill modified in some points to meet the wishes of the Lords: the Lords, though not perfectly contented with the new bill, passed it without any alteration; and the royal assent was immediately given. The fourth of May, a date long remembered over the whole kingdom and especially in the capital, was fixed as the day on which the government would cease to receive the clipped money in payment of taxes.

The principles of the Recoinage Act are excellent. But some of the details, both of that Act and of a supplementary Act which was passed at a later period of the session, seem to prove that Montague had not fully considered what legislation can, and what it cannot, effect. For example, he persuaded the Parliament to enact that it should be penal to give or take more than twenty two shillings for a guinea. It may be confidently affirmed that this enactment was not suggested or approved by Locke. He well knew that the high price of gold was not the evil which afflicted the State, but merely a symptom of that evil, and that a fall in the price of gold would inevitably follow, and could by no human power or ingenuity be made to precede, the recoinage of the silver. In fact, the penalty seems to have produced no effect whatever. Till the milled silver was in circulation, the guinea continued, in spite of the law, to pass for thirty shillings. When the milled silver became plentiful, the guinea fell; and did not stop at twenty two shillings, but continued till it reached twenty one shillings and sixpence.

Early in February the panic which had been caused by the first debates on the currency subsided; and, from that time till the fourth of May, the want of money was not very severely felt. The recoinage began. Ten furnaces were erected in the garden behind the Treasury, which was then a part of Whitehall, and which lay between the Banquetting House and the river. Every day huge heaps of pared and defaced crowns and shillings were turned into massy ingots which were instantly sent off to the mint in the Tower.

DARIEN

IT is necessary to go back some years for the purpose of tracing the origin and progress of this quarrel. Few portions of our history are more interesting or instructive: but few have been more obscured and distorted by passion and prejudice. The story is an exciting one; and it has generally been told by writers whose judgment had been perverted by strong national partiality. Their invectives and lamentations have still to be temperately examined; and it may well be doubted whether, even now, after the lapse of more than a century and a half, feelings hardly compatible with temperate examination will not be stirred up in many minds by the name of Darien. In truth that name is associated with calamities so cruel that the recollection of them may not unnaturally disturb the equipoise even of a fair and sedate mind.

The man who brought these calamities on his country was not a mere visionary or a mere swindler. He was that William Paterson whose name is honourably associated with the auspicious commencement of a new era in English commerce and in English finance. His plan of a national bank, having been examined and approved by the most eminent statesmen who sate in the Parliament house at Westminster and by the most eminent merchants who walked the Exchange of London, had been carried into execution with signal success. He thought, and perhaps thought with reason, that his services had been ill requited. He was, indeed, one of the original Directors of the great corporation which owed its existence to him; but he was not reelected. It may easily be believed that his colleagues, citizens of ample fortune and of long experience in the practical part of trade, aldermen, wardens of companies, heads of firms well known in every Burse throughout the civilised world, were not well pleased to see among them in Grocers' Hall a foreign adventurer whose whole capital consisted in an inventive brain and a persuasive tongue. Some of them were probably weak enough to dislike him for being a Scot: some were probably mean enough to be jealous of his parts and knowledge: and even persons who were not unfavourably disposed to him might have discovered, before they had known him long, that, with all his cleverness, he was deficient in common sense; that his mind was full of schemes which, at the first glance, had a specious aspect, but which, on closer examination, appeared to be impracticable or pernicious; and that the benefit which the public had derived from one happy project formed by him would be very dearly purchased if it were taken for granted that all his other projects must be equally happy. Disgusted by what he considered as the ingratitude of the English, he repaired to the Continent, in the hope that he might be able to interest the traders of the Hanse Towns and the princes of the German Empire in his plans. From the Continent he returned unsuccessful to London; and then at length the thought that he might be more justly appreciated by his countrymen than by strangers seems to have risen in his mind. Just at this time he fell in with Fletcher of Saltoun, who happened to be in England. These eccentric men soon became intimate. Each of them had his monomania; and the two monomanias suited each other perfectly. Fletcher's whole soul was possessed by a sore, jealous, punctilious patriotism. His heart was ulcerated by the thought of the poverty, the feebleness, the political insignificance of Scotland, and of the indignities which she had suffered at the hand of her powerful and opulent neighbour. When he talked of her wrongs his dark meagre face took its sternest expression: his habitual frown grew blacker; and his eyes flashed more than their wonted fire. Paterson, on the other hand, firmly believed himself to have discovered the means of making any state which would follow his counsel great and prosperous in a time which, when compared with the life of an individual, could hardly be called long, and which, in the life of a nation, was but as a moment. There is not the least reason to believe that he was dishonest. Indeed he would have found more difficulty in deceiving others had he not begun by deceiving himself. His faith in his own schemes was strong even to martyrdom; and the eloquence with which he illustrated and defended them had all the charm of sincerity and of enthusiasm. Very seldom has any blunder committed by fools, or any villany devised by impostors, brought on any society miseries so great as the dreams of these two friends, both of them men of integrity and both of them men of parts, were destined to bring on Scotland.

In 1695 the pair went down together to their native country.

The Parliament of that country was then about to meet under the presidency of Tweeddale, an old acquaintance and country neighbour of Fletcher. On Tweeddale the first attack was made. He was a shrewd, cautious, old politician. Yet it should seem that he was not able to hold out against the skill and energy of the assailants. Perhaps, however, he was not altogether a dupe. The public mind was at that moment violently agitated. Men of all parties were clamouring for an inquiry into the slaughter of Glencoe. There was reason to fear that the session which was about to commence would be stormy. In such circumstances the Lord High Commissioner might think that it would be prudent to appease the anger of the Estates by offering an almost irresistible bait to their cupidity. If such was the policy of Tweeddale, it was, for the moment, eminently successful. The Parliament, which met burning with indignation, was soothed into good humour. The blood of the murdered Macdonalds continued to cry for vengeance in vain. The schemes of Paterson, brought forward under the patronage of the ministers of the Crown, were sanctioned by the unanimous voice of the Legislature.

The great projector was the idol of the whole nation. Men spoke to him with more profound respect than to the Lord High Commissioner. His antechamber was crowded with solicitors desirous to catch some drops of that golden shower of which he was supposed to be the dispenser. To be seen walking with him in the High Street, to be honoured by him with a private interview of a quarter of an hour, were enviable distinctions. He, after the fashion of all the false prophets who have deluded themselves and others, drew new faith in his own lie from the credulity of his disciples. His countenance, his voice, his gestures, indicated boundless self-importance. When he appeared in public he looked,—such is the language of one who probably had often seen him,—like Atlas conscious that a world was on his shoulders. But the airs which he gave himself only heightened the respect and admiration which he inspired. His demeanour was regarded as a model. Scotchmen who wished to be thought wise looked as like Paterson as they could.

His plan, though as yet disclosed to the public only by glimpses, was applauded by all classes, factions and sects, lords, merchants, advocates, divines, Whigs and Jacobites, Cameronians and Episcopalians. In truth, of all the ten thousand bubbles of which history has preserved the memory, none was ever more skilfully puffed into existence; none ever soared higher, or glittered more brilliantly; and none ever burst with a more lamentable explosion.

There was, however, a certain mixture of truth in the magnificent day dream which produced such fatal effects.

Scotland was, indeed, not blessed with a mild climate or a fertile soil. But the richest spots that had ever existed on the face of the earth had been spots quite as little favoured by nature. It was on a bare rock, surrounded by deep sea, that the streets of Tyre were piled up to a dizzy height. On that sterile crag were woven the robes of Persian satraps and Sicilian tyrants: there were fashioned silver bowls and chargers for the banquets of kings: and there Pomeranian amber was set in Lydian gold to adorn the necks of queens. In the warehouses were collected the fine linen of Egypt and the odorous gums of Arabia; the ivory of India, and the tin of Britain. In the port lay fleets of great ships which had weathered the storms of the Euxine and the Atlantic. Powerful and wealthy colonies in distant parts of the world looked up with filial reverence to the little island; and despots, who trampled on the laws and outraged the feelings of all the nations between the Hydaspes and the Ægean, condescended to court the population of that busy hive. At a later period, on a dreary bank formed by the soil which the Alpine streams swept down to the Adriatic, rose the palaces of Venice. Within a space which would not have been thought large enough for one of the parks of a rude northern baron were collected riches far exceeding those of a northern kingdom. In almost every one of the private dwellings which fringed the Great Canal were to be seen plate, mirrors, jewellery, tapestry, paintings, carving, such as might move the envy of the master of Holyrood. In the arsenal were munitions of war sufficient to maintain a contest against the whole power of the Ottoman Empire. And, before the grandeur of Venice had declined, another commonwealth, still less favoured, if possible, by nature, had rapidly risen to a power and opulence which the whole civilised world contemplated with envy and admiration. On a desolate marsh overhung by fogs and exhaling diseases, a marsh where there was neither wood nor stone, neither firm earth nor drinkable water, a marsh from which the ocean on one side and the Rhine on the other were with difficulty kept out by art, was to be found the most prosperous community in Europe. The wealth which was collected within five miles of the Stadthouse of Amsterdam would purchase the fee simple of Scotland. And why should this be? Was there any reason to believe that nature had bestowed on the Phœnician, on the Venetian, or on the Hollander, a larger measure of activity, of ingenuity, of forethought, of self command, than on the citizen of Edinburgh or Glasgow? The truth was that, in all those qualities which conduce to success in life, and especially in commercial life, the Scot had never been surpassed; perhaps he had never been equalled. All that was necessary was that his energy should take a proper direction; and a proper direction Paterson undertook to give.

His esoteric project was the original project of Christopher Columbus, extended and modified. Columbus had hoped to establish a communication between our quarter of the world and India across the great western ocean. But he was stopped by an unexpected obstacle. The American continent, stretching far north and far south into cold and inhospitable regions, presented what seemed an insurmountable barrier to his progress; and, in the same year in which he first set foot on that continent, Gama reached Malabar by doubling the Cape of Good Hope. The consequence was that during two hundred years the trade of Europe with the remoter parts of Asia had been carried on by rounding the immense peninsula of Africa. Paterson now revived the project of Columbus, and persuaded himself and others that it was possible to carry that project into effect in such a manner as to make his country the greatest emporium that had ever existed on our globe.

For this purpose it was necessary to occupy in America some spot which might be a resting place between Scotland and India. It was true that almost every habitable part of America had already been seized by some European power. Paterson, however, imagined that one province, the most important of all, had been overlooked by the short-sighted cupidity of vulgar politicians and vulgar traders. The isthmus which joined the two great continents of the New World remained, according to him, unappropriated. Great Spanish vice-royalties, he said, lay on the east and on the west; but the mountains and forests of Darien were abandoned to rude tribes which followed their own usages and obeyed their own princes. He had been in that part of the world, in what character was not quite clear. Some said that he had gone thither to convert the Indians, and some that he had gone thither to rob the Spaniards. But, missionary or pirate, he had visited Darien, and had brought away none but delightful recollections. The havens, he averred, were capacious and secure: the sea swarmed with turtle: the country was so mountainous that, within nine degrees of the equator, the climate was temperate; and yet the inequalities of the ground offered no impediment to the conveyance of goods. Nothing would be easier than to construct roads along which a string of mules or a wheeled carriage might in the course of a single day pass from sea to sea. The soil was, to the depth of several feet, a rich black mould, on which a profusion of valuable herbs and fruits grew spontaneously, and on which all the choicest productions of tropical regions might easily be raised by human industry and art; and yet the exuberant fertility of the earth had not tainted the purity of the air. Considered merely as a place of residence, the isthmus was a paradise. A colony placed there could not fail to prosper, even if it had no wealth except what was derived from agriculture. But agriculture was a secondary object in the colonization of Darien. Let but that precious neck of land be occupied by an intelligent, an enterprising, a thrifty race; and, in a few years, the whole trade between India and Europe must be drawn to that point. The tedious and perilous passage round Africa would soon be abandoned. The merchant would no longer expose his cargoes to the mountainous billows and capricious gales of the Antarctic seas. The greater part of the voyage from Europe to Darien, and the whole voyage from Darien to the richest kingdoms of Asia, would be a rapid yet easy gliding before the trade winds over blue and sparkling waters. The voyage back across the Pacific would, in the latitude of Japan, be almost equally speedy and pleasant. Time, labour, money, would be saved. The returns would come in more quickly. Fewer hands would be required to navigate the ships. The loss of a vessel would be a rare event. The trade would increase fast. In a short time it would double; and it would all pass through Darien. Whoever possessed that door of the sea, that key of the universe,—such were the bold figures which Paterson loved to employ,—would give law to both hemispheres; and would, by peaceful arts, without shedding one drop of blood, establish an empire as splendid as that of Cyrus or Alexander. Of the kingdoms of Europe, Scotland was, as yet, the poorest and the least considered. If she would but occupy Darien, if she would but become one great free port, one great warehouse for the wealth which the soil of Darien might produce, and for the still greater wealth which would be poured into Darien from Canton and Siam, from Ceylon and the Moluccas, from the mouths of the Ganges and the Gulf of Cambay, she would at once take her place in the first rank among nations. No rival would be able to contend with her either in the West Indian or in the East Indian trade. The beggarly country, as it had been insolently called by the inhabitants of warmer and more fruitful regions, would be the great mart for the choicest luxuries, sugar, rum, coffee, chocolate, tobacco, the tea and porcelain of China, the muslin of Dacca, the shawls of Cashmere, the diamonds of Golconda, the pearls of Karrack, the delicious birds' nests of Nicobar, cinnamon and pepper, ivory and sandal wood. From Scotland would come all the finest jewels and brocade worn by duchesses at the balls of St. James's and Versailles. From Scotland would come all the saltpetre which would furnish the means of war to the fleets and armies of contending potentates. And on all the vast riches which would be constantly passing through the little kingdom a toll would be paid which would remain behind. There would be a prosperity such as might seem fabulous, a prosperity of which every Scotchman, from the peer to the cadie, would partake. Soon, all along the now desolate shores of the Forth and Clyde, villas and pleasure grounds would be as thick as along the edges of the Dutch canals. Edinburgh would vie with London and Paris; and the baillie of Glasgow or Dundee would have as stately and well furnished a mansion, and as fine a gallery of pictures, as any burgomaster of Amsterdam.

This magnificent plan was at first but partially disclosed to the public. A colony was to be planted: a vast trade was to be opened between both the Indies and Scotland: but the name of Darien was as yet pronounced only in whispers by Paterson and by his most confidential friends. He had however shown enough to excite boundless hopes and desires. How well he succeeded in inspiring others with his own feelings is sufficiently proved by the memorable Act to which the Lord High Commissioner gave the Royal sanction on the 26th of June 1695. By this Act some persons who were named, and such other persons as should join with them, were formed into a corporation, which was to be named the Company of Scotland trading to Africa and the Indies. The amount of the capital to be employed was not fixed by law; but it was provided that one half of the stock at least must be held by Scotchmen resident in Scotland, and that no stock which had been originally held by a Scotchman resident in Scotland should ever be transferred to any but a Scotchman resident in Scotland. An entire monopoly of the trade with Asia, Africa and America, for a term of thirty one years, was granted to the Company. All goods imported by the Company were during twenty one years to be duty free, with the exception of foreign sugar and tobacco. Sugar and tobacco grown on the Company's own plantations were exempted from all taxation. Every member and every servant of the Company was to be privileged against impressment and arrest. If any of these privileged persons was impressed or arrested, the Company was authorised to release him, and to demand the assistance both of the civil and of the military power. The Company was authorised to take possession of unoccupied territories in any part of Asia, Africa or America, and there to plant colonies, to build towns and forts, to impose taxes, and to provide magazines, arms and ammunition, to raise troops, to wage war, to conclude treaties; and the King was made to promise that, if any foreign state should injure the Company, he would interpose, and would, at the public charge, obtain reparation. Lastly it was provided that, in order to give greater security and solemnity to this most exorbitant grant, the whole substance of the Act should be set forth in Letters Patent to which the Chancellor was directed to put the Great Seal without delay.

The letters were drawn: the Great Seal was affixed: the subscription books were opened; the shares were fixed at a hundred pounds sterling each; and from the Pentland Firth to the Solway Firth every man who had a hundred pounds was impatient to put down his name. About two hundred and twenty thousand pounds were actually paid up. This may not, at first sight, appear a large sum to those who remember the bubbles of 1825 and of 1845, and would assuredly not have sufficed to defray the charge of three months of war with Spain. Yet the effort was marvellous when it may be affirmed with confidence that the Scotch people voluntarily contributed for the colonisation of Darien a larger proportion of their substance than any other people ever, in the same space of time, voluntarily contributed to any commercial undertaking. A great part of Scotland was then as poor and rude as Iceland now is. There were five or six shires which did not altogether contain so many guineas and crowns as were tossed about every day by the shovels of a single goldsmith in Lombard Street. Even the nobles had very little ready money. They generally took a large part of their rents in kind, and were thus able, on their own domains, to live plentifully and hospitably. But there were many esquires in Kent and Somersetshire who received from their tenants a greater quantity of gold and silver than a Duke of Gordon or a Marquess of Atholl drew from extensive provinces. The pecuniary remuneration of the clergy was such as would have moved the pity of the most needy curate who thought it a privilege to drink his ale and smoke his pipe in the kitchen of an English manor house. Even in the fertile Merse there were parishes of which the minister received only from four to eight pounds sterling in cash. The official income of the Lord President of the Court of Session was only five hundred a year; that of the Lord Justice Clerk only four hundred a year. The land tax of the whole kingdom was fixed some years later by the Treaty of Union at little more than half the land tax of the single county of Norfolk. Four hundred thousand pounds probably bore as great a ratio to the wealth of Scotland then as forty millions would bear now.

The list of the members of the Darien Company deserves to be examined. The number of shareholders was about fourteen hundred. The largest quantity of stock registered in one name was three thousand pounds. The heads of three noble houses took three thousand pounds each, the Duke of Hamilton, the Duke of Queensbury and Lord Belhaven, a man of ability, spirit and patriotism, who had entered into the design with enthusiasm not inferior to that of Fletcher. Argyle held fifteen hundred pounds. John Dalrymple, but too well known as the Master of Stair, had just succeeded to his father's title and estate, and was now Viscount Stair. He put down his name for a thousand pounds. The number of Scotch peers who subscribed was between thirty and forty. The City of Edinburgh, in its corporate capacity, took three thousand pounds, the City of Glasgow three thousand, the City of Perth two thousand. But the great majority of the subscribers contributed only one hundred or two hundred pounds each. A very few divines who were settled in the capital or in other large towns were able to purchase shares. It is melancholy to see in the roll the name of more than one professional man whose paternal anxiety led him to lay out probably all his hardly earned savings in purchasing a hundred pound share for each of his children. If, indeed, Paterson's predictions had been verified, such a share would, according to the notions of that age and country, have been a handsome portion for the daughter of a writer or a surgeon.

That the Scotch are a people eminently intelligent, wary, resolute and self possessed is obvious to the most superficial observation. That they are a people peculiarly liable to dangerous fits of passion and delusions of the imagination is less generally acknowledged, but is not less true. The whole kingdom seemed to have gone mad. Paterson had acquired an influence resembling rather that of the founder of a new religion, that of a Mahomet, that of a Joseph Smith, than that of a commercial projector. Blind faith in a religion, fanatical zeal for a religion, are too common to astonish us. But such faith and zeal seem strangely out of place in the transactions of the money market. It is true that we are judging after the event. But before the event materials sufficient for the forming of a sound judgment were within the reach of all who cared to use them. It seems incredible that men of sense, who had only a vague and general notion of Paterson's scheme, should have staked everything on the success of that scheme. It seems more incredible still that men to whom the details of that scheme had been confided should not have looked into any of the common books of history or geography in which an account of Darien might have been found, and should not have asked themselves the simple question, whether

Spain was likely to endure a Scotch colony in the heart of her
Transatlantic dominions. It was notorious that she claimed the
sovereignty of the isthmus on specious, nay on solid, grounds. A
Spaniard had been the first discoverer of the coast of Darien. A
Spaniard had built a town and established a government on that
coast. A Spaniard had, with great labour and peril, crossed the
mountainous neck of land, had seen rolling beneath him the vast
Pacific, never before revealed to European eyes, had descended,
sword in hand, into the waves up to his girdle, and had there
solemnly taken possession of sea and shore in the name of the
Crown of Castile. It was true that the region which Paterson
described as a paradise had been found by the first Castilian settlers
to be a land of misery and death. The poisonous air, exhaled from
rank jungle and stagnant water, had compelled them to remove to
the neighbouring haven of Panama; and the Red Indians had been
contemptuously permitted to live after their own fashion on the
pestilential soil. But that soil was still considered, and might well
be considered, by Spain as her own. In many countries there were
tracts of morass, of mountain, of forest, in which governments did
not think it worth while to be at the expense of maintaining order,
and in which rude tribes enjoyed by connivance a kind of independence. It was not necessary for the members of the Company of
Scotland trading to Africa and the Indies to look very far for an
example. In some highland districts, not more than a hundred
miles from Edinburgh, dwelt clans which had always regarded the
authority of King, Parliament, Privy Council and Court of Session,
quite as little as the aboriginal population of Darien regarded the
authority of the Spanish Viceroys and Audiences. Yet it would
surely have been thought an outrageous violation of public law in
the King of Spain to take possession of Appin and Lochaber. And
would it be a less outrageous violation of public law in the Scots to
seize on a province in the very centre of his possessions, on the plea
that this province was in the same state in which Appin and Lochaber had been during centuries?

So grossly unjust was Paterson's scheme; and yet it was less unjust than impolitic. Torpid as Spain had become, there was still
one point on which she was exquisitely sensitive. The slightest
encroachment of any other European power even on the outskirts of
her American dominions sufficed to disturb her repose and to brace
her paralysed nerves. To imagine that she would tamely suffer
adventurers from one of the most insignificant kingdoms of the Old
World to form a settlement in the midst of her empire, within a
day's sail of Portobello on one side and of Carthagena on the other,

was ludicrously absurd. She would have been just as likely to let them take possession of the Escurial. It was, therefore, evident that, before the new Company could even begin its commercial operations, there must be a war with Spain and a complete triumph over Spain. What means had the Company of waging such a war, and what chance of achieving such a triumph? The ordinary revenue of Scotland in time of peace was between sixty and seventy thousand a year. The extraordinary supplies granted to the Crown during the war with France had amounted perhaps to as much more. Spain, it is true, was no longer the Spain of Pavia and Lepanto. But, even in her decay, she possessed in Europe resources which exceeded thirty fold those of Scotland; and in America, where the struggle must take place, the disproportion was still greater. The Spanish fleets and arsenals were doubtless in wretched condition. But there were Spanish fleets; there were Spanish arsenals. The galleons, which sailed every year from Seville to the neighbourhood of Darien and from the neighbourhood of Darien back to Seville, were in tolerable condition, and formed, by themselves, a considerable armament. Scotland had not a single ship of the line, nor a single dockyard where such a ship could be built. A marine sufficient to overpower that of Spain must be, not merely equipped and manned, but created. An armed force sufficient to defend the isthmus against the whole power of the viceroyalties of Mexico and Peru must be sent over five thousand miles of ocean. What was the charge of such an expedition likely to be? Oliver had, in the preceding generation, wrested a West Indian island from Spain: but, in order to do this, Oliver, a man who thoroughly understood the administration of war, who wasted nothing, and who was excellently served, had been forced to spend, in a single year, on his navy alone, twenty times the ordinary revenue of Scotland; and, since his days, war had been constantly becoming more and more costly.

It was plain that Scotland could not alone support the charge of a contest with the enemy whom Paterson was bent on provoking. And what assistance was she likely to have from abroad? Undoubtedly the vast colonial empire and the narrow colonial policy of Spain were regarded with an evil eye by more than one great maritime power. But there was no great maritime power which would not far rather have seen the isthmus between the Atlantic and the Pacific in the hands of Spain than in the hands of the Darien Company. Lewis could not but dread whatever tended to aggrandise a state governed by William. To Holland the East India trade was as the apple of her eye. She had been the chief gainer by the discoveries of Gama; and it might be expected that she would do all that could be done by craft, and, if need were, by violence, rather than suffer any rival to be to her what she had been to Venice. England remained; and Paterson was sanguine enough to flatter himself that England might be induced to lend her powerful aid to the Company. He and Lord Belhaven repaired to London, opened an office in Clement's Lane, formed a Board of Directors auxiliary to the Central Board at Edinburgh, and invited the capitalists of the Royal Exchange to subscribe for the stock which had not been reserved for Scotchmen resident in Scotland. A few moneyed men were allured by the bait: but the clamour of the City was loud and menacing; and from the City a feeling of indignation spread fast through the country. In this feeling there was undoubtedly a large mixture of evil. National antipathy operated on some minds, religious antipathy on others. But it is impossible to deny that the anger which Paterson's schemes excited throughout the south of the island was, in the main, just and reasonable. Though it was not yet generally known in what precise spot his colony was to be planted, there could be little doubt that he intended to occupy some part of America; and there could be as little doubt that such occupation would be resisted. There would be a maritime war; and such a war Scotland had no means of carrying on. The state of her finances was such that she must be quite unable to fit out even a single squadron of moderate size. Before the conflict had lasted three months, she would have neither money nor credit left. These things were obvious to every coffeehouse politician; and it was impossible to believe that they had escaped the notice of men so able and well informed as some who sate in the Privy Council and Parliament at Edinburgh. In one way only could the conduct of these schemers be explained. They meant to make a dupe and a tool of the Southron. The two British kingdoms were so closely connected, physically and politically, that it was scarcely possible for one of them to be at peace with a power with which the other was at war. If the Scotch drew King William into a quarrel, England must, from regard to her own dignity which was bound up with his, support him in it. She was to be tricked into a bloody and expensive contest in the event of which she had no interest; nay, into a contest in which victory would be a greater calamity to her than defeat. She was to lavish her wealth and the lives of her seamen, in order that a set of cunning foreigners might enjoy a monopoly by which she would be the chief sufferer. She was to conquer and defend provinces for this Scotch Corporation; and her reward was to be that her merchants were to be undersold, her customers decoyed away, her exchequer beggared. There would by an end to the disputes between the old East India Company and the new East India Company; for both Companies would be ruined alike. The two great springs of revenue would be dried up together. What would be the receipt of the Customs, what of the Excise, when vast magazines of sugar, rum, tobacco, coffee, chocolate, tea, spices, silks, muslins, all duty free, should be formed along the estuaries of the Forth and of the Clyde, and along the border from the mouth of the Esk to the mouth of the Tweed? What army, what fleet, would be sufficient to protect the interests of the government and of the fair trader when the whole kingdom of Scotland should be turned into one great smuggling establishment? Paterson's plan was simply this, that England should first spend millions in defence of the trade of his Company, and should then be plundered of twice as many millions by means of that very trade.

The cry of the city and of the nation was soon echoed by the legislature. When the Parliament met for the first time after the general election of 1695, Rochester called the attention of the Lords to the constitution and designs of the Company. Several witnesses were summoned to the bar, and gave evidence which produced a powerful effect on the House. "If these Scots are to have their way," said one peer, "I shall go and settle in Scotland, and not stay here to be made a beggar." The Lords resolved to represent strongly to the King the injustice of requiring England to exert her power in support of an enterprise which, if successful, must be fatal to her commerce and to her finances. A representation was drawn up and communicated to the Commons. The Commons eagerly concurred, and complimented the Peers on the promptitude with which their Lordships had, on this occasion, stood forth to protect the public interests. The two Houses went up together to Kensington with the address. William had been under the walls of Namur when the Act for incorporating the Company had been touched with his sceptre at Edinburgh, and had known nothing about that Act till his attention had been called to it by the clamour of his English subjects. He now said, in plain terms, that he had been ill served in Scotland, but that he would try to find a remedy for the evil which had been brought to his notice. The Lord High Commissioner Tweeddale and Secretary Johnstone were immediately dismissed. But the Act which had been passed by their management still continued to be law in Scotland; nor was it in their master's power to undo what they had done.

The Commons were not content with addressing the throne. They instituted an inquiry into the proceedings of the Scotch

Company in London. Belhaven made his escape to his own country, and was there beyond the reach of the Serjeant-at-Arms. But Paterson and some of his confederates were severely examined. It soon appeared that the Board which was sitting in Clement's Lane had done things which were certainly imprudent and perhaps illegal. The Act of Incorporation empowered the directors to take and to administer to their servants an oath of fidelity. But that Act was on the south of the Tweed a nullity. Nevertheless the directors had, in the heart of the City of London, taken and administered this oath, and had thus, by implication, asserted that the powers conferred on them by the legislature of Scotland accompanied them to England. It was resolved that they had been guilty of a high crime and misdemeanour, and that they should be impeached. A committee was appointed to frame articles of impeachment; but the task proved a difficult one; and the prosecution was suffered to drop, not however till the few English capitalists who had at first been friendly to Paterson's project had been terrified into renouncing all connection with him.

Now, surely, if not before, Paterson ought to have seen that his project could end in nothing but shame to himself and ruin to his worshippers. From the first it had been clear that England alone could protect his company against the enmity of Spain; and it was now clear that Spain would be a less formidable enemy than England. It was impossible that his plan could excite greater indignation in the Council of the Indies at Madrid, or in the House of Trade at Seville, than it had excited in London. Unhappily he was given over to a strong delusion; and the blind multitude eagerly followed their blind leader. Indeed his dupes were maddened by that which should have sobered them. The proceedings of the Parliament which sate at Westminster, proceedings just and reasonable in substance, but in manner doubtless harsh and insolent, had roused the angry passions of a nation, feeble indeed in numbers and in material resources, but eminently high spirited. The proverbial pride of the Scotch was too much for their proverbial shrewdness. The votes of the English Lords and Commons were treated with marked contempt. The populace of Edinburgh burned Rochester in effigy. Money was poured faster than ever into the treasury of the Company. A stately house, in Milne Square, then the most modern and fashionable part of Edinburgh, was purchased and fitted up at once as an office and a warehouse. Ships adapted both for war and for trade were required: but the means of building such ships did not exist in Scotland; and no firm in the south of the island was disposed to enter into a contract which might not improbably be considered by the House of Commons as an impeachable offence. It was necessary to have recourse to the dockyards of Amsterdam and Hamburg. At an expense of fifty thousand pounds a few vessels were procured, the largest of which would hardly have ranked as sixtieth in the English navy; and with this force, a force not sufficient to keep the pirates of Sallee in check, the Company threw down the gauntlet to all the maritime powers in the world.

It was not till the summer of 1698 that all was ready for the expedition which was to change the face of the globe. The number of seamen and colonists who embarked at Leith was twelve hundred. Of the colonists many were younger sons of honourable families, or officers who had been disbanded since the peace. It was impossible to find room for all who were desirous of emigrating. It is said that some persons who had vainly applied for a passage hid themselves in dark corners about the ships, and, when discovered, refused to depart, clung to the rigging, and were at last taken on shore by main force. This infatuation is the more extraordinary because few of the adventurers knew to what place they were going. All that was quite certain was that a colony was to be planted somewhere, and to be named Caledonia. The general opinion was that the fleet would steer for some part of the coast of America. But this opinion was not universal. At the Dutch Embassy in Saint James's Square there was an uneasy suspicion that the new Caledonia would be founded among those Eastern spice islands with which Amsterdam had long carried on a lucrative commerce.

The supreme direction of the expedition was entrusted to a Council of Seven. Two Presbyterian chaplains and a precentor were on board. A cargo had been laid in which was afterwards the subject of much mirth to the enemies of the Company, slippers innumerable, four thousand periwigs of all kinds from plain bobs to those magnificent structures which, in that age, towered high above the foreheads and descended to the elbows of men of fashion, bales of Scotch woollen stuffs which nobody within the tropics could wear, and many hundreds of English bibles which neither Spaniard nor Indian could read. Paterson, flushed with pride and hope, not only accompanied the expedition, but took with him his wife, a comely dame, whose heart he had won in London, where she had presided over one of the great coffeehouses in the neighbourhood of the Royal Exchange. At length on the twenty-fifth of July the ships, followed by many tearful eyes, and commended to heaven in many vain prayers, sailed out of the estuary of the Forth.

The voyage was much longer than a voyage to the Antipodes

now is; and the adventurers suffered much. The rations were scanty: there were bitter complaints both of the bread and of the meat; and, when the little fleet, after passing round the Orkneys and Ireland, touched at Madeira, those gentlemen who had fine clothes among their baggage were glad to exchange embroidered coats and laced waistcoats for provisions and wine. From Madeira the adventurers ran across the Atlantic, landed on an uninhabited islet lying between Porto Rico and St. Thomas, took possession of this desolate spot in the name of the Company, set up a tent, and hoisted the white cross of St. Andrew. Soon, however, they were warned off by an officer who was sent from St. Thomas to inform them that they were trespassing on the territory of the King of Denmark. They proceeded on their voyage, having obtained the services of an old buccaneer who knew the coast of Central America well. Under his pilotage they anchored on the first of November close to the Isthmus of Darien. One of the greatest princes of the country soon came on board. The courtiers who attended him, ten or twelve in number, were stark naked: but he was distinguished by a red coat, a pair of cotton drawers, and an old hat. He had a Spanish name, spoke Spanish, and affected the grave deportment of a Spanish don. The Scotch propitiated Andreas, as he was called, by a present of a new hat blazing with gold lace, and assured him that, if he would trade with them, they would treat him better than the Castilians had done.

A few hours later the chiefs of the expedition went on shore, took formal possession of the country, and named it Caledonia. They were pleased with the aspect of a small peninsula about three miles in length and a quarter of a mile in breadth, and determined to fix here the city of New Edinburgh, destined, as they hoped, to be the great emporium of both Indies. The peninsula terminated in a low promontory of about thirty acres, which might easily be turned into an island by digging a trench. The trench was dug; and on the ground thus separated from the main land a fort was constructed: fifty guns were placed on the ramparts; and within the enclosure houses were speedily built and thatched with palm leaves.

Negotiations were opened with the chieftains, as they were called, who governed the neighbouring tribes. Among these savage rulers were found as insatiable a cupidity, as watchful a jealousy, and as punctilious a pride, as among the potentates whose disputes had seemed likely to make the Congress of Ryswick eternal. One prince hated the Spaniards because a fine rifle had been taken away from him by the Governor of Portobello on the plea that such a weapon was too good for a red man. Another loved the Spaniards because they had given him a stick tipped with silver. On the whole, the new comers succeeded in making friends of the aboriginal race. One mighty monarch, the Lewis the Great of the isthmus, who wore with pride a cap of white reeds lined with red silk and adorned with an ostrich feather, seemed well inclined to the strangers, received them hospitably in a palace built of canes and covered with palmetto royal, and regaled them with calabashes of a sort of ale brewed from Indian corn and potatoes. Another chief set his mark to a treaty of peace and alliance with the colony. A third consented to become a vassal of the Company, received with great delight a commission embellished with gold thread and flowered riband, and swallowed to the health of his new masters not a few bumpers of their own brandy.

Meanwhile the internal government of the colony was organised according to a plan devised by the directors at Edinburgh. The settlers were divided into bands of fifty or sixty: each band chose a representative; and thus was formed an assembly which took the magnificent name of Parliament. This Parliament speedily framed a curious code. The first article provided that the precepts, instructions, examples, commands and prohibitions expressed and contained in the Holy Scriptures should have the full force and effect of laws in New Caledonia, an enactment which proves that those who drew it up either did not know what the Holy Scriptures contained or did not know what a law meant. There is another provision which shows not less clearly how far these legislators were from understanding the first principles of legislation. "Benefits received and good services done shall always be generously and thankfully compensated, whether a prior bargain hath been made or not; and, if it shall happen to be otherwise, and the Benefactor obliged justly to complain of the ingratitude, the Ungrateful shall in such case be obliged to give threefold satisfaction at the least." An article much more creditable to the little Parliament, and much needed in a community which was likely to be constantly at war, prohibits, on pain of death, the violation of female captives.

By this time all the Antilles and all the shores of the Gulf of Mexico were in a ferment. The new colony was the object of universal hatred. The Spaniards began to fit out armaments. The chiefs of the French dependencies in the West Indies eagerly offered assistance to the Spaniards. The governors of the English settlements put forth proclamations interdicting all communication with this nest of buccaneers. Just at this time, the Dolphin, a vessel of fourteen guns, which was the property of the Scotch

Company, was driven on shore by stress of weather under the walls of Carthagena. The ship and cargo were confiscated, the crew imprisoned and put in irons. Some of the sailors were treated as slaves, and compelled to sweep the streets and to work on the fortifications. Others, and among them the captain, were sent to Seville to be tried for piracy. Soon an envoy with a flag of truce arrived at Carthagena, and, in the name of the Council of Caledonia, demanded the release of the prisoners. He delivered to the authorities a letter threatening them with the vengeance of the King of Great Britain, and a copy of the Act of Parliament by which the Company had been created. The Castilian governor, who probably knew that William, as Sovereign of England, would not, and, as Sovereign of Scotland, could not, protect the squatters who had occupied Darien, flung away both letter and Act of Parliament with a gesture of contempt, called for a guard, and was with difficulty dissuaded from throwing the messenger into a dungeon. The Council of Caledonia, in great indignation, issued letters of mark and reprisal against Spanish vessels. What every man of common sense must have foreseen had taken place. The Scottish flag had been but a few months planted on the walls of New Edinburgh; and already a war, which Scotland, without the help of England, was utterly unable to sustain, had begun.

By this time it was known in Europe that the mysterious voyage of the adventurers from the Forth had ended at Darien. The ambassador of the Catholic King repaired to Kensington, and complained bitterly to William of this outrageous violation of the law of nations. Preparations were made in the Spanish ports for an expedition against the intruders; and in no Spanish port were there more fervent wishes for the success of that expedition than in the cities of London and Bristol. In Scotland, on the other hand, the exultation was boundless. In the parish churches all over the kingdom the ministers gave public thanks to God for having vouchsafed thus far to protect and bless the infant colony. At some places a day was set apart for religious exercises on this account. In every borough bells were rung; bonfires were lighted; and candles were placed in the windows at night. During some months all the reports which arrived from the other side of the Atlantic were such as to excite hope and joy in the north of the island, and alarm and envy in the south. The colonists, it was asserted, had found rich gold mines, mines in which the precious metal was far more abundant and in a far purer state than on the coast of Guinea. Provisions were plentiful. The rainy season had not proved unhealthy. The settlement was well fortified. Sixty guns were mounted on the ramparts. An immense crop of Indian corn was expected. The aboriginal tribes were friendly. Emigrants from various quarters were coming in. The population of Caledonia had already increased from twelve hundred to ten thousand. The riches of the country,— these are the words of a newspaper of that time,—were great beyond imagination. The mania in Scotland rose to the highest point. Munitions of war and implements of agriculture were provided in large quantities. Multitudes were impatient to emigrate to the land of promise.

In August 1699 four ships, with thirteen hundred men on board, were despatched by the Company to Caledonia. The spiritual care of these emigrants was entrusted to divines of the Church of Scotland. One of these was that Alexander Shields whose Hind Let Loose proves that in his zeal for the Covenant he had forgotten the Gospel. To another, John Borland, we owe the best account of the voyage which is now extant. The General Assembly had charged the chaplains to divide the colonists into congregations, to appoint ruling elders, to constitute a presbytery, and to labour for the propagation of divine truth among the Pagan inhabitants of Darien. The second expedition sailed as the first had sailed, amidst the acclamations and blessings of all Scotland. During the earlier part of September the whole nation was dreaming a delightful dream of prosperity and glory; and triumphing, somewhat maliciously, in the vexation of the English. But, before the close of that month, it began to be rumoured about Lombard Street and Cheapside that letters had arrived from Jamaica with strange news. The colony from which so much had been hoped and dreaded was no more. It had disappeared from the face of the earth. The report spread to Edinburgh, but was received there with scornful incredulity. It was an impudent lie devised by some Englishmen who could not bear to see that, in spite of the votes of the English Parliament, in spite of the proclamations of the governors of the English colonies, Caledonia was waxing great and opulent. Nay, the inventor of the fable was named. It was declared to be quite certain that Secretary Vernon was the man. On the fourth of October was put forth a vehement contradiction of the story. On the fifth the whole truth was known. Letters were received from New York announcing that a few miserable men, the remains of the colony which was to have been the garden, the warehouse, the mart, of the whole world, their bones peeping through their skin, and hunger and fever written in their faces, had arrived in the Hudson.

The grief, the dismay and the rage of those who had a few hours before fancied themselves masters of all the wealth of both Indies may easily be imagined. The Directors, in their fury, lost all self command, and, in their official letters, railed at the betrayers of Scotland, the white-livered deserters. The truth is that those who used these hard words were far more deserving of blame than the wretches whom they had sent to destruction, and whom they now reviled for not staying to be utterly destroyed. Nothing had happened but what might easily have been foreseen. The Company had, in childish reliance on the word of an enthusiastic projector, and in defiance of facts known to every educated man in Europe, taken it for granted that emigrants born and bred within ten degrees of the Arctic Circle would enjoy excellent health within ten degrees of the Equator. Nay, statesmen and scholars had been deluded into the belief that a country which, as they might have read in books so common as those of Hakluyt and Purchas, was noted even among tropical countries for its insalubrity, and had been abandoned by the Spaniards solely on account of its insalubrity, was a Montpelier. Nor had any of Paterson's dupes considered how colonists from Fife or Lothian, who had never in their lives known what it was to feel the heat of a distressing midsummer day, could endure the labour of breaking clods and carrying burdens under the fierce blaze of a vertical sun. It ought to have been remembered that such colonists would have to do for themselves what English, French, Dutch, and Spanish colonists employed Negroes or Indians to do for them. It was seldom indeed that a white freeman in Barbadoes or Martinique, in Guiana or at Panama, was employed in severe bodily labour. But the Scotch who settled at Darien must at first be without slaves, and must therefore dig the trench round their town, build their houses, cultivate their fields, hew wood, and draw water, with their own hands. Such toil in such an atmosphere was too much for them. The provisions which they had brought out had been of no good quality, and had not been improved by lapse of time or by change of climate. The yams and plantains did not suit stomachs accustomed to good oatmeal. The flesh of wild animals and the green fat of the turtle, a luxury then unknown in Europe, went but a small way; and supplies were not to be expected from any foreign settlement. During the cool months, however, which immediately followed the occupation of the isthmus there were few deaths. But, before the equinox, disease began to make fearful havoc in the little community. The mortality gradually rose to ten or twelve a day. Both the clergymen who had accompanied the expedition died. Paterson buried his wife in that soil which, as he had assured his too credulous countrymen, exhaled health and vigour. He was himself stretched on his pallet by an intermittent fever. Still he would not admit that the climate of his promised land was bad. There could not be a purer air. This was merely the seasoning which people who passed from one country to another must expect. In November all would be well again. But the rate at which the emigrants died was such that none of them seemed likely to live till November. Those who were not laid on their beds were yellow, lean, feeble, hardly able to move the sick and to bury the dead, and quite unable to repel the expected attack of the Spaniards. The cry of the whole community was that death was all around them, and that they must, while they still had strength to weigh an anchor or spread a sail, fly to some less fatal region. The men and provisions were equally distributed among three ships, the Caledonia, the Unicorn, and the Saint Andrew. Paterson, though still too ill to sit in the Council, begged hard that he might be left behind with twenty or thirty companions to keep up a show of possession, and to await the next arrivals from Scotland. So small a number of people, he said, might easily subsist by catching fish and turtles. But his offer was disregarded: he was carried, utterly helpless, on board of the Saint Andrew; and the vessels stood out to sea.

The voyage was horrible. Scarcely any Guinea slave ship has ever had such a middle passage. Of two hundred and fifty persons who were on board of the Saint Andrew, one hundred and fifty fed the sharks of the Atlantic before Sandy Hook was in sight. The Unicorn lost almost all its officers, and about a hundred and forty men. The Caledonia, the healthiest ship of the three, threw overboard a hundred corpses. The squalid survivors, as if they were not sufficiently miserable, raged fiercely against one another. Charges of incapacity, cruelty, brutal insolence, were hurled backward and forward. The rigid Presbyterians attributed the calamities of the colony to the wickedness of Jacobites, Prelatists, Sabbathbreakers, Atheists, who hated in others that image of God which was wanting in themselves. The accused malignants, on the other hand, complained bitterly of the impertinence of meddling fanatics and hypocrites. Paterson was cruelly reviled, and was unable to defend himself. He had been completely prostrated by bodily and mental suffering. He looked like a skeleton. His heart was broken. His inventive faculties and his plausible eloquence were no more; and he seemed to have sunk into second childhood.

Meanwhile the second expedition had been on the seas. It reached Darien about four months after the first settlers had fled.

The new comers had fully expected to find a flourishing young town, secure fortifications, cultivated fields, and a cordial welcome. They found a wilderness. The castle of New Edinburgh was in ruins. The huts had been burned. The site marked out for the proud capital which was to have been the Tyre, the Venice, the Amsterdam of the eighteenth century was overgrown with jungle, and inhabited only by the sloth and the baboon. The hearts of the adventurers sank within them. For their fleet had been fitted out, not to plant a colony, but to recruit a colony already planted and supposed to be prospering. They were therefore worse provided with every necessary of life than their predecessors had been. Some feeble attempts, however, were made to restore what had perished. A new fort was constructed on the old ground; and within the ramparts was built a hamlet, consisting of eighty or ninety cabins, generally of twelve feet by ten. But the work went on languidly. The alacrity which is the effect of hope, the strength which is the effect of union, were alike wanting to the little community. From the councillors down to the humblest settlers all was despondency and discontent. The stock of provisions was scanty. The stewards embezzled great part of it. The rations were small; and soon there was a cry that they were unfairly distributed. Factions were formed. Plots were laid. One ringleader of the malecontents was hanged. The Scotch were generally, as they still are, a religious people; and it might therefore have been expected that the influence of the divines to whom the spiritual charge of the colony had been confided would have been employed with advantage for the preserving of order and the calming of evil passions. Unfortunately those divines seem to have been at war with almost all the rest of the society. They described their companions as the most profligate of mankind, and declared that it was impossible to constitute a presbytery according to the directions of the General Assembly; for that persons fit to be ruling elders of a Christian Church were not to be found among the twelve or thirteen hundred emigrants. Where the blame lay it is now impossible to decide. All that can with confidence be said is that either the clergymen must have been most unreasonably and most uncharitably austere, or the laymen must have been most unfavourable specimens of the nation and class to which they belonged.

It may be added that the provision by the General Assembly for the spiritual wants of the colony was as defective as the provision made for temporal wants by the directors of the Company. Nearly one third of the emigrants who sailed with the second expedition were Highlanders, who did not understand a word of English; and not one of the four chaplains could speak a word of Gaelic. It was only through interpreters that a pastor could communicate with a large portion of the Christian flock of which he had charge. Even by the help of interpreters he could not impart religious instruction to those heathen tribes which the Church of Scotland had solemnly recommended to his care. In fact, the colonists left behind them no mark that baptized men had set foot on Darien, except a few Anglo-Saxon curses, which, having been uttered more frequently and with greater energy than any other words in our language, had caught the ear and been retained in the memory of the native population of the isthmus.

The months which immediately followed the arrival of the new comers were the coolest and most salubrious of the year. But, even in those months, the pestilential influence of a tropical sun, shining on swamps rank with impenetrable thickets of black mangroves, began to be felt. The mortality was great; and it was but too clear that, before the summer was far advanced, the second colony would, like the first, have to choose between death and flight. But the agony of the inevitable dissolution was shortened by violence. A fleet of eleven vessels under the flag of Castile anchored off New Edinburgh. At the same time an irregular army of Spaniards, creoles, negroes, mulattoes and Indians marched across the isthmus from Panama; and the fort was blockaded at once by sea and land.

A drummer soon came with a message from the besiegers, but a message which was utterly unintelligible to the besieged. Even after all that we have seen of the perverse imbecility of the directors of the Company, it must be thought strange that they should have sent a colony to a remote part of the world, where it was certain that there must be constant intercourse, peaceable or hostile, with Spaniards, and yet should not have taken care that there should be in the whole colony a single person who knew a little Spanish.

With some difficulty a negotiation was carried on in such French and such Latin as the two parties could furnish. Before the end of March a treaty was signed by which the Scotch bound themselves to evacuate Darien in fourteen days; and on the eleventh of April they departed, a much less numerous body than when they arrived. In little more than four months, although the healthiest months of the year, three hundred men out of thirteen hundred had been swept away by disease. Of the survivors very few lived to see their native country again. Two of the ships perished at sea. Many of the adventurers, who had left their homes flushed with hopes of speedy opulence, were glad to hire themselves out to the planters of Jamaica, and laid their bones in that land of exile. Shields died there, worn out and heart broken. Borland was the only minister who came back. In his curious and interesting narrative, he expresses his feelings, after the fashion of the school in which he had been bred, by grotesque allusions to the Old Testament, and by a profusion of Hebrew words. On his first arrival, he tells us, he found New Edinburgh a Ziklag. He had subsequently been compelled to dwell in the tents of Kedar. Once, indeed, during his sojourn, he had fallen in with a Beer-lahai-roi, and had set up his Ebenezer: but in general Darien was to him a Magor Missabib, a Kibroth-hattaavah. The sad story is introduced with the words in which a great man of old, delivered over to the malice of the Evil Power, was informed of the death of his children and of the ruin of his fortunes: "I alone am escaped to tell thee."

ESSAYS

HISTORICAL, LITERARY AND CONTROVERSIAL

SEVEN of the essays which follow were first printed in the *Edinburgh Review*. The dates of the issues in which they appeared are as follow:

Machiavelli: March 1827.
Mill on Government: March 1829.
Moore's Life of Byron: June 1830.
William Pitt, Earl of Chatham: January 1834.
Gladstone on Church and State: April 1839.
Lord Clive: January 1840.
Warren Hastings: October 1841.

Unauthorised American volumes of Macaulay's essays from the *Edinburgh Review* began appearing in 1841, and he felt obliged to bring out an authoritative edition, *Critical and Historical Essays, Contributed to the Edinburgh Review*, which Longman published in three volumes in 1843. Macaulay made no serious changes in the text, his object being

> that every Essay should now appear as it probably would have appeared when it was first published, if [the author] had then been allowed an additional day or two to revise the proof-sheets, with the assistance of a good library.

This text has been followed in all the essays mentioned above except the review of Mill's *Essay on Government*, which Macaulay omitted with one or two others from the *Critical and Historical Essays*

> not because he is disposed to retract a single doctrine which they contain; but because he is unwilling to offer what might be regarded as an affront to the memory of one from whose opinions he still widely dissents, but to whose talents and virtues he admits that he formerly did not do justice. Serious as are the faults of the Essay on Government, a critic, while noticing those faults, should have abstained from using contemptuous language respecting the historian of British India.

The text here used is therefore that of the *Edinburgh Review*.

The two remaining essays, on Samuel Johnson and William Pitt, were written in December 1856 and January 1859 for the eighth edition of the *Encyclopædia Britannica* (Adam and Charles Black, 1853–61). They are reprinted here from the text of the copy at Britannica House, which the present publishers of the *Encyclopædia* have kindly made available.

I. *Historical Essays*

MACHIAVELLI

(MARCH 1827)

Œuvres complètes de MACHIAVEL, *traduites par* J. V. PÉRIER, Paris, 1825.

THOSE who have attended to the practice of our literary tribunal are well aware that, by means of certain legal fictions similar to those of Westminster Hall, we are frequently enabled to take cognisance of cases lying beyond the sphere of our original jurisdiction. We need hardly say, therefore, that in the present instance M. Périer is merely a Richard Roe, who will not be mentioned in any subsequent stage of the proceedings, and whose name is used for the sole purpose of bringing Machiavelli into court.

We doubt whether any name in literary history be so generally odious as that of the man whose character and writings we now propose to consider. The terms in which he is commonly described would seem to import that he was the Tempter, the Evil Principle, the discoverer of ambition and revenge, the original inventor of perjury, and that, before the publication of his fatal Prince, there had never been a hypocrite, a tyrant, or a traitor, a simulated virtue, or a convenient crime. One writer gravely assures us that Maurice of Saxony learned all his fraudulent policy from that execrable volume. Another remarks that, since it was translated into Turkish, the Sultans have been more addicted than formerly to the custom of strangling their brothers. Lord Lyttelton charges the poor Florentine with the manifold treasons of the House of Guise, and with the massacre of St. Bartholomew. Several authors have hinted that the Gunpowder Plot is to be primarily attributed to his doctrines, and seem to think that his effigy ought to be substituted for that of Guy Faux, in those processions by which the ingenuous youth of England annually commemorate the preservation of the Three Estates. The Church of Rome has pronounced his works accursed things. Nor have our own countrymen been backward in testifying their opinion of his merits. Out of his surname they have coined an epithet for a knave, and out of his Christian name a synonyme for the Devil.[1]

It is indeed scarcely possible for any person not well acquainted with the history and literature of Italy to read without horror and amazement the celebrated treatise which has brought so much obloquy on the name of Machiavelli. Such a display of wickedness, naked yet not ashamed, such cool, judicious, scientific atrocity, seem rather to belong to a fiend than to the most depraved of men. Principles which the most hardened ruffian would scarcely hint to his most trusted accomplice, or avow, without the disguise of some palliating sophism, even to his own mind, are professed without the slightest circumlocution, and assumed as the fundamental axioms of all political science.

It is not strange that ordinary readers should regard the author of such a book as the most depraved and shameless of human beings. Wise men, however, have always been inclined to look with great suspicion on the angels and dæmons of the multitude: and in the present instance, several circumstances have led even superficial observers to question the justice of the vulgar decision. It is notorious that Machiavelli was, through life, a zealous republican. In the same year in which he composed his manual of King-craft, he suffered imprisonment and torture in the cause of public liberty. It seems inconceivable that the martyr of freedom should have designedly acted as the apostle of tyranny. Several eminent writers have, therefore, endeavoured to detect in this unfortunate performance some concealed meaning, more consistent with the character and conduct of the author than that which appears at the first glance.

One hypothesis is that Machiavelli intended to practise on the young Lorenzo de Medici a fraud similar to that which Sunderland is said to have employed against our James the Second, and that he urged his pupil to violent and perfidious measures, as the surest means of accelerating the moment of deliverance and revenge. Another supposition, which Lord Bacon seems to countenance, is that the treatise was merely a piece of grave irony, intended to warn nations against the arts of ambitious men. It would be easy to show that neither of these solutions is consistent with many

[1] Nick Machiavel had ne'er a trick,
Tho' he gave his name to our old Nick.
Hudibras, Part III. Canto I.

But, we believe, there is a schism on this subject among the antiquarians.

passages in The Prince itself. But the most decisive refutation is that which is furnished by the other works of Machiavelli. In all the writings which he gave to the public, and in all those which the research of editors has, in the course of three centuries, discovered, in his Comedies, designed for the entertainment of the multitude, in his Comments on Livy, intended for the perusal of the most enthusiastic patriots of Florence, in his History, inscribed to one of the most amiable and estimable of the Popes, in his public despatches, in his private memoranda, the same obliquity of moral principle for which The Prince is so severely censured is more or less discernible. We doubt whether it would be possible to find, in all the many volumes of his compositions, a single expression indicating that dissimulation and treachery had ever struck him as discreditable.

After this, it may seem ridiculous to say that we are acquainted with few writings which exhibit so much elevation of sentiment, so pure and warm a zeal for the public good, or so just a view of the duties and rights of citizens, as those of Machiavelli. Yet so it is. And even from The Prince itself we could select many passages in support of this remark. To a reader of our age and country this inconsistency is, at first, perfectly bewildering. The whole man seems to be an enigma, a grotesque assemblage of incongruous qualities, selfishness and generosity, cruelty and benevolence, craft and simplicity, abject villany and romantic heroism. One sentence is such as a veteran diplomatist would scarcely write in cipher for the direction of his most confidential spy; the next seems to be extracted from a theme composed by an ardent schoolboy on the death of Leonidas. An act of dexterous perfidy, and an act of patriotic self-devotion, call forth the same kind and the same degree of respectful admiration. The moral sensibility of the writer seems at once to be morbidly obtuse and morbidly acute. Two characters altogether dissimilar are united in him. They are not merely joined, but interwoven. They are the warp and the woof of his mind; and their combination, like that of the variegated threads in shot silk, gives to the whole texture a glancing and ever changing appearance. The explanation might have been easy, if he had been a very weak or a very affected man. But he was evidently neither the one nor the other. His works prove, beyond all contradiction, that his understanding was strong, his taste pure, and his sense of the ridiculous exquisitely keen.

This is strange: and yet the strangest is behind. There is no reason whatever to think, that those amongst whom he lived saw any thing shocking or incongruous in his writings. Abundant proofs remain of the high estimation in which both his works and his person were held by the most respectable among his contemporaries. Clement the Seventh patronised the publication of those very books which the Council of Trent, in the following generation, pronounced unfit for the perusal of Christians. Some members of the democratical party censured the Secretary for dedicating The Prince to a patron who bore the unpopular name of Medici. But to those immoral doctrines which have since called forth such severe reprehensions no exception appears to have been taken. The cry against them was first raised beyond the Alps, and seems to have been heard with amazement in Italy. The earliest assailant, as far as we are aware, was a countryman of our own, Cardinal Pole. The author of the Anti-Machiavelli was a French Protestant.

It is, therefore, in the state of moral feeling among the Italians of those times that we must seek for the real explanation of what seems most mysterious in the life and writings of this remarkable man. As this is a subject which suggests many interesting considerations, both political and metaphysical, we shall make no apology for discussing it at some length.

During the gloomy and disastrous centuries which followed the downfall of the Roman Empire, Italy had preserved, in a far greater degree than any other part of Western Europe, the traces of ancient civilisation. The night which descended upon her was the night of an Arctic summer. The dawn began to reappear before the last reflection of the preceding sunset had faded from the horizon. It was in the time of the French Merovingians and of the Saxon Heptarchy that ignorance and ferocity seemed to have done their worst. Yet even then the Neapolitan provinces, recognising the authority of the Eastern Empire, preserved something of Eastern knowledge and refinement. Rome, protected by the sacred character of her Pontiffs, enjoyed at least comparative security and repose. Even in those regions where the sanguinary Lombards had fixed their monarchy, there was incomparably more of wealth, of information, of physical comfort, and of social order, than could be found in Gaul, Britain, or Germany.

That which most distinguished Italy from the neighbouring countries was the importance which the population of the towns, at a very early period, began to acquire. Some cities had been founded in wild and remote situations, by fugitives who had escaped from the rage of the barbarians. Such were Venice and Genoa, which preserved their freedom by their obscurity, till they became able to preserve it by their power. Other cities seem to have retained, under all the changing dynasties of invaders, under Odoacer and Theodoric, Narses and Alboin, the municipal institutions which had been conferred on them by the liberal policy of the Great Republic. In provinces which the central government was too feeble either to protect or to oppress, these institutions gradually acquired stability and vigour. The citizens, defended by their walls, and governed by their own magistrates and their own by-laws, enjoyed a considerable share of republican independence. Thus a strong democratic spirit was called into action. The Carlovingian sovereigns were too imbecile to subdue it. The generous policy of Otho encouraged it. It might perhaps have been suppressed by a close coalition between the Church and the Empire. It was fostered and invigorated by their disputes. In the twelfth century it attained its full vigour, and, after a long and doubtful conflict, triumphed over the abilities and courage of the Swabian Princes.

The assistance of the Ecclesiastical Power had greatly contributed to the success of the Guelfs. That success would, however, have been a doubtful good, if its only effect had been to substitute a moral for a political servitude, and to exalt the Popes at the expense of the Cæsars. Happily the public mind of Italy had long contained the seeds of free opinions, which were now rapidly developed by the genial influence of free institutions. The people of that country had observed the whole machinery of the church, its saints and its miracles, its lofty pretensions and its splendid ceremonial, its worthless blessings and its harmless curses, too long and too closely to be duped. They stood behind the scenes on which others were gazing with childish awe and interest. They witnessed the arrangement of the pullies, and the manufacture of the thunders. They saw the natural faces and heard the natural voices of the actors. Distant nations looked on the Pope as the vicegerent of the Almighty, the oracle of the All-wise, the umpire from whose decisions, in the disputes either of theologians or of kings, no Christian ought to appeal. The Italians were acquainted with all the follies of his youth, and with all the dishonest arts by which he had attained power. They knew how often he had employed the keys of the church to release himself from the most sacred engagements, and its wealth to pamper his mistresses and nephews. The doctrines and rites of the established religion they treated with decent reverence. But though they still called themselves Catholics, they had ceased to be Papists. Those spiritual arms which carried terror into the palaces and camps of the proudest sovereigns excited only contempt in the immediate neighbourhood of the Vatican.

Alexander, when he commanded our Henry the Second to submit to the lash before the tomb of a rebellious subject, was himself an exile. The Romans, apprehending that he entertained designs against their liberties, had driven him from their city; and, though he solemnly promised to confine himself for the future to his spiritual functions, they still refused to readmit him.

In every other part of Europe, a large and powerful privileged class trampled on the people and defied the government. But, in the most flourishing parts of Italy, the feudal nobles were reduced to comparative insignificance. In some districts they took shelter under the protection of the powerful commonwealths which they were unable to oppose, and gradually sank into the mass of burghers. In other places they possessed great influence; but it was an influence widely different from that which was exercised by the aristocracy of any Transalpine kingdom. They were not petty princes, but eminent citizens. Instead of strengthening their fastnesses among the mountains, they embellished their palaces in the market-place. The state of society in the Neapolitan dominions, and in some parts of the Ecclesiastical State, more nearly resembled that which existed in the great monarchies of Europe. But the governments of Lombardy and Tuscany, through all their revolutions, preserved a different character. A people, when assembled in a town, is far more formidable to its rulers than when dispersed over a wide extent of country. The most arbitrary of the Cæsars found it necessary to feed and divert the inhabitants of their unwieldy capital at the expense of the provinces. The citizens of Madrid have more than once besieged their sovereign in his own palace, and extorted from him the most humiliating concessions. The Sultans have often been compelled to propitiate the furious rabble of Constantinople with the head of an unpopular Vizier. From the same cause there was a certain tinge of democracy in the monarchies and aristocracies of Northern Italy.

Thus liberty, partially indeed and transiently, revisited Italy; and with liberty came commerce and empire, science and taste, all the comforts and all the ornaments of life. The Crusades, from which the inhabitants of other countries gained nothing but relics and wounds, brought to the rising commonwealths of the Adriatic and Tyrrhene seas a large increase of wealth, dominion, and knowledge. The moral and the geographical position of those commonwealths enabled them to profit alike by the barbarism of the West and by the civilisation of the East. Italian ships covered every sea. Italian factories rose on every shore. The tables of Italian money-changers were set in every city. Manufactures flourished. Banks were established. The operations of the commercial machine were facilitated by many useful and beautiful inventions. We doubt whether any country of Europe, our own excepted, have at the present time reached so high a point of wealth and civilisation as some parts of Italy had attained four hundred years ago. Historians rarely descend to those details from which alone the real state of a community can be collected. Hence posterity is too often deceived by the vague hyperboles of poets and rhetoricians, who mistake the splendour of a court for the happiness of a people. Fortunately, John Villani has given us an ample and precise account of the state of Florence in the early part of the fourteenth century. The revenue of the Republic amounted to three hundred thousand florins, a sum which, allowing for the depreciation of the precious metals, was at least equivalent to six hundred thousand pounds sterling; a larger sum than England and Ireland, two centuries ago, yielded annually to Elizabeth. The manufacture of wool alone employed two hundred factories and thirty thousand workmen. The cloth annually produced sold, at an average, for twelve hundred thousand florins; a sum fully equal, in exchangeable value, to two millions and a half of our money. Four hundred thousand florins were annually coined. Eighty banks conducted the commercial operations, not of Florence only, but of all Europe. The transactions of these establishments were sometimes of a magnitude which may surprise even the contemporaries of the Barings and the Rothschilds. Two houses advanced to Edward the Third of England upwards of three hundred thousand marks, at a time when the mark contained more silver than fifty shillings of the present day, and when the value of silver was more than quadruple of what it now is. The city and its environs contained a hundred and seventy thousand inhabitants. In the various schools about ten thousand children were taught to read; twelve hundred studied arithmetic; six hundred received a learned education.

The progress of elegant literature and of the fine arts was proportioned to that of the public prosperity. Under the despotic successors of Augustus, all the fields of the intellect had been turned into arid wastes, still marked out by formal boundaries, still retaining the traces of old cultivation, but yielding neither flowers nor fruit. The deluge of barbarism came. It swept away all the landmarks. It obliterated all the signs of former tillage. But it fertilised while it devastated. When it receded, the wilderness was as the garden of God, rejoicing on every side, laughing, clapping its hands, pouring forth, in spontaneous abundance, every thing brilliant, or fragrant, or nourishing. A new language, characterized by simple sweetness and simple energy, had attained perfection. No tongue ever furnished more gorgeous and vivid tints to poetry; nor was it long before a poet appeared, who knew how to employ them. Early in the fourteenth century came forth the Divine Comedy, beyond comparison the greatest work of imagination which had appeared since the poems of Homer. The following generation produced indeed no second Dante: but it was eminently distinguished by general intellectual activity. The study of the Latin writers had never been wholly neglected in Italy. But Petrarch introduced a more profound, liberal, and elegant scholarship, and communicated to his countrymen that enthusiasm for the literature, the history, and the antiquities of Rome, which divided his own heart with a frigid mistress and a more frigid Muse. Boccaccio turned their attention to the more sublime and graceful models of Greece.

From this time, the admiration of learning and genius became almost an idolatry among the people of Italy. Kings and republics, cardinals and doges, vied with each other in honouring and flattering Petrarch. Embassies from rival states solicited the honour of his instructions. His coronation agitated the Court of Naples and the people of Rome as much as the most important political transaction could have done. To collect books and antiques, to found professorships, to patronise men of learning, became almost universal fashions among the great. The spirit of literary research allied itself to that of commercial enterprise. Every place to which the merchant princes of Florence extended their gigantic traffic, from the bazars of the Tigris to the monasteries of the Clyde, was ransacked for medals and manuscripts. Architecture, painting, and sculpture, were munificently encouraged. Indeed it would be difficult to name an Italian of eminence, during the period of which we speak, who, whatever may have been his general character, did not at least affect a love of letters and of the arts.

Knowledge and public prosperity continued to advance together. Both attained their meridian in the age of Lorenzo the Magnificent. We cannot refrain from quoting the splendid passage, in which the Tuscan Thucydides describes the state of Italy at that period. "Ridotta tutta in somma pace e tranquillità, coltivata non meno ne' luoghi più montuosi e più sterili che nelle pianure e regioni più fertili, nè sottoposta ad altro imperio che de' suoi medesimi, non solo era abbondantissima d'abitatori e di ricchezze; ma illustrata sommamente dalla magnificenza di molti principi, dallo splendore di molte nobilissime e bellissime città, dalla sedia e maestà della religione, fioriva d' uomini prestantissimi nell' amministrazione delle cose pubbliche, e d'ingegni molto nobili in tutte le scienze, ed in qualunque arte preclara ed industriosa." When we peruse this just and splendid description, we can scarcely persuade ourselves that we are reading of times in which the annals of England and France present us only with a frightful spectacle of poverty, barbarity, and ignorance. From the oppressions of illiterate masters, and the sufferings of a degraded peasantry, it is delightful to turn to the opulent and enlightened States of Italy, to the vast and magnificent cities, the ports, the arsenals, the villas, the museums, the libraries, the marts filled with every article of comfort or luxury, the factories swarming with artisans, the Apennines covered with rich cultivation up to their very summits, the Po wafting the harvests of Lombardy to the granaries of Venice, and carrying back the silks of Bengal and the furs of Siberia to the palaces of Milan. With peculiar pleasure, every cultivated mind must repose on the fair, the happy, the glorious Florence, the halls which rang with the mirth of Pulci, the cell where twinkled the midnight lamp of Politian, the statues on which the young eye of Michael Angelo glared with the frenzy of a kindred inspiration, the gardens in which Lorenzo meditated some sparkling song for the May-day dance of the Etrurian virgins. Alas, for the beautiful city! Alas, for the wit and the learning, the genius and the love!

> "Le donne, e i cavalier, gli affanni, e gli agi,
> Che ne 'nvogliava amore e cortesia
> Là dove i cuor son fatti sì malvagi."

A time was at hand, when all the seven vials of the Apocalypse were to be poured forth and shaken out over those pleasant countries, a time of slaughter, famine, beggary, infamy, slavery, despair.

In the Italian States, as in many natural bodies, untimely decrepitude was the penalty of precocious maturity. Their early greatness, and their early decline, are principally to be attributed to the same cause, the preponderance which the towns acquired in the political system.

In a community of hunters or of shepherds, every man easily and necessarily becomes a soldier. His ordinary avocations are perfectly compatible with all the duties of military service. However remote may be the expedition on which he is bound, he finds it easy to transport with him the stock from which he derives his subsistence. The whole people is an army; the whole year a march. Such was the state of society which facilitated the gigantic conquests of Attila and Tamerlane.

But a people which subsists by the cultivation of the earth is in a very different situation. The husbandman is bound to the soil on which he labours. A long campaign would be ruinous to him. Still his pursuits are such as give to his frame both the active and the passive strength necessary to a soldier. Nor do they, at least in the infancy of agricultural science, demand his uninterrupted attention. At particular times of the year he is almost wholly unemployed, and can, without injury to himself, afford the time necessary for a short expedition. Thus the legions of Rome were supplied during its earlier wars. The season during which the fields did not require the presence of the cultivators sufficed for a short inroad and a battle. These operations, too frequently interrupted to produce decisive results, yet served to keep up among the people a degree of discipline and courage which rendered them, not only secure, but formidable. The archers and billmen of the middle ages, who, with provisions for forty days at their backs, left the fields for the camp, were troops of the same description.

But when commerce and manufactures begin to flourish a great change takes place. The sedentary habits of the desk and the loom render the exertions and hardships of war insupportable. The business of traders and artisans requires their constant presence and attention. In such a community there is little superfluous time; but there is generally much superfluous money. Some members of the society are, therefore, hired to relieve the rest from a task inconsistent with their habits and engagements.

The history of Greece is, in this, as in many other respects, the best commentary on the history of Italy. Five hundred years before the Christian era, the citizens of the republics round the Ægean Sea formed perhaps the finest militia that ever existed. As wealth and refinement advanced, the system underwent a gradual alteration. The Ionian States were the first in which commerce and the arts were cultivated, and the first in which the ancient discipline decayed. Within eighty years after the battle of Platæa, mercenary troops were every where plying for battles and sieges. In the time of Demosthenes, it was scarcely possible to persuade or compel the Athenians to enlist for foreign service. The laws of Lycurgus prohibited trade and manufactures. The Spartans, therefore, continued to form a national force long after their neighbours had begun to hire soldiers. But their military spirit declined with their singular institutions. In the second century before Christ, Greece contained only one nation of warriors, the savage highlanders of Ætolia, who were some generations behind their countrymen in civilisation and intelligence.

All the causes which produced these effects among the Greeks acted still more strongly on the modern Italians. Instead of a power like Sparta, in its nature warlike, they had amongst them an ecclesiastical state, in its nature pacific. Where there are numerous slaves, every freeman is induced by the strongest motives to familiarise himself with the use of arms. The commonwealths of Italy did not, like those of Greece, swarm with thousands of these household enemies. Lastly, the mode in which military operations were conducted during the prosperous times of Italy was peculiarly unfavourable to the formation of an efficient militia. Men covered with iron from head to foot, armed with ponderous lances, and mounted on horses of the largest breed, were considered as composing the strength of an army. The infantry was regarded as comparatively worthless, and was neglected till it became really so. These tactics maintained their ground for centuries in most parts of Europe. That foot soldiers could withstand the charge of heavy cavalry was thought utterly impossible, till, towards the close of the fifteenth century, the rude mountaineers of Switzerland dissolved the spell, and astounded the most experienced generals by receiving the dreaded shock on an impenetrable forest of pikes.

The use of the Grecian spear, the Roman sword, or the modern bayonet, might be acquired with comparative ease. But nothing short of the daily exercise of years could train the man at arms to support his ponderous panoply, and manage his unwieldy weapon. Throughout Europe this most important branch of war became a separate profession. Beyond the Alps, indeed, though a profession, it was not generally a trade. It was the duty and the amusement of a large class of country gentlemen. It was the service by which they held their lands, and the diversion by which, in the absence of mental resources, they beguiled their leisure. But in the Northern States of Italy, as we have already remarked, the growing power of the cities, where it had not exterminated this order of men, had completely changed their habits. Here, therefore, the practice of employing mercenaries became universal, at a time when it was almost unknown in other countries.

When war becomes the trade of a separate class, the least dangerous course left to a government is to form that class into a standing army. It is scarcely possible, that men can pass their lives in the service of one state, without feeling some interest in its greatness. Its victories are their victories. Its defeats are their defeats. The contract loses something of its mercantile character. The services of the soldier are considered as the effects of patriotic zeal, his pay as the tribute of national gratitude. To betray the power which employs him, to be even remiss in its service, are in his eyes the most atrocious and degrading of crimes.

When the princes and commonwealths of Italy began to use hired troops, their wisest course would have been to form separate military establishments. Unhappily this was not done. The mercenary warriors of the Peninsula, instead of being attached to the service of different powers, were regarded as the common property of all. The connection between the state and its defenders was reduced to the most simple and naked traffic. The adventurer brought his horse, his weapons, his strength, and his experience, into the market. Whether the King of Naples or the Duke of Milan, the Pope or the Signory of Florence, struck the bargain, was to him a matter of perfect indifference. He was for the highest wages and the longest term. When the campaign for which he had contracted was finished, there was neither law nor punctilio to prevent him from instantly turning his arms against his late masters. The soldier was altogether disjoined from the citizen and from the subject.

The natural consequences followed. Left to the conduct of men who neither loved those whom they defended nor hated those whom they opposed, who were often bound by stronger ties to the army against which they fought than to the state which they served, who lost by the termination of the conflict, and gained by its prolongation, war completely changed its character. Every man came into the field of battle impressed with the knowledge that, in a few days, he might be taking the pay of the power against which he was then employed, and fighting by the side of his enemies against his associates. The strongest interests and the strongest feelings concurred to mitigate the hostility of those who had lately been brethren in arms, and who might soon be brethren in arms once more. Their common profession was a bond of union not to be forgotten even when they were engaged in the service of contending parties. Hence it was that operations, languid and indecisive beyond any recorded in history, marches and counter-marches, pillaging expeditions and blockades, bloodless capitulations and equally bloodless combats, make up the military history of Italy during the course of nearly two centuries. Mighty armies fight from sunrise to sunset. A great victory is won. Thousands of prisoners are taken; and hardly a life is lost. A pitched battle seems to have been really less dangerous than an ordinary civil tumult.

Courage was now no longer necessary even to the military character. Men grew old in camps, and acquired the highest renown by their warlike achievements, without being once required to face serious danger. The political consequences are too well known.

The richest and most enlightened part of the world was left un-defended to the assaults of every barbarous invader, to the brutality of Switzerland, the insolence of France, and the fierce rapacity of Arragon. The moral effects which followed from this state of things, were still more remarkable.

Among the rude nations which lay beyond the Alps, valour was absolutely indispensable. Without it, none could be eminent; few could be secure. Cowardice was, therefore, naturally considered as the foulest reproach. Among the polished Italians, enriched by commerce, governed by law, and passionately attached to literature, every thing was done by superiority of intelligence. Their very wars, more pacific than the peace of their neighbours, required rather civil than military qualifications. Hence, while courage was the point of honour in other countries, ingenuity became the point of honour in Italy.

From these principles were deduced, by processes strictly analogous, two opposite systems of fashionable morality. Through the greater part of Europe, the vices which peculiarly belong to timid dispositions, and which are the natural defence of weakness, fraud and hypocrisy, have always been most disreputable. On the other hand, the excesses of haughty and daring spirits have been treated with indulgence, and even with respect. The Italians regarded with corresponding lenity those crimes which require self-command, address, quick observation, fertile invention, and profound knowledge of human nature.

Such a prince as our Henry the Fifth would have been the idol of the North. The follies of his youth, the selfish ambition of his manhood, the Lollards roasted at slow fires, the prisoners massacred on the field of battle, the expiring lease of priestcraft renewed for another century, the dreadful legacy of a causeless and hopeless war bequeathed to a people who had no interest in its event, every thing is forgotten but the victory of Agincourt. Francis Sforza, on the other hand, was the model of Italian heroes. He made his employers and his rivals alike his tools. He first overpowered his open enemies by the help of faithless allies; he then armed himself against his allies with the spoils taken from his enemies. By his incomparable dexterity, he raised himself from the precarious and dependent situation of a military adventurer to the first throne of Italy. To such a man much was forgiven, hollow friendship, un-generous enmity, violated faith. Such are the opposite errors which men commit, when their morality is not a science but a taste, when they abandon eternal principles for accidental associations.

We have illustrated our meaning by an instance taken from

history. We will select another from fiction. Othello murders his wife; he gives orders for the murder of his lieutenant; he ends by murdering himself. Yet he never loses the esteem and affection of Northern readers. His intrepid and ardent spirit redeems every thing. The unsuspecting confidence with which he listens to his adviser, the agony with which he shrinks from the thought of shame, the tempest of passion with which he commits his crimes, and the haughty fearlessness with which he avows them, give an extraordinary interest to his character. Iago, on the contrary, is the object of universal loathing. Many are inclined to suspect that Shakspeare has been seduced into an exaggeration unusual with him, and has drawn a monster who has no archetype in human nature. Now we suspect, that an Italian audience, in the fifteenth century, would have felt very differently. Othello would have inspired nothing but detestation and contempt. The folly with which he trusts the friendly professions of a man whose promotion he had obstructed, the credulity with which he takes unsupported assertions, and trivial circumstances, for unanswerable proofs, the violence with which he silences the exculpation till the exculpation can only aggravate his misery, would have excited the abhorrence and disgust of the spectators. The conduct of Iago they would assuredly have condemned; but they would have condemned it as we condemn that of his victim. Something of interest and respect would have mingled with their disapprobation. The readiness of the traitor's wit, the clearness of his judgment, the skill with which he penetrates the dispositions of others and conceals his own, would have insured to him a certain portion of their esteem.

So wide was the difference between the Italians and their neighbours. A similar difference existed between the Greeks of the second century before Christ, and their masters the Romans. The conquerors, brave and resolute, faithful to their engagements, and strongly influenced by religious feelings, were, at the same time, ignorant, arbitrary, and cruel. With the vanquished people were deposited all the art, the science, and the literature of the Western world. In poetry, in philosophy, in painting, in architecture, in sculpture, they had no rivals. Their manners were polished, their perceptions acute, their invention ready; they were tolerant, affable, humane; but of courage and sincerity they were almost utterly destitute. Every rude centurion consoled himself for his intellectual inferiority, by remarking that knowledge and taste seemed only to make men atheists, cowards, and slaves. The distinction long continued to be strongly marked, and furnished an admirable subject for the fierce sarcasms of Juvenal.

The citizen of an Italian commonwealth was the Greek of the time of Juvenal, and the Greek of the time of Pericles, joined in one. Like the former, he was timid and pliable, artful and mean. But, like the latter, he had a country. Its independence and prosperity were dear to him. If his character were degraded by some base crimes, it was, on the other hand, ennobled by public spirit and by an honourable ambition.

A vice sanctioned by the general opinion is merely a vice. The evil terminates in itself. A vice condemned by the general opinion produces a pernicious effect on the whole character. The former is a local malady, the latter a constitutional taint. When the reputation of the offender is lost, he too often flings the remains of his virtue after it in despair. The Highland gentleman who, a century ago, lived by taking black mail from his neighbours, committed the same crime for which Wild was accompanied to Tyburn by the huzzas of two hundred thousand people. But there can be no doubt that he was a much less depraved man than Wild. The deed for which Mrs. Brownrigg was hanged sinks into nothing, when compared with the conduct of the Roman who treated the public to a hundred pair of gladiators. Yet we should greatly wrong such a Roman if we supposed that his disposition was as cruel as that of Mrs. Brownrigg. In our own country, a woman forfeits her place in society by what, in a man, is too commonly considered as an honourable distinction, and, at worst, as a venial error. The consequence is notorious. The moral principle of a woman is frequently more impaired by a single lapse from virtue than that of a man by twenty years of intrigues. Classical antiquity would furnish us with instances stronger, if possible, than those to which we have referred.

We must apply this principle to the case before us. Habits of dissimulation and falsehood, no doubt, mark a man of our age and country as utterly worthless and abandoned. But it by no means follows that a similar judgment would be just in the case of an Italian of the middle ages. On the contrary, we frequently find those faults which we are accustomed to consider as certain indications of a mind altogether depraved, in company with great and good qualities, with generosity, with benevolence, with disinterestedness. From such a state of society, Palamedes, in the admirable dialogue of Hume, might have drawn illustrations of his theory as striking as any of those with which Fourli furnished him. These are not, we well know, the lessons which historians are generally most careful to teach, or readers most willing to learn. But they are not therefore useless. How Philip disposed his troops at

Chæronea, where Hannibal crossed the Alps, whether Mary blew up Darnley, or Siquier shot Charles the Twelfth, and ten thousand other questions of the same description, are in themselves unimportant. The inquiry may amuse us, but the decision leaves us no wiser. He alone reads history aright who, observing how powerfully circumstances influence the feelings and opinions of men, how often vices pass into virtues and paradoxes into axioms, learns to distinguish what is accidental and transitory in human nature from what is essential and immutable.

In this respect no history suggests more important reflections than that of the Tuscan and Lombard commonwealths. The character of the Italian statesman seems, at first sight, a collection of contradictions, a phantom as monstrous as the portress of hell in Milton, half divinity, half snake, majestic and beautiful above, grovelling and poisonous below. We see a man whose thoughts and words have no connexion with each other, who never hesitates at an oath when he wishes to seduce, who never wants a pretext when he is inclined to betray. His cruelties spring, not from the heat of blood, or the insanity of uncontrolled power, but from deep and cool meditation. His passions, like well trained troops, are impetuous by rule, and in their most headstrong fury never forget the discipline to which they have been accustomed. His whole soul is occupied with vast and complicated schemes of ambition: yet his aspect and language exhibit nothing but philosophical moderation. Hatred and revenge eat into his heart: yet every look is a cordial smile, every gesture a familiar caress. He never excites the suspicion of his adversaries by petty provocations. His purpose is disclosed only when it is accomplished. His face is unruffled, his speech is courteous, till vigilance is laid asleep, till a vital point is exposed, till a sure aim is taken; and then he strikes, for the first and last time. Military courage, the boast of the sottish German, of the frivolous and prating Frenchman, of the romantic and arrogant Spaniard, he neither possesses nor values. He shuns danger, not because he is insensible to shame, but because, in the society in which he lives, timidity has ceased to be shameful. To do an injury openly is, in his estimation, as wicked as to do it secretly, and far less profitable. With him the most honourable means are those which are the surest, the speediest, and the darkest. He cannot comprehend how a man should scruple to deceive those whom he does not scruple to destroy. He would think it madness to declare open hostilities against rivals whom he might stab in a friendly embrace, or poison in a consecrated wafer.

Yet this man, black with the vices which we consider as most loathsome, traitor, hypocrite, coward, assassin, was by no means destitute even of those virtues which we generally consider as indicating superior elevation of character. In civil courage, in perseverance, in presence of mind, those barbarous warriors, who were foremost in the battle or the breach, were far his inferiors. Even the dangers which he avoided with a caution almost pusillanimous never confused his perceptions, never paralysed his inventive faculties, never wrung out one secret from his smooth tongue and his inscrutable brow. Though a dangerous enemy, and a still more dangerous accomplice, he could be a just and beneficent ruler. With so much unfairness in his policy, there was an extraordinary degree of fairness in his intellect. Indifferent to truth in the transactions of life, he was honestly devoted to truth in the researches of speculation. Wanton cruelty was not in his nature. On the contrary, where no political object was at stake, his disposition was soft and humane. The susceptibility of his nerves and the activity of his imagination inclined him to sympathise with the feelings of others, and to delight in the charities and courtesies of social life. Perpetually descending to actions which might seem to mark a mind diseased through all its faculties, he had nevertheless an exquisite sensibility, both for the natural and the moral sublime, for every graceful and every lofty conception. Habits of petty intrigue and dissimulation might have rendered him incapable of great general views, but that the expanding effect of his philosophical studies counteracted the narrowing tendency. He had the keenest enjoyment of wit, eloquence, and poetry. The fine arts profited alike by the severity of his judgment, and by the liberality of his patronage. The portraits of some of the remarkable Italians of those times are perfectly in harmony with this description. Ample and majestic foreheads, brows strong and dark, but not frowning, eyes of which the calm full gaze, while it expresses nothing, seems to discern every thing, cheeks pale with thought and sedentary habits, lips formed with feminine delicacy, but compressed with more than masculine decision, mark out men at once enterprising and timid, men equally skilled in detecting the purposes of others, and in concealing their own, men who must have been formidable enemies and unsafe allies, but men, at the same time, whose tempers were mild and equable, and who possessed an amplitude and subtlety of intellect which would have rendered them eminent either in active or in contemplative life, and fitted them either to govern or to instruct mankind.

Every age and every nation has certain characteristic vices, which prevail almost universally, which scarcely any person scruples to avow, and which even rigid moralists but faintly censure. Succeeding generations change the fashion of their morals, with the fashion of their hats and their coaches; take some other kind of wickedness under their patronage, and wonder at the depravity of their ancestors. Nor is this all. Posterity, that high court of appeal which is never tired of eulogising its own justice and discernment, acts on such occasions like a Roman dictator after a general mutiny. Finding the delinquents too numerous to be all punished, it selects some of them at hazard, to bear the whole penalty of an offence in which they are not more deeply implicated than those who escape. Whether decimation be a convenient mode of military execution, we know not; but we solemnly protest against the introduction of such a principle into the philosophy of history.

In the present instance, the lot has fallen on Machiavelli, a man whose public conduct was upright and honourable, whose views of morality, where they differed from those of the persons around him, seemed to have differed for the better, and whose only fault was, that, having adopted some of the maxims then generally received, he arranged them more luminously, and expressed them more forcibly, than any other writer.

Having now, we hope, in some degree cleared the personal character of Machiavelli, we come to the consideration of his works. As a poet, he is not entitled to a high place; but his comedies deserve attention.

The Mandragola, in particular, is superior to the best of Goldoni, and inferior only to the best of Molière. It is the work of a man who, if he had devoted himself to the drama, would probably have attained the highest eminence, and produced a permanent and salutary effect on the national taste. This we infer, not so much from the degree, as from the kind of its excellence. There are compositions which indicate still greater talent, and which are perused with still greater delight, from which we should have drawn very different conclusions. Books quite worthless are quite harmless. The sure sign of the general decline of an art is the frequent occurrence, not of deformity, but of misplaced beauty. In general, tragedy is corrupted by eloquence, and comedy by wit.

The real object of the drama is the exhibition of human character. This, we conceive, is no arbitrary canon, originating in local and temporary associations, like those canons which regulate the number of acts in a play, or of syllables in a line. To this fundamental law every other regulation is subordinate. The situations which most signally develop character form the best plot. The mother tongue of the passions is the best style.

This principle, rightly understood, does not debar the poet from any grace of composition. There is no style in which some man may not, under some circumstances, express himself. There is therefore no style which the drama rejects, none which it does not occasionally require. It is in the discernment of place, of time, and of person, that the inferior artists fail. The fantastic rhapsody of Mercutio, the elaborate declamation of Antony, are, where Shakspeare has placed them, natural and pleasing. But Dryden would have made Mercutio challenge Tybalt, in hyperboles as fanciful as those in which he describes the chariot of Mab. Corneille would have represented Antony as scolding and coaxing Cleopatra with all the measured rhetoric of a funeral oration.

No writers have injured the Comedy of England so deeply as Congreve and Sheridan. Both were men of splendid wit and polished taste. Unhappily, they made all their characters in their own likeness. Their works bear the same relation to the legitimate drama which a transparency bears to a painting. There are no delicate touches, no hues imperceptibly fading into each other: the whole is lighted up with an universal glare. Outlines and tints are forgotten in the common blaze which illuminates all. The flowers and fruits of the intellect abound; but it is the abundance of a jungle, not of a garden, unwholesome, bewildering, unprofitable from its very plenty, rank from its very fragrance. Every fop, every boor, every valet, is a man of wit. The very butts and dupes, Tattle, Witwould, Puff, Acres, outshine the whole Hotel of Rambouillet. To prove the whole system of this school erroneous, it is only necessary to apply the test which dissolved the enchanted Florimel, to place the true by the false Thalia, to contrast the most celebrated characters which have been drawn by the writers of whom we speak with the Bastard in King John, or the Nurse in Romeo and Juliet. It was not surely from want of wit that Shakspeare adopted so different a manner. Benedick and Beatrice throw Mirabel and Millamant into the shade. All the good sayings of the facetious houses of Absolute and Surface might have been clipped from the single character of Falstaff without being missed. It would have been easy for that fertile mind to have given Bardolph and Shallow as much wit as Prince Hal, and to have made Dogberry and Verges retort on each other in sparkling epigrams. But he knew that such indiscriminate prodigality was, to use his own admirable language, "from the purpose of playing, whose end, both at the first and now, was, and is, to hold, as it were, the mirror up to Nature."

This digression will enable our readers to understand what we mean when we say that, in the Mandragola, Machiavelli has proved that he completely understood the nature of the dramatic art, and possessed talents which would have enabled him to excel in it. By the correct and vigorous delineation of human nature, it produces interest without a pleasing or skilful plot, and laughter without the least ambition of wit. The lover, not a very delicate or generous lover, and his adviser the parasite, are drawn with spirit. The hypocritical confessor is an admirable portrait. He is, if we mistake not, the original of Father Dominic, the best comic character of Dryden. But old Nicias is the glory of the piece. We cannot call to mind any thing that resembles him. The follies which Molière ridicules are those of affectation, not those of fatuity. Coxcombs and pedants, not absolute simpletons, are his game. Shakspeare has indeed a vast assortment of fools; but the precise species of which we speak is not, if we remember right, to be found there. Shallow is a fool. But his animal spirits supply, to a certain degree, the place of cleverness. His talk is to that of Sir John what soda water is to champagne. It has the effervescence, though not the body or the flavour. Slender and Sir Andrew Aguecheek are fools, troubled with an uneasy consciousness of their folly, which, in the latter, produces meekness and docility, and in the former, awkwardness, obstinacy, and confusion. Cloten is an arrogant fool, Osric a foppish fool, Ajax a savage fool; but Nicias is, as Thersites says of Patroclus, a fool positive. His mind is occupied by no strong feeling; it takes every character, and retains none; its aspect is diversified, not by passions, but by faint and transitory semblances of passion, a mock joy, a mock fear, a mock love, a mock pride, which chase each other like shadows over its surface, and vanish as soon as they appear. He is just idiot enough to be an object, not of pity or horror, but of ridicule. He bears some resemblance to poor Calandrino, whose mishaps, as recounted by Boccaccio, have made all Europe merry for more than four centuries. He perhaps resembles still more closely Simon da Villa, to whom Bruno and Buffalmacco promised the love of the Countess Civillari. Nicias is, like Simon, of a learned profession; and the dignity with which he wears the doctoral fur, renders his absurdities infinitely more grotesque. The old Tuscan is the very language for such a being. Its peculiar simplicity gives even to the most forcible reasoning and the most brilliant wit an infantine air, generally delightful, but to a foreign reader sometimes a little ludicrous. Heroes and states-men seem to lisp when they use it. It becomes Nicias incomparably, and renders all his silliness infinitely more silly.

We may add, that the verses with which the Mandragola is

interspersed, appear to us to be the most spirited and correct of all that Machiavelli has written in metre. He seems to have entertained the same opinion; for he has introduced some of them in other places. The contemporaries of the author were not blind to the merits of this striking piece. It was acted at Florence with the greatest success. Leo the Tenth was among its admirers, and by his order it was represented at Rome.[1]

The Clizia is an imitation of the Casina of Plautus, which is itself an imitation of the lost κληρουμένοι of Diphilus. Plautus was, unquestionably, one of the best Latin writers; but the Casina is by no means one of his best plays; nor is it one which offers great facilities to an imitator. The story is as alien from modern habits of life, as the manner in which it is developed from the modern fashion of composition. The lover remains in the country and the heroine in her chamber during the whole action, leaving their fate to be decided by a foolish father, a cunning mother, and two knavish servants. Machiavelli has executed his task with judgment and taste. He has accommodated the plot to a different state of society, and has very dexterously connected it with the history of his own times. The relation of the trick put on the doting old lover is exquisitely humorous. It is far superior to the corresponding passage in the Latin comedy, and scarcely yields to the account which Falstaff gives of his ducking.

Two other comedies without titles, the one in prose, the other in verse, appear among the works of Machiavelli. The former is very short, lively enough, but of no great value. The latter we can scarcely believe to be genuine. Neither its merits nor its defects remind us of the reputed author. It was first printed in 1796, from a manuscript discovered in the celebrated library of the Strozzi. Its genuineness, if we have been rightly informed, is established solely by the comparison of hands. Our suspicions are strengthened by the circumstance, that the same manuscript contained a description of the plague of 1527, which has also, in consequence, been added to the works of Machiavelli. Of this last composition, the strongest external evidence would scarcely induce us to believe him guilty. Nothing was ever written more detestable in matter and manner. The narrations, the reflections, the jokes, the lamentations, are all the very worst of their respective kinds, at once trite and affected, threadbare tinsel from the Rag-fairs and Monmouth-

[1] Nothing can be more evident than that Paulus Jovius designates the Mandragola under the name of the Nicias. We should not have noticed what is so perfectly obvious, were it not that this natural and palpable misnomer has led the sagacious and industrious Bayle into a gross error.

streets of literature. A foolish schoolboy might write such a piece, and, after he had written it, think it much finer than the incomparable introduction of the Decameron. But that a shrewd statesman, whose earliest works are characterised by manliness of thought and language, should, at near sixty years of age, descend to such puerility, is utterly inconceivable.

The little novel of Belphegor is pleasantly conceived, and pleasantly told. But the extravagance of the satire in some measure injures its effect. Machiavelli was unhappily married; and his wish to avenge his own cause and that of his brethren in misfortune, carried him beyond even the license of fiction. Jonson seems to have combined some hints taken from this tale, with others from Boccaccio, in the plot of The Devil is an Ass, a play which, though not the most highly finished of his compositions, is perhaps that which exhibits the strongest proofs of genius.

The political correspondence of Machiavelli, first published in 1767, is unquestionably genuine, and highly valuable. The unhappy circumstances in which his country was placed during the greater part of his public life gave extraordinary encouragement to diplomatic talents. From the moment that Charles the Eighth descended from the Alps, the whole character of Italian politics was changed. The governments of the Peninsula ceased to form an independent system. Drawn from their old orbit by the attraction of the larger bodies which now approached them, they became mere satellites of France and Spain. All their disputes, internal and external, were decided by foreign influence. The contests of opposite factions were carried on, not as formerly in the senate-house or in the market-place, but in the antechambers of Louis and Ferdinand. Under these circumstances, the prosperity of the Italian States depended far more on the ability of their foreign agents, than on the conduct of those who were entrusted with the domestic administration. The ambassador had to discharge functions far more delicate than transmitting orders of knighthood, introducing tourists, or presenting his brethren with the homage of his high consideration. He was an advocate to whose management the dearest interests of his clients were intrusted, a spy clothed with an inviolable character. Instead of consulting, by a reserved manner and ambiguous style, the dignity of those whom he represented, he was to plunge into all the intrigues of the court at which he resided, to discover and flatter every weakness of the prince, and of the favourite who governed the prince, and of the lacquey who governed the favourite. He was to compliment the mistress and bribe the confessor, to panegyrize or supplicate, to laugh or weep, to accommodate himself to every caprice, to lull every suspicion, to treasure every hint, to be every thing, to observe every thing, to endure every thing. High as the art of political intrigue had been carried in Italy, these were times which required it all.

On these arduous errands Machiavelli was frequently employed. He was sent to treat with the King of the Romans and with the Duke of Valentinois. He was twice ambassador at the Court of Rome, and thrice at that of France. In these missions, and in several others of inferior importance, he acquitted himself with great dexterity. His despatches form one of the most amusing and instructive collections extant. The narratives are clear and agreeably written; the remarks on men and things clever and judicious. The conversations are reported in a spirited and characteristic manner. We find ourselves introduced into the presence of the men who, during twenty eventful years, swayed the destinies of Europe. Their wit and their folly, their fretfulness and their merriment are exposed to us. We are admitted to overhear their chat, and to watch their familiar gestures. It is interesting and curious to recognise, in circumstances which elude the notice of historians, the feeble violence and shallow cunning of Louis the Twelfth; the bustling insignificance of Maximilian, cursed with an impotent pruriency for renown, rash yet timid, obstinate yet fickle, always in a hurry, yet always too late; the fierce and haughty energy which gave dignity to the eccentricities of Julius; the soft and graceful manners which masked the insatiable ambition and the implacable hatred of Cæsar Borgia.

We have mentioned Cæsar Borgia. It is impossible not to pause for a moment on the name of a man in whom the political morality of Italy was so strongly personified, partially blended with the sterner lineaments of the Spanish character. On two important occasions Machiavelli was admitted to his society; once, at the moment when Cæsar's splendid villany achieved its most signal triumph, when he caught in one snare and crushed at one blow all his most formidable rivals; and again when, exhausted by disease and overwhelmed by misfortunes, which no human prudence could have averted, he was the prisoner of the deadliest enemy of his house. These interviews between the greatest speculative and the greatest practical statesman of the age are fully described in the correspondence, and form perhaps the most interesting part of it. From some passages in The Prince, and perhaps also from some indistinct traditions, several writers have supposed a connexion between those remarkable men much closer than ever existed. The Envoy has even been accused of prompting the crimes of the artful

M—9

and merciless tyrant. But from the official documents it is clear that their intercourse, though ostensibly amicable, was in reality hostile. It cannot be doubted, however, that the imagination of Machiavelli was strongly impressed, and his speculations on government coloured, by the observations which he made on the singular character and equally singular fortunes of a man who under such disadvantages had achieved such exploits; who, when sensuality, varied through innumerable forms, could no longer stimulate his sated mind, found a more powerful and durable excitement in the intense thirst of empire and revenge; who emerged from the sloth and luxury of the Roman purple the first prince and general of the age; who, trained in an unwarlike profession, formed a gallant army out of the dregs of an unwarlike people; who, after acquiring sovereignty by destroying his enemies, acquired popularity by destroying his tools; who had begun to employ for the most salutary ends the power which he had attained by the most atrocious means; who tolerated within the sphere of his iron despotism no plunderer or oppressor but himself; and who fell at last amidst the mingled curses and regrets of a people of whom his genius had been the wonder, and might have been the salvation. Some of those crimes of Borgia which to us appear the most odious would not, from causes which we have already considered, have struck an Italian of the fifteenth century with equal horror. Patriotic feeling also might induce Machiavelli to look with some indulgence and regret on the memory of the only leader who could have defended the independence of Italy against the confederate spoilers of Cambray.

On this subject Machiavelli felt most strongly. Indeed the expulsion of the foreign tyrants, and the restoration of that golden age which had preceded the irruption of Charles the Eighth, were projects which, at that time, fascinated all the master-spirits of Italy. The magnificent vision delighted the great but ill-regulated mind of Julius. It divided with manuscripts and sauces, painters and falcons, the attention of the frivolous Leo. It prompted the generous treason of Morone. It imparted a transient energy to the feeble mind and body of the last Sforza. It excited for one moment an honest ambition in the false heart of Pescara. Ferocity and insolence were not among the vices of the national character. To the discriminating cruelties of politicians, committed for great ends on select victims, the moral code of the Italians was too indulgent. But though they might have recourse to barbarity as an expedient, they did not require it as a stimulant. They turned with loathing from the atrocity of the strangers who seemed to love blood for its own sake, who, not content with subjugating, were impatient to destroy, who found a fiendish pleasure in razing magnificent cities, cutting the throats of enemies who cried for quarter, or suffocating an unarmed population by thousands in the caverns to which it had fled for safety. Such were the cruelties which daily excited the terror and disgust of a people among whom, till lately, the worst that a soldier had to fear in a pitched battle was the loss of his horse and the expense of his ransom. The swinish intemperance of Switzerland, the wolfish avarice of Spain, the gross licentiousness of the French, indulged in violation of hospitality, of decency, of love itself, the wanton inhumanity which was common to all the invaders, had made them objects of deadly hatred to the inhabitants of the Peninsula. The wealth which had been accumulated during centuries of prosperity and repose was rapidly melting away. The intellectual superiority of the oppressed people only rendered them more keenly sensible of their political degradation. Literature and taste, indeed, still disguised with a flush of hectic loveliness and brilliancy the ravages of an incurable decay. The iron had not yet entered into the soul. The time was not yet come when eloquence was to be gagged, and reason to be hoodwinked, when the harp of the poet was to be hung on the willows of Arno, and the right hand of the painter to forget its cunning. Yet a discerning eye might even then have seen that genius and learning would not long survive the state of things from which they had sprung, and that the great men whose talents gave lustre to that melancholy period had been formed under the influence of happier days, and would leave no successors behind them. The times which shine with the greatest splendour in literary history are not always those to which the human mind is most indebted. Of this we may be convinced, by comparing the generation which follows them with that which had preceded them. The first fruits which are reaped under a bad system often spring from seed sown under a good one. Thus it was, in some measure, with the Augustan age. Thus it was with the age of Raphael and Ariosto, of Aldus and Vida.

Machiavelli deeply regretted the misfortunes of his country, and clearly discerned the cause and the remedy. It was the military system of the Italian people which had extinguished their valour and discipline, and left their wealth an easy prey to every foreign plunderer. The Secretary projected a scheme, alike honourable to his heart and to his intellect, for abolishing the use of mercenary troops, and for organizing a national militia.

The exertions which he made to effect this great object ought alone to rescue his name from obloquy. Though his situation and his habits were pacific, he studied with intense assiduity the theory of war. He made himself master of all its details. The Florentine government entered into his views. A council of war was appointed. Levies were decreed. The indefatigable minister flew from place to place in order to superintend the execution of his design. The times were, in some respects, favourable to the experiment. The system of military tactics had undergone a great revolution. The cavalry was no longer considered as forming the strength of an army. The hours which a citizen could spare from his ordinary employments, though by no means sufficient to familiarise him with the exercise of a man-at-arms, might render him an useful foot-soldier. The dread of a foreign yoke, of plunder, massacre, and conflagration, might have conquered that repugnance to military pursuits which both the industry and the idleness of great towns commonly generate. For a time the scheme promised well. The new troops acquitted themselves respectably in the field. Machiavelli looked with parental rapture on the success of his plan, and began to hope that the arms of Italy might once more be formidable to the barbarians of the Tagus and the Rhine. But the tide of misfortune came on before the barriers which should have withstood it were prepared. For a time, indeed, Florence might be considered as peculiarly fortunate. Famine and sword and pestilence had devasted the fertile plains and stately cities of the Po. All the curses denounced of old against Tyre seemed to have fallen on Venice. Her merchants already stood afar off, lamenting for their great city. The time seemed near when the sea-weed should overgrow her silent Rialto, and the fisherman wash his nets in her deserted arsenal. Naples had been four times conquered and reconquered by tyrants equally indifferent to its welfare, and equally greedy for its spoils. Florence, as yet, had only to endure degradation and extortion, to submit to the mandates of foreign powers, to buy over and over again, at an enormous price, what was already justly her own, to return thanks for being wronged, and to ask pardon for being in the right. She was at length deprived of the blessings even of this infamous and servile repose. Her military and political institutions were swept away together. The Medici returned, in the train of foreign invaders, from their long exile. The policy of Machiavelli was abandoned; and his public services were requited with poverty, imprisonment, and torture.

The fallen statesman still clung to his project with unabated ardour. With the view of vindicating it from some popular objections and of refuting some prevailing errors on the subject of military science, he wrote his seven books on the Art of War. This excellent work is in the form of a dialogue. The opinions of the writer are put into the mouth of Fabrizio Colonna, a powerful nobleman of the Ecclesiastical State, and an officer of distinguished merit in the service of the king of Spain. Colonna visits Florence on his way from Lombardy to his own domains. He is invited to meet some friends at the house of Cosimo Rucellai, an amiable and accomplished young man, whose early death Machiavelli feelingly deplores. After partaking of an elegant entertainment, they retire from the heat into the most shady recesses of the garden. Fabrizio is struck by the sight of some uncommon plants. Cosimo says that, though rare in modern days, they are frequently mentioned by the classical authors, and that his grandfather, like many other Italians, amused himself with practising the ancient methods of gardening. Fabrizio expresses his regret that those who, in later times, affected the manners of the old Romans should select for imitation the most trifling pursuits. This leads to a conversation on the decline of military discipline and on the best means of restoring it. The institution of the Florentine militia is ably defended; and several improvements are suggested in the details.

The Swiss and the Spaniards were, at that time, regarded as the best soldiers in Europe. The Swiss battalion consisted of pikemen, and bore a close resemblance to the Greek phalanx. The Spaniards, like the soldiers of Rome, were armed with the sword and the shield. The victories of Flamininus and Æmilius over the Macedonian kings seem to prove the superiority of the weapons used by the legions. The same experiment had been recently tried with the same result at the battle of Ravenna, one of those tremendous days into which human folly and wickedness compress the whole devastation of a famine or a plague. In that memorable conflict, the infantry of Arragon, the old companions of Gonsalvo, deserted by all their allies, hewed a passage through the thickest of the imperial pikes, and effected an unbroken retreat, in the face of the gendarmerie of De Foix, and the renowned artillery of Este. Fabrizio, or rather Machiavelli, proposes to combine the two systems, to arm the foremost lines with the pike for the purpose of repulsing cavalry, and those in the rear with the sword, as being a weapon better adapted for every other purpose. Throughout the work, the author expresses the highest admiration of the military science of the ancient Romans, and the greatest contempt for the maxims which had been in vogue amongst the Italian commanders of the preceding generation. He prefers infantry to cavalry, and fortified camps to fortified towns. He is inclined to substitute rapid movements and decisive engagements for the languid and dilatory operations of his countrymen. He attaches very little importance to the invention of gunpowder. Indeed he seems to think that it ought scarcely to produce any change in the mode of arming or of disposing troops. The general testimony of historians, it must be allowed, seems to prove that the ill-constructed and ill-served artillery of those times, though useful in a siege, was of little value on the field of battle.

Of the tactics of Machiavelli we will not venture to give an opinion: but we are certain that his book is most able and interesting. As a commentary on the history of his times, it is invaluable. The ingenuity, the grace, and the perspicuity of the style, and the eloquence and animation of particular passages must give pleasure even to readers who take no interest in the subject.

The Prince and the Discourses on Livy were written after the fall of the Republican Government. The former was dedicated to the Young Lorenzo de Medici. This circumstance seems to have disgusted the contemporaries of the writer far more than the doctrines which have rendered the name of the work odious in later times. It was considered as an indication of political apostasy. The fact however seems to have been that Machiavelli, despairing of the liberty of Florence, was inclined to support any government which might preserve her independence. The interval which separated a democracy and a despotism, Soderini and Lorenzo, seemed to vanish when compared with the difference between the former and the present state of Italy, between the security, the opulence, and the repose which she had enjoyed under its native rulers, and the misery in which she had been plunged since the fatal year in which the first foreign tyrant had descended from the Alps. The noble and pathetic exhortation with which The Prince concludes shows how strongly the writer felt upon this subject.

The Prince traces the progress of an ambitious man, the Discourses the progress of an ambitious people. The same principles on which, in the former work, the elevation of an individual is explained, are applied, in the latter, to the longer duration and more complex interests of a society. To a modern statesman the form of the Discourses may appear to be puerile. In truth Livy is not an historian on whom implicit reliance can be placed, even in cases where he must have possessed considerable means of information. And the first Decade, to which Machiavelli has confined himself, is scarcely entitled to more credit than our Chronicle of British Kings who reigned before the Roman invasion. But the commentator is indebted to Livy for little more than a few texts which he might as easily have extracted from the Vulgate or the Decameron. The whole train of thought is original.

On the peculiar immorality which has rendered The Prince unpopular, and which is almost equally discernible in the Discourses, we have already given our opinion at length. We have attempted to show that it belonged rather to the age than to the man, that it was a partial taint, and by no means implied general depravity. We cannot however deny that it is a great blemish, and that it considerably diminishes the pleasure which, in other respects, those works must afford to every intelligent mind.

It is, indeed, impossible to conceive a more healthful and vigorous constitution of the understanding than that which these works indicate. The qualities of the active and the contemplative statesman appear to have been blended in the mind of the writer into a rare and exquisite harmony. His skill in the details of business had not been acquired at the expense of his general powers. It had not rendered his mind less comprehensive; but it had served to correct his speculations, and to impart to them that vivid and practical character which so widely distinguishes them from the vague theories of most political philosophers.

Every man who has seen the world knows that nothing is so useless as a general maxim. If it be very moral and very true, it may serve for a copy to a charity-boy. If, like those of Rochefoucault, it be sparkling and whimsical, it may make an excellent motto for an essay. But few indeed of the many wise apophthegms which have been uttered, from the time of the Seven Sages of Greece to that of Poor Richard, have prevented a single foolish action. We give the highest and the most peculiar praise to the precepts of Machiavelli when we say that they may frequently be of real use in regulating conduct, not so much because they are more just or more profound than those which might be culled from other authors, as because they can be more readily applied to the problems of real life.

There are errors in these works. But they are errors which a writer, situated like Machiavelli, could scarcely avoid. They arise, for the most part, from a single defect which appears to us to pervade his whole system. In his political scheme, the means had been more deeply considered than the ends. The great principle, that societies and laws exist only for the purpose of increasing the sum of private happiness, is not recognised with sufficient clearness. The good of the body, distinct from the good of the members, and sometimes hardly compatible with the good of the members, seems to be the object which he proposes to himself. Of all political fallacies, this has perhaps had the widest and the most mischievous operation. The state of society in the little commonwealths of Greece, the close connexion and mutual dependence of the citizens, and the severity of the laws of war, tended to encourage an opinion which, under such circumstances, could hardly be called erroneous. The interests of every individual were inseparably bound up with those of the state. An invasion destroyed his corn-fields and vineyards, drove him from his home, and compelled him to encounter all the hardships of a military life. A treaty of peace restored him to security and comfort. A victory doubled the number of his slaves. A defeat perhaps made him a slave himself. When Pericles, in the Peloponnesian war, told the Athenians that, if their country triumphed, their private losses would speedily be repaired, but that, if their arms failed of success, every individual amongst them would probably be ruined, he spoke no more than the truth. He spoke to men whom the tribute of vanquished cities supplied with food and clothing, with the luxury of the bath and the amusements of the theatre, on whom the greatness of their country conferred rank, and before whom the members of less prosperous communities trembled; to men who, in case of a change in the public fortunes, would, at least, be deprived of every comfort and every distinction which they enjoyed. To be butchered on the smoking ruins of their city, to be dragged in chains to a slave-market, too see one child torn from them to dig in the quarries of Sicily, and another to guard the harams of Persepolis, these were the frequent and probable consequences of national calamities. Hence, among the Greeks, patriotism became a governing principle, or rather an ungovernable passion. Their legislators and their philosophers took it for granted that, in providing for the strength and greatness of the state, they sufficiently provided for the happiness of the people. The writers of the Roman empire lived under despots, into whose dominion a hundred nations were melted down, and whose gardens would have covered the little commonwealths of Phlius and Platæa. Yet they continued to employ the same language, and to cant about the duty of sacrificing every thing to a country to which they owed nothing.

Causes similar to those which had influenced the disposition of the Greeks operated powerfully on the less vigorous and daring character of the Italians. The Italians, like the Greeks, were members of small communities. Every man was deeply interested in the welfare of the society to which he belonged, a partaker in its wealth and its poverty, in its glory and its shame. In the age of Machiavelli this was peculiarly the case. Public events had produced an immense sum of misery to private citizens. The Northern invaders had brought want to their boards, infamy to their beds, fire to their roofs, and the knife to their throats. It was natural that a man who lived in times like these should overrate the importance of those measures by which a nation is rendered formidable to its neighbours, and undervalue those which make it prosperous within itself.

Nothing is more remarkable in the political treatises of Machiavelli than the fairness of mind which they indicate. It appears where the author is in the wrong, almost as strongly as where he is in the right. He never advances a false opinion because it is new or splendid, because he can clothe it in a happy phrase, or defend it by an ingenious sophism. His errors are at once explained by a reference to the circumstances in which he was placed. They evidently were not sought out; they lay in his way, and could scarcely be avoided. Such mistakes must necessarily be committed by early speculators in every science.

In this respect it is amusing to compare The Prince and the Discourses with the Spirit of Laws. Montesquieu enjoys, perhaps, a wider celebrity than any political writer of modern Europe. Something he doubtless owes to his merit, but much more to his fortune. He had the good luck of a Valentine. He caught the eye of the French nation, at the moment when it was waking from the long sleep of political and religious bigotry; and, in consequence, he became a favourite. The English, at that time, considered a Frenchman who talked about constitutional checks and fundamental laws as a prodigy not less astonishing than the learned pig or the musical infant. Specious but shallow, studious of effect, indifferent to truth, eager to build a system, but careless of collecting those materials out of which alone a sound and durable system can be built, the lively President constructed theories as rapidly and as slightly as card-houses, no sooner projected than completed, no sooner completed than blown away, no sooner blown away than forgotten. Machiavelli errs only because his experience, acquired in a very peculiar state of society, could not always enable him to calculate the effect of institutions differing from those of which he had observed the operation. Montesquieu errs, because he has a fine thing to say, and is resolved to say it. If the phænomena which lie before him will not suit his purpose, all history must be ransacked. If nothing established by authentic testimony can be racked or chipped to suit his Procrustean hypothesis, he puts up with some monstrous fable about Siam, or Bantam, or Japan, told by writers compared with whom Lucian and Gulliver were veracious, liars by a double right, as travellers and as Jesuits.

Propriety of thought, and propriety of diction, are commonly found together. Obscurity and affectation are the two greatest faults of style. Obscurity of expression generally springs from confusion of ideas; and the same wish to dazzle at any cost which produces affectation in the manner of a writer is likely to produce sophistry in his reasonings. The judicious and candid mind of Machiavelli shows itself in his luminous, manly, and polished language. The style of Montesquieu, on the other hand, indicates in every page a lively and ingenious, but an unsound mind. Every trick of expression, from the mysterious conciseness of an oracle to the flippancy of a Parisian coxcomb, is employed to disguise the fallacy of some positions, and the triteness of others. Absurdities are brightened into epigrams; truisms are darkened into enigmas. It is with difficulty that the strongest eye can sustain the glare with which some parts are illuminated, or penetrate the shade in which others are concealed.

The political works of Machiavelli derive a peculiar interest from the mournful earnestness which he manifests whenever he touches on topics connected with the calamities of his native land. It is difficult to conceive any situation more painful than that of a great man, condemned to watch the lingering agony of an exhausted country, to tend it during the alternate fits of stupefaction and raving which precede its dissolution, and to see the symptoms of vitality disappear one by one, till nothing is left but coldness, darkness, and corruption. To this joyless and thankless duty was Machiavelli called. In the energetic language of the prophet, he was "mad for the sight of his eyes which he saw," disunion in the council, effeminacy in the camp, liberty extinguished, commerce decaying, national honour sullied, an enlightened and flourishing people given over to the ferocity of ignorant savages. Though his opinions had not escaped the contagion of that political immorality which was common among his countrymen, his natural disposition seems to have been rather stern and impetuous than pliant and artful. When the misery and degradation of Florence and the foul outrage which he had himself sustained recur to his mind, the smooth craft of his profession and his nation is exchanged for the honest bitterness of scorn and anger. He speaks like one sick of the calamitous times and abject people among whom his lot is cast. He pines for the strength and glory of ancient Rome, for the fasces of Brutus and the sword of Scipio, the gravity of the curule chair, and the bloody pomp of the triumphal sacrifice. He seems to be transported back to the days when eight hundred thousand Italian warriors sprung to arms at the rumour of a Gallic invasion. He breathes all the spirit of those intrepid and haughty senators who forgot the dearest ties of nature in the claims of public duty, who looked with disdain on the elephants and on the gold of Pyrrhus, and listened with unaltered composure to the tremendous tidings of Cannæ. Like an ancient temple deformed by the barbarous architecture of a later age, his character acquires an interest from the very circumstances which debase it. The original proportions are rendered more striking by the contrast which they present to the mean and incongruous additions.

The influence of the sentiments which we have described was not apparent in his writings alone. His enthusiasm, barred from the career which it would have selected for itself, seems to have found a vent in desperate levity. He enjoyed a vindictive pleasure in outraging the opinions of a society which he despised. He became careless of the decencies which were expected from a man so highly distinguished in the literary and political world. The sarcastic bitterness of his conversation disgusted those who were more inclined to accuse his licentiousness than their own degeneracy, and who were unable to conceive the strength of those emotions which are concealed by the jests of the wretched, and by the follies of the wise.

The historical works of Machiavelli still remain to be considered. The life of Castruccio Castracani will occupy us for a very short time, and would scarcely have demanded our notice, had it not attracted a much greater share of public attention than it deserves. Few books, indeed, could be more interesting than a careful and judicious account, from such a pen, of the illustrious Prince of Lucca, the most eminent of those Italian chiefs, who, like Pisistratus and Gelon, acquired a power felt rather than seen, and resting, not on law or on prescription, but on the public favour and on their great personal qualities. Such a work would exhibit to us the real nature of that species of sovereignty, so singular and so often misunderstood, which the Greeks denominated tyranny, and which, modified in some degree by the feudal system, reappeared in the commonwealths of Lombardy and Tuscany. But this little composition of Machiavelli is in no sense a history. It has no pretensions to fidelity. It is a trifle, and not a very successful trifle. It is scarcely more authentic than the novel of Belphegor, and is very much duller.

The last great work of this illustrious man was the history of his native city. It was written by command of the Pope, who, as chief of the house of Medici, was at that time sovereign of Florence. The characters of Cosmo, of Piero, and of Lorenzo, are, however, treated with a freedom and impartiality equally honourable to the writer and to the patron. The miseries and humiliations of dependence, the bread which is more bitter than every other food, the stairs which are more painful than every other ascent, had not broken the spirit of Machiavelli. The most corrupting post in a corrupting profession had not depraved the generous heart of Clement.

The History does not appear to be the fruit of much industry or research. It is unquestionably inaccurate. But it is elegant, lively, and picturesque, beyond any other in the Italian language. The reader, we believe, carries away from it a more vivid and a more faithful impression of the national character and manners than from more correct accounts. The truth is, that the book belongs rather to ancient than to modern literature. It is in the style, not of Davila and Clarendon, but of Herodotus and Tacitus. The classical histories may almost be called romances founded in fact. The relation is, no doubt, in all its principal points, strictly true. But the numerous little incidents which heighten the interest, the words, the gestures, the looks, are evidently furnished by the imagination of the author. The fashion of later times is different. A more exact narrative is given by the writer. It may be doubted whether more exact notions are conveyed to the reader. The best portraits are perhaps those in which there is a slight mixture of caricature, and we are not certain, that the best histories are not those in which a little of the exaggeration of fictitious narrative is judiciously employed. Something is lost in accuracy; but much is gained in effect. The fainter lines are neglected; but the great characteristic features are imprinted on the mind for ever.

The History terminates with the death of Lorenzo de' Medici. Machiavelli had, it seems, intended to continue his narrative to a later period. But his death prevented the execution of his design; and the melancholy task of recording the desolation and shame of Italy devolved on Guicciardini.

Machiavelli lived long enough to see the commencement of the last struggle for Florentine liberty. Soon after his death monarchy was finally established, not such a monarchy as that of which Cosmo had laid the foundations deep in the institutions and feelings of his countrymen, and which Lorenzo had embellished with the trophies of every science and every art; but a loathsome tyranny, proud and mean, cruel and feeble, bigotted and lascivious. The character of Machiavelli was hateful to the new masters of Italy; and those parts of his theory which were in strict accordance with their own daily practice afforded a pretext for blackening his memory. His works were misrepresented by the learned, misconstrued by the ignorant, censured by the church, abused, with all the rancour of simulated virtue, by the tools of a base government, and the priests of a baser superstition. The name of the man whose genius had illuminated all the dark places of policy, and to whose patriotic wisdom an oppressed people had owed their last chance of emancipation and revenge, passed into a proverb of infamy. For more than two hundred years his bones lay undistinguished. At length, an English nobleman paid the last honours to the greatest statesman of Florence. In the church of Santa Croce a monument was erected to his memory, which is contemplated with reverence by all who can distinguish the virtues of a great mind through the corruptions of a degenerate age, and which will be approached with still deeper homage when the object to which his public life was devoted shall be attained, when the foreign yoke shall be broken, when a second Procida shall avenge the wrongs of Naples, when a happier Rienzi shall restore the good estate of Rome, when the streets of Florence and Bologna shall again resound with their ancient war cry, *Popolo; popolo; muoiano i tiranni!*

WILLIAM PITT, EARL OF CHATHAM

(JANUARY 1834)

A History of the Right Honourable William Pitt, Earl of Chatham, containing his Speeches in Parliament, a considerable portion of his Correspondence when Secretary of State, upon French, Spanish, and American Affairs, never before published; and an Account of the principal Events and Persons of his time, connected with his Life, Sentiments, and Administration. By the REV. FRANCIS THACKERAY, A.M. 2 vols. 4to. London: 1827.

THOUGH several years have elapsed since the publication of this work, it is still, we believe, a new publication to most of our readers. Nor are we surprised at this. The book is large, and the style heavy. The information which Mr. Thackeray has obtained from the State Paper Office is new; but much of it is very uninteresting. The rest of his narrative is very little better than Gifford's or Tomline's Life of the second Pitt, and tells us little or nothing that may not be found quite as well told in the Parliamentary History, the Annual Register, and other works equally common.

Almost every mechanical employment, it is said, has a tendency to injure some one or other of the bodily organs of the artisan. Grinders of cutlery die of consumption; weavers are stunted in their growth; smiths become blear-eyed. In the same manner almost every intellectual employment has a tendency to produce some intellectual malady. Biographers, translators, editors, all, in short, who employ themselves in illustrating the lives or the writings of others, are peculiarly exposed to the *Lues Boswelliana,* or disease of admiration. But we scarcely remember ever to have seen a patient so far gone in this distemper as Mr. Thackeray. He is not satisfied with forcing us to confess that Pitt was a great orator, a vigorous minister, an honourable and high-spirited gentleman. He will have it, that all virtues and all accomplishments met in his hero. In spite of Gods, men, and columns, Pitt must be a poet, a poet capable of producing a heroic poem of the first order; and we are assured that we ought to find many charms in such lines as these:—

> "Midst all the tumults of the warring sphere,
>   My light-charged bark may haply *glide*;
> Some gale may waft, some conscious thought shall cheer,
>   And the small freight unanxious *glide*."[1]

Pitt was in the army for a few months in time of peace. Mr. Thackeray accordingly insists on our confessing that, if the young cornet had remained in the service, he would have been one of the ablest commanders that ever lived. But this is not all. Pitt, it seems, was not merely a great poet *in esse*, and a great general *in posse*, but a finished example of moral excellence, the just man made perfect. He was in the right when he attempted to establish an inquisition, and to give bounties for perjury, in order to get Walpole's head. He was in the right when he declared Walpole to have been an excellent minister. He was in the right when, being in Opposition, he maintained that no peace ought to be made with Spain, till she should formally renounce the right of search. He was in the right when, being in office, he silently acquiesced in a treaty by which Spain did not renounce the right of search. When he left the Duke of Newcastle, when he coalesced with the Duke of Newcastle, when he thundered against subsidies, when he lavished subsidies with unexampled profusion, when he execrated the Hanoverian connexion, when he declared that Hanover ought to be as dear to us as Hampshire, he was still invariably speaking the language of a virtuous and enlightened statesman.

The truth is that there scarcely ever lived a person who had so little claim to this sort of praise as Pitt. He was undoubtedly a great man. But his was not a complete and well-proportioned greatness. The public life of Hampden or of Somers resembles a regular drama, which can be criticized as a whole, and every scene

---

[1] The quotation is faithfully made from Mr. Thackeray. Perhaps Pitt wrote *guide* in the fourth line.

of which is to be viewed in connexion with the main action. The public life of Pitt, on the other hand, is a rude though striking piece, a piece abounding in incongruities, a piece without any unity of plan, but redeemed by some noble passages, the effect of which is increased by the tameness or extravagance of what precedes and of what follows. His opinions were unfixed. His conduct at some of the most important conjunctures of his life was evidently determined by pride and resentment. He had one fault, which of all human faults is most rarely found in company with true greatness. He was extremely affected. He was an almost solitary instance of a man of real genius, and of a brave, lofty, and commanding spirit, without simplicity of character. He was an actor in the Closet, an actor at Council, an actor in Parliament; and even in private society he could not lay aside his theatrical tones and attitudes. We know that one of the most distinguished of his partisans often complained that he could never obtain admittance to Lord Chatham's room till every thing was ready for the representation, till the dresses and properties were all correctly disposed, till the light was thrown with Rembrandt-like effect on the head of the illustrious performer, till the flannels had been arranged with the air of a Grecian drapery, and the crutch placed as gracefully as that of Belisarius or Lear.

Yet, with all his faults and affectations, Pitt had, in a very extraordinary degree, many of the elements of greatness. He had splendid talents, strong passions, quick sensibility, and vehement enthusiasm for the grand and the beautiful. There was something about him which ennobled tergiversation itself. He often went wrong, very wrong. But, to quote the language of Wordsworth,

> "He still retained,
> 'Mid such abasement, what he had received
> From nature, an intense and glowing mind."

In an age of low and dirty prostitution, in the age of Doddington and Sandys, it was something to have a man who might perhaps, under some strong excitement, have been tempted to ruin his country, but who never would have stooped to pilfer from her, a man whose errors arose, not from a sordid desire of gain, but from a fierce thirst for power, for glory, and for vengeance. History owes to him this attestation, that, at a time when any thing short of direct embezzlement of the public money was considered as quite fair in public men, he showed the most scrupulous disinterestedness, that, at a time when it seemed to be generally taken for granted that Government could be upheld only by the basest and most immoral arts, he appealed to the better and nobler parts of human nature, that he made a brave and splendid attempt to do, by means of public opinion, what no other statesman of his day thought it possible to do, except by means of corruption, that he looked for support, not, like the Pelhams, to a strong aristocratical connexion, not, like Bute, to the personal favour of the Sovereign, but to the middle class of Englishmen, that he inspired that class with a firm confidence in his integrity and ability, that, backed by them, he forced an unwilling court and an unwilling oligarchy to admit him to an ample share of power, and that he used his power in such a manner as clearly proved him to have sought it, not for the sake of profit or patronage, but from a wish to establish for himself a great and durable reputation by means of eminent services rendered to the state.

The family of Pitt was wealthy and respectable. His grandfather was Governor of Madras, and brought back from India that celebrated diamond which the Regent Orleans, by the advice of Saint-Simon, purchased for upwards of two millions of livres, and which is still considered as the most precious of the crown jewels of France. Governor Pitt bought estates and rotten boroughs, and sat in the House of Commons for Old Sarum. His son Robert was at one time member for Old Sarum, and at another for Oakhampton. Robert had two sons. Thomas, the elder, inherited the estates and the parliamentary interest of his father. The second was the celebrated William Pitt.

He was born in November 1708. About the early part of his life little more is known than that he was educated at Eton, and that at seventeen he was entered at Trinity College Oxford. During the second year of his residence at the University, George the First died; and the event was, after the fashion of that generation, celebrated by the Oxonians in many very middling copies of verses. On this occasion Pitt published some Latin lines, which Mr. Thackeray has preserved. They prove that the young student had but a very limited knowledge even of the mechanical part of his art. All true Etonians will hear with concern that their illustrious schoolfellow is guilty of making the first syllable in *labenti* short.[1] The matter of the poem is as worthless as that of any college exercise that was ever written before or since. There is, of course, much about Mars, Themis, Neptune, and Cocytus. The Muses are earnestly entreated to weep over the urn of Cæsar; for Cæsar, says

[1] So Mr. Thackeray has printed the poem. But it may be charitably hoped that Pitt wrote *labanti*.

the Poet, loved the Muses; Cæsar, who could not read a line of Pope, and who loved nothing but punch and fat women.

Pitt had been, from his school-days, cruelly tormented by the gout, and was at last advised to travel for his health. He accordingly left Oxford without taking a degree, and visited France and Italy. He returned, however, without having received much benefit from his excursion, and continued, till the close of his life, to suffer most severely from his constitutional malady.

His father was now dead, and had left very little to the younger children. It was necessary that William should choose a profession. He decided for the army, and a cornet's commission was procured for him in the Blues.

But, small as his fortune was, his family had both the power and the inclination to serve him. At the general election of 1734, his elder brother Thomas was chosen both for Old Sarum and for Oakhampton. When Parliament met in 1735, Thomas made his election to serve for Oakhampton, and William was returned for Old Sarum.

Walpole had now been, during fourteen years, at the head of affairs. He had risen to power under the most favourable circumstances. The whole of the Whig party, of that party which professed peculiar attachment to the principles of the Revolution, and which exclusively enjoyed the confidence of the reigning house, had been united in support of his administration. Happily for him, he had been out of office when the South-Sea Act was passed; and, though he does not appear to have foreseen all the consequences of that measure, he had strenuously opposed it, as he opposed all the measures, good and bad, of Sunderland's administration. When the South-Sea Company were voting dividends of fifty per cent, when a hundred pounds of their stock were selling for eleven hundred pounds, when Threadneedle Street was daily crowded with the coaches of dukes and prelates, when divines and philosophers turned gamblers, when a thousand kindred bubbles were daily blown into existence, the periwig company, and the Spanish-jackass company, and the quicksilver-fixation company, Walpole's calm good sense preserved him from the general infatuation. He condemned the prevailing madness in public, and turned a considerable sum by taking advantage of it in private. When the crash came, when ten thousand families were reduced to beggary in a day, when the people, in the frenzy of their rage and despair, clamoured, not only against the lower agents in the juggle, but against the Hanoverian favourites, against the English ministers, against the King himself, when Parliament met, eager for confiscation and blood, when members of the House of Commons proposed that the directors should be treated like parricides in ancient Rome, tied up in sacks, and thrown into the Thames, Walpole was the man on whom all parties turned their eyes. Four years before he had been driven from power by the intrigues of Sunderland and Stanhope, and the lead in the House of Commons had been intrusted to Craggs and Aislabie. Stanhope was no more. Aislabie was expelled from Parliament on account of his disgraceful conduct regarding the South-Sea scheme. Craggs was saved by a timely death from a similar mark of infamy. A large minority in the House of Commons voted for a severe censure on Sunderland who, finding it impossible to withstand the force of the prevailing sentiment, retired from office, and outlived his retirement but a very short time. The schism which had divided the Whig party was now completely healed. Walpole had no opposition to encounter except that of the Tories; and the Tories were naturally regarded by the King with the strongest suspicion and dislike.

For a time business went on with a smoothness and a despatch such as had not been known since the days of the Tudors. During the session of 1724, for example, there was hardly a single division except on private bills. It is not impossible that, by taking the course which Pelham afterwards took, by admitting into the Government all the rising talents and ambition of the Whig party, and by making room here and there for a Tory not unfriendly to the House of Brunswick, Walpole might have averted the tremendous conflict in which he passed the later years of his administration, and in which he was at length vanquished. The Opposition which overthrew him was an Opposition created by his own policy, by his own insatiable love of power.

In the very act of forming his Ministry he turned one of the ablest and most attached of his supporters into a deadly enemy. Pulteney had strong public and private claims to a high situation in the new arrangement. His fortune was immense. His private character was respectable. He was already a distinguished speaker. He had acquired official experience in an important post. He had been, through all changes of fortune, a consistent Whig. When the Whig party was split into two sections, Pulteney had resigned a valuable place, and had followed the fortunes of Walpole. Yet, when Walpole returned to power, Pulteney was not invited to take office. An angry discussion took place between the friends. The minister offered a peerage. It was impossible for Pulteney not to discern the motive of such an offer. He indignantly refused to accept it. For some time he continued to brood over his wrongs, and to watch for an opportunity of revenge. As soon as a favourable conjuncture arrived he joined the minority, and became the greatest leader of Opposition that the House of Commons had ever seen.

Of all the Members of the Cabinet Carteret was the most eloquent and accomplished. His talents for debate were of the first order; his knowledge of foreign affairs was superior to that of any living statesman; his attachment to the Protestant succession was undoubted. But there was not room in one Government for him and Walpole. Carteret retired, and was, from that time forward, one of the most persevering and formidable enemies of his old colleague.

If there was any man with whom Walpole could have consented to make a partition of power, that man was Lord Townshend. They were distant kinsmen by birth, near kinsmen by marriage. They had been friends from childhood. They had been schoolfellows at Eton. They were country-neighbours in Norfolk. They had been in office together under Godolphin. They had gone into Opposition together when Harley rose to power. They had been persecuted by the same House of Commons. They had, after the death of Anne, been recalled together to office. They had again been driven out together by Sunderland, and had again come back together when the influence of Sunderland had declined. Their opinions on public affairs almost always coincided. They were both men of frank, generous, and compassionate natures. Their intercourse had been for many years affectionate and cordial. But the ties of blood, of marriage, and of friendship, the memory of mutual services, the memory of common triumphs and common disasters, were insufficient to restrain that ambition which domineered over all the virtues and vices of Walpole. He was resolved, to use his own metaphor, that the firm of the house should be, not Townshend and Walpole, but Walpole and Townshend. At length the rivals proceeded to personal abuse before a large company, seized each other by the collar, and grasped their swords. The women squalled. The men parted the combatants. By friendly intervention the scandal of a duel between cousins, brothers-in-law, old friends, and old colleagues, was prevented. But the disputants could not long continue to act together. Townshend retired, and, with rare moderation and public spirit, refused to take any part in politics. He could not, he said, trust his temper. He feared that the recollection of his private wrongs might impel him to follow the example of Pulteney, and to oppose measures which he thought generally beneficial to the country. He therefore never visited London after his resignation, but passed the closing years of his life in dignity and repose among his trees and pictures at Rainham.

Next went Chesterfield. He too was a Whig and a friend of the Protestant succession. He was an orator, a courtier, a wit, and a man of letters. He was at the head of *ton* in days when, in order to be at the head of *ton*, it was not sufficient to be dull and supercilious. It was evident that he submitted impatiently to the ascendency of Walpole. He murmured against the Excise Bill. His brothers voted against it in the House of Commons. The minister acted with characteristic caution and characteristic energy; caution in the conduct of public affairs; energy where his own supremacy was concerned. He withdrew his Bill, and turned out all his hostile or wavering colleagues. Chesterfield was stopped on the great stair-case of St. James's, and summoned to deliver up the staff which he bore as Lord Steward of the Household. A crowd of noble and powerful functionaries, the Dukes of Montrose and Bolton, Lord Burlington, Lord Stair, Lord Cobham, Lord Marchmont, Lord Clinton, were at the same time dismissed from the service of the Crown.

Not long after these events the Opposition was reinforced by the Duke of Argyle, a man vainglorious indeed and fickle, but brave, eloquent, and popular. It was in a great measure owing to his exertions that the Act of Settlement had been peaceably carried into effect in England immediately after the death of Anne, and that the Jacobite rebellion which, during the following year, broke out in Scotland, had been suppressed. He too carried over to the minority the aid of his great name, his talents, and his paramount influence in his native country.

In each of these cases taken separately, a skilful defender of Walpole might perhaps make out a case for him. But when we see that during a long course of years all the footsteps are turned the same way, that all the most eminent of those public men who agreed with the minister in their general views of policy left him, one after another, with sore and irritated minds, we find it impossible not to believe that the real explanation of the phænomenon is to be found in the words of his son, "Sir Robert Walpole loved power so much that he would not endure a rival." Hume has described this famous minister with great felicity in one short sentence,—"moderate in exercising power, not equitable in engrossing it." Kind-hearted, jovial, and placable as Walpole was, he was yet a man with whom no person of high pretensions and high spirit could long continue to act. He had, therefore, to stand

against an Opposition containing all the most accomplished statesmen of the age, with no better support than that which he received
from persons like his brother Horace or Henry Pelham, whose
industrious mediocrity gave no cause for jealousy, or from clever
adventurers, whose situation and character diminished the dread
which their talents might have inspired. To this last class belonged
Fox, who was too poor to live without office; Sir William Yonge, of
whom Walpole himself said, that nothing but such parts could
buoy up such a character, and that nothing but such a character
could drag down such parts; and Winnington, whose private morals
lay, justly or unjustly, under imputations of the worst kind.

The discontented Whigs were, not perhaps in number, but
certainly in ability, experience, and weight, by far the most important part of the Opposition. The Tories furnished little more
than rows of ponderous foxhunters, fat with Staffordshire or
Devonshire ale, men who drank to the king over the water and
believed that all the fundholders were Jews, men whose religion
consisted in hating the Dissenters, and whose political researches
had led them to fear, like Squire Western, that their land might be
sent over to Hanover to be put in the sinking-fund. The eloquence
of these zealous squires, the remnant of the once formidable
October Club, seldom went beyond a hearty Aye or No. Very few
members of this party had distinguished themselves much in
Parliament, or could, under any circumstances, have been called
to fill any high office; and those few had generally, like Sir William
Wyndham, learned in the company of their new associates the
doctrines of toleration and political liberty, and might indeed with
strict propriety be called Whigs.

It was to the Whigs in Opposition, the patriots, as they were
called, that the most distinguished of the English youth who at this
season entered into public life attached themselves. These inexperienced politicians felt all the enthusiasm which the name of
liberty naturally excites in young and ardent minds. They conceived that the theory of the Tory Opposition and the practice of
Walpole's Government were alike inconsistent with the principles
of liberty. They accordingly repaired to the standard which
Pulteney had set up. While opposing the Whig minister, they professed a firm adherence to the purest doctrines of Whiggism. He
was the schismatic; they were the true Catholics, the peculiar
people, the depositaries of the orthodox faith of Hampden and
Russell, the one sect which, amidst the corruptions generated by
time and by the long possession of power, had preserved inviolate
the principles of the Revolution. Of the young men who attached

themselves to this portion of the Opposition the most distinguished were Lyttelton and Pitt.

When Pitt entered Parliament, the whole political world was attentively watching the progress of an event which soon added great strength to the Opposition, and particularly to that section of the Opposition in which the young statesman enrolled himself. The Prince of Wales was gradually becoming more and more estranged from his father and his father's ministers, and more and more friendly to the patriots.

Nothing is more natural than that, in a monarchy where a constitutional Opposition exists, the heir-apparent of the throne should put himself at the head of that Opposition. He is impelled to such a course by every feeling of ambition and of vanity. He cannot be more than second in the estimation of the party which is in. He is sure to be the first member of the party which is out. The highest favour which the existing administration can expect from him is that he will not discard them. But, if he joins the Opposition, all his associates expect that he will promote them; and the feelings which men entertain towards one from whom they hope to obtain great advantages which they have not are far warmer than the feelings with which they regard one who, at the very utmost, can only leave them in possession of what they already have. An heir-apparent, therefore, who wishes to enjoy, in the highest perfection, all the pleasure that can be derived from eloquent flattery and profound respect will always join those who are struggling to force themselves into power. This is, we believe, the true explanation of a fact which Lord Granville attributed to some natural peculiarity in the illustrious house of Brunswick. "This family," said he at Council, we suppose after his daily half-gallon of Burgundy, "always has quarrelled, and always will quarrel, from generation to generation." He should have known something of the matter; for he had been a favourite with three successive generations of the royal house. We cannot quite admit his explanation; but the fact is indisputable. Since the accession of George the First, there have been four Princes of Wales, and they have all been almost constantly in Opposition.

Whatever might have been the motives which induced Prince Frederick to join the party opposed to Sir Robert Walpole, his support infused into many members of that party a courage and an energy of which they stood greatly in need. Hitherto it had been impossible for the discontented Whigs not to feel some misgivings when they found themselves dividing, night after night, with uncompromising Jacobites who were known to be in constant communication with the exiled family, or with Tories who had impeached Somers, who had murmured against Harley and St. John as too remiss in the cause of the Church and the landed interest, and who, if they were not inclined to attack the reigning family, yet considered the introduction of that family as, at best, only the less of two great evils, as a necessary but painful and humiliating preservative against Popery. The minister might plausibly say that Pulteney and Carteret, in the hope of gratifying their own appetite for office and for revenge, did not scruple to serve the purposes of a faction hostile to the Protestant succession. The appearance of Frederick at the head of the patriots silenced this reproach. The leaders of the Opposition might now boast that their course was sanctioned by a person as deeply interested as the King himself in maintaining the Act of Settlement, and that, instead of serving the purposes of the Tory party, they had brought that party over to the side of Whiggism. It must indeed be admitted that, though both the King and the Prince behaved in a manner little to their honour, though the father acted harshly, the son disrespectfully, and both childishly, the royal family was rather strengthened than weakened by the disagreement of its two most distinguished members. A large class of politicians, who had considered themselves as placed under sentence of perpetual exclusion from office, and who, in their despair, had been almost ready to join in a counter-revolution, as the only mode of removing the proscription under which they lay, now saw with pleasure an easier and safer road to power opening before them, and thought it far better to wait till, in the natural course of things, the Crown should descend to the heir of the House of Brunswick, than to risk their lands and their necks in a rising for the House of Stuart. The situation of the royal family resembled the situation of those Scotch families in which father and son took opposite sides during the rebellion, in order that, come what might, the estate might not be forfeited.

In April 1736 Frederick was married to the Princess of Saxe Gotha, with whom he afterwards lived on terms very similar to those on which his father had lived with Queen Caroline. The Prince adored his wife, and thought her in mind and person the most attractive of her sex. But he thought that conjugal fidelity was an unprincely virtue; and, in order to be like Henry the Fourth and the Regent Orleans, he affected a libertinism for which he had no taste, and frequently quitted the only woman whom he loved for ugly and disagreeable mistresses.

The address which the House of Commons presented to the King on occasion of the Prince's marriage was moved, not by the

minister, but by Pulteney, the leader of the Whigs in Opposition.
It was on this motion that Pitt, who had not broken silence during
the session in which he took his seat, addressed the House for the
first time. "A contemporary historian," says Mr. Thackeray,
"describes Mr. Pitt's first speech as superior even to the models of
ancient eloquence. According to Tindal, it was more ornamented
than the speeches of Demosthenes, and less diffuse than those of
Cicero." This unmeaning phrase has been a hundred times quoted.
That it should ever have been quoted, except to be laughed at, is
strange. The vogue which it has obtained may serve to show in
how slovenly a way most people are content to think. Did Tindal,
who first used it, or Archdeacon Coxe and Mr. Thackeray, who
have borrowed it, ever in their lives hear any speaking which did
not deserve the same compliment? Did they ever hear speaking
less ornamented than that of Demosthenes, or more diffuse than
that of Cicero? We know no living orator, from Lord Brougham
down to Mr. Hunt, who is not entitled to the same eulogy. It would
be no very flattering compliment to a man's figure to say, that he
was taller than the Polish Count, and shorter than Giant O'Brien,
fatter than the *Anatomie Vivante*, and more slender than Daniel
Lambert.

Pitt's speech, as it is reported in the Gentleman's Magazine,
certainly deserves Tindal's compliment, and deserves no other. It
is just as empty and wordy as a maiden speech on such an occasion
might be expected to be. But the fluency and the personal advantages of the young orator instantly caught the ear and eye of his
audience. He was, from the day of his first appearance, always
heard with attention; and exercise soon developed the great powers
which he possessed.

In our time, the audience of a member of Parliament is the
nation. The three or four hundred persons who may be present
while a speech is delivered may be pleased or disgusted by the voice
and action of the orator; but, in the reports which are read the next
day by hundreds of thousands, the difference between the noblest
and the meanest figure, between the richest and the shrillest tones,
between the most graceful and the most uncouth gesture, altogether
vanishes. A hundred years ago, scarcely any report of what passed
within the walls of the House of Commons was suffered to get
abroad. In those times, therefore, the impression which a speaker
might make on the persons who actually heard him was every thing.
His fame out of doors depended entirely on the report of those who
were within the doors. In the Parliaments of that time, therefore,
as in the ancient commonwealths, those qualifications which en-

hance the immediate effect of a speech, were far more important ingredients in the composition of an orator than at present. All those qualifications Pitt possessed in the highest degree. On the stage, he would have been the finest Brutus or Coriolanus ever seen. Those who saw him in his decay, when his health was broken, when his mind was untuned, when he had been removed from that stormy assembly of which he thoroughly knew the temper and over which he possessed unbounded influence to a small, a torpid, and an unfriendly audience, say that his speaking was then, for the most part, a low, monotonous muttering, audible only to those who sate close to him, that, when violently excited, he sometimes raised his voice for a few minutes, but that it soon sank again into an unintelligible murmur. Such was the Earl of Chatham; but such was not William Pitt. His figure, when he first appeared in Parliament, was strikingly graceful and commanding, his features high and noble, his eye full of fire. His voice, even when it sank to a whisper, was heard to the remotest benches; and when he strained it to its full extent, the sound rose like the swell of the organ of a great cathedral, shook the house with its peal, and was heard through lobbies and down staircases, to the Court of Requests and the precincts of Westminster Hall. He cultivated all these eminent advantages with the most assiduous care. His action is described by a very malignant observer as equal to that of Garrick. His play of countenance was wonderful: he frequently disconcerted a hostile orator by a single glance of indignation or scorn. Every tone, from the impassioned cry to the thrilling aside, was perfectly at his command. It is by no means improbable that the pains which he took to improve his great personal advantages had, in some respects, a prejudicial operation, and tended to nourish in him that passion for theatrical effect which, as we have already remarked, was one of the most conspicuous blemishes in his character.

But it was not solely or principally to outward accomplishments that Pitt owed the vast influence which, during nearly thirty years, he exercised over the House of Commons. He was undoubtedly a great orator; and, from the descriptions of his contemporaries, and the fragments of his speeches which still remain, it is not difficult to discover the nature and extent of his oratorical powers.

He was no speaker of set speeches. His few prepared discourses were complete failures. The elaborate panegyric which he pronounced on General Wolfe was considered as the very worst of all his performances. "No man," says a critic who had often heard him, "ever knew so little what he was going to say." Indeed his facility amounted to a vice. He was not the master, but the slave of his own speech. So little self-command had he when once he felt the impulse, that he did not like to take part in a debate when his mind was full of an important secret of state. "I must sit still," he once said to Lord Shelburne on such an occasion; "for, when once I am up, every thing that is in my mind comes out."

Yet he was not a great debater. That he should not have been so when first he entered the House of Commons is not strange. Scarcely any person has ever become so without long practice, and many failures. It was by slow degrees, as Burke said, that the late Mr. Fox became the most brilliant and powerful debater that ever lived. Mr. Fox himself attributed his own success to the resolution which he formed when very young, of speaking, well or ill, at least once every night. "During five whole sessions," he used to say, "I spoke every night but one; and I regret only that I did not speak on that night too." Indeed, with the exception of Mr. Stanley, whose knowledge of the science of parliamentary defence resembles an instinct, it would be difficult to name any eminent debater who has not made himself a master of his art at the expense of his audience.

But as this art is one which even the ablest men have seldom acquired without long practice, so it is one which men of respectable abilities, with assiduous and intrepid practice, seldom fail to acquire. It is singular that in such an art, Pitt, a man of splendid talents, of great fluency, of great boldness, a man whose whole life was passed in parliamentary conflict, a man who, during several years, was the leading minister of the Crown in the House of Commons, should never have attained to high excellence. He spoke without premeditation; but his speech followed the course of his own thoughts and not the course of the previous discussion. He could, indeed, treasure up in his memory some detached expression of a hostile orator, and make it the text for lively ridicule or solemn reprehension. Some of the most celebrated bursts of his eloquence were called forth by an unguarded word, a laugh, or a cheer. But this was the only sort of reply in which he appears to have excelled. He was perhaps the only great English orator who did not think it any advantage to have the last word, and who generally spoke by choice before his most formidable opponents. His merit was almost entirely rhetorical. He did not succeed either in exposition or in refutation; but his speeches abounded with lively illustrations, striking apophthegms, well told anecdotes, happy allusions, passionate appeals. His invective and sarcasm were terrific. Perhaps no English orator was ever so much feared.

But that which gave most effect to his declamation was the air of sincerity, of vehement feeling, of moral elevation, which belonged to all that he said. His style was not always in the purest taste. Several contemporary judges pronounced it too florid. Walpole, in the midst of the rapturous eulogy which he pronounces on one of Pitt's greatest orations, owns that some of the metaphors were too forced. Some of Pitt's quotations and classical stories are too trite for a clever schoolboy. But these were niceties for which the audience cared little. The enthusiasm of the orator infected all who heard him; his ardour and his noble bearing put fire into the most frigid conceit, and gave dignity to the most puerile allusion.

His powers soon began to give annoyance to the Government; and Walpole determined to make an example of the patriotic cornet. Pitt was accordingly dismissed from the service. Mr. Thackeray says that the minister took this step, because he plainly saw that it would have been vain to think of buying over so honourable and disinterested an opponent. We do not dispute Pitt's integrity; but we do not know what proof he had given of it when he was turned out of the army; and we are sure that Walpole was not likely to give credit for inflexible honesty to a young adventurer who had never had an opportunity of refusing any thing. The truth is, that it was not Walpole's practice to buy off enemies. Mr. Burke truly says, in the Appeal to the Old Whigs, that Walpole gained very few over from the Opposition. Indeed that great minister knew his business far too well. He knew that for one mouth which is stopped with a place, fifty other mouths will be instantly opened. He knew that it would have been very bad policy in him to give the world to understand that more was to be got by thwarting his measures than by supporting them. These maxims are as old as the origin of parliamentary corruption in England. Pepys learned them, as he tells us, from the counsellors of Charles the Second.

Pitt was no loser. He was made Groom of the Bedchamber to the Prince of Wales, and continued to declaim against the ministers with unabated violence and with increasing ability. The question of maritime right, then agitated between Spain and England, called forth all his powers. He clamoured for war with a vehemence which it is not easy to reconcile with reason or humanity, but which appears to Mr. Thackeray worthy of the highest admiration. We will not stop to argue a point on which we had long thought that all well-informed people were agreed. We could easily show, we think, that, if any respect be due to international law, if right, where societies of men are concerned, be any thing but another name for might, if we do not adopt the doctrine of the Buccaneers, which seems to be also the doctrine of Mr. Thackeray, that treaties mean nothing within thirty degrees of the line, the war with Spain was altogether unjustifiable. But the truth is, that the promoters of that war have saved the historian the trouble of trying them. They have pleaded guilty. "I have seen," says Burke, "and with some care examined, the original documents concerning certain important transactions of those times. They perfectly satisfied me of the extreme injustice of that war, and of the falsehood of the colours which Walpole, to his ruin, and guided by a mistaken policy, suffered to be daubed over that measure. Some years after, it was my fortune to converse with many of the principal actors against that minister, and with those who principally excited that clamour. None of them, no not one, did in the least defend the measure, or attempt to justify their conduct. They condemned it as freely as they would have done in commenting upon any proceeding in history in which they were totally unconcerned." Pitt, on subsequent occasions, gave ample proof that he was one of those tardy penitents. But his conduct, even where it appeared most criminal to himself, appears admirable to his biographer.

The elections of 1741 were unfavourable to Walpole; and after a long and obstinate struggle he found it necessary to resign. The Duke of Newcastle and Lord Hardwicke opened a negotiation with the leading patriots, in the hope of forming an administration on a Whig basis. At this conjuncture, Pitt and those persons who were most nearly connected with him, acted in a manner very little to their honour. They attempted to come to an understanding with Walpole, and offered, if he would use his influence with the King in their favour, to screen him from prosecution. They even went so far as to engage for the concurrence of the Prince of Wales. But Walpole knew that the assistance of the Boys, as he called the young patriots, would avail him nothing if Pulteney and Carteret should prove intractable, and would be superfluous if the great leaders of the Opposition could be gained. He, therefore, declined the proposal. It is remarkable that Mr. Thackeray, who has thought it worth while to preserve Pitt's bad college verses, has not even alluded to this story, a story which is supported by strong testimony, and which may be found in so common a book as Coxe's Life of Walpole.

The new arrangements disappointed almost every member of the Opposition, and none more than Pitt. He was not invited to become a placeman; and he therefore stuck firmly to his old trade of patriot. Fortunate it was for him that he did so. Had he taken office at this time, he would in all probability have shared largely in the unpopularity of Pulteney, Sandys, and Carteret. He was now the fiercest and most implacable of those who called for vengeance on

Walpole. He spoke with great energy and ability in favour of the most unjust and violent propositions which the enemies of the fallen minister could invent. He urged the House of Commons to appoint a secret tribunal for the purpose of investigating the conduct of the late first Lord of the Treasury. This was done. The great majority of the inquisitors were notoriously hostile to the accused statesman. Yet they were compelled to own that they could find no fault in him. They therefore called for new powers, for a bill of indemnity to witnesses, or, in plain words, for a bill to reward all who might give evidence, true or false, against the Earl of Orford. This bill Pitt supported, Pitt, who had himself offered to be a screen between Lord Orford and public justice. These are melancholy facts. Mr. Thackeray omits them, or hurries over them as fast as he can; and, as eulogy is his business, he is in the right to do so. But, though there are many parts of the life of Pitt which it is more agreeable to contemplate, we know none more instructive. What must have been the general state of political morality, when a young man, considered, and justly considered, as the most public-spirited and spotless statesman of his time, could attempt to force his way into office by means so disgraceful!

The Bill of Indemnity was rejected by the Lords. Walpole withdrew himself quietly from the public eye; and the ample space which he had left vacant was soon occupied by Carteret. Against Carteret Pitt began to thunder with as much zeal as he had ever manifested against Sir Robert. To Carteret he transferred most of the hard names which were familiar to his eloquence, sole minister, wicked minister, odious minister, execrable minister. The chief topic of Pitt's invective was the favour shown to the German dominions of the House of Brunswick. He attacked with great violence, and with an ability which raised him to the very first rank among the Parliamentary speakers, the practice of paying Hanoverian troops with English money. The House of Commons had lately lost some of its most distinguished ornaments. Walpole and Pulteney had accepted peerages; Sir William Wyndham was dead; and among the rising men none could be considered as, on the whole, a match for Pitt.

During the recess of 1744, the old Duchess of Marlborough died. She carried to her grave the reputation of being decidedly the best hater of her time. Yet her love had been infinitely more destructive than her hatred. More than thirty years before, her temper had ruined the party to which she belonged and the husband whom she adored. Time had made her neither wiser nor kinder. Whoever was at any moment great and prosperous was the object of her fiercest detestation. She had hated Walpole: she now hated Carteret. Pope, long before her death, predicted the fate of her vast property.

> "To heirs unknown descends the unguarded store,
> Or wanders, heaven-directed, to the poor."

Pitt was then one of the poor; and to him Heaven directed a portion of the wealth of the haughty Dowager. She left him a legacy of ten thousand pounds, in consideration of "the noble defence he had made for the support of the laws of England, and to prevent the ruin of his country."

The will was made in August. The Duchess died in October. In November Pitt was a courtier. The Pelhams had forced the King, much against his will, to part with Lord Carteret, who had now become Earl Granville. They proceeded, after this victory, to form the Government on that basis, called by the cant name of "the broad bottom." Lyttelton had a seat at the Treasury, and several other friends of Pitt were provided for. But Pitt himself was, for the present, forced to be content with promises. The King resented most highly some expressions which the ardent orator had used in the debate on the Hanoverian troops. But Newcastle and Pelham expressed the strongest confidence that time and their exertions would soften the royal displeasure.

Pitt, on his part, omitted nothing that might facilitate his admission to office. He resigned his place in the household of Prince Frederick, and, when Parliament met, exerted his eloquence in support of the Government. The Pelhams were really sincere in their endeavours to remove the strong prejudices which had taken root in the King's mind. They knew that Pitt was not a man to be deceived with ease or offended with impunity. They were afraid that they should not be long able to put him off with promises. Nor was it their interest so to put him off. There was a strong tie between him and them. He was the enemy of their enemy. The brothers hated and dreaded the eloquent, aspiring, and imperious Granville. They had traced his intrigues in many quarters. They knew his influence over the royal mind. They knew that, as soon as a favourable opportunity should arrive, he would be recalled to the head of affairs. They resolved to bring things to a crisis; and the question on which they took issue with their master was, whether Pitt should or should not be admitted to office? They chose their time with more skill than generosity. It was when rebellion was actually raging in Britain, when the Pretender was

master of the northern extremity of the island, that they tendered
their resignations. The King found himself deserted, in one day,
by the whole strength of that party which had placed his family on
the throne. Lord Granville tried to form a government; but it soon
appeared that the Parliamentary interest of the Pelhams was
irresistible; and that the King's favourite statesman could count
only on about thirty Lords and eighty members of the House of
Commons. The scheme was given up. Granville went away
laughing. The ministers came back stronger than ever; and the
King was now no longer able to refuse any thing that they might be
pleased to demand. He could only mutter that it was very hard
that Newcastle, who was not fit to be chamberlain to the most
insignificant prince in Germany, should dictate to the King of
England.

One concession the ministers graciously made. They agreed
that Pitt should not be placed in a situation in which it would be
necessary for him to have frequent interviews with the King.
Instead, therefore, of making their new ally Secretary-at-War, as
they had intended, they appointed him Vice-Treasurer of Ireland,
and in a few months promoted him to the office of Paymaster of the
Forces.

This was, at that time, one of the most lucrative offices in the
Government. The salary was but a small part of the emolument
which the Paymaster derived from his place. He was allowed to
keep a large sum, which, even in time of peace, was seldom less than
one hundred thousand pounds, constantly in his hands; and the
interest on this sum he might appropriate to his own use. This
practice was not secret, nor was it considered as disreputable. It
was the practice of men of undoubted honour, both before and
after the time of Pitt. He, however, refused to accept one farthing
beyond the salary which the law had annexed to his office. It had
been usual for foreign princes who received the pay of England to
give to the Paymaster of the Forces a small per centage on the
subsidies. These ignominious vails Pitt resolutely declined.

Disinterestedness of this kind was, in his days, very rare. His
conduct surprised and amused politicians. It excited the warmest
admiration throughout the body of the people. In spite of the
inconsistencies of which Pitt had been guilty, in spite of the strange
contrast between his violence in Opposition and his tameness in
office, he still possessed a large share of the public confidence. The
motives which may lead a politician to change his connexions or his
general line of conduct are often obscure; but disinterestedness in
pecuniary matters every body can understand. Pitt was thenceforth

considered as a man who was proof to all sordid temptations. If he acted ill, it might be from an error in judgment; it might be from resentment; it might be from ambition. But, poor as he was, he had vindicated himself from all suspicion of covetousness.

Eight quiet years followed, eight years during which the minority, which had been feeble ever since Lord Granville had been overthrown, continued to dwindle till it became almost invisible. Peace was made with France and Spain in 1748. Prince Frederick died in 1751; and with him died the very semblance of Opposition. All the most distinguished survivors of the party which had supported Walpole and of the party which had opposed him were united under his successor. The fiery and vehement spirit of Pitt had for a time been laid to rest. He silently acquiesced in that very system of Continental measures which he had lately condemned. He ceased to talk disrespectfully about Hanover. He did not object to the treaty with Spain, though that treaty left us exactly where we had been when he uttered his spirit-stirring harangues against the pacific policy of Walpole. Now and then glimpses of his former self appeared; but they were few and transient. Pelham knew with whom he had to deal, and felt that an ally, so little used to control, and so capable of inflicting injury, might well be indulged in an occasional fit of waywardness.

Two men, little, if at all, inferior to Pitt in powers of mind, held, like him, subordinate offices in the government. One of these, Murray, was successively Solicitor-General and Attorney-General. This distinguished person far surpassed Pitt in correctness of taste, in power of reasoning, in depth and variety of knowledge. His parliamentary eloquence never blazed into sudden flashes of dazzling brilliancy; but its clear, placid, and mellow splendour was never for an instant overclouded. Intellectually he was, we believe, fully equal to Pitt; but he was deficient in the moral qualities to which Pitt owed most of his success. Murray wanted the energy, the courage, the all-grasping and all-risking ambition, which make men great in stirring times. His heart was a little cold, his temper cautious even to timidity, his manners decorous even to formality. He never exposed his fortunes or his fame to any risk which he could avoid. At one time he might, in all probability, have been Prime Minister. But the object of his wishes was the judicial bench. The situation of Chief Justice might not be so splendid as that of First Lord of the Treasury; but it was dignified; it was quiet; it was secure; and therefore it was the favourite situation of Murray.

Fox, the father of the great man whose mighty efforts in the cause of peace, of truth, and of liberty, have made that name immortal, was Secretary-at-War. He was a favourite with the King, with the Duke of Cumberland, and with some of the most powerful members of the great Whig connexion. His parliamentary talents were of the highest order. As a speaker, he was in almost all respects the very opposite of Pitt. His figure was ungraceful; his face, as Reynolds and Nollekens have preserved it to us, indicated a strong understanding; but the features were coarse, and the general aspect dark and lowering. His manner was awkward; his delivery was hesitating; he was often at a stand for want of a word; but as a debater, as a master of that keen, weighty, manly logic, which is suited to the discussion of political questions, he has perhaps never been surpassed except by his son. In reply he was as decidedly superior to Pitt as in declamation he was Pitt's inferior. Intellectually, the balance was nearly even between the rivals. But here, again, the moral qualities of Pitt turned the scale. Fox had undoubtedly many virtues. In natural disposition, as well as in talents, he bore a great resemblance to his more celebrated son. He had the same sweetness of temper, the same strong passions, the same openness, boldness, and impetuosity, the same cordiality towards friends, the same placability towards enemies. No man was more warmly or justly beloved by his family or by his associates. But unhappily he had been trained in a bad political school, in a school, the doctrines of which were, that political virtue is the mere coquetry of political prostitution, that every patriot has his price, that government can be carried on only by means of corruption, and that the state is given as a prey to statesmen. These maxims were too much in vogue throughout the lower ranks of Walpole's party, and were too much encouraged by Walpole himself, who, from contempt of what is in our day vulgarly called *humbug*, often ran extravagantly and offensively into the opposite extreme. The loose political morality of Fox presented a remarkable contrast to the ostentatious purity of Pitt. The nation distrusted the former, and placed implicit confidence in the latter. But almost all the statesmen of the age had still to learn that the confidence of the nation was worth having. While things went on quietly, while there was no Opposition, while every thing was given by the favour of a small ruling junto, Fox had a decided advantage over Pitt; but when dangerous times came, when Europe was convulsed with war, when Parliament was broken up into factions, when the public mind was violently excited, the favourite of the people rose to supreme power, while his rival sank into insignificance.

Early in the year 1754 Henry Pelham died unexpectedly. "Now I shall have no more peace," exclaimed the old King, when he heard the news. He was in the right. Pelham had succeeded in bringing together and keeping together all the talents of the kingdom. By his death, the highest post to which an English subject can aspire was left vacant; and, at the same moment, the influence which had yoked together and reined in so many turbulent and ambitious spirits was withdrawn.

Within a week after Pelham's death, it was determined that the Duke of Newcastle should be placed at the head of the Treasury; but the arrangement was still far from complete. Who was to be the leading Minister of the Crown in the House of Commons? Was the office to be intrusted to a man of eminent talents? And would not such a man in such a place demand and obtain a larger share of power and patronage than Newcastle would be disposed to concede? Was a mere drudge to be employed? And what probability was there that a mere drudge would be able to manage a large and stormy assembly, abounding with able and experienced men?

Pope has said of that wretched miser Sir John Cutler,

> "Cutler saw tenants break and houses fall
> For very want: he could not build a wall."

Newcastle's love of power resembled Cutler's love of money. It was an avarice which thwarted itself, a penny-wise and pound-foolish cupidity. An immediate outlay was so painful to him that he would not venture to make the most desirable improvement. If he could have found it in his heart to cede at once a portion of his authority, he might probably have ensured the continuance of what remained. But he thought it better to construct a weak and rotten government, which tottered at the smallest breath, and fell in the first storm, than to pay the necessary price for sound and durable materials. He wished to find some person who would be willing to accept the lead of the House of Commons on terms similar to those on which Secretary Craggs had acted under Sunderland, five-and-thirty years before. Craggs could hardly be called a minister. He was a mere agent for the minister. He was not trusted with the higher secrets of state, but obeyed implicitly the directions of his superior, and was, to use Doddington's expression, merely Lord Sunderland's man. But times were changed. Since the days of Sunderland, the importance of the House of Commons had been constantly on the increase. During many years, the person who conducted the business of the Government in that House had almost always been Prime Minister. Under these circumstances, it was not to be supposed that any person who possessed the talents necessary for the situation, would stoop to accept it on such terms as Newcastle was disposed to offer.

Pitt was ill at Bath; and, had he been well and in London, neither the King nor Newcastle would have been disposed to make any overtures to him. The cool and wary Murray had set his heart on professional objects. Negotiations were opened with Fox. Newcastle behaved like himself, that is to say, childishly and basely. The proposition which he made was, that Fox should be Secretary of State, with the lead of the House of Commons; that the disposal of the secret-service-money, or, in plain words, the business of buying members of Parliament, should be left to the First Lord of the Treasury; but that Fox should be exactly informed of the way in which this fund was employed.

To these conditions Fox assented. But the next day every thing was in confusion. Newcastle had changed his mind. The conversation which took place between Fox and the Duke is one of the most curious in English history. "My brother," said Newcastle, "when he was at the Treasury, never told any body what he did with the secret-service-money. No more will I." The answer was obvious. Pelham had been, not only First Lord of the Treasury, but also manager of the House of Commons; and it was therefore unnecessary for him to confide to any other person his dealings with the members of that house. "But how," said Fox, "can I lead in the Commons without information on this head? How can I talk to gentlemen when I do not know which of them have received gratifications and which have not? And who," he continued, "is to have the disposal of places?"—"I myself," said the Duke.—"How then am I to manage the House of Commons?"—"Oh, let the members of the House of Commons come to me." Fox then mentioned the general election which was approaching, and asked how the ministerial boroughs were to be filled up. "Do not trouble yourself," said Newcastle; "that is all settled." This was too much for human nature to bear. Fox refused to accept the Secretaryship of State on such terms; and the Duke confided the management of the House of Commons to a dull, harmless man, whose name is almost forgotten in our time, Sir Thomas Robinson.

When Pitt returned from Bath he affected great moderation, though his haughty soul was boiling with resentment. He did not complain of the manner in which he had been passed by, but said openly that, in his opinion, Fox was the fittest man to lead the House of Commons. The rivals, reconciled by their common interest and their common enmities, concerted a plan of operations for the next session. "Sir Thomas Robinson lead us!" said Pitt to Fox. "The Duke might as well send his jack-boot to lead us."

The elections of 1754 were favourable to the administration. But the aspect of foreign affairs was threatening. In India the English and the French had been employed, ever since the peace of Aix-la-Chapelle, in cutting each other's throats. They had lately taken to the same practice in America. It might have been foreseen that stirring times were at hand, times which would call for abilities very different from those of Newcastle and Robinson.

In November the Parliament met; and before the end of that month the new Secretary of State had been so unmercifully baited by the Paymaster of the Forces and the Secretary-at-War that he was thoroughly sick of his situation. Fox attacked him with great force and acrimony. Pitt affected a kind of contemptuous tenderness for Sir Thomas, and directed his attacks principally against Newcastle. On one occasion, he asked in tones of thunder whether Parliament sat only to register the edicts of one too-powerful subject? The Duke was scared out of his wits. He was afraid to dismiss the mutineers; he was afraid to promote them; but it was absolutely necessary to do something. Fox, as the less proud and intractable of the refractory pair, was preferred. A seat in the Cabinet was offered to him, on condition that he would give efficient support to the ministry in Parliament. In an evil hour for his fame and his fortunes he accepted the offer, and abandoned his connexion with Pitt, who never forgave this desertion.

Sir Thomas, assisted by Fox, contrived to get through the business of the year without much trouble. Pitt was waiting his time. The negotiations pending between France and England took every day a more unfavourable aspect. Towards the close of the session the King sent a message to inform the House of Commons that he had found it necessary to make preparations for war. The House returned an address of thanks, and passed a vote of credit. During the recess, the old animosity of both nations was inflamed by a series of disastrous events. An English force was cut off in America; and several French merchantmen were taken in the West Indian seas. It was plain that an appeal to arms was at hand.

The first object of the King was to secure Hanover; and Newcastle was disposed to gratify his master. Treaties were concluded, after the fashion of those times, with several petty German princes, who bound themselves to find soldiers if England would find money; and, as it was suspected that Frederic the Second had set his heart on the electoral dominions of his uncle, Russia was hired to keep Prussia in awe.

When the stipulations of these treaties were made known, there arose throughout the kingdom a murmur from which a judicious observer might easily prognosticate the approach of a tempest. Newcastle encountered strong opposition, even from those whom he had always considered as his tools. Legge, the Chancellor of the Exchequer, refused to sign the Treasury warrants which were necessary to give effect to the treaties. Those persons who were supposed to possess the confidence of the young Prince of Wales and of his mother held very menacing language. In this perplexity Newcastle sent for Pitt, hugged him, patted him, smirked at him, wept over him, and lisped out the highest compliments and the most splendid promises. The King, who had hitherto been as sulky as possible, would be civil to him at the levee; he should be brought into the Cabinet; he should be consulted about every thing; if he would only be so good as to support the Hessian subsidy in the House of Commons. Pitt coldly declined the proffered seat in the Cabinet, expressed the highest love and reverence for the King, and said that, if his Majesty felt a strong personal interest in the Hessian treaty, he would so far deviate from the line which he had traced out for himself as to give that treaty his support. "Well, and the Russian subsidy," said Newcastle. "No," said Pitt, "not a system of subsidies." The Duke summoned Lord Hardwicke to his aid; but Pitt was inflexible. Murray would do nothing. Robinson could do nothing. It was necessary to have recourse to Fox. He became Secretary of State, with the full authority of a leader in the House of Commons; and Sir Thomas was pensioned off on the Irish establishment.

In November 1755 the Houses met. Public expectation was wound up to the height. After ten quiet years there was to be an Opposition, countenanced by the heir-apparent of the throne, and headed by the most brilliant orator of the age. The debate on the address was long remembered as one of the greatest parliamentary conflicts of that generation. It began at three in the afternoon, and lasted till five the next morning. It was on this night that Gerard Hamilton delivered that single speech from which his nickname was derived. His eloquence threw into the shade every orator except Pitt, who declaimed against the subsidies for an hour and a half with extraordinary energy and effect. Those powers which had formerly spread terror through the majorities of Walpole and Carteret were now displayed in their highest perfection before an audience long unaccustomed to such exhibitions. One fragment of this celebrated oration remains in a state of tolerable preservation. It is the comparison between the coalition of Fox and Newcastle, and the junction of the Rhone and the Saone. "At Lyons," said Pitt, "I was taken to see the place where the two rivers meet, the one gentle, feeble, languid, and, though languid, yet of no depth, the other a boisterous and impetuous torrent; but different as they are, they meet at last." The amendment moved by the Opposition was rejected by a great majority; and Pitt and Legge were immediately dismissed from their offices.

During several months the contest in the House of Commons was extremely sharp. Warm debates took place on the estimates, debates still warmer on the subsidiary treaties. The Government succeeded in every division; but the fame of Pitt's eloquence, and the influence of his lofty and determined character, continued to increase through the Session; and the events which followed the prorogation made it utterly impossible for any other person to manage the Parliament or the country.

The war began in every part of the world with events disastrous to England, and even more shameful than disastrous. But the most humiliating of these events was the loss of Minorca. The Duke of Richelieu, an old fop who had passed his life from sixteen to sixty in seducing women for whom he cared not one straw, landed on that island, and succeeded in reducing it. Admiral Byng was sent from Gibraltar to throw succours into Port-Mahon; but he did not think fit to engage the French squadron, and sailed back without having effected his purpose. The people were inflamed to madness. A storm broke forth, which appalled even those who remembered the days of Excise and of South-Sea. The shops were filled with libels and caricatures. The walls were covered with placards. The city of London called for vengeance, and the cry was echoed from every corner of the kingdom. Dorsetshire, Huntingdonshire, Bedfordshire, Buckinghamshire, Somersetshire, Lancashire, Suffolk, Shropshire, Surrey, sent up strong addresses to the throne, and instructed their representatives to vote for a strict inquiry into the causes of the late disasters. In the great towns the feeling was as strong as in the counties. In some of the instructions it was even recommended that the supplies should be stopped.

The nation was in a state of angry and sullen despondency, almost unparalleled in history. People have, in all ages, been in the habit of talking about the good old times of their ancestors, and the degeneracy of their contemporaries. This is in general merely a cant. But in 1756 it was something more. At this time appeared Brown's Estimate, a book now remembered only by the allusions in Cowper's Table Talk and in Burke's Letters on a Regicide Peace. It was universally read, admired, and believed. The author fully convinced his readers that they were a race of cowards and scoundrels; that nothing could save them; that they were on the point of being enslaved by their enemies, and that they richly deserved their fate. Such were the speculations to which ready credence was given at the outset of the most glorious war in which England had ever been engaged.

Newcastle now began to tremble for his place, and for the only thing which was dearer to him than his place, his neck. The people were not in a mood to be trifled with. Their cry was for blood. For this once they might be contented with the sacrifice of Byng. But what if fresh disasters should take place? What if an unfriendly sovereign should ascend the throne? What if a hostile House of Commons should be chosen?

At length, in October, the decisive crisis came. The new Secretary of State had been long sick of the perfidy and levity of the First Lord of the Treasury, and began to fear that he might be made a scapegoat to save the old intriguer who, imbecile as he seemed, never wanted dexterity where danger was to be avoided. Fox threw up his office. Newcastle had recourse to Murray; but Murray had now within his reach the favourite object of his ambition. The situation of Chief-Justice of the King's Bench was vacant; and the Attorney-General was fully resolved to obtain it, or to go into Opposition. Newcastle offered him any terms, the Duchy of Lancaster for life, a tellership of the Exchequer, any amount of pension, two thousand a year, six thousand a year. When the ministers found that Murray's mind was made up, they pressed for delay, the delay of a session, a month, a week, a day. Would he only make his appearance once more in the House of Commons? Would he only speak in favour of the address? He was inexorable, and peremptorily said that they might give or withhold the Chief-Justiceship, but that he would be Attorney-General no longer.

Newcastle now contrived to overcome the prejudices of the King, and overtures were made to Pitt, through Lord Hardwicke. Pitt knew his power, and showed that he knew it. He demanded as an indispensable condition that Newcastle should be altogether excluded from the new arrangement.

The Duke was now in a state of ludicrous distress. He ran about chattering and crying, asking advice and listening to none. In the meantime, the Session drew near. The public excitement was unabated. Nobody could be found to face Pitt and Fox in the House of Commons. Newcastle's heart failed him, and he tendered his resignation.

The King sent for Fox, and directed him to form the plan of an administration in concert with Pitt. But Pitt had not forgotten old injuries, and positively refused to act with Fox.

The King now applied to the Duke of Devonshire, and this mediator succeeded in making an arrangement. He consented to take the Treasury. Pitt became Secretary of State, with the lead of the House of Commons. The Great Seal was put into commission. Legge returned to the Exchequer; and Lord Temple, whose sister Pitt had lately married, was placed at the head of the Admiralty.

It was clear from the first that this administration would last but a very short time. It lasted not quite five months; and, during those five months, Pitt and Lord Temple were treated with rudeness by the King, and found but feeble support in the House of Commons. It is a remarkable fact, that the Opposition prevented the reelection of some of the new ministers. Pitt, who sat for one of the boroughs which were in the Pelham interest, found some difficulty in obtaining a seat after his acceptance of the seals. So destitute was the new Government of that sort of influence without which no government could then be durable. One of the arguments most frequently urged against the Reform Bill was that, under a system of popular representation, men whose presence in the House of Commons was necessary to the conducting of public business might often find it impossible to find seats. Should this inconvenience ever be felt, there cannot be the slightest difficulty in devising and applying a remedy. But those who threatened us with this evil ought to have remembered that, under the old system, a great man called to power at a great crisis by the voice of the whole nation was in danger of being excluded, by an aristocratical cabal, from that House of which he was the most distinguished ornament.

The most important event of this short administration was the trial of Byng. On that subject public opinion is still divided. We think the punishment of the Admiral altogether unjust and absurd. Treachery, cowardice, ignorance amounting to what lawyers have called *crassa ignorantia*, are fit objects of severe penal inflictions. But Byng was not found guilty of treachery, of cowardice, or of gross ignorance of his profession. He died for doing what the most loyal subject, the most intrepid warrior, the most experienced seaman, might have done. He died for an error in judgment, an error, such as the greatest commanders, Frederic, Napoleon, Wellington, have often committed, and have often acknowledged. Such errors are not proper objects of punishment, for this reason, that the punishing of such errors tends not to prevent them, but to produce them. The dread of an ignominious death may stimulate sluggishness to exertion, may keep a traitor to his standard, may prevent a coward from running away, but it has no tendency to bring out those qualities which enable men to form prompt and judicious decisions in great emergencies. The best marksman may be expected to fail when the apple which is to be his mark is set on his child's head. We cannot conceive anything more likely to deprive an officer of his self-possession at the time when he most needs it than the knowledge that, if the judgment of his superiors should not agree with his, he will be executed with every circumstance of shame. Queens, it has often been said, run far greater risk in childbed than private women, merely because their medical attendants are more anxious. The surgeon who attended Marie Louise was altogether unnerved by his emotions. "Compose yourself," said Bonaparte; "imagine that you are assisting a poor girl in the Faubourg St. Antoine." This was surely a far wiser course than that of the Eastern king in the Arabian Nights' Entertainments, who proclaimed that the physicians who failed to cure his daughter should have their heads chopped off. Bonaparte knew mankind well; and, as he acted towards this surgeon, he acted towards his officers. No sovereign was ever so indulgent to mere errors of judgment; and it is certain that no sovereign ever had in his service so many military men fit for the highest commands.

Pitt acted a brave and honest part on this occasion. He ventured to put both his power and his popularity to hazard, and spoke manfully for Byng, both in Parliament and in the royal presence. But the King was inexorable. "The House of Commons, Sir," said Pitt, "seems inclined to mercy." "Sir," answered the King, "you have taught me to look for the sense of my people in other places than the House of Commons." The saying has more point than most of those which are recorded of George the Second, and, though sarcastically meant, contains a high and just compliment to Pitt.

The King disliked Pitt, but absolutely hated Temple. The new Secretary of State, his Majesty said, had never read Vatel, and was tedious and pompous, but respectful. The First Lord of the Admiralty was grossly impertinent. Walpole tells one story, which, we fear, is much too good to be true. He assures us that Temple entertained his royal master with an elaborate parallel between Byng's behaviour at Minorca, and his Majesty's behaviour at Oudenarde, in which the advantage was all on the side of the Admiral.

This state of things could not last. Early in April, Pitt and all his

M—10*

friends were turned out, and Newcastle was summoned to St.
James's. But the public discontent was not extinguished. It had
subsided when Pitt was called to power. But it still glowed under
the embers; and it now burst at once into a flame. The stocks fell.
The Common Council met. The freedom of the city was voted to
Pitt. All the greatest corporate towns followed the example. "For
some weeks," says Walpole, "it rained gold boxes."

This was the turning point of Pitt's life. It might have been
expected that a man of so haughty and vehement a nature, treated
so ungraciously by the Court, and supported so enthusiastically by
the people, would have eagerly taken the first opportunity of showing
his power and gratifying his resentment; and an opportunity was
not wanting. The members for many counties and large towns had
been instructed to vote for an inquiry into the circumstances which
had produced the miscarriage of the preceding year. A motion for
inquiry had been carried in the House of Commons, without
opposition; and, a few days after Pitt's dismissal, the investigation
commenced. Newcastle and his colleagues obtained a vote of
acquittal; but the minority was so strong that they could not
venture to ask for a vote of approbation, as they had at first intended; and it was thought by some shrewd observers that, if Pitt
had exerted himself to the utmost of his power, the inquiry might
have ended in a censure, if not in an impeachment.

Pitt showed on this occasion a moderation and self-government
which were not habitual to him. He had found by experience, that
he could not stand alone. His eloquence and his popularity had
done much, very much for him. Without rank, without fortune,
without borough interest, hated by the King, hated by the aristocracy, he was a person of the first importance in the state. He
had been suffered to form a ministry, and to pronounce sentence of
exclusion on all his rivals, on the most powerful nobleman of the
Whig party, on the ablest debater in the House of Commons. And
he now found that he had gone too far. The English Constitution
was not, indeed, without a popular element. But other elements
generally predominated. The confidence and admiration of the
nation might make a statesman formidable at the head of an Opposition, might load him with framed and glazed parchments and gold
boxes, might possibly, under very peculiar circumstances, such as
those of the preceding year, raise him for a time to power. But,
constituted as Parliament then was, the favourite of the people
could not depend on a majority in the people's own House. The
Duke of Newcastle, however contemptible in morals, manners, and
understanding, was a dangerous enemy. His rank, his wealth, his

unrivalled parliamentary interest, would alone have made him important. But this was not all. The Whig aristocracy regarded him as their leader. His long possession of power had given him a kind of prescriptive right to possess it still. The House of Commons had been elected when he was at the head of affairs. The members for the ministerial boroughs had all been nominated by him. The public offices swarmed with his creatures.

Pitt desired power, and he desired it, we really believe, from high and generous motives. He was, in the strict sense of the word, a patriot. He had none of that philanthropy which the great French writers of his time preached to all the nations of Europe. He loved England as an Athenian loved the City of the Violet Crown, as a Roman loved the City of the Seven Hills. He saw his country insulted and defeated. He saw the national spirit sinking. Yet he knew what the resources of the empire, vigorously employed, could effect; and he felt that he was the man to employ them vigorously. "My Lord," he said to the Duke of Devonshire, "I am sure that I can save this country, and that nobody else can."

Desiring, then, to be in power, and feeling that his abilities and the public confidence were not alone sufficient to keep him in power against the wishes of the Court and of the aristocracy, he began to think of a coalition with Newcastle.

Newcastle was equally disposed to a reconciliation. He, too, had profited by his recent experience. He had found that the Court and the aristocracy, though powerful, were not every thing in the state. A strong oligarchical connexion, a great borough interest, ample patronage, and secret-service-money, might, in quiet times, be all that a minister needed; but it was unsafe to trust wholly to such support in time of war, of discontent, and of agitation. The composition of the House of Commons was not wholly aristocratical; and, whatever be the composition of large deliberative assemblies, their spirit is always in some degree popular. Where there are free debates, eloquence must have admirers, and reason must make converts. Where there is a free press, the governors must live in constant awe of the opinions of the governed.

Thus these two men, so unlike in character, so lately mortal enemies, were necessary to each other. Newcastle had fallen in November, for want of that public confidence which Pitt possessed and of that parliamentary support which Pitt was better qualified than any man of his time to give. Pitt had fallen in April, for want of that species of influence which Newcastle had passed his whole life in acquiring and hoarding. Neither of them had power enough to support himself. Each of them had power enough to overturn the other. Their union would be irresistible. Neither the King nor any party in the state would be able to stand against them.

Under these circumstances, Pitt was not disposed to proceed to extremities against his predecessors in office. Something, however, was due to consistency; and something was necessary for the preservation of his popularity. He did little; but that little he did in such a manner as to produce great effect. He came down to the House in all the pomp of gout, his legs swathed in flannels, his arm dangling in a sling. He kept his seat, through several fatiguing days, in spite of pain and languor. He uttered a few sharp and vehement sentences; but, during the greater part of the discussion, his language was unusually gentle.

When the inquiry had terminated without a vote either of approbation or of censure, the great obstacle to a coalition was removed. Many obstacles, however, remained. The King was still rejoicing in his deliverance from the proud and aspiring minister who had been forced on him by the cry of the nation. His Majesty's indignation was excited to the highest point when it appeared that Newcastle who had, during thirty years, been loaded with marks of royal favour, and who had bound himself, by a solemn promise, never to coalesce with Pitt, was meditating a new perfidy. Of all the statesmen of that age, Fox had the largest share of royal favour. A coalition between Fox and Newcastle was the arrangement which the King wished to bring about. But the Duke was too cunning to fall into such a snare. As a speaker in Parliament, Fox might perhaps be, on the whole, as useful to an administration as his great rival; but he was one of the most unpopular men in England. Then, again, Newcastle felt all that jealousy of Fox which, according to the proverb, generally exists between two of a trade. Fox would certainly intermeddle with that department which the Duke was most desirous to reserve entire to himself, the jobbing department. Pitt, on the other hand, was quite willing to leave the drudgery of corruption to any who might be inclined to undertake it.

During eleven weeks England remained without a ministry; and in the meantime Parliament was sitting, and a war was raging. The prejudices of the King, the haughtiness of Pitt, the jealousy, levity, and treachery of Newcastle, delayed the settlement. Pitt knew the Duke too well to trust him without security. The Duke loved power too much to be inclined to give security. While they were haggling, the King was in vain attempting to produce a final rupture between them, or to form a Government without them. At one time he applied to Lord Waldégrave, an honest and sensible man, but unpractised in affairs. Lord Waldégrave had the courage to accept the Treasury, but soon found that no administration formed by him had the smallest chance of standing a single week.

At length the King's pertinacity yielded to the necessity of the case. After exclaiming with great bitterness, and with some justice, against the Whigs, who ought, he said, to be ashamed to talk about liberty while they submitted to be the footmen of the Duke of Newcastle, his Majesty submitted. The influence of Leicester House prevailed on Pitt to abate a little, and but a little, of his high demands; and all at once, out of the chaos in which parties had for some time been rising, falling, meeting, separating, arose a government as strong at home as that of Pelham, as successful abroad as that of Godolphin.

Newcastle took the Treasury. Pitt was Secretary of State, with the lead in the House of Commons, and with the supreme direction of the war and of foreign affairs. Fox, the only man who could have given much annoyance to the new Government, was silenced with the office of Paymaster, which, during the continuance of that war, was probably the most lucrative place in the whole Government. He was poor, and the situation was tempting; yet it cannot but seem extraordinary that a man who had played a first part in politics, and whose abilities had been found not unequal to that part, who had sat in the Cabinet, who had led the House of Commons, who had been twice intrusted by the King with the office of forming a ministry, who was regarded as the rival of Pitt, and who at one time seemed likely to be a successful rival, should have consented, for the sake of emolument, to take a subordinate place, and to give silent votes for all the measures of a government to the deliberations of which he was not summoned.

The first measures of the new administration were characterized rather by vigour than by judgment. Expeditions were sent against different parts of the French coast with little success. The small island of Aix was taken, Rochefort threatened, a few ships burned in the harbour of St. Maloes, and a few guns and mortars brought home as trophies from the fortifications of Cherbourg. But soon conquests of a very different kind filled the kingdom with pride and rejoicing. A succession of victories, undoubtedly brilliant, and, as it was thought, not barren, raised to the highest point the fame of the minister to whom the conduct of the war had been intrusted. In July 1758 Louisburg fell. The whole island of Cape Breton was reduced. The fleet to which the court of Versailles had confided the defence of French America was destroyed. The captured standards were borne in triumph from Kensington Palace to the city, and were suspended in St. Paul's Church, amidst the roar of guns and kettle-drums, and the shouts of an immense multitude. Addresses of congratulation came in from all the great towns of England. Parliament met only to decree thanks and monuments, and to bestow, without one murmur, supplies more than double of those which had been given during the war of the Grand Alliance.

The year 1759 opened with the conquest of Goree. Next fell Guadaloupe; then Ticonderoga; then Niagara. The Toulon squadron was completely defeated by Boscawen off Cape Lagos. But the greatest exploit of the year was the achievement of Wolfe on the heights of Abraham. The news of his glorious death and of the fall of Quebec reached London in the very week in which the Houses met. All was joy and triumph. Envy and faction were forced to join in the general applause. Whigs and Tories vied with each other in extolling the genius and energy of Pitt. His colleagues were never talked of or thought of. The House of Commons, the nation, the colonies, our allies, our enemies, had their eyes fixed on him alone.

Scarcely had Parliament voted a monument to Wolfe when another great event called for fresh rejoicings. The Brest fleet, under the command of Conflans, had put out to sea. It was overtaken by an English squadron under Hawke. Conflans attempted to take shelter close under the French coast. The shore was rocky: the night was black: the wind was furious: the waves of the Bay of Biscay ran high. But Pitt had infused into every branch of the service a spirit which had long been unknown. No British seaman was disposed to err on the same side with Byng. The pilot told Hawke that the attack could not be made without the greatest danger. "You have done your duty in remonstrating," answered Hawke; "I will answer for every thing. I command you to lay me alongside the French admiral." Two French ships of the line struck. Four were destroyed. The rest hid themselves in the rivers of Britanny.

The year 1760 came; and still triumph followed triumph. Montreal was taken; the whole province of Canada was subjugated; the French fleets underwent a succession of disasters in the seas of Europe and America.

In the mean time conquests equalling in rapidity, and far surpassing in magnitude, those of Cortes and Pizarro, had been achieved in the East. In the space of three years the English had founded a mighty empire. The French had been defeated in every part of India. Chandernagore had surrendered to Clive, Pondicherry to Coote. Throughout Bengal, Bahar, Orissa, and the Carnatic, the authority of the East India Company was more absolute than that of Acbar or Aurungzebe had ever been.

On the continent of Europe the odds were against England. We had but one important ally, the King of Prussia; and he was attacked, not only by France, but also by Russia and Austria. Yet even on the Continent the energy of Pitt triumphed over all difficulties. Vehemently as he had condemned the practice of subsidising foreign princes, he now carried that practice farther than Carteret himself would have ventured to do. The active and able Sovereign of Prussia received such pecuniary assistance as enabled him to maintain the conflict on equal terms against his powerful enemies. On no subject had Pitt ever spoken with so much eloquence and ardour as on the mischiefs of the Hanoverian connexion. He now declared, not without much show of reason, that it would be unworthy of the English people to suffer their King to be deprived of his electoral dominions in an English quarrel. He assured his countrymen that they should be no losers, and that he would conquer America for them in Germany. By taking this line he conciliated the King, and lost no part of his influence with the nation. In Parliament, such was the ascendency which his eloquence, his success, his high situation, his pride, and his intrepidity had obtained for him, that he took liberties with the House of which there had been no example, and which have never since been imitated. No orator could there venture to reproach him with inconsistency. One unfortunate man made the attempt, and was so much disconcerted by the scornful demeanour of the minister that he stammered, stopped, and sat down. Even the old Tory country gentlemen, to whom the very name of Hanover had been odious, gave their hearty Ayes to subsidy after subsidy. In a lively contemporary satire, much more lively indeed than delicate, this remarkable conversion is not unhappily described.

> "No more they make a fiddle-faddle
>   About a Hessian horse or saddle.
> No more of continental measures;
> No more of wasting British treasures.
> Ten millions, and a vote of credit,
>   'Tis right. He can't be wrong who did it."

The success of Pitt's continental measures was such as might have been expected from their vigour. When he came into power, Hanover was in imminent danger; and, before he had been in office three months, the whole electorate was in the hands of France.

But the face of affairs was speedily changed. The invaders were driven out. An army, partly English, partly Hanoverian, partly composed of soldiers furnished by the petty princes of Germany, was placed under the command of Prince Ferdinand of Brunswick. The French were beaten in 1758 at Crevelt. In 1759, they received a still more complete and humiliating defeat at Minden.

In the mean time, the nation exhibited all the signs of wealth and prosperity. The merchants of London had never been more thriving. The importance of several great commercial and manufacturing towns, of Glasgow in particular, dates from this period. The fine inscription on the monument of Lord Chatham in Guildhall records the general opinion of the citizens of London, that under his administration commerce had been "united with and made to flourish by war."

It must be owned that these signs of prosperity were in some degree delusive. It must be owned that some of our conquests were rather splendid than useful. It must be owned that the expense of the war never entered into Pitt's consideration. Perhaps it would be more correct to say that the cost of his victories increased the pleasure with which he contemplated them. Unlike other men in his situation, he loved to exaggerate the sums which the nation was laying out under his direction. He was proud of the sacrifices and efforts which his eloquence and his success had induced his countrymen to make. The price at which he purchased faithful service and complete victory, though far smaller than that which his son, the most profuse and incapable of war ministers, paid for treachery, defeat, and shame, was long and severely felt by the nation.

Even as a war minister, Pitt is scarcely entitled to all the praise which his contemporaries lavished on him. We, perhaps from ignorance, cannot discern in his arrangements any appearance of profound or dexterous combination. Several of his expeditions, particularly those which were sent to the coast of France, were at once costly and absurd. Our Indian conquests, though they add to the splendour of the period during which he was at the head of affairs, were not planned by him. He had undoubtedly great energy, great determination, great means at his command. His temper was enterprising; and, situated as he was, he had only to follow his temper. The wealth of a rich nation, the valour of a brave nation were ready to support him in every attempt.

In one respect, however, he deserved all the praise that he has ever received. The success of our arms was perhaps owing less to the skill of his dispositions than to the national resources and the national spirit. But that the national spirit rose to the emergency, that the national resources were contributed with unexampled cheerfulness, this was undoubtedly his work. The ardour of his soul had set the whole kingdom on fire. It inflamed every soldier who dragged the cannon up the heights of Quebec, and every sailor who boarded the French ships among the rocks of Britanny. The minister, before he had been long in office, had imparted to the commanders whom he employed his own impetuous, adventurous, and defying character. They, like him, were disposed to risk every thing, to play double or quits to the last, to think nothing done while any thing remained undone, fail rather than not to attempt. For the errors of rashness there might be indulgence. For over-caution, for faults like those of Lord George Sackville, there was no mercy. In other times, and against other enemies, this mode of warfare might have failed. But the state of the French government and of the French nation gave every advantage to Pitt. The fops and intriguers of Versailles were appalled and bewildered by his vigour. A panic spread through all ranks of society. Our enemies soon considered it as a settled thing that they were always to be beaten. Thus victory begot victory; till, at last, wherever the forces of the two nations met, they met with disdainful confidence on the one side, and with a craven fear on the other.

The situation which Pitt occupied at the close of the reign of George the Second was the most enviable ever occupied by any public man in English history. He had conciliated the King; he domineered over the House of Commons; he was adored by the people; he was admired by all Europe. He was the first English-man of his time; and he had made England the first country in the world. The Great Commoner, the name by which he was often designated, might look down with scorn on coronets and garters. The nation was drunk with joy and pride. The Parliament was as quiet as it had been under Pelham. The old party distinctions were almost effaced; nor was their place yet supplied by distinctions of a still more important kind. A new generation of country squires and rectors had arisen who knew not the Stuarts. The Dissenters were tolerated; the Catholics not cruelly persecuted. The Church was drowsy and indulgent. The great civil and religious conflict which began at the Reformation seemed to have terminated in universal repose. Whigs and Tories, Churchmen and Puritans, spoke with equal reverence of the constitution, and with equal enthusiasm of the talents, virtues, and services of the minister.

A few years sufficed to change the whole aspect of affairs. A nation convulsed by faction, a throne assailed by the fiercest invective, a House of Commons hated and despised by the nation, England set against Scotland, Britain set against America, a rival legislature sitting beyond the Atlantic, English blood shed by English bayonets, our armies capitulating, our conquests wrested from us, our enemies hastening to take vengeance for past humiliation, our flag scarcely able to maintain itself in our own seas, such was the spectacle which Pitt lived to see. But the history of this great revolution requires far more space than we can at present bestow. We leave the Great Commoner in the zenith of his glory. It is not impossible that we may take some other opportunity of tracing his life to its melancholy, yet not inglorious close.

LORD CLIVE

(JANUARY 1840)

The Life of Robert Lord Clive; collected from the Family Papers, communicated by the Earl of Powis. By MAJOR-GENERAL SIR JOHN MALCOLM, K.C.B. 3 vols. 8vo. London: 1836.

WE have always thought it strange that, while the history of the Spanish empire in America is familiarly known to all the nations of Europe, the great actions of our countrymen in the East should, even among ourselves, excite little interest. Every schoolboy knows who imprisoned Montezuma, and who strangled Atahualpa. But we doubt whether one in ten, even among English gentlemen of highly cultivated minds, can tell who won the battle of Buxar, who perpetrated the massacre of Patna, whether Sujah Dowlah ruled in Oude or in Travancore, or whether Holkar was a Hindoo or a Mussulman. Yet the victories of Cortes were gained over savages who had no letters, who were ignorant of the use of metals, who had not broken in a single animal to labour, who wielded no better weapons than those which could be made out of sticks, flints, and fish-bones, who regarded a horse-soldier as a monster, half man and half beast, who took a harquebusier for a sorcerer, able to scatter the thunder and lightning of the skies. The people of India, when we subdued them, were ten times as numerous as the Americans whom the Spaniards vanquished, and were at the same time quite as highly civilised as the victorious Spaniards. They had reared cities larger and fairer than Saragossa or Toledo, and buildings more beautiful and costly than the cathedral of Seville. They could show bankers richer than the richest firms of Barcelona or Cadiz, viceroys whose splendour far surpassed that of Ferdinand the Catholic, myriads of cavalry and long trains of artillery which would have astonished the Great Captain. It might have been expected, that every Englishman who takes any interest in any part of history would be curious to know how a handful of his countrymen, separated from their home by an immense ocean, subjugated, in the course of a few years, one of the greatest empires in the world. Yet, unless we greatly err, this subject is, to most readers, not only insipid, but positively distasteful.

Perhaps the fault lies partly with the historians. Mr. Mill's book, though it has undoubtedly great and rare merit, is not sufficiently animated and picturesque to attract those who read for amusement. Orme, inferior to no English historian in style and power of painting, is minute even to tediousness. In one volume he allots, on an average, a closely printed quarto page to the events of every forty-eight hours. The consequence is, that his narrative, though one of the most authentic and one of the most finely written in our language, has never been very popular, and is now scarcely ever read.

We fear that the volumes before us will not much attract those readers whom Orme and Mill have repelled. The materials placed at the disposal of Sir John Malcolm by the late Lord Powis were indeed of great value. But we cannot say that they have been very skilfully worked up. It would, however, be unjust to criticize with severity a work which, if the author had lived to complete and revise it, would probably have been improved by condensation and by a better arrangement. We are more disposed to perform the pleasing duty of expressing our gratitude to the noble family to which the public owes so much useful and curious information.

The effect of the book, even when we make the largest allowance for the partiality of those who have furnished and of those who have digested the materials, is, on the whole, greatly to raise the character of Lord Clive. We are far indeed from sympathizing with Sir John Malcolm, whose love passes the love of biographers, and who can see nothing but wisdom and justice in the actions of his idol. But we are at least equally far from concurring in the severe judgment of Mr. Mill, who seems to us to show less discrimination in his account of Clive than in any other part of his valuable work. Clive, like most men who are born with strong passions and tried by strong temptations, committed great faults. But every person who takes a fair and enlightened view of his whole career must admit that our island, so fertile in heroes and statesmen, has scarcely ever produced a man more truly great either in arms or in council.

The Clives had been settled, ever since the twelfth century, on an estate of no great value, near Market-Drayton, in Shropshire.

In the reign of George the First, this moderate but ancient inheritance was possessed by Mr. Richard Clive, who seems to have been a plain man of no great tact or capacity. He had been bred to the law, and divided his time between professional business and the avocations of a small proprietor. He married a lady from Manchester, of the name of Gaskill, and became the father of a very numerous family. His eldest son, Robert, the founder of the British empire in India, was born at the old seat of his ancestors on the twenty-ninth of September 1725.

Some lineaments of the character of the man were early discerned in the child. There remain letters written by his relations when he was in his seventh year; and from these letters it appears that, even at that early age, his strong will and his fiery passions, sustained by a constitutional intrepidity which sometimes seemed hardly compatible with soundness of mind, had begun to cause great uneasiness to his family. "Fighting," says one of his uncles, "to which he is out of measure addicted, gives his temper such a fierceness and imperiousness, that he flies out on every trifling occasion." The old people of the neighbourhood still remember to have heard from their parents how Bob Clive climbed to the top of the lofty steeple of Market-Drayton, and with what terror the inhabitants saw him seated on a stone spout near the summit. They also relate how he formed all the idle lads of the town into a kind of predatory army, and compelled the shopkeepers to submit to a tribute of apples and halfpence, in consideration of which he guaranteed the security of their windows. He was sent from school to school, making very little progress in his learning, and gaining for himself every where the character of an exceedingly naughty boy. One of his masters, it is said, was sagacious enough to prophesy that the idle lad would make a great figure in the world. But the general opinion seems to have been that poor Robert was a dunce, if not a reprobate. His family expected nothing good from such slender parts and such a headstrong temper. It is not strange, therefore, that they gladly accepted for him, when he was in his eighteenth year, a writership in the service of the East India Company, and shipped him off to make a fortune or to die of a fever at Madras.

Far different were the prospects of Clive from those of the youths whom the East India College now annually sends to the Presidencies of our Asiatic empire. The Company was then purely a trading corporation. Its territory consisted of a few square miles, for which rent was paid to the native governments. Its troops were scarcely numerous enough to man the batteries of three or four ill-constructed forts, which had been erected for the protection of the warehouses. The natives, who composed a considerable part of these little garrisons, had not yet been trained in the discipline of Europe, and were armed, some with swords and shields, some with bows and arrows. The business of the servant of the Company was not, as now, to conduct the judicial, financial, and diplomatic business of a great country, but to take stock, to make advances to weavers, to ship cargoes, and above all to keep an eye on private traders who dared to infringe the monopoly. The younger clerks were so miserably paid that they could scarcely subsist without incurring debt; the elder enriched themselves by trading on their own account; and those who lived to rise to the top of the service often accumulated considerable fortunes.

Madras, to which Clive had been appointed, was, at this time, perhaps the first in importance of the Company's settlements. In the preceding century, Fort St. George had arisen on a barren spot beaten by a raging surf; and in the neighbourhood a town, inhabited by many thousands of natives, had sprung up, as towns spring up in the East, with the rapidity of the prophet's gourd. There were already in the suburbs many white villas, each surrounded by its garden, whither the wealthy agents of the Company retired, after the labours of the desk and the warehouse, to enjoy the cool breeze which springs up at sunset from the Bay of Bengal. The habits of these mercantile grandees appear to have been more profuse, luxurious, and ostentatious, than those of the high judicial and political functionaries who have succeeded them. But comfort was far less understood. Many devices which now mitigate the heat of the climate, preserve health, and prolong life, were unknown. There was far less intercourse with Europe than at present. The voyage by the Cape, which in our time has often been performed within three months, was then very seldom accomplished in six, and was sometimes protracted to more than a year. Consequently, the Anglo-Indian was then much more estranged from his country, much more addicted to Oriental usages, and much less fitted to mix in society after his return to Europe, than the Anglo-Indian of the present day.

Within the fort and its precincts, the English governors exercised, by permission of the native rulers, an extensive authority, such as every great Indian landowner exercised within his own domain. But they had never dreamed of claiming independent power. The surrounding country was governed by the Nabob of the Carnatic, a deputy of the Viceroy of the Deccan, commonly called the Nizam, who was himself only a deputy of the mighty prince designated by our ancestors as the Great Mogul. Those names, once so august and formidable, still remain. There is still a Nabob of the Carnatic, who lives on a pension allowed to him by the English out of the revenues of the province which his ancestors ruled. There is still a Nizam, whose capital is overawed by a British cantonment, and to whom a British resident gives, under the name of advice, commands which are not to be disputed. There is still a Mogul, who is permitted to play at holding courts and receiving petitions, but who has less power to help or hurt than the youngest civil servant of the Company.

Clive's voyage was unusually tedious even for that age. The ship remained some months at the Brazils, where the young adventurer picked up some knowledge of Portuguese, and spent all his pocket-money. He did not arrive in India till more than a year after he had left England. His situation at Madras was most painful. His funds were exhausted. His pay was small. He had contracted debts. He was wretchedly lodged, no small calamity in a climate which can be made tolerable to an European only by spacious and well placed apartments. He had been furnished with letters of recommendation to a gentleman who might have assisted him; but when he landed at Fort St. George he found that this gentleman had sailed for England. The lad's shy and haughty disposition withheld him from introducing himself to strangers. He was several months in India before he became acquainted with a single family. The climate affected his health and spirits. His duties were of a kind ill suited to his ardent and daring character. He pined for his home, and in his letters to his relations expressed his feelings in language softer and more pensive than we should have expected, either from the waywardness of his boyhood, or from the inflexible sternness of his later years. "I have not enjoyed," says he, "one happy day since I left my native country:" and again, "I must confess, at intervals, when I think of my dear native England, it affects me in a very particular manner. . . . If I should be so far blest as to revisit again my own country, but more especially Manchester, the centre of all my wishes, all that I could hope or desire for would be presented before me in one view."

One solace he found of the most respectable kind. The Governor possessed a good library, and permitted Clive to have access to it. The young man devoted much of his leisure to reading, and acquired at this time almost all the knowledge of books that he ever possessed. As a boy he had been too idle, as a man he soon became too busy, for literary pursuits.

But neither climate nor poverty, neither study nor the sorrows of a home-sick exile, could tame the desperate audacity of his spirit. He behaved to his official superiors as he had behaved to his schoolmasters, and was several times in danger of losing his situation. Twice, while residing in the Writers' Buildings, he attempted to destroy himself; and twice the pistol which he snapped at his own head failed to go off. This circumstance, it is said, affected him as a similar escape affected Wallenstein. After satisfying himself that the pistol was really well loaded, he burst forth into an exclamation that surely he was reserved for something great.

About this time an event which at first seemed likely to destroy all his hopes in life suddenly opened before him a new path to eminence. Europe had been, during some years, distracted by the war of the Austrian succession. George the Second was the steady ally of Maria Theresa. The house of Bourbon took the opposite side. Though England was even then the first of maritime powers, she was not, as she has since become, more than a match on the sea for all the nations of the world together; and she found it difficult to maintain a contest against the united navies of France and Spain. In the eastern seas France obtained the ascendency. Labourdonnais, governor of Mauritius, a man of eminent talents and virtues, conducted an expedition to the continent of India in spite of the opposition of the British fleet, landed, assembled an army, appeared before Madras, and compelled the town and fort to capitulate. The keys were delivered up; the French colours were displayed on Fort St. George; and the contents of the Company's warehouses were seized as prize of war by the conquerors. It was stipulated by the capitulation that the English inhabitants should be prisoners of war on parole, and that the town should remain in the hands of the French till it should be ransomed. Labourdonnais pledged his honour that only a moderate ransom should be required.

But the success of Labourdonnais had awakened the jealousy of his countryman, Dupleix, governor of Pondicherry. Dupleix, moreover, had already begun to revolve gigantic schemes, with which the restoration of Madras to the English was by no means compatible. He declared that Labourdonnais had gone beyond his powers; that conquests made by the French arms on the continent of India were at the disposal of the governor of Pondicherry alone; and that Madras should be rased to the ground. Labourdonnais was compelled to yield. The anger which the breach of the capitulation excited among the English was increased by the ungenerous manner in which Dupleix treated the principal servants of the Company. The governor and several of the first gentlemen of Fort St. George were carried under a guard to Pondicherry, and conducted through the town in a triumphal procession under the eyes of fifty thousand spectators. It was with reason thought that this gross violation of public faith absolved the inhabitants of Madras from the engagements into which they had entered with Labourdonnais. Clive fled from the town by night in the disguise of a Mussulman, and took refuge at Fort St. David, one of the small English settlements subordinate to Madras.

The circumstances in which he was now placed naturally led him to adopt a profession better suited to his restless and intrepid spirit than the business of examining packages and casting accounts. He solicited and obtained an ensign's commission in the service of the Company, and at twenty-one entered on his military career. His personal courage, of which he had, while still a writer, given signal proof by a desperate duel with a military bully who was the terror of Fort St. David, speedily made him conspicuous even among hundreds of brave men. He soon began to show in his new calling other qualities which had not before been discerned in him, judgment, sagacity, deference to legitimate authority. He distinguished himself highly in several operations against the French, and was particularly noticed by Major Lawrence, who was then considered as the ablest British officer in India.

Clive had been only a few months in the army when intelligence arrived that peace had been concluded between Great Britain and France. Dupleix was in consequence compelled to restore Madras to the English Company; and the young ensign was at liberty to resume his former business. He did indeed return for a short time to his desk. He again quitted it in order to assist Major Lawrence in some petty hostilities with the natives, and then again returned to it. While he was thus wavering between a military and a commercial life, events took place which decided his choice. The politics of India assumed a new aspect. There was peace between the English and French Crowns; but there arose between the English and French Companies trading to the East a war most eventful and important, a war in which the prize was nothing less than the magnificent inheritance of the house of Tamerlane.

The empire which Baber and his Moguls reared in the sixteenth century was long one of the most extensive and splendid in the world. In no European kingdom was so large a population subject to a single prince, or so large a revenue poured into the treasury. The beauty and magnificence of the buildings erected by the sovereigns of Hindostan, amazed even travellers who had seen St. Peter's. The innumerable retinues and gorgeous decorations which surrounded the throne of Delhi dazzled even eyes which were accustomed to the pomp of Versailles. Some of the great viceroys who held their posts by virtue of commissions from the Mogul ruled as many subjects as the King of France or the Emperor of Germany. Even the deputies of these deputies might well rank, as to extent of territory and amount of revenue, with the Grand Duke of Tuscany, or the Elector of Saxony.

There can be little doubt that this great empire, powerful and prosperous as it appears on a superficial view, was yet, even in its best days, far worse governed than the worst governed parts of Europe now are. The administration was tainted with all the vices of Oriental despotism and with all the vices inseparable from the domination of race over race. The conflicting pretensions of the princes of the royal house produced a long series of crimes and public disasters. Ambitious lieutenants of the sovereign sometimes aspired to independence. Fierce tribes of Hindoos, impatient of a foreign yoke, frequently withheld tribute, repelled the armies of the government from the mountain fastnesses, and poured down in arms on the cultivated plains. In spite, however, of much constant maladministration, in spite of occasional convulsions which shook the whole frame of society, this great monarchy, on the whole, retained, during some generations, an outward appearance of unity, majesty, and energy. But, throughout the long reign of Aurungzebe, the state, notwithstanding all that the vigour and policy of the prince could effect, was hastening to dissolution. After his death, which took place in the year 1707, the ruin was fearfully rapid. Violent shocks from without cooperated with an incurable decay which was fast proceeding within; and in a few years the empire had undergone utter decomposition.

The history of the successors of Theodosius bears no small analogy to that of the successors of Aurungzebe. But perhaps the fall of the Carlovingians furnishes the nearest parallel to the fall of the Moguls. Charlemagne was scarcely interred when the imbecility and the disputes of his descendants began to bring contempt on themselves and destruction on their subjects. The wide dominion of the Franks was severed into a thousand pieces. Nothing more than a nominal dignity was left to the abject heirs of an illustrious name, Charles the Bald, and Charles the Fat, and Charles the Simple. Fierce invaders, differing from each other in race, language, and religion, flocked, as if by concert, from the farthest corners of the earth, to plunder provinces which the government could no longer defend. The pirates of the Northern Sea extended their ravages from the Elbe to the Pyrenees, and at length fixed their seat in the rich valley of the Seine. The Hungarian, in

whom the trembling monks fancied that they recognised the Gog
or Magog of prophecy, carried back the plunder of the cities of
Lombardy to the depth of the Pannonian forests. The Saracen
ruled in Sicily, desolated the fertile plains of Campania, and spread
terror even to the walls of Rome. In the midst of these sufferings, a
great internal change passed upon the empire. The corruption of
death began to ferment into new forms of life. While the great
body, as a whole, was torpid and passive, every separate member
began to feel with a sense, and to move with an energy all its own.
Just here, in the most barren and dreary tract of European history,
all feudal privileges, all modern nobility, take their source. It is to
this point that we trace the power of those princes who, nominally
vassals, but really independent, long governed, with the titles of
dukes, marquesses, and counts, almost every part of the dominions
which had obeyed Charlemagne.

Such or nearly such was the change which passed on the Mogul
empire during the forty years which followed the death of Aurungzebe. A succession of nominal sovereigns, sunk in indolence and
debauchery, sauntered away life in secluded palaces, chewing bang,
fondling concubines, and listening to buffoons. A succession of
ferocious invaders descended through the western passes, to prey
on the defenceless wealth of Hindostan. A Persian conqueror
crossed the Indus, marched through the gates of Delhi, and bore
away in triumph those treasures of which the magnificence had
astounded Roe and Bernier, the Peacock Throne, on which the
richest jewels of Golconda had been disposed by the most skilful
hands of Europe, and the inestimable Mountain of Light, which,
after many strange vicissitudes, lately shone in the bracelet of
Runjeet Sing, and is now destined to adorn the hideous idol of
Orissa. The Afghan soon followed to complete the work of devastation which the Persian had begun. The warlike tribes of Rajpootana
threw off the Mussulman yoke. A band of mercenary soldiers
occupied Rohilcund. The Seiks ruled on the Indus. The Jauts
spread dismay along the Jumna. The highlands which border on
the western sea-coast of India poured forth a yet more formidable
race, a race which was long the terror of every native power, and
which, after many desperate and doubtful struggles, yielded only
to the fortune and genius of England. It was under the reign of
Aurungzebe that this wild clan of plunderers first descended from
their mountains; and soon after his death, every corner of his wide
empire learned to tremble at the mighty name of the Mahrattas.
Many fertile viceroyalties were entirely subdued by them. Their
dominions stretched across the peninsula from sea to sea. Mahratta

captains reigned at Poonah, at Gualior, in Guzerat, in Berar, and in Tanjore. Nor did they, though they had become great sovereigns, therefore cease to be freebooters. They still retained the predatory habits of their forefathers. Every region which was not subject to their rule was wasted by their incursions. Wherever their kettle-drums were heard, the peasant threw his bag of rice on his shoulder, hid his small savings in his girdle, and fled with his wife and children to the mountains or the jungles, to the milder neighbour-hood of the hyæna and the tiger. Many provinces redeemed their harvests by the payment of an annual ransom. Even the wretched phantom who still bore the imperial title stooped to pay this ignominious black-mail. The camp-fires of one rapacious leader were seen from the walls of the palace of Delhi. Another, at the head of his innumerable cavalry, descended year after year on the rice-fields of Bengal. Even the European factors trembled for their magazines. Less than a hundred years ago, it was thought necessary to fortify Calcutta against the horsemen of Berar; and the name of the Mahratta ditch still preserves the memory of the danger.

Wherever the viceroys of the Mogul retained authority they became sovereigns. They might still acknowledge in words the superiority of the house of Tamerlane; as a Count of Flanders or a Duke of Burgundy might have acknowledged the superiority of the most helpless driveller among the later Carlovingians. They might occasionally send to their titular sovereign a complimentary present, or solicit from him a title of honour. In truth, however, they were no longer lieutenants removable at pleasure, but indepen-dent hereditary princes. In this way originated those great Mussul-man houses which formerly ruled Bengal and the Carnatic, and those which still, though in a state of vassalage, exercise some of the powers of royalty at Lucknow and Hyderabad.

In what was this confusion to end? Was the strife to continue during centuries? Was it to terminate in the rise of another great monarchy? Was the Mussulman or the Mahratta to be the Lord of India? Was another Baber to descend from the mountains, and to lead the hardy tribes of Cabul and Chorasan against a wealthier and less warlike race? None of these events seemed improbable. But scarcely any man, however sagacious, would have thought it possible that a trading company, separated from India by fifteen thousand miles of sea, and possessing in India only a few acres for purposes of commerce, would, in less than a hundred years, spread its empire from Cape Comorin to the eternal snow of the Hima-layas; would compel Mahratta and Mahommedan to forget their mutual feuds in common subjection; would tame down even those wild races which had resisted the most powerful of the Moguls; and, having united under its laws a hundred millions of subjects, would carry its victorious arms far to the east of the Burrampooter, and far to the west of the Hydaspes, dictate terms of peace at the gates of Ava, and seat its vassal on the throne of Candahar.

The man who first saw that it was possible to found an European empire on the ruins of the Mogul monarchy was Dupleix. His restless, capacious, and inventive mind had formed this scheme, at a time when the ablest servants of the English Company were busied only about invoices and bills of lading. Nor had he only proposed to himself the end. He had also a just and distinct view of the means by which it was to be attained. He clearly saw that the greatest force which the princes of India could bring into the field would be no match for a small body of men trained in the discipline, and guided by the tactics, of the West. He saw also that the natives of India might, under European commanders, be formed into armies, such as Saxe or Frederic would be proud to command. He was perfectly aware that the most easy and convenient way in which an European adventurer could exercise sovereignty in India, was to govern the motions, and to speak through the mouth of some glittering puppet dignified by the title of Nabob or Nizam. The arts both of war and policy, which a few years later were employed with such signal success by the English, were first understood and practised by this ingenious and aspiring Frenchman.

The situation of India was such that scarcely any aggression could be without a pretext, either in old laws or in recent practice. All rights were in a state of utter uncertainty; and the Europeans who took part in the disputes of the natives confounded the confusion, by applying to Asiatic politics the public law of the West and analogies drawn from the feudal system. If it was convenient to treat a Nabob as an independent prince, there was an excellent plea for doing so. He was independent in fact. If it was convenient to treat him as a mere deputy of the Court of Delhi, there was no difficulty; for he was so in theory. If it was convenient to consider his office as an hereditary dignity, or as a dignity held during life only, or as a dignity held only during the good pleasure of the Mogul, arguments and precedents might be found for every one of those views. The party who had the heir of Baber in their hands represented him as the undoubted, the legitimate, the absolute sovereign, whom all subordinate authorities were bound to obey. The party against whom his name was used did not want plausible pretexts for maintaining that the empire was *de facto* dissolved, and that, though it might be decent to treat the Mogul with respect, as a venerable relic of an order of things which had passed away, it was absurd to regard him as the real master of Hindostan.

In the year 1748, died one of the most powerful of the new masters of India, the great Nizam al Mulk, Viceroy of the Deccan. His authority descended to his son, Nazir Jung. Of the provinces subject to this high functionary, the Carnatic was the wealthiest and the most extensive. It was governed by an ancient Nabob, whose name the English corrupted into Anaverdy Khan.

But there were pretenders to the government both of the vice-royalty and of the subordinate province. Mirzapha Jung, a grandson of Nizam al Mulk, appeared as the competitor of Nazir Jung. Chunda Sahib, son-in-law of a former Nabob of the Carnatic, disputed the title of Anaverdy Khan. In the unsettled state of Indian law, it was easy for both Mirzapha Jung and Chunda Sahib to make out something like a claim of right. In a society altogether disorganized, they had no difficulty in finding greedy adventurers to follow their standards. They united their interests, invaded the Carnatic, and applied for assistance to the French, whose fame had been raised by their success against the English in the recent war on the coast of Coromandel.

Nothing could have happened more pleasing to the subtle and ambitious Dupleix. To make a Nabob of the Carnatic, to make a Viceroy of the Deccan, to rule under their names the whole of southern India; this was indeed an attractive prospect. He allied himself with the pretenders, and sent four hundred French soldiers, and two thousand sepoys, disciplined after the European fashion, to the assistance of his confederates. A battle was fought. The French distinguished themselves greatly. Anaverdy Khan was defeated and slain. His son, Mahommed Ali, who was afterwards well known in England as the Nabob of Arcot, and who owes to the eloquence of Burke a most unenviable immortality, fled with a scanty remnant of his army to Trichinopoly; and the conquerors became at once masters of almost every part of the Carnatic.

This was but the beginning of the greatness of Dupleix. After some months of fighting, negotiation, and intrigue, his ability and good fortune seemed to have prevailed every where. Nazir Jung perished by the hands of his own followers; Mirzapha Jung was master of the Deccan; and the triumph of French arms and French policy was complete. At Pondicherry all was exultation and festivity. Salutes were fired from the batteries, and *Te Deum* sung in the churches. The new Nizam came thither to visit his allies; and the ceremony of his installation was performed there with great pomp. Dupleix, dressed in the garb worn by Mahommedans of the highest rank, entered the town in the same palanquin with the Nizam, and, in the pageant which followed, took precedence of all the court. He was declared Governor of India from the river Kristna to Cape Comorin, a country about as large as France, with authority superior even to that of Chunda Sahib. He was entrusted with the command of seven thousand cavalry. It was announced that no mint would be suffered to exist in the Carnatic except that at Pondicherry. A large portion of the treasures which former Viceroys of the Deccan had accumulated found its way into the coffers of the French governor. It was rumoured that he had received two hundred thousand pounds sterling in money, besides many valuable jewels. In fact, there could scarcely be any limit to his gains. He now ruled thirty millions of people with almost absolute power. No honour or emolument could be obtained from the government but by his intervention. No petition, unless signed by him, was perused by the Nizam.

Mirzapha Jung survived his elevation only a few months. But another prince of the same house was raised to the throne by French influence, and ratified all the promises of his predecessor. Dupleix was now the greatest potentate in India. His countrymen boasted that his name was mentioned with awe even in the chambers of the palace of Delhi. The native population looked with amazement on the progress which, in the short space of four years, an European adventurer had made towards dominion in Asia. Nor was the vain-glorious Frenchman content with the reality of power. He loved to display his greatness with arrogant ostentation before the eyes of his subjects and of his rivals. Near the spot where his policy had obtained its chief triumph, by the fall of Nazir Jung and the eleva-tion of Mirzapha, he determined to erect a column, on the four sides of which four pompous inscriptions, in four languages, should proclaim his glory to all the nations of the East. Medals stamped with emblems of his successes were buried beneath the foundations of this stately pillar, and round it arose a town bearing the haughty name of Dupleix Fatihabad, which is, being interpreted, the City of the Victory of Dupleix.

The English had made some feeble and irresolute attempts to stop the rapid and brilliant career of the rival Company, and con-tinued to recognise Mahommed Ali as Nabob of the Carnatic. But the dominions of Mahommed Ali consisted of Trichinopoly alone; and Trichinopoly was now invested by Chunda Sahib and his French auxiliaries. To raise the siege seemed impossible. The small force which was then at Madras had no commander. Major Lawrence had returned to England; and not a single officer of established character remained in the settlement. The natives had learned to look with contempt on the mighty nation which was soon to conquer and to rule them. They had seen the French colours flying on Fort St. George; they had seen the chiefs of the English factory led in triumph through the streets of Pondicherry; they had seen the arms and counsels of Dupleix everywhere successful, while the opposition which the authorities of Madras had made to his progress, had served only to expose their own weakness, and to heighten his glory. At this moment, the valour and genius of an obscure English youth suddenly turned the tide of fortune.

Clive was now twenty-five years old. After hesitating for some time between a military and a commercial life, he had at length been placed in a post which partook of both characters, that of commissary to the troops, with the rank of captain. The present emergency called forth all his powers. He represented to his superiors that, unless some vigorous effort were made, Trichinopoly would fall, the house of Anaverdy Khan would perish, and the French would become the real masters of the whole peninsula of India. It was absolutely necessary to strike some daring blow. If an attack were made on Arcot, the capital of the Carnatic, and the favourite residence of the Nabobs, it was not impossible that the siege of Trichinopoly would be raised. The heads of the English settlement, now thoroughly alarmed by the success of Dupleix, and apprehensive that, in the event of a new war between France and Great Britain, Madras would be instantly taken and destroyed, approved of Clive's plan, and intrusted the execution of it to himself. The young captain was put at the head of two hundred English soldiers, and three hundred sepoys, armed and disciplined after the European fashion. Of the eight officers who commanded this little force under him, only two had ever been in action, and four of the eight were factors of the Company, whom Clive's example had induced to offer their services. The weather was stormy; but Clive pushed on, through thunder, lightning, and rain, to the gates of Arcot. The garrison, in a panic, evacuated the fort, and the English entered it without a blow.

But Clive well knew that he should not be suffered to retain undisturbed possession of his conquest. He instantly began to collect provisions, to throw up works, and to make preparations for sustaining a siege. The garrison, which had fled at his approach, had now recovered from its dismay, and, having been swollen by large reinforcements from the neighbourhood to a force of three thousand men, encamped close to the town. At dead of night, Clive marched out of the fort, attacked the camp by surprise, slew great numbers, dispersed the rest, and returned to his quarters without having lost a single man.

The intelligence of these events was soon carried to Chunda Sahib who, with his French allies, was besieging Trichinopoly. He immediately detached four thousand men from his camp, and sent them to Arcot. They were speedily joined by the remains of the force which Clive had lately scattered. They were further strengthened by two thousand men from Vellore, and by a still more important reinforcement of a hundred and fifty French soldiers whom Dupleix despatched from Pondicherry. The whole of this army, amounting to about ten thousand men, was under the command of Rajah Sahib, son of Chunda Sahib.

Rajah Sahib proceeded to invest the fort of Arcot, which seemed quite incapable of sustaining a siege. The walls were ruinous, the ditches dry, the ramparts too narrow to admit the guns, the battlements too low to protect the soldiers. The little garrison had been greatly reduced by casualties. It now consisted of a hundred and twenty Europeans and two hundred sepoys. Only four officers were left; the stock of provisions was scanty; and the commander, who had to conduct the defence under circumstances so discouraging, was a young man of five and twenty, who had been bred a book-keeper.

During fifty days the siege went on. During fifty days the young captain maintained the defence, with a firmness, vigilance, and ability which would have done honour to the oldest marshal in Europe. The breach, however, increased day by day. The garrison began to feel the pressure of hunger. Under such circumstances, any troops so scantily provided with officers might have been expected to show signs of insubordination; and the danger was peculiarly great in a force composed of men differing widely from each other in extraction, colour, language, manners, and religion. But the devotion of the little band to its chief surpassed any thing that is related of the Tenth Legion of Cæsar, or of the Old Guard of Napoleon. The sepoys came to Clive, not to complain of their scanty fare, but to propose that all the grain should be given to the Europeans, who required more nourishment than the natives of Asia. The thin gruel, they said, which was strained away from the rice, would suffice for themselves. History contains no more touching instance of military fidelity, or of the influence of a commanding mind.

An attempt made by the government of Madras to relieve the place had failed. But there was hope from another quarter. A body of six thousand Mahrattas, half soldiers, half robbers, under the command of a chief named Morari Row, had been hired to assist Mahommed Ali; but thinking the French power irresistible, and the triumph of Chunda Sahib certain, they had hitherto remained inactive on the frontiers of the Carnatic. The fame of the defence of Arcot roused them from their torpor. Morari Row declared that he had never before believed that Englishmen could fight, but that he would willingly help them since he saw that they had spirit to help themselves. Rajah Sahib learned that the Mahrattas were in motion. It was necessary for him to be expeditious. He first tried negotiation. He offered large bribes to Clive, which were rejected with scorn. He vowed that, if his proposals were not accepted, he would instantly storm the fort, and put every man in it to the sword. Clive told him in reply, with characteristic haughtiness, that his father was an usurper, that his army was a rabble, and that he would do well to think twice before he sent such poltroons into a breach defended by English soldiers.

Rajah Sahib determined to storm the fort. The day was well suited to a bold military enterprise. It was the great Mahommedan festival which is sacred to the memory of Hosein the son of Ali. The history of Islam contains nothing more touching than the event which gave rise to that solemnity. The mournful legend relates how the chief of the Fatimites, when all his brave followers had perished round him, drank his latest draught of water, and uttered his latest prayer, how the assassins carried his head in triumph, how the tyrant smote the lifeless lips with his staff, and how a few old men recollected with tears that they had seen those lips pressed to the lips of the Prophet of God. After the lapse of near twelve centuries, the recurrence of this solemn season excites the fiercest and saddest emotions in the bosoms of the devout Moslem of India. They work themselves up to such agonies of rage and lamentation that some, it is said, have given up the ghost from the mere effect of mental excitement. They believe that whoever, during this festival, falls in arms against the infidels, atones by his death for all the sins of his life, and passes at once to the garden of the Houris. It was at this time that Rajah Sahib determined to assault Arcot. Stimulating drugs were employed to aid the effect of religious zeal, and the besiegers, drunk with enthusiasm, drunk with bang, rushed furiously to the attack.

Clive had received secret intelligence of the design, had made his arrangements, and, exhausted by fatigue, had thrown himself on his bed. He was awakened by the alarm, and was instantly at his post. The enemy advanced driving before them elephants whose foreheads were armed with iron plates. It was expected that the gates would yield to the shock of these living battering-rams. But the huge beasts no sooner felt the English musket-balls than they turned round, and rushed furiously away, tramping on the multitude which had urged them forward. A raft was launched on the water which filled one part of the ditch. Clive, perceiving that his gunners at that post did not understand their business, took the management of a piece of artillery himself, and cleared the raft in a few minutes. Where the moat was dry, the assailants mounted with great boldness; but they were received with a fire so heavy and so well-directed, that it soon quelled the courage even of fanaticism and of intoxication. The rear ranks of the English kept the front ranks supplied with a constant succession of loaded muskets, and every shot told on the living mass below. After three desperate onsets, the besiegers retired behind the ditch.

The struggle lasted about an hour. Four hundred of the assailants fell. The garrison lost only five or six men. The besieged passed an anxious night, looking for a renewal of the attack. But when day broke, the enemy were no more to be seen. They had retired, leaving to the English several guns and a large quantity of ammunition.

The news was received at Fort St. George with transports of joy and pride. Clive was justly regarded as a man equal to any command. Two hundred English soldiers, and seven hundred sepoys were sent to him, and with this force he instantly commenced offensive operations. He took the fort of Timery, effected a junction with a division of Morari Row's army, and hastened, by forced marches, to attack Rajah Sahib, who was at the head of about five thousand men, of whom three hundred were French. The action was sharp; but Clive gained a complete victory. The military chest of Rajah Sahib fell into the hands of the conquerors. Six hundred sepoys, who had served in the enemy's army, came over to Clive's quarters, and were taken into the British service. Conjeveram surrendered without a blow. The governor of Arnee deserted Chunda Sahib, and recognised the title of Mahommed Ali.

Had the entire direction of the war been entrusted to Clive, it would probably have been brought to a speedy close. But the timidity and incapacity which appeared in all the movements of the English, except where he was personally present, protracted the struggle. The Mahrattas muttered that his soldiers were of a different race from the British whom they found elsewhere. The effect of this languor was that in no long time Rajah Sahib, at the head of a considerable army, in which were four hundred French troops, appeared almost under the guns of Fort St. George, and laid waste the villas and gardens of the gentlemen of the English settlement. But he was again encountered and defeated by Clive. More than a hundred of the French were killed or taken, a loss more serious than that of thousands of natives. The victorious army marched from the field of battle to Fort St. David. On the road lay the City of the Victory of Dupleix, and the stately monument which was designed to commemorate the triumphs of France in the East. Clive ordered both the city and the monument to be rased to the ground. He was induced, we believe, to take this step, not by personal or national malevolence, but by a just and profound policy. The town and its pompous name, the pillar and its vaunting inscriptions, were among the devices by which Dupleix had laid the public mind of India under a spell. This spell it was Clive's business to break. The natives had been taught that France was confessedly the first power in Europe, and that the English did not presume to dispute her supremacy. No measure could be more effectual for the removing of this delusion than the public and solemn demolition of the French trophies.

The government of Madras, encouraged by these events, determined to send a strong detachment, under Clive, to reinforce the garrison of Trichinopoly. But just at this conjuncture, Major Lawrence arrived from England, and assumed the chief command. From the waywardness and impatience of control which had characterized Clive, both at school and in the counting-house, it might have been expected that he would not, after such achievements, act with zeal and good humour in a subordinate capacity. But Lawrence had early treated him with kindness; and it is bare justice to Clive to say that, proud and overbearing as he was, kindness was never thrown away upon him. He cheerfully placed himself under the orders of his old friend, and exerted himself as strenuously in the second post as he could have done in the first. Lawrence well knew the value of such assistance. Though himself gifted with no intellectual faculty higher than plain good sense, he fully appreciated the powers of his brilliant coadjutor. Though he had made a methodical study of military tactics, and, like all men regularly bred to a profession, was disposed to look with disdain on interlopers, he had yet liberality enough to acknowledge that Clive was an exception to common rules. "Some people," he wrote, "are pleased to term Captain Clive fortunate and lucky; but, in my opinion, from the knowledge I have of the gentleman, he deserved and might expect from his conduct every thing as it fell out;—a man of an undaunted resolution, of a cool temper, and of a presence of mind which never left him in the greatest danger—

born a soldier; for, without a military education of any sort, or much conversing with any of the profession, from his judgment and good sense, he led on an army like an experienced officer and a brave soldier, with a prudence that certainly warranted success."

The French had no commander to oppose to the two friends. Dupleix, not inferior in talents for negotiation and intrigue to any European who has borne a part in the revolutions of India, was not qualified to direct in person military operations. He had not been bred a soldier, and had no inclination to become one. His enemies accused him of personal cowardice; and he defended himself in a strain worthy of Captain Bobadil. He kept away from shot, he said, because silence and tranquillity were propitious to his genius, and he found it difficult to pursue his meditations amidst the noise of fire-arms. He was thus under the necessity of entrusting to others the execution of his great warlike designs; and he bitterly complained that he was ill served. He had indeed been assisted by one officer of eminent merit, the celebrated Bussy. But Bussy had marched northward with the Nizam, and was fully employed in looking after his own interests, and those of France, at the court of that prince. Among the officers who remained with Dupleix, there was not a single man of capacity; and many of them were boys, at whose ignorance and folly the common soldiers laughed.

The English triumphed every where. The besiegers of Trichinopoly were themselves besieged and compelled to capitulate. Chunda Sahib fell into the hands of the Mahrattas, and was put to death, at the instigation probably of his competitor, Mahommed Ali. The spirit of Dupleix, however, was unconquerable, and his resources inexhaustible. From his employers in Europe, he no longer received help or countenance. They condemned his policy. They gave him no pecuniary assistance. They sent him for troops only the sweepings of the galleys. Yet still he persisted, intrigued, bribed, promised, lavished his private fortune, strained his credit, procured new diplomas from Delhi, raised up new enemies to the government of Madras on every side, and found tools even among the allies of the English Company. But all was in vain. Slowly, but steadily, the power of Britain continued to increase, and that of France to decline.

The health of Clive had never been good during his residence in India; and his constitution was now so much impaired that he determined to return to England. Before his departure he undertook a service of considerable difficulty, and performed it with his usual vigour and dexterity. The forts of Covelong and Chingleput were occupied by French garrisons. It was determined to send a force against them. But the only force available for this purpose was of such a description that no officer but Clive would risk his reputation by commanding it. It consisted of five hundred newly-levied sepoys, and two hundred recruits who had just landed from England, and who were the worst and lowest wretches that the Company's crimps could pick up in the flash-houses of London. Clive, ill and exhausted as he was, undertook to make an army of this undisciplined rabble, and marched with them to Covelong. A shot from the fort killed one of these extraordinary soldiers; on which all the rest faced about and ran away, and it was with the greatest difficulty that Clive rallied them. On another occasion, the noise of a gun terrified the sentinels so much that one of them was found, some hours later, at the bottom of a well. Clive gradually accustomed them to danger, and, by exposing himself constantly in the most perilous situations, shamed them into courage. He at length succeeded in forming a respectable force out of his unpromising materials. Covelong fell. Clive learned that a strong detachment was marching to relieve it from Chingleput. He took measures to prevent the enemy from learning that they were too late, laid an ambuscade for them on the road, killed a hundred of them with one fire, took three hundred prisoners, pursued the fugitives to the gates of Chingleput, laid siege instantly to that fastness, reputed one of the strongest in India, made a breach, and was on the point of storming when the French commandant capitulated and retired with his men.

Clive returned to Madras victorious, but in a state of health which rendered it impossible for him to remain there long. He married at this time a young lady of the name of Maskelyne, sister of the eminent mathematician, who long held the post of Astronomer Royal. She is described as handsome and accomplished; and her husband's letters, it is said, contain proofs that he was devotedly attached to her.

Almost immediately after the marriage, Clive embarked with his bride for England. He returned a very different person from the poor slighted boy who had been sent out ten years before to seek his fortune. He was only twenty-seven; yet his country already respected him as one of her first soldiers. There was then general peace in Europe. The Carnatic was the only part of the world where the English and French were in arms against each other. The vast schemes of Dupleix had excited no small uneasiness in the city of London; and the rapid turn of fortune, which was chiefly owing to the courage and talents of Clive, had been hailed with great delight. The young captain was known at the India House by the honourable nickname of General Clive, and was toasted by that appellation at the feasts of the Directors. On his arrival in England, he found himself an object of general interest and admiration. The East India Company thanked him for his services in the warmest terms, and bestowed on him a sword set with diamonds. With rare delicacy, he refused to receive this token of gratitude, unless a similar compliment were paid to his friend and commander, Lawrence.

It may easily be supposed that Clive was most cordially welcomed home by his family, who were delighted by his success, though they seem to have been hardly able to comprehend how their naughty idle Bobby had become so great a man. His father had been singularly hard of belief. Not until the news of the defence of Arcot arrived in England was the old gentleman heard to growl out that, after all, the booby had something in him. His expressions of approbation became stronger and stronger as news arrived of one brilliant exploit after another; and he was at length immoderately fond and proud of his son.

Clive's relations had very substantial reasons for rejoicing at his return. Considerable sums of prize-money had fallen to his share; and he had brought home a moderate fortune, part of which he expended in extricating his father from pecuniary difficulties, and in redeeming the family estate. The remainder he appears to have dissipated in the course of about two years. He lived splendidly, dressed gaily even for those times, kept a carriage and saddle horses, and, not content with these ways of getting rid of his money, resorted to the most speedy and effectual of all modes of evacuation, a contested election followed by a petition.

At the time of the general election of 1754, the government was in a very singular state. There was scarcely any formal opposition. The Jacobites had been cowed by the issue of the last rebellion. The Tory party had fallen into utter contempt. It had been deserted by all the men of talents who had belonged to it, and had scarcely given a symptom of life during some years. The small faction which had been held together by the influence and promises of Prince Frederic, had been dispersed by his death. Almost every public man of distinguished talents in the kingdom, whatever his early connections might have been, was in office, and called himself a Whig. But this extraordinary appearance of concord was quite delusive. The administration itself was distracted by bitter enmities and conflicting pretensions. The chief object of its members was to depress and supplant each other. The prime minister, Newcastle, weak, timid, jealous, and perfidious, was at once detested and despised by some of the most important members of his government, and by none more than by Henry Fox, the Secretary at War. This able, daring, and ambitious man seized every opportunity of crossing the First Lord of the Treasury, from whom he well knew that he had little to dread and little to hope; for Newcastle was through life equally afraid of breaking with men of parts and of promoting them.

Newcastle had set his heart on returning two members for St. Michael, one of those wretched Cornish boroughs which were swept away by the Reform Act in 1832. He was opposed by Lord Sandwich, whose influence had long been paramount there; and Fox exerted himself strenuously in Sandwich's behalf. Clive, who had been introduced to Fox, and very kindly received by him, was brought forward on the Sandwich interest, and was returned. But a petition was presented against the return, and was backed by the whole influence of the Duke of Newcastle.

The case was heard, according to the usage of that time, before a committee of the whole House. Questions respecting elections were then considered merely as party questions. Judicial impartiality was not even affected. Sir Robert Walpole was in the habit of saying openly that, in election battles, there ought to be no quarter. On the present occasion the excitement was great. The matter really at issue was, not whether Clive had been properly or improperly returned, but whether Newcastle or Fox was to be master of the New House of Commons, and consequently first minister. The contest was long and obstinate, and success seemed to lean sometimes to one side and sometimes to the other. Fox put forth all his rare powers of debate, beat half the lawyers in the House at their own weapons, and carried division after division against the whole influence of the Treasury. The committee decided in Clive's favour. But when the resolution was reported to the House, things took a different course. The remnant of the Tory Opposition, contemptible as it was, had yet sufficient weight to turn the scale between the nicely balanced parties of Newcastle and Fox. Newcastle the Tories could only despise. Fox they hated, as the boldest and most subtle politician and the ablest debater among the Whigs, as the steady friend of Walpole, as the devoted adherent of the Duke of Cumberland. After wavering till the last moment, they determined to vote in a body with the Prime Minister's friends. The consequence was that the House, by a small majority, rescinded the decision of the committee, and Clive was unseated.

Ejected from Parliament, and straitened in his means, he naturally began to look again towards India. The Company and the

Government were eager to avail themselves of his services. A treaty favourable to England had indeed been concluded in the Carnatic. Dupleix had been superseded, and had returned with the wreck of his immense fortune to Europe, where calumny and chicanery soon hunted him to his grave. But many signs indicated that a war between France and Great Britain was at hand; and it was therefore thought desirable to send an able commander to the Company's settlements in India. The Directors appointed Clive governor of Fort St. David. The King gave him the commission of a lieutenant-colonel in the British army, and in 1755 he again sailed for Asia.

The first service on which he was employed after his return to the East was the reduction of the stronghold of Gheriah. This fortress, built on a craggy promontory, and almost surrounded by the ocean, was the den of a pirate named Angria, whose barks had long been the terror of the Arabian Gulf. Admiral Watson, who commanded the English squadron in the Eastern seas, burned Angria's fleet, while Clive attacked the fastness by land. The place soon fell, and a booty of a hundred and fifty thousand pounds sterling was divided among the conquerors.

After this exploit, Clive proceeded to his government of Fort St. David. Before he had been there two months, he received intelligence which called forth all the energy of his bold and active mind.

Of the provinces which had been subject to the house of Tamerlane, the wealthiest was Bengal. No part of India possessed such natural advantages both for agriculture and for commerce. The Ganges, rushing through a hundred channels to the sea, has formed a vast plain of rich mould which, even under the tropical sky, rivals the verdure of an English April. The rice fields yield an increase such as is elsewhere unknown. Spices, sugar, vegetable oils, are produced with marvellous exuberance. The rivers afford an inexhaustible supply of fish. The desolate islands along the sea-coast, overgrown by noxious vegetation, and swarming with deer and tigers, supply the cultivated districts with abundance of salt. The great stream which fertilises the soil is, at the same time, the chief highway of Eastern commerce. On its banks, and on those of its tributary waters, are the wealthiest marts, the most splendid capitals, and the most sacred shrines of India. The tyranny of man had for ages struggled in vain against the overflowing bounty of nature. In spite of the Mussulman despot and of the Mahratta freebooter, Bengal was known through the East as the garden of Eden, as the rich kingdom. Its population multiplied exceedingly.

Distant provinces were nourished from the overflowing of its granaries; and the noble ladies of London and Paris were clothed in the delicate produce of its looms. The race by whom this rich tract was peopled, enervated by a soft climate and accustomed to peaceful avocations, bore the same relation to other Asiatics which the Asiatics generally bear to the bold and energetic children of Europe. The Castilians have a proverb, that in Valencia the earth is water and the men women; and the description is at least equally applicable to the vast plain of the Lower Ganges. Whatever the Bengalee does he does languidly. His favourite pursuits are sedentary. He shrinks from bodily exertion; and, though voluble in dispute, and singularly pertinacious in the war of chicane, he seldom engages in a personal conflict, and scarcely ever enlists as a soldier. We doubt whether there be a hundred genuine Bengalees in the whole army of the East India Company. There never, perhaps, existed a people so thoroughly fitted by nature and by habit for a foreign yoke.

The great commercial companies of Europe had long possessed factories in Bengal. The French were settled, as they still are, at Chandernagore on the Hoogley. Higher up the stream the Dutch traders held Chinsurah. Nearer to the sea, the English had built Fort William. A church and ample warehouses rose in the vicinity. A row of spacious houses, belonging to the chief factors of the East India Company, lined the banks of the river; and in the neighbourhood had sprung up a large and busy native town, where some Hindoo merchants of great opulence had fixed their abode. But the tract now covered by the palaces of Chowringhee contained only a few miserable huts thatched with straw. A jungle, abandoned to water-fowl and alligators, covered the site of the present Citadel, and the Course, which is now daily crowded at sunset with the gayest equipages of Calcutta. For the ground on which the settlement stood, the English, like other great landholders, paid rent to the government; and they were, like other great landholders, permitted to exercise a certain jurisdiction within their domain.

The great province of Bengal, together with Orissa and Bahar, had long been governed by a viceroy, whom the English called Aliverdy Khan, and who, like the other viceroys of the Mogul, had become virtually independent. He died in 1756, and the sovereignty descended to his grandson, a youth under twenty years of age, who bore the name of Surajah Dowlah. Oriental despots are perhaps the worst class of human beings; and this unhappy boy was one of the worst specimens of his class. His understanding was naturally feeble, and his temper naturally unamiable. His education had been such as would have enervated even a vigorous intellect and perverted even a generous disposition. He was unreasonable, because nobody ever dared to reason with him, and selfish, because he had never been made to feel himself dependent on the good-will of others. Early debauchery had unnerved his body and his mind. He indulged immoderately in the use of ardent spirits, which inflamed his weak brain almost to madness. His chosen companions were flatterers, sprung from the dregs of the people, and recommended by nothing but buffoonery and servility. It is said that he had arrived at that last stage of human depravity, when cruelty becomes pleasing for its own sake, when the sight of pain as pain, where no advantage is to be gained, no offence punished, no danger averted, is an agreeable excitement. It had early been his amusement to torture beasts and birds; and, when he grew up, he enjoyed with still keener relish the misery of his fellow-creatures.

From a child Surajah Dowlah had hated the English. It was his whim to do so; and his whims were never opposed. He had also formed a very exaggerated notion of the wealth which might be obtained by plundering them; and his feeble and uncultivated mind was incapable of perceiving that the riches of Calcutta, had they been even greater than he imagined, would not compensate him for what he must lose, if the European trade, of which Bengal was a chief seat, should be driven by his violence to some other quarter. Pretexts for a quarrel were readily found. The English, in expectation of a war with France, had begun to fortify their settlement without special permission from the Nabob. A rich native whom he longed to plunder, had taken refuge at Calcutta, and had not been delivered up. On such grounds as these Surajah Dowlah marched with a great army against Fort William.

The servants of the Company at Madras had been forced by Dupleix to become statesmen and soldiers. Those in Bengal were still mere traders, and were terrified and bewildered by the approaching danger. The governor, who had heard much of Surajah Dowlah's cruelty, was frightened out of his wits, jumped into a boat, and took refuge in the nearest ship. The military commandant thought that he could not do better than follow so good an example. The fort was taken after a feeble resistance; and great numbers of the English fell into the hands of the conquerors. The Nabob seated himself with regal pomp in the principal hall of the factory, and ordered Mr. Holwell, the first in rank among the prisoners, to be brought before him. His Highness abused the insolence of the English, and grumbled at the smallness of the treasure which he had found; but promised to spare their lives, and retired to rest.

Then was committed that great crime, memorable for its singular atrocity, memorable for the tremendous retribution by which it was followed. The English captives were left at the mercy of the guards; and the guards determined to secure them for the night in the prison of the garrison, a chamber known by the fearful name of the Black Hole. Even for a single European malefactor, that dungeon would, in such a climate, have been too close and narrow. The space was only twenty feet square. The air-holes were small and obstructed. It was the summer solstice, the season when the fierce heat of Bengal can scarcely be rendered tolerable to natives of England by lofty halls and by the constant waving of fans. The number of the prisoners was one hundred and forty-six. When they were ordered to enter the cell, they imagined that the soldiers were joking; and, being in high spirits on account of the promise of the Nabob to spare their lives, they laughed and jested at the absurdity of the notion. They soon discovered their mistake. They expostulated; they entreated; but in vain. The guards threatened to cut down all who hesitated. The captives were driven into the cell at the point of the sword, and the door was instantly shut and locked upon them.

Nothing in history or fiction, not even the story which Ugolino told in the sea of everlasting ice, after he had wiped his bloody lips on the scalp of his murderer, approaches the horrors which were recounted by the few survivors of that night. They cried for mercy. They strove to burst the door. Holwell who, even in that extremity, retained some presence of mind, offered large bribes to the gaolers. But the answer was that nothing could be done without the Nabob's orders, that the Nabob was asleep, and that he would be angry if anybody woke him. Then the prisoners went mad with despair. They trampled each other down, fought for the places at the windows, fought for the pittance of water with which the cruel mercy of the murderers mocked their agonies, raved, prayed, blasphemed, implored the guards to fire among them. The gaolers in the mean time held lights to the bars, and shouted with laughter at the frantic struggles of their victims. At length the tumult died away in low gaspings and moanings. The day broke. The Nabob had slept off his debauch, and permitted the door to be opened. But it was some time before the soldiers could make a lane for the survivors, by piling up on each side the heaps of corpses on which the burning climate had already begun to do its loathsome work. When at length a passage was made, twenty-three ghastly figures, such as their own mothers would not have known, staggered one by one out of the charnel-house. A pit was instantly dug. The dead bodies, a hundred and twenty-three in number, were flung into it promiscuously, and covered up.

But these things which, after the lapse of more than eighty years, cannot be told or read without horror, awakened neither remorse nor pity in the bosom of the savage Nabob. He inflicted no punishment on the murderers. He shewed no tenderness to the survivors. Some of them, indeed, from whom nothing was to be got, were suffered to depart; but those from whom it was thought that any thing could be extorted were treated with execrable cruelty. Holwell, unable to walk, was carried before the tyrant, who reproached him, threatened him, and sent him up the country in irons, together with some other gentlemen who were suspected of knowing more than they chose to tell about the treasures of the Company. These persons, still bowed down by the sufferings of that great agony, were lodged in miserable sheds, and fed only with grain and water, till at length the intercessions of the female relations of the Nabob procured their release. One Englishwoman had survived that night. She was placed in the haram of the Prince at Moorshedabad.

Surajah Dowlah, in the mean time, sent letters to his nominal sovereign at Delhi, describing the late conquest in the most pompous language. He placed a garrison in Fort William, forbade any Englishman to dwell in the neighbourhood, and directed that, in memory of his great actions, Calcutta should thenceforward be called Alinagore, that is to say, the Port of God.

In August the news of the fall of Calcutta reached Madras, and excited the fiercest and bitterest resentment. The cry of the whole settlement was for vengeance. Within forty-eight hours after the arrival of the intelligence it was determined that an expedition should be sent to the Hoogley, and that Clive should be at the head of the land forces. The naval armament was under the command of Admiral Watson. Nine hundred English infantry, fine troops and full of spirit, and fifteen hundred sepoys, composed the army which sailed to punish a Prince who had more subjects than Louis the Fifteenth or the Empress Maria Theresa. In October the expedition sailed; but it had to make its way against adverse winds, and did not reach Bengal till December.

The Nabob was revelling in fancied security at Moorshedabad. He was so profoundly ignorant of the state of foreign countries that he often used to say that there were not ten thousand men in all Europe; and it had never occurred to him as possible, that the English would dare to invade his dominions. But, though undisturbed by any fear of their military power, he began to miss them greatly. His revenues fell off; and his ministers succeeded in making him understand that a ruler may sometimes find it more profitable to protect traders in the open enjoyment of their gains than to put them to the torture for the purpose of discovering hidden chests of gold and jewels. He was already disposed to permit the Company to resume its mercantile operations in his country, when he received the news that an English armament was in the Hoogley. He instantly ordered all his troops to assemble at Moorshedabad, and marched towards Calcutta.

Clive had commenced operations with his usual vigour. He took Budgebudge, routed the garrison of Fort William, recovered Calcutta, stormed and sacked Hoogley. The Nabob, already disposed to make some concessions to the English, was confirmed in his pacific disposition by these proofs of their power and spirit. He accordingly made overtures to the chiefs of the invading armament, and offered to restore the factory, and to give compensation to those whom he had despoiled.

Clive's profession was war; and he felt that there was something discreditable in an accommodation with Surajah Dowlah. But his power was limited. A committee, chiefly composed of servants of the Company who had fled from Calcutta, had the principal direction of affairs; and these persons were eager to be restored to their posts and compensated for their losses. The government of Madras, apprised that war had commenced in Europe, and apprehensive of an attack from the French, became impatient for the return of the armament. The promises of the Nabob were large, the chances of a contest doubtful; and Clive consented to treat, though he expressed his regret that things should not be concluded in so glorious a manner as he could have wished.

With this negotiation commences a new chapter in the life of Clive. Hitherto he had been merely a soldier, carrying into effect, with eminent ability and valour, the plans of others. Henceforth he is to be chiefly regarded as a statesman; and his military movements are to be considered as subordinate to his political designs. That in his new capacity he displayed great talents, and obtained great success, is unquestionable. But it is also unquestionable, that the transactions in which he now began to take a part have left a stain on his moral character.

We can by no means agree with Sir John Malcolm, who is obstinately resolved to see nothing but honour and integrity in the conduct of his hero. But we can as little agree with Mr. Mill, who has gone so far as to say that Clive was a man "to whom deception, when it suited his purpose, never cost a pang." Clive seems to us to have been constitutionally the very opposite of a knave, bold even to temerity, sincere even to indiscretion, hearty in friendship, open in enmity. Neither in his private life, nor in those parts of his public life in which he had to do with his countrymen, do we find any signs of a propensity to cunning. On the contrary, in all the disputes in which he was engaged as an Englishman against Englishmen, from his boxing-matches at school to those stormy altercations at the India House and in Parliament amidst which his later years were passed, his very faults were those of a high and magnanimous spirit. The truth seems to have been that he considered Oriental politics as a game in which nothing was unfair. He knew that the standard of morality among the natives of India differed widely from that established in England. He knew that he had to deal with men destitute of what in Europe is called honour, with men who would give any promise without hesitation and break any promise without shame, with men who would unscrupulously employ corruption, perjury, forgery, to compass their ends. His letters show that the great difference between Asiatic and European morality was constantly in his thoughts. He seems to have imagined, most erroneously in our opinion, that he could effect nothing against such adversaries, if he was content to be bound by ties from which they were free, if he went on telling truth, and hearing none, if he fulfilled, to his own hurt, all his engagements with confederates who never kept an engagement that was not to their advantage. Accordingly this man, in the other parts of his life an honourable English gentleman and soldier, was no sooner matched against an Indian intriguer, than he became himself an Indian intriguer, and descended, without scruple, to falsehood, to hypocritical caresses, to the substitution of documents, and to the counterfeiting of hands.

The negotiations between the English and the Nabob were carried on chiefly by two agents, Mr. Watts, a servant of the Company, and a Bengalee of the name of Omichund. This Omichund had been one of the wealthiest native merchants resident at Calcutta, and had sustained great losses in consequence of the Nabob's expedition against that place. In the course of his commercial transactions, he had seen much of the English, and was peculiarly qualified to serve as a medium of communication between them and a native court. He possessed great influence with his own race, and had in large measure the Hindoo talents, quick observation, tact, dexterity, perseverance, and the Hindoo vices, servility, greediness, and treachery.

The Nabob behaved with all the faithlessness of an Indian statesman, and with all the levity of a boy whose mind had been enfeebled by power and self-indulgence. He promised, retracted, hesitated, evaded. At one time he advanced with his army in a threatening manner towards Calcutta; but when he saw the resolute front which the English presented, he fell back in alarm, and consented to make peace with them on their own terms. The treaty was no sooner concluded than he formed new designs against them. He intrigued with the French authorities at Chandernagore. He invited Bussy to march from the Deccan to the Hoogley, and to drive the English out of Bengal. All this was well known to Clive and Watson. They determined accordingly to strike a decisive blow, and to attack Chandernagore, before the force there could be strengthened by new arrivals, either from the south of India or from Europe. Watson directed the expedition by water, Clive by land. The success of the combined movements was rapid and complete. The fort, the garrison, the artillery, the military stores, all fell into the hands of the English. Near five hundred European troops were among the prisoners.

The Nabob had feared and hated the English, even while he was still able to oppose to them their French rivals. The French were now vanquished; and he began to regard the English with still greater fear and still greater hatred. His weak and unprincipled mind oscillated between servility and insolence. One day he sent a large sum to Calcutta, as part of the compensation due for the wrongs which he had committed. The next day he sent a present of jewels to Bussy, exhorting that distinguished officer to hasten to protect Bengal "against Clive, the daring in war, on whom," says his highness, "may all bad fortune attend." He ordered his army to march against the English. He countermanded his orders. He tore Clive's letters. He then sent answers in the most florid language of compliment. He ordered Watts out of his presence, and threatened to impale him. He again sent for Watts, and begged pardon for the insult. In the mean time, his wretched maladministration, his folly, his dissolute manners, and his love of the lowest company, had disgusted all classes of his subjects, soldiers, traders, civil functionaries, the proud and ostentatious Mahommedans, the timid, supple, and parsimonious Hindoos. A formidable confederacy was formed against him, in which were included Roydullub, the minister of finance, Meer Jaffier, the principal commander of the troops, and Jugget Seit, the richest banker in India. The plot was confided to the English agents, and a communication was opened between the malcontents at Moorshedabad and the committee at Calcutta.

In the committee there was much hesitation; but Clive's voice was given in favour of the conspirators, and his vigour and firmness bore down all opposition. It was determined that the English should lend their powerful assistance to depose Surajah Dowlah, and to place Meer Jaffier on the throne of Bengal. In return, Meer Jaffier promised ample compensation to the Company and its servants, and a liberal donative to the army, the navy, and the committee. The odious vices of Surajah Dowlah, the wrongs which the English had suffered at his hands, the dangers to which our trade must have been exposed had he continued to reign, appear to us fully to justify the resolution of deposing him. But nothing can justify the dissimulation which Clive stooped to practise. He wrote to Surajah Dowlah in terms so affectionate that they for a time lulled that weak prince into perfect security. The same courier who carried this "soothing letter," as Clive calls it, to the Nabob, carried to Mr. Watts a letter in the following terms: "Tell Meer Jaffier to fear nothing. I will join him with five thousand men who never turned their backs. Assure him I will march night and day to his assistance, and stand by him as long as I have a man left."

It was impossible that a plot which had so many ramifications should long remain entirely concealed. Enough reached the ears of the Nabob to arouse his suspicions. But he was soon quieted by the fictions and artifices which the inventive genius of Omichund produced with miraculous readiness. All was going well; the plot was nearly ripe; when Clive learned that Omichund was likely to play false. The artful Bengalee had been promised a liberal compensation for all that he had lost at Calcutta. But this would not satisfy him. His services had been great. He held the thread of the whole intrigue. By one word breathed in the ear of Surajah Dowlah, he could undo all that he had done. The lives of Watts, of Meer Jaffier, of all the conspirators, were at his mercy; and he determined to take advantage of his situation and to make his own terms. He demanded three hundred thousand pounds sterling as the price of his secrecy and of his assistance. The committee, incensed by the treachery and appalled by the danger, knew not what course to take. But Clive was more than Omichund's match in Omichund's own arts. The man, he said, was a villain. Any artifice which would defeat such knavery was justifiable. The best course would be to promise what was asked. Omichund would soon be at their mercy; and then they might punish him by withholding from him, not only the bribe which he now demanded, but also the compensation which all the other sufferers of Calcutta were to receive.

His advice was taken. But how was the wary and sagacious

Hindoo to be deceived? He had demanded that an article touching his claims should be inserted in the treaty between Meer Jaffier and the English, and he would not be satisfied unless he saw it with his own eyes. Clive had an expedient ready. Two treaties were drawn up, one on white paper, the other on red, the former real, the latter fictitious. In the former Omichund's name was not mentioned; the latter, which was to be shown to him, contained a stipulation in his favour.

But another difficulty arose. Admiral Watson had scruples about signing the red treaty. Omichund's vigilance and acuteness were such that the absence of so important a name would probably awaken his suspicions. But Clive was not a man to do anything by halves. We almost blush to write it. He forged Admiral Watson's name.

All was now ready for action. Mr. Watts fled secretly from Moorshedabad. Clive put his troops in motion, and wrote to the Nabob in a tone very different from that of his previous letters. He set forth all the wrongs which the British had suffered, offered to submit the points in dispute to the arbitration of Meer Jaffier, and concluded by announcing that, as the rains were about to set in, he and his men would do themselves the honour of waiting on his highness for an answer.

Surajah Dowlah instantly assembled his whole force, and marched to encounter the English. It had been agreed that Meer Jaffier should separate himself from the Nabob, and carry over his division to Clive. But, as the decisive moment approached, the fears of the conspirator overpowered his ambition. Clive had advanced to Cossimbuzar; the Nabob lay with a mighty power a few miles off at Plassey; and still Meer Jaffier delayed to fulfil his engagements, and returned evasive answers to the earnest remonstrances of the English general.

Clive was in a painfully anxious situation. He could place no confidence in the sincerity or in the courage of his confederate: and, whatever confidence he might place in his own military talents, and in the valour and discipline of his troops, it was no light thing to engage an army twenty times as numerous as his own. Before him lay a river over which it was easy to advance, but over which, if things went ill, not one of his little band would ever return. On this occasion, for the first and for the last time, his dauntless spirit, during a few hours, shrank from the fearful responsibility of making a decision. He called a council of war. The majority pronounced against fighting; and Clive declared his concurrence with the majority. Long afterwards, he said that he had never called but one council of war, and that, if he had taken the advice of that council, the British would never have been masters of Bengal. But scarcely had the meeting broken up when he was himself again. He retired alone under the shade of some trees, and passed near an hour there in thought. He came back determined to put every thing to the hazard, and gave orders that all should be in readiness for passing the river on the morrow.

The river was passed; and, at the close of a toilsome day's march, the army, long after sunset, took up its quarters in a grove of mango-trees near Plassey, within a mile of the enemy. Clive was unable to sleep: he heard, through the whole night, the sound of drums and cymbals from the vast camp of the Nabob. It is not strange that even his stout heart should now and then have sunk, when he reflected against what odds, and for what a prize, he was in a few hours to contend.

Nor was the rest of Surajah Dowlah more peaceful. His mind, at once weak and stormy, was distracted by wild and horrible apprehensions. Appalled by the greatness and nearness of the crisis, distrusting his captains, dreading every one who approached him, dreading to be left alone, he sat gloomily in his tent, haunted, a Greek poet would have said, by the furies of those who had cursed him with their last breath in the Black Hole.

The day broke, the day which was to decide the fate of India. At sunrise the army of the Nabob, pouring through many openings from the camp, began to move towards the grove where the English lay. Forty thousand infantry, armed with firelocks, pikes, swords, bows and arrows, covered the plain. They were accompanied by fifty pieces of ordnance of the largest size, each tugged by a long team of white oxen, and each pushed on from behind by an elephant. Some smaller guns, under the direction of a few French auxiliaries, were perhaps more formidable. The cavalry were fifteen thousand, drawn, not from the effeminate population of Bengal, but from the bolder race which inhabits the northern provinces; and the practised eye of Clive could perceive that both the men and the horses were more powerful than those of the Carnatic. The force which he had to oppose to this great multitude consisted of only three thousand men. But of these nearly a thousand were English; and all were led by English officers, and trained in the English discipline. Conspicuous in the ranks of the little army were the men of the Thirty-Ninth Regiment, which still bears on its colours, amidst many honourable additions won under Wellington in Spain and Gascony, the name of Plassey, and the proud motto, *Primus in Indis*.

The battle commenced with a cannonade in which the artillery of the Nabob did scarcely any execution, while the few field-pieces of the English produced great effect. Several of the most distinguished officers in Surajah Dowlah's service fell. Disorder began to spread through his ranks. His own terror increased every moment. One of the conspirators urged on him the expediency of retreating. The insidious advice, agreeing as it did with what his own terrors suggested, was readily received. He ordered his army to fall back, and this order decided his fate. Clive snatched the moment, and ordered his troops to advance. The confused and dispirited multitude gave way before the onset of disciplined valour. No mob attacked by regular soldiers was ever more completely routed. The little band of Frenchmen, who alone ventured to confront the English, were swept down the stream of fugitives. In an hour the forces of Surajah Dowlah were dispersed, never to reassemble. Only five hundred of the vanquished were slain. But their camp, their guns, their baggage, innumerable waggons, innumerable cattle, remained in the power of the conquerors. With the loss of twenty-two soldiers killed and fifty wounded, Clive had scattered an army of near sixty thousand men, and subdued an empire larger and more populous than Great Britain.

Meer Jaffier had given no assistance to the English during the action. But, as soon as he saw that the fate of the day was decided, he drew off his division of the army, and, when the battle was over, sent his congratulations to his ally. The next morning he repaired to the English quarters, not a little uneasy as to the reception which awaited him there. He gave evident signs of alarm when a guard was drawn out to receive him with the honours due to his rank. But his apprehensions were speedily removed. Clive came forward to meet him, embraced him, saluted him as Nabob of the three great provinces of Bengal, Bahar, and Orissa, listened graciously to his apologies, and advised him to march without delay to Moorshedabad.

Surajah Dowlah had fled from the field of battle with all the speed with which a fleet camel could carry him, and arrived at Moorshedabad in little more than twenty-four hours. There he called his councillors round him. The wisest advised him to put himself into the hands of the English, from whom he had nothing worse to fear than deposition and confinement. But he attributed this suggestion to treachery. Others urged him to try the chance of war again. He approved the advice, and issued orders accordingly. But he wanted spirit to adhere even during one day to a manly resolution. He learned that Meer Jaffier had arrived; and his terrors became insupportable. Disguised in a mean dress, with a casket of jewels in his hand, he let himself down at night from a window of his palace, and, accompanied by only two attendants, embarked on the river for Patna.

In a few days Clive arrived at Moorshedabad, escorted by two hundred English soldiers and three hundred sepoys. For his residence had been assigned a palace, which was surrounded by a garden so spacious that all the troops who accompanied him could conveniently encamp within it. The ceremony of the installation of Meer Jaffier was instantly performed. Clive led the new Nabob to the seat of honour, placed him on it, presented to him, after the immemorial fashion of the East, an offering of gold, and then, turning to the natives who filled the hall, congratulated them on the good fortune which had freed them from a tyrant. He was compelled on this occasion to use the services of an interpreter; for it is remarkable that, long as he resided in India, intimately acquainted as he was with Indian politics and with the Indian character, and adored as he was by his Indian soldiery, he never learned to express himself with facility in any Indian language. He is said indeed to have been sometimes under the necessity of employing, in his intercourse with natives of India, the smattering of Portuguese which he had acquired, when a lad, in Brazil.

The new sovereign was now called upon to fulfil the engagements into which he had entered with his allies. A conference was held at the house of Jugget Seit, the great banker, for the purpose of making the necessary arrangements. Omichund came thither, fully believing himself to stand high in the favour of Clive who, with dissimulation surpassing even the dissimulation of Bengal, had up to that day treated him with undiminished kindness. The white treaty was produced and read. Clive then turned to Mr. Scrafton, one of the servants of the Company, and said in English, "It is now time to undeceive Omichund." "Omichund," said Mr. Scrafton in Hindostanee, "the red treaty is a trick. You are to have nothing." Omichund fell back insensible into the arms of his attendants. He revived; but his mind was irreparably ruined. Clive, who, though little troubled by scruples of conscience in his dealings with Indian politicians, was not inhuman, seems to have been touched. He saw Omichund a few days later, spoke to him kindly, advised him to make a pilgrimage to one of the great temples of India, in the hope that change of scene might restore his health, and was even disposed, notwithstanding all that had passed, again to employ his talents in the public service. But, from the moment of that sudden shock, the unhappy man sank gradually into idiocy. He, who had formerly been distinguished by the strength of his understanding and the simplicity of his habits, now squandered the remains of his fortune on childish trinkets, and loved to exhibit himself dressed in rich garments, and hung with precious stones. In this abject state he languished a few months, and then died.

We should not think it necessary to offer any remarks for the purpose of directing the judgment of our readers with respect to this transaction, had not Sir John Malcolm undertaken to defend it in all its parts. He regrets, indeed, that it was necessary to employ means so liable to abuse as forgery; but he will not admit than any blame attaches to those who deceived the deceiver. He thinks that the English were not bound to keep faith with one who kept no faith with them, and that, if they had fulfilled their engagements with the wily Bengalee, so signal an example of successful treason would have produced a crowd of imitators. Now, we will not discuss this point on any rigid principles of morality. Indeed, it is quite unnecessary to do so; for, looking at the question as a question of expediency in the lowest sense of the word, and using no arguments but such as Machiavelli might have employed in his conferences with Borgia, we are convinced that Clive was altogether in the wrong, and that he committed, not merely a crime, but a blunder. That honesty is the best policy is a maxim which we firmly believe to be generally correct, even with respect to the temporal interest of individuals; but, with respect to societies, the rule is subject to still fewer exceptions, and that for this reason, that the life of societies is longer than the life of individuals. It is possible to mention men who have owed great worldly prosperity to breaches of private faith. But we doubt whether it be possible to mention a state which has on the whole been a gainer by a breach of public faith. The entire history of British India is an illustration of the great truth, that it is not prudent to oppose perfidy to perfidy, and that the most efficient weapon with which men can encounter falsehood is truth. During a long course of years, the English rulers of India, surrounded by allies and enemies whom no engagement could bind, have generally acted with sincerity and uprightness; and the event has proved that sincerity and uprightness are wisdom. English valour and English intelligence have done less to extend and to preserve our Oriental empire than English veracity. All that we could have gained by imitating the doublings, the evasions, the fictions, the perjuries which have been employed against us, is as nothing, when compared with what we have gained by being the one power in India on whose word reliance can be placed. No oath which superstition can devise, no hostage however precious, inspires a hundredth part of the confidence which is produced by the "yea, yea," and "nay, nay," of a British envoy. No fastness, however strong by art or nature, gives to its inmates a security like that enjoyed by the chief who, passing through the territories of powerful and deadly enemies, is armed with the British guarantee. The mightiest princes of the East can scarcely, by the offer of enormous usury, draw forth any portion of the wealth which is concealed under the hearths of their subjects. The British Government offers little more than four per cent.; and avarice hastens to bring forth tens of millions of rupees from its most secret repositories. A hostile monarch may promise mountains of gold to our sepoys, on condition that they will desert the standard of the Company. The Company promises only a moderate pension after a long service. But every sepoy knows that the promise of the Company will be kept: he knows that if he lives a hundred years his rice and salt are as secure as the salary of the Governor-General: and he knows that there is not another state in India which would not, in spite of the most solemn vows, leave him to die of hunger in a ditch as soon as he had ceased to be useful. The greatest advantage which a government can possess is to be the one trustworthy government in the midst of governments which nobody can trust. This advantage we enjoy in Asia. Had we acted during the last two generations on the principles which Sir John Malcolm appears to have considered as sound, had we, as often as we had to deal with people like Omichund, retaliated by lying, and forging, and breaking faith, after their fashion, it is our firm belief that no courage or capacity could have upheld our empire.

Sir John Malcolm admits that Clive's breach of faith could be justified only by the strongest necessity. As we think that breach of faith not only unnecessary, but most inexpedient, we need hardly say that we altogether condemn it.

Omichund was not the only victim of the revolution. Surajah Dowlah was taken a few days after his flight, and was brought before Meer Jaffier. There he flung himself on the ground in convulsions of fear, and with tears and loud cries implored the mercy which he had never shown. Meer Jaffier hesitated; but his son Meeran, a youth of seventeen, who in feebleness of brain and savageness of nature greatly resembled the wretched captive, was implacable. Surajah Dowlah was led into a secret chamber, to which in a short time the ministers of death were sent. In this act the English bore no part; and Meer Jaffier understood so much of their feelings, that he thought it necessary to apologise to them for having avenged them on their most malignant enemy.

The shower of wealth now fell copiously on the Company and its servants. A sum of eight hundred thousand pounds sterling, in coined silver, was sent down the river from Moorshedabad to Fort William. The fleet which conveyed this treasure consisted of more than a hundred boats, and performed its triumphal voyage with flags flying and music playing. Calcutta, which a few months before had been desolate, was now more prosperous than ever. Trade revived; and the signs of affluence appeared in every English house. As to Clive, there was no limit to his acquisitions but his own moderation. The treasury of Bengal was thrown open to him. There were piled up, after the usage of Indian princes, immense masses of coin, among which might not seldom be detected the florins and byzants with which, before any European ship had turned the Cape of Good Hope, the Venetians purchased the stuffs and spices of the East. Clive walked between heaps of gold and silver, crowned with rubies and diamonds, and was at liberty to help himself. He accepted between two and three hundred thousand pounds.

The pecuniary transactions between Meer Jaffier and Clive were sixteen years later condemned by the public voice, and severely criticised in Parliament. They are vehemently defended by Sir John Malcolm. The accusers of the victorious general represented his gains as the wages of corruption, or as plunder extorted at the point of the sword from a helpless ally. The biographer, on the other hand, considers these great acquisitions as free gifts, honourable alike to the donor and to the receiver, and compares them to the rewards bestowed by foreign powers on Marlborough, on Nelson, and on Wellington. It had always, he says, been customary in the East to give and receive presents; and there was, as yet, no Act of Parliament positively prohibiting English functionaries in India from profiting by this Asiatic usage. This reasoning, we own, does not quite satisfy us. We do not suspect Clive of selling the interests of his employers or his country; but we cannot acquit him of having done what, if not in itself evil, was yet of evil example. Nothing is more clear than that a general ought to be the servant of his own government, and of no other. It follows that whatever rewards he receives for his services ought to be given either by his own government, or with the full knowledge and approbation of his own government. This rule ought to be strictly maintained even with respect to the merest bauble, with respect to a cross, a medal, or a yard of coloured riband. But how can any government be well served, if those who command its forces are at liberty, without its permission, without its privity, to accept princely fortunes from its allies? It is idle to say that there was then no Act of Parliament prohibiting the practice of taking presents from Asiatic sovereigns. It is not on the Act which was passed at a later period for the purpose of preventing any such taking of presents, but on grounds which were valid before that Act was passed, on grounds of common law and common sense, that we arraign the conduct of Clive. There is no Act that we know of, prohibiting the Secretary of State for Foreign Affairs from being in the pay of continental powers. But it is not the less true that a Secretary who should receive a secret pension from France would grossly violate his duty, and would deserve severe punishment. Sir John Malcolm compares the conduct of Clive with that of the Duke of Wellington. Suppose,—and we beg pardon for putting such a supposition even for the sake of argument,—that the Duke of Wellington had, after the campaign of 1815, and while he commanded the army of occupation in France, privately accepted two hundred thousand pounds from Louis the Eighteenth, as a mark of gratitude for the great services which his Grace had rendered to the House of Bourbon; what would be thought of such a transaction? Yet the statute-book no more forbids the taking of presents in Europe now than it forbade the taking of presents in Asia then.

At the same time, it must be admitted that, in Clive's case, there were many extenuating circumstances. He considered himself as the general, not of the Crown, but of the Company. The Company had, by implication at least, authorised its agents to enrich themselves by means of the liberality of the native princes, and by other means still more objectionable. It was hardly to be expected that the servant should entertain stricter notions of his duty than were entertained by his masters. Though Clive did not distinctly acquaint his employers with what had taken place, and request their sanction, he did not, on the other hand, by studied concealment, show that he was conscious of having done wrong. On the contrary, he avowed with the greatest openness that the Nabob's bounty had raised him to affluence. Lastly, though we think that he ought not in such a way to have taken any thing, we must admit that he deserves praise for having taken so little. He accepted twenty lacs of rupees. It would have cost him only a word to make the twenty forty. It was a very easy exercise of virtue to declaim in England against Clive's rapacity; but not one in a hundred of his accusers would have shown so much self-command in the treasury of Moorshedabad.

Meer Jaffier could be upheld on the throne only by the hand which had placed him on it. He was not, indeed, a mere boy; nor had he been so unfortunate as to be born in the purple. He was not therefore quite so imbecile or quite so depraved as his predecessor had been. But he had none of the talents or virtues which his post required; and his son and heir, Meeran, was another Surajah Dowlah. The recent revolution had unsettled the minds of men. Many chiefs were in open insurrection against the new Nabob. The viceroy of the rich and powerful province of Oude who, like the other viceroys of the Mogul, was now in truth an independent sovereign, menaced Bengal with invasion. Nothing but the talents and authority of Clive could support the tottering government. While things were in this state a ship arrived with despatches which had been written at the India House before the news of the battle of Plassey had reached London. The Directors had determined to place the English settlements in Bengal under a government constituted in the most cumbrous and absurd manner; and, to make the matter worse, no place in the arrangement was assigned to Clive. The persons who were selected to form this new government, greatly to their honour, took on themselves the responsibility of disobeying these preposterous orders, and invited Clive to exercise the supreme authority. He consented; and it soon appeared that the servants of the Company had only anticipated the wishes of their employers. The Directors, on receiving news of Clive's brilliant success, instantly appointed him governor of their possessions in Bengal, with the highest marks of gratitude and esteem. His power was now boundless, and far surpassed even that which Dupleix had attained in the south of India. Meer Jaffier regarded him with slavish awe. On one occasion, the Nabob spoke with severity to a native chief of high rank, whose followers had been engaged in a brawl with some of the Company's sepoys. "Are you yet to learn," he said, "who that Colonel Clive is, and in what station God has placed him?" The chief, who, as a famous jester and an old friend of Meer Jaffier, could venture to take liberties, answered, "I affront the Colonel! I, who never get up in the morning without making three low bows to his jackass!" This was hardly an exaggeration. Europeans and natives were alike at Clive's feet. The English regarded him as the only man who could force Meer Jaffier to keep his engagements with them. Meer Jaffier regarded him as the only man who could protect the new dynasty against turbulent subjects and encroaching neighbours.

It is but justice to say that Clive used his power ably and vigorously for the advantage of his country. He sent forth an expedition against the tract lying to the north of the Carnatic. In this tract the French still had the ascendency; and it was important to dislodge them. The conduct of the enterprise was entrusted to an officer of the name of Forde, who was then little known, but in whom the keen eye of the governor had detected military talents of a high order. The success of the expedition was rapid and splendid.

While a considerable part of the army of Bengal was thus engaged at a distance, a new and formidable danger menaced the western frontier. The Great Mogul was a prisoner at Delhi in the hands of a subject. His eldest son, named Shah Alum, destined to be, during many years, the sport of adverse fortune, and to be a tool in the hands, first of the Mahrattas, and then of the English, had fled from the palace of his father. His birth was still revered in India. Some powerful princes, the Nabob of Oude in particular, were inclined to favour him. Shah Alum found it easy to draw to his standard great numbers of the military adventurers with whom every part of the country swarmed. An army of forty thousand men, of various races and religions, Mahrattas, Rohillas, Jauts, and Afghans, was speedily assembled round him; and he formed the design of overthrowing the upstart whom the English had elevated to a throne, and of establishing his own authority throughout Bengal, Orissa, and Bahar.

Meer Jaffier's terror was extreme; and the only expedient which occurred to him was to purchase, by the payment of a large sum of money, an accommodation with Shah Alum. This expedient had been repeatedly employed by those who, before him, had ruled the rich and unwarlike provinces near the mouth of the Ganges. But Clive treated the suggestion with a scorn worthy of his strong sense and dauntless courage. "If you do this," he wrote, "you will have the Nabob of Oude, the Mahrattas, and many more, come from all parts of the confines of your country, who will bully you out of money till you have none left in your treasury. I beg your excellency will rely on the fidelity of the English, and of those troops which are attached to you." He wrote in a similar strain to the governor of Patna, a brave native soldier, whom he highly esteemed. "Come to no terms; defend your city to the last. Rest assured that the English are stanch and firm friends, and that they never desert a cause in which they have once taken a part."

He kept his word. Shah Alum had invested Patna, and was on the point of proceeding to storm, when he learned that the Colonel was advancing by forced marches. The whole army which was approaching consisted of only four hundred and fifty Europeans, and two thousand five hundred sepoys. But Clive and his Englishmen were now objects of dread over all the East. As soon as his advanced guard appeared, the besiegers fled before him. A few

French adventurers who were about the person of the prince advised him to try the chance of battle; but in vain. In a few days this great army, which had been regarded with so much uneasiness by the court of Moorshedabad, melted away before the mere terror of the British name.

The conqueror returned in triumph to Fort William. The joy of Meer Jaffier was as unbounded as his fears had been, and led him to bestow on his preserver a princely token of gratitude. The quit-rent which the East India Company was bound to pay to the Nabob for the extensive lands held by them to the south of Calcutta amounted to near thirty thousand pounds sterling a year. The whole of this splendid estate, sufficient to support with dignity the highest rank of the British peerage, was now conferred on Clive for life.

This present we think Clive justified in accepting. It was a present which, from its very nature, could be no secret. In fact, the Company itself was his tenant, and, by its acquiescence, signified its approbation of Meer Jaffier's grant.

But the gratitude of Meer Jaffier did not last long. He had for some time felt that the powerful ally who had set him up might pull him down, and had been looking round for support against the formidable strength by which he had himself been hitherto supported. He knew that it would be impossible to find among the natives of India any force which would look the Colonel's little army in the face. The French power in Bengal was extinct. But the fame of the Dutch had anciently been great in the Eastern seas; and it was not yet distinctly known in Asia how much the power of Holland had declined in Europe. Secret communications passed between the court of Moorshedabad, and the Dutch factory at Chinsurah; and urgent letters were sent from Chinsurah, exhorting the government of Batavia to fit out an expedition which might balance the power of the English in Bengal. The authorities of Batavia, eager to extend the influence of their country, and still more eager to obtain for themselves a share of the wealth which had recently raised so many English adventurers to opulence, equipped a powerful armament. Seven large ships from Java arrived unexpectedly in the Hoogley. The military force on board amounted to fifteen hundred men, of whom about one half were Europeans. The enterprise was well timed. Clive had sent such large detachments to oppose the French in the Carnatic that his army was now inferior in number to that of the Dutch. He knew that Meer Jaffier secretly favoured the invaders. He knew that he took on himself a serious responsibility if he attacked the forces of a friendly power;

that the English ministers could not wish to see a war with Holland added to that in which they were already engaged with France; that they might disavow his acts; that they might punish him. He had recently remitted a great part of his fortune to Europe, through the Dutch East India Company; and he had therefore a strong interest in avoiding any quarrel. But he was satisfied, that if he suffered the Batavian armament to pass up the river and to join the garrison of Chinsurah, Meer Jaffier would throw himself into the arms of these new allies, and that the English ascendency in Bengal would be exposed to most serious danger. He took his resolution with characteristic boldness, and was most ably seconded by his officers, particularly by Colonel Forde, to whom the most important part of the operations was entrusted. The Dutch attempted to force a passage. The English encountered them both by land and water. On both elements the enemy had a great superiority of force. On both they were signally defeated. Their ships were taken. Their troops were put to a total rout. Almost all the European soldiers, who constituted the main strength of the invading army, were killed or taken. The conquerors sat down before Chinsurah; and the chiefs of that settlement, now thoroughly humbled, consented to the terms which Clive dictated. They engaged to build no fortifications, and to raise no troops beyond a small force necessary for the police of their factories; and it was distinctly provided that any violation of these covenants should be punished with instant expulsion from Bengal.

Three months after this great victory, Clive sailed for England. At home, honours and rewards awaited him, not indeed equal to his claims or to his ambition, but still such as, when his age, his rank in the army, and his original place in society are considered, must be pronounced rare and splendid. He was raised to the Irish peerage, and encouraged to expect an English title. George the Third, who had just ascended the throne, received him with great distinction. The ministers paid him marked attention; and Pitt, whose influence in the House of Commons and in the country was unbounded, was eager to mark his regard for one whose exploits had contributed so much to the lustre of that memorable period. The great orator had already in Parliament described Clive as a heaven-born general, as a man who, bred to the labour of the desk, had displayed a military genius which might excite the admiration of the King of Prussia. There were then no reporters in the gallery; but these words, emphatically spoken by the first statesman of the age, had passed from mouth to mouth, had been transmitted to Clive in Bengal, and had greatly delighted and flattered him.

Indeed, since the death of Wolfe, Clive was the only English general of whom his countrymen had much reason to be proud. The Duke of Cumberland had been generally unfortunate; and his single victory, having been gained over his countrymen, and used with merciless severity, had been more fatal to his popularity than his many defeats. Conway, versed in the learning of his profession, and personally courageous, wanted vigour and capacity. Granby, honest, generous, and as brave as a lion, had neither science nor genius. Sackville, inferior in knowledge and abilities to none of his contemporaries, had incurred, unjustly as we believe, the imputation most fatal to the character of a soldier. It was under the command of a foreign general that the British had triumphed at Minden and Warburg. The people therefore, as was natural, greeted with pride and delight a captain of their own, whose native courage and self-taught skill had placed him on a level with the great tacticians of Germany.

The wealth of Clive was such as enabled him to vie with the first grandees of England. There remains proof that he had remitted more than a hundred and eighty thousand pounds through the Dutch East India Company, and more than forty thousand pounds through the English Company. The amount which he had sent home through private houses was also considerable. He had invested great sums in jewels, then a very common mode of remittance from India. His purchases of diamonds, at Madras alone, amounted to twenty-five thousand pounds. Besides a great mass of ready money, he had his Indian estate, valued by himself at twenty-seven thousand a-year. His whole annual income, in the opinion of Sir John Malcolm, who is desirous to state it as low as possible, exceeded forty thousand pounds; and incomes of forty thousand pounds at the time of the accession of George the Third were at least as rare as incomes of a hundred thousand pounds now. We may safely affirm that no Englishman who started with nothing has ever, in any line of life, created such a fortune at the early age of thirty-four.

It would be unjust not to add that Clive made a creditable use of his riches. As soon as the battle of Plassey had laid the foundation of his fortune, he sent ten thousand pounds to his sisters, bestowed as much more on other poor friends and relations, ordered his agent to pay eight hundred a-year to his parents, and to insist that they should keep a carriage, and settled five hundred a-year on his old commander Lawrence, whose means were very slender. The whole sum which Clive expended in this manner may be calculated at fifty thousand pounds.

He now set himself to cultivate Parliamentary interest. His purchases of land seem to have been made in a great measure with that view, and, after the general election of 1761, he found himself in the House of Commons, at the head of a body of dependents whose support must have been important to any administration. In English politics, however, he did not take a prominent part. His first attachments, as we have seen, were to Mr. Fox; at a later period he was attracted by the genius and success of Mr. Pitt; but finally he connected himself in the closest manner with George Grenville. Early in the session of 1764, when the illegal and impolitic persecution of that worthless demagogue Wilkes had strongly excited the public mind, the town was amused by an anecdote, which we have seen in some unpublished memoirs of Horace Walpole. Old Mr. Richard Clive, who, since his son's elevation, had been introduced into society for which his former habits had not well fitted him, presented himself at the levee. The King asked him where Lord Clive was. "He will be in town very soon," said the old gentleman, loud enough to be heard by the whole circle, "and then your Majesty will have another vote."

But in truth all Clive's views were directed towards the country in which he had so eminently distinguished himself as a soldier and a statesman; and it was by considerations relating to India that his conduct as a public man in England was regulated. The power of the Company, though an anomaly, is in our time, we are firmly persuaded, a beneficial anomaly. In the time of Clive, it was not merely an anomaly, but a nuisance. There was no Board of Control. The Directors were for the most part mere traders, ignorant of general politics, ignorant of the peculiarities of the empire which had strangely become subject to them. The Court of Proprietors, wherever it chose to interfere, was able to have its way. That court was more numerous, as well as more powerful than at present; for then every share of five hundred pounds conferred a vote. The meetings were large, stormy, even riotous, the debates indecently virulent. All the turbulence of a Westminster election, all the trickery and corruption of a Grampound election, disgraced the proceedings of this assembly on questions of the most solemn importance. Fictitious votes were manufactured on a gigantic scale. Clive himself laid out a hundred thousand pounds in the purchase of stock, which he then divided among nominal proprietors on whom he could depend, and whom he brought down in his train to every discussion and every ballot. Others did the same, though not to quite so enormous an extent.

The interest taken by the public of England in Indian questions was then far greater than at present, and the reason is obvious. At present a writer enters the service young; he climbs slowly; he is fortunate if, at forty-five, he can return to his country with an annuity of a thousand a-year, and with savings amounting to thirty thousand pounds. A great quantity of wealth is made by English functionaries in India; but no single functionary makes a very large fortune, and what is made is slowly, hardly, and honestly earned. Only four or five high political offices are reserved for public men from England. The residencies, the secretaryships, the seats in the boards of revenue and in the Sudder courts, are all filled by men who have given the best years of life to the service of the Company; nor can any talents however splendid or any connexions however powerful obtain those lucrative posts for any person who has not entered by the regular door, and mounted by the regular gradations. Seventy years ago, less money was brought home from the East than in our time. But it was divided among a very much smaller number of persons, and immense sums were often accumulated in a few months. Any Englishman, whatever his age might be, might hope to be one of the lucky emigrants. If he made a good speech in Leadenhall Street, or published a clever pamphlet in defence of the chairman, he might be sent out in the Company's service, and might return in three or four years as rich as Pigot or as Clive. Thus the India House was a lottery-office, which invited every body to take a chance, and held out ducal fortunes as the prizes destined for the lucky few. As soon as it was known that there was a part of the world where a lieutenant-colonel had one morning received as a present an estate as large as that of the Earl of Bath or the Marquis of Rockingham, and where it seemed that such a trifle as ten or twenty thousand pounds was to be had by any British functionary for the asking, society began to exhibit all the symptoms of the South Sea year, a feverish excitement, an ungovernable impatience to be rich, a contempt for slow, sure, and moderate gains.

At the head of the preponderating party in the India House, had long stood a powerful, able, and ambitious Director of the name of Sulivan. He had conceived a strong jealousy of Clive, and remembered with bitterness the audacity with which the late governor of Bengal had repeatedly set at nought the authority of the distant Directors of the Company. An apparent reconciliation took place after Clive's arrival; but enmity remained deeply rooted in the hearts of both. The whole body of Directors was then chosen annually. At the election of 1763, Clive attempted to break down the power of the dominant faction. The contest was carried on with a violence which he describes as tremendous. Sulivan was victorious, and hastened to take his revenge. The grant of rent which Clive had received from Meer Jaffier was, in the opinion of the best English lawyers, valid. It had been made by exactly the same authority from which the Company had received their chief possessions in Bengal, and the Company had long acquiesced in it. The Directors, however, most unjustly determined to confiscate it, and Clive was forced to file a bill in Chancery against them.

But a great and sudden turn in affairs was at hand. Every ship from Bengal had for some time brought alarming tidings. The internal misgovernment of the province had reached such a point that it could go no further. What, indeed, was to be expected from a body of public servants exposed to temptation such that, as Clive once said, flesh and blood could not bear it, armed with irresistible power, and responsible only to the corrupt, turbulent, distracted, ill-informed Company, situated at such a distance that the average interval between the sending of a despatch and the receipt of an answer was above a year and a half? Accordingly, during the five years which followed the departure of Clive from Bengal, the misgovernment of the English was carried to a point such as seems hardly compatible with the very existence of society. The Roman proconsul, who, in a year or two, squeezed out of a province the means of rearing marble palaces and baths on the shores of Campania, of drinking from amber, of feasting on singing birds, of exhibiting armies of gladiators and flocks of camelopards, the Spanish viceroy, who, leaving behind him the curses of Mexico or Lima, entered Madrid with a long train of gilded coaches, and of sumpter-horses trapped and shod with silver, were now outdone. Cruelty, indeed, properly so called, was not among the vices of the servants of the Company. But cruelty itself could hardly have produced greater evils than sprang from their unprincipled eagerness to be rich. They pulled down their creature, Meer Jaffier. They set up in his place another Nabob, named Meer Cossim. But Meer Cossim had talents and a will; and, though sufficiently inclined to oppress his subjects himself, he could not bear to see them ground to the dust by oppressions which yielded him no profit, nay, which destroyed his revenue in its very source. The English accordingly pulled down Meer Cossim, and set up Meer Jaffier again; and Meer Cossim, after revenging himself by a massacre surpassing in atrocity that of the Black Hole, fled to the dominions of the Nabob of Oude. At every one of these revolutions, the new prince divided among his foreign masters whatever could be scraped together from the treasury of his fallen predecessor. The immense population of his dominions was given up as a prey to those who had made him a sovereign, and who could unmake him. The servants of the Company obtained, not for their employers, but for themselves, a monopoly of almost the whole internal trade. They forced the natives to buy dear and to sell cheap. They insulted with impunity the tribunals, the police, and the fiscal authorities of the country. They covered with their protection a set of native dependents who ranged through the provinces, spreading desolation and terror wherever they appeared. Every servant of a British factor was armed with all the power of his master; and his master was armed with all the power of the Company. Enormous fortunes were thus rapidly accumulated at Calcutta, while thirty millions of human beings were reduced to the extremity of wretchedness. They had been accustomed to live under tyranny, but never under tyranny like this. They found the little finger of the Company thicker than the loins of Surajah Dowlah. Under their old masters they had at least one resource: when the evil became insupportable, the people rose and pulled down the government. But the English government was not to be so shaken off. That government, oppressive as the most oppressive form of barbarian despotism, was strong with all the strength of civilisation. It resembled the government of evil Genii, rather than the government of human tyrants. Even despair could not inspire the soft Bengalee with courage to confront men of English breed, the hereditary nobility of mankind, whose skill and valour had so often triumphed in spite of tenfold odds. The unhappy race never attempted resistance. Sometimes they submitted in patient misery. Sometimes they fled from the white man, as their fathers had been used to fly from the Mahratta; and the palanquin of the English traveller was often carried through silent villages and towns, which the report of his approach had made desolate.

The foreign lords of Bengal were naturally objects of hatred to all the neighbouring powers; and to all the haughty race presented a dauntless front. Their armies, every where outnumbered, were every where victorious. A succession of commanders, formed in the school of Clive, still maintained the fame of their country. "It must be acknowledged," says the Mussulman historian of those times, "that this nation's presence of mind, firmness of temper, and undaunted bravery, are past all question. They join the most resolute courage to the most cautious prudence; nor have they their equals in the art of ranging themselves in battle array and fighting in order. If to so many military qualifications they knew how to join the arts of government, if they exerted as much ingenuity and solicitude in relieving the people of God, as they do in whatever concerns their military affairs, no nation in the world would be preferable to them, or worthier of command. But the people under their dominion groan every where, and are reduced to poverty and distress. Oh God! come to the assistance of thine afflicted servants, and deliver them from the oppressions which they suffer."

It was impossible, however, that even the military establishment should long continue exempt from the vices which pervaded every other part of the government. Rapacity, luxury, and the spirit of insubordination, spread from the civil service to the officers of the army, and from the officers to the soldiers. The evil continued to grow till every mess-room became the seat of conspiracy and cabal, and till the sepoys could be kept in order only by wholesale executions.

At length the state of things in Bengal began to excite uneasiness at home. A succession of revolutions; a disorganized administration; the natives pillaged, yet the Company not enriched; every fleet bringing back fortunate adventurers who were able to purchase manors and to build stately dwellings, yet bringing back also alarming accounts of the financial prospects of the government; war on the frontiers; disaffection in the army; the national character disgraced by excesses resembling those of Verres and Pizarro; such was the spectacle which dismayed those who were conversant with Indian affairs. The general cry was that Clive, and Clive alone, could save the empire which he had founded.

This feeling manifested itself in the strongest manner at a very full General Court of Proprietors. Men of all parties, forgetting their feuds and trembling for their dividends, exclaimed that Clive was the man whom the crisis required, that the oppressive proceedings which had been adopted respecting his estate ought to be dropped, and that he ought to be entreated to return to India.

Clive rose. As to his estate, he said, he would make such propositions to the Directors as would, he trusted, lead to an amicable settlement. But there was a still greater difficulty. It was proper to tell them that he never would undertake the government of Bengal while his enemy Sulivan was chairman of the Company. The tumult was violent. Sulivan could scarcely obtain a hearing. An overwhelming majority of the assembly was on Clive's side. Sulivan wished to try the result of a ballot. But, according to the by-laws of the Company, there can be no ballot except on a requisition signed by nine proprietors; and, though hundreds were present, nine persons could not be found to set their hands to such a requisition.

Clive was in consequence nominated Governor and Commander-in-Chief of the British possessions in Bengal. But he adhered to his declaration, and refused to enter on his office till the event of the next election of Directors should be known. The contest was obstinate; but Clive triumphed. Sulivan, lately absolute master of the India House, was within a vote of losing his own seat; and both the chairman and the deputy-chairman were friends of the new governor.

Such were the circumstances under which Lord Clive sailed for the third and last time to India. In May 1765 he reached Calcutta; and he found the whole machine of government even more fearfully disorganized than he had anticipated. Meer Jaffier, who had some time before lost his eldest son Meeran, had died while Clive was on his voyage out. The English functionaries at Calcutta had already received from home strict orders not to accept presents from the native princes. But, eager for gain, and unaccustomed to respect the commands of their distant, ignorant, and negligent masters, they again set up the throne of Bengal to sale. About one hundred and forty thousand pounds sterling were distributed among nine of the most powerful servants of the Company; and, in consideration of this bribe, an infant son of the deceased Nabob was placed on the seat of his father. The news of the ignominious bargain met Clive on his arrival. In a private letter, written immediately after his landing to an intimate friend, he poured out his feelings in language which, proceeding from a man so daring, so resolute, and so little given to theatrical display of sentiment, seems to us singularly touching. "Alas!" he says, "how is the English name sunk! I could not avoid paying the tribute of a few tears to the departed and lost fame of the British nation—irrecoverably so, I fear. However, I do declare, by that great Being who is the searcher of all hearts, and to whom we must be accountable if there be a hereafter, that I am come out with a mind superior to all corruption, and that I am determined to destroy these great and growing evils, or perish in the attempt."

The Council met, and Clive stated to them his full determination to make a thorough reform, and to use for that purpose the whole of the ample authority, civil and military, which had been confided to him. Johnstone, one of the boldest and worst men in the assembly, made some show of opposition. Clive interrupted him, and haughtily demanded whether he meant to question the power of the new government. Johnstone was cowed, and disclaimed any such intention. All the faces round the board grew long and pale; and not another syllable of dissent was uttered.

Clive redeemed his pledge. He remained in India about a year and a half; and in that short time effected one of the most extensive, difficult, and salutary reforms that ever was accomplished by any statesman. This was the part of his life on which he afterwards looked back with most pride. He had it in his power to triple his already splendid fortune: to connive at abuses while pretending to remove them; to conciliate the good-will of all the English in Bengal, by giving up to their rapacity a helpless and timid race, who knew not where lay the island which sent forth their oppressors, and whose complaints had little chance of being heard across fifteen thousand miles of ocean. He knew that, if he applied himself in earnest to the work of reformation, he should raise every bad passion in arms against him. He knew how unscrupulous, how implacable, would be the hatred of those ravenous adventurers who, having counted on accumulating in a few months fortunes sufficient to support peerages, should find all their hopes frustrated. But he had chosen the good part; and he called up all the force of his mind for a battle far harder than that of Plassey. At first success seemed hopeless; but soon all obstacles began to bend before that iron courage and that vehement will. The receiving of presents from the natives was rigidly prohibited. The private trade of the servants of the Company was put down. The whole settlement seemed to be set, as one man, against these measures. But the inexorable governor declared that, if he could not find support at Fort William, he would procure it elsewhere, and sent for some civil servants from Madras to assist him in carrying on the administration. The most factious of his opponents he turned out of their offices. The rest submitted to what was inevitable; and in a very short time all resistance was quelled.

But Clive was far too wise a man not to see that the recent abuses were partly to be ascribed to a cause which could not fail to produce similar abuses as soon as the pressure of his strong hand was withdrawn. The Company had followed a mistaken policy with respect to the remuneration of its servants. The salaries were too low to afford even those indulgences which are necessary to the health and comfort of Europeans in a tropical climate. To lay by a rupee from such scanty pay was impossible. It could not be supposed that men of even average abilities would consent to pass the best years of life in exile, under a burning sun, for no other consideration than these stinted wages. It had accordingly been understood, from a very early period, that the Company's agents were at liberty to enrich themselves by their private trade. This practice had been seriously injurious to the commercial interests of the corporation. That very intelligent observer, Sir Thomas Roe, in the reign of James the First, strongly urged the Directors to apply a remedy to the abuse. "Absolutely prohibit the private trade," said he; "for your business will be better done. I know this is harsh. Men profess they come not for bare wages. But you will take away this plea if you give great wages to their content; and then you know what you part from."

In spite of this excellent advice, the Company adhered to the old system, paid low salaries, and connived at the indirect gains of the agents. The pay of a member of Council was only three hundred pounds a-year. Yet it was notorious that such a functionary could not live in India for less than ten times that sum; and it could not be expected that he would be content to live even handsomely in India without laying up something against the time of his return to England. This system, before the conquest of Bengal, might affect the amount of the dividends payable to the proprietors, but could do little harm in any other way. But the Company was now a ruling body. Its servants might still be called factors, junior merchants, senior merchants. But they were in truth proconsuls, proprætors, procurators of extensive regions. They had immense power. Their regular pay was universally admitted to be insufficient. They were, by the ancient usage of the service, and by the implied permission of their employers, warranted in enriching themselves by indirect means; and this had been the origin of the frightful oppression and corruption which had desolated Bengal. Clive saw clearly that it was absurd to give men power, and to require them to live in penury. He justly concluded that no reform could be effectual which should not be coupled with a plan for liberally remunerating the civil servants of the Company. The Directors, he knew, were not disposed to sanction any increase of the salaries out of their own treasury. The only course which remained open to the governor was one which exposed him to much misrepresentation, but which we think him fully justified in adopting. He appropriated to the support of the service the monopoly of salt, which has formed, down to our own time, a principal head of Indian revenue; and he divided the proceeds according to a scale which seems to have been not unreasonably fixed. He was in consequence accused by his enemies, and has been accused by historians, of disobeying his instructions, of violating his promises, of authorizing that very abuse which it was his special mission to destroy, namely, the trade of the Company's servants. But every discerning and impartial judge will admit, that there was really nothing in common between the system which he set up and that which he was sent to destroy. The monopoly of salt had been a source of revenue to the governments of India before Clive was born. It continued to be so long after his death. The civil servants were clearly entitled to a maintenance out of the revenue; and all that Clive did was to charge a particular portion of the revenue with their maintenance. He thus, while he put an end to the practices by which gigantic fortunes had been rapidly accumulated, gave to every British functionary employed in the East the means of slowly, but surely, acquiring a competence. Yet, such is the injustice of mankind that none of those acts which are the real stains of his life has drawn on him so much obloquy as this measure, which was in truth a reform necessary to the success of all his other reforms.

He had quelled the opposition of the civil service: that of the army was more formidable. Some of the retrenchments which had been ordered by the Directors affected the interests of the military service; and a storm arose, such as even Cæsar would not willingly have faced. It was no light thing to encounter the resistance of those who held the power of the sword, in a country governed only by the sword. Two hundred English officers engaged in a conspiracy against the government, and determined to resign their commissions on the same day, not doubting that Clive would grant any terms rather than see the army, on which alone the British empire in the East rested, left without commanders. They little knew the unconquerable spirit with which they had to deal. Clive had still a few officers round his person on whom he could rely. He sent to Fort St. George for a fresh supply. He gave commissions even to mercantile agents who were disposed to support him at this crisis; and he sent orders that every officer who resigned should be instantly brought up to Calcutta. The conspirators found that they had miscalculated. The governor was inexorable. The troops were steady. The sepoys, over whom Clive had always possessed extraordinary influence, stood by him with unshaken fidelity. The leaders in the plot were arrested, tried, and cashiered. The rest, humbled and dispirited, begged to be permitted to withdraw their resignations. Many of them declared their repentance even with tears. The younger offenders Clive treated with lenity. To the ringleaders he was inflexibly severe; but his severity was pure from all taint of private malevolence. While he sternly upheld the just authority of his office, he passed by personal insults and injuries with magnanimous disdain. One of the conspirators was accused of having planned the assassination of the governor; but Clive would not listen to the charge. "The officers," he said, "are Englishmen, not assassins."

While he reformed the civil service and established his authority over the army, he was equally successful in his foreign policy. His landing on Indian ground was the signal for immediate peace. The Nabob of Oude, with a large army, lay at that time on the frontier of Bahar. He had been joined by many Afghans and Mahrattas, and there was no small reason to expect a general coalition of all the native powers against the English. But the name of Clive quelled in an instant all opposition. The enemy implored peace in the humblest language, and submitted to such terms as the new governor chose to dictate.

At the same time, the government of Bengal was placed on a new footing. The power of the English in that province had hitherto been altogether undefined. It was unknown to the ancient constitution of the empire, and it had been ascertained by no compact. It resembled the power which, in the last decrepitude of the Western Empire, was exercised over Italy by the great chiefs of foreign mercenaries, the Ricimers and the Odoacers, who put up and pulled down at their pleasure a succession of insignificant princes, dignified with the names of Cæsar and Augustus. But as in Italy, so in India, the warlike strangers at length found it expedient to give to a domination which had been established by arms the sanction of law and ancient prescription. Theodoric thought it politic to obtain from the distant court of Byzantium a commission appointing him ruler of Italy; and Clive, in the same manner, applied to the Court of Delhi for a formal grant of the powers of which he already possessed the reality. The Mogul was absolutely helpless; and, though he murmured, had reason to be well pleased that the English were disposed to give solid rupees which he never could have extorted from them, in exchange for a few Persian characters which cost him nothing. A bargain was speedily struck; and the titular sovereign of Hindostan issued a warrant, empowering the Company to collect and administer the revenues of Bengal, Orissa, and Bahar.

There was still a Nabob, who stood to the British authorities in the same relation in which the last drivelling Chilperics and Childerics of the Merovingian line stood to their able and vigorous Mayors of the Palace, to Charles Martel and to Pepin. At one time Clive had almost made up his mind to discard this phantom altogether; but he afterwards thought that it might be convenient still to use the name of the Nabob, particularly in dealings with other European nations. The French, the Dutch, and the Danes, would, he conceived, submit far more readily to the authority of the native Prince, whom they had always been accustomed to respect, than to that of a rival trading corporation. This policy may, at that time, have been judicious. But the pretence was soon found to be too flimsy to impose on anybody; and it was altogether laid aside. The heir of Meer Jaffier still resides at Moorshedabad, the ancient capital of his house, still bears the title of Nabob, is still accosted by the English as "Your Highness," and is still suffered to retain a portion of the regal state which surrounded his ancestors. A pension of a hundred and sixty thousand pounds a-year is annually paid to him by the government. His carriage is surrounded by guards, and preceded by attendants with silver maces. His person and his dwelling are exempted from the ordinary authority of the ministers of justice. But he has not the smallest share of political power, and is, in fact, only a noble and wealthy subject of the Company.

It would have been easy for Clive, during his second administration in Bengal, to accumulate riches such as no subject in Europe possessed. He might indeed, without subjecting the rich inhabitants of the province to any pressure beyond that to which their mildest rulers had accustomed them, have received presents to the amount of three hundred thousand pounds a-year. The neighbouring princes would gladly have paid any price for his favour. But he appears to have strictly adhered to the rules which he had laid down for the guidance of others. The Rajah of Benares offered him diamonds of great value. The Nabob of Oude pressed him to accept a large sum of money and a casket of costly jewels. Clive courteously, but peremptorily refused: and it should be observed that he made no merit of his refusal, and that the facts did not come to light till after his death. He kept an exact account of his salary, of his share of the profits accruing from the trade in salt, and of those presents which, according to the fashion of the East, it would be churlish to refuse. Out of the sum arising from these resources, he defrayed the expenses of his situation. The surplus he divided among a few attached friends who had accompanied him to India. He always boasted, and, as far as we can judge, he boasted with truth, that his last administration diminished instead of increasing his fortune.

One large sum indeed he accepted. Meer Jaffier had left him by will above sixty thousand pounds sterling in specie and jewels: and the rules which had been recently laid down extended only to presents from the living, and did not affect legacies from the dead. Clive took the money, but not for himself. He made the whole over to the Company, in trust for officers and soldiers invalided in their service. The fund which still bears his name owes its origin to this princely donation.

After a stay of eighteen months, the state of his health made it necessary for him to return to Europe. At the close of January 1767 he quitted for the last time the country on whose destinies he had exercised so mighty an influence.

His second return from Bengal was not, like his first, greeted by the acclamations of his countrymen. Numerous causes were already at work which embittered the remaining years of his life and hurried him to an untimely grave. His old enemies at the India House were still powerful and active; and they had been reinforced by a large band of allies whose violence far exceeded their own. The whole crew of pilferers and oppressors from whom he had rescued Bengal persecuted him with the implacable rancour which belongs to such abject natures. Many of them even invested their property in India stock, merely that they might be better able to annoy the man whose firmness had set bounds to their rapacity. Lying newspapers were set up for no purpose but to abuse him; and the temper of the public mind was then such, that these arts, which under ordinary circumstances would have been ineffectual against truth and merit, produced an extraordinary impression.

The great events which had taken place in India had called into existence a new class of Englishmen, to whom their countrymen gave the name of Nabobs. These persons had generally sprung from families neither ancient nor opulent; they had generally been sent at an early age to the East; and they had there acquired large fortunes, which they had brought back to their native land. It was natural that, not having had much opportunity of mixing with the best society, they should exhibit some of the awkwardness and some of the pomposity of upstarts. It was natural that, during their sojourn in Asia, they should have acquired some tastes and habits surprising, if not disgusting, to persons who never had quitted Europe. It was natural that, having enjoyed great consideration in the East, they should not be disposed to sink into obscurity at home; and as they had money, and had not birth or high connexion, it was natural that they should display a little obtrusively the single advantage which they possessed. Wherever they settled there was a kind of feud between them and the old nobility and gentry, similar to that which raged in France between the farmer-general and the marquis. This enmity to the aristocracy long continued to distinguish the servants of the Company. More than twenty years after the time of which we are now speaking, Burke pronounced that among the Jacobins might be reckoned "the East Indians almost to a man, who cannot bear to find that their present importance does not bear a proportion to their wealth."

M—12*

The Nabobs soon became a most unpopular class of men. Some of them had in the East displayed eminent talents, and rendered great services to the state; but at home their talents were not shown to advantage, and their services were little known. That they had sprung from obscurity, that they had acquired great wealth, that they exhibited it insolently, that they spent it extravagantly, that they raised the price of every thing in their neighbourhood, from fresh eggs to rotten boroughs, that their liveries outshone those of dukes, that their coaches were finer than that of the Lord Mayor, that the examples of their large and ill governed households corrupted half the servants in the country, that some of them, with all their magnificence, could not catch the tone of good society, but, in spite of the stud and the crowd of menials, of the plate and the Dresden china, of the venison and the Burgundy, were still low men; these were things which excited, both in the class from which they had sprung and in the class into which they attempted to force themselves, the bitter aversion which is the effect of mingled envy and contempt. But when it was also rumoured that the fortune which had enabled its possessor to eclipse the Lord-Lieutenant on the race-ground, or to carry the county against the head of a house as old as Domesday Book, had been accumulated by violating public faith, by deposing legitimate princes, by reducing whole provinces to beggary, all the higher and better as well as all the low and evil parts of human nature were stirred against the wretch who had obtained by guilt and dishonour the riches which he now lavished with arrogant and inelegant profusion. The unfortunate Nabob seemed to be made up of those foibles against which comedy has pointed the most merciless ridicule, and of those crimes which have thrown the deepest gloom over tragedy, of Turcaret and Nero, of Monsieur Jourdain and Richard the Third. A tempest of execration and derision, such as can be compared only to that outbreak of public feeling against the Puritans which took place at the time of the Restoration, burst on the servants of the Company. The humane man was horror-struck at the way in which they had got their money, the thrifty man at the way in which they spent it. The dilettante sneered at their want of taste. The maccaroni blackballed them as vulgar fellows. Writers the most unlike in sentiment and style, Methodists and libertines, philosophers and buffoons, were for once on the same side. It is hardly too much to say that, during a space of about thirty years, the whole lighter literature of England was coloured by the feelings which we have described. Foote brought on the stage an Anglo-Indian chief, dissolute, ungenerous, and tyrannical, ashamed of the humble friends of his youth, hating the aristocracy, yet childishly eager to be numbered among them, squandering his wealth on pandars and flatterers, tricking out his chairmen with the most costly hothouse flowers, and astounding the ignorant with jargon about rupees, lacs, and jaghires. Mackenzie, with more delicate humour, depicted a plain country family raised by the Indian acquisitions of one of its members to sudden opulence, and exciting derision by an awkward mimicry of the manners of the great. Cowper, in that lofty expostulation which glows with the very spirit of the Hebrew poets, placed the oppression of India foremost in the list of those national crimes for which God had punished England with years of disastrous war, with discomfiture in her own seas, and with the loss of her transatlantic empire. If any of our readers will take the trouble to search in the dusty recesses of circulating libraries for some novel published sixty years ago, the chance is that the villain or sub-villain of the story will prove to be a savage old Nabob, with an immense fortune, a tawny complexion, a bad liver, and a worse heart.

Such, as far as we can now judge, was the feeling of the country respecting Nabobs in general. And Clive was eminently the Nabob, the ablest, the most celebrated, the highest in rank, the highest in fortune, of all the fraternity. His wealth was exhibited in a manner which could not fail to excite odium. He lived with great magnificence in Berkeley Square. He reared one palace in Shropshire and another at Claremont. His parliamentary influence might vie with that of the greatest families. But in all this splendour and power envy found something to sneer at. On some of his relations wealth and dignity seem to have sat as awkwardly as on Mackenzie's Margery Mushroom. Nor was he himself, with all his great qualities, free from those weaknesses which the satirists of that age represented as characteristic of his whole class. In the field, indeed, his habits were remarkably simple. He was constantly on horseback, was never seen but in his uniform, never wore silk, never entered a palanquin, and was content with the plainest fare. But when he was no longer at the head of an army, he laid aside this Spartan temperance for the ostentatious luxury of a Sybarite. Though his person was ungraceful, and though his harsh features were redeemed from vulgar ugliness only by their stern, dauntless, and commanding expression, he was fond of rich and gay clothing, and replenished his wardrobe with absurd profusion. Sir John Malcolm gives us a letter worthy of Sir Matthew Mite, in which Clive orders "two hundred shirts, the best and finest that can be got for love or money." A few follies of this description, grossly exaggerated by report, produced an unfavourable impression on the public mind. But this was not the worst. Black stories, of which the greater part were pure inventions, were circulated respecting his conduct in the East. He had to bear the whole odium, not only of those bad acts to which he had once or twice stooped, but of all the bad acts of all the English in India, of bad acts committed when he was absent, nay, of bad acts which he had manfully opposed and severely punished. The very abuses against which he had waged an honest, resolute, and successful war, were laid to his account. He was, in fact, regarded as the personification of all the vices and weaknesses which the public, with or without reason, ascribed to the English adventurers in Asia. We have ourselves heard old men, who knew nothing of his history, but who still retained the prejudices conceived in their youth, talk of him as an incarnate fiend. Johnson always held this language. Brown, whom Clive employed to lay out his pleasure grounds, was amazed to see in the house of his noble employer a chest which had once been filled with gold from the treasury of Moorshedabad, and could not understand how the conscience of the criminal could suffer him to sleep with such an object so near to his bedchamber. The peasantry of Surrey looked with mysterious horror on the stately house which was rising at Claremont, and whispered that the great wicked lord had ordered the walls to be made so thick in order to keep out the devil, who would one day carry him bodily away. Among the gaping clowns who drank in this frightful story was a worthless ugly lad of the name of Hunter, since widely known as William Huntington, S.S.; and the superstition which was strangely mingled with the knavery of that remarkable impostor seems to have derived no small nutriment from the tales which he heard of the life and character of Clive.

In the mean time, the impulse which Clive had given to the administration of Bengal was constantly becoming fainter and fainter. His policy was to a great extent abandoned; the abuses which he had suppressed began to revive; and at length the evils which a bad government had engendered were aggravated by one of those fearful visitations which the best government cannot avert. In the summer of 1770, the rains failed; the earth was parched up; the tanks were empty; the rivers shrank within their beds; and a famine, such as is known only in countries where every household depends for support on its own little patch of cultivation, filled the whole valley of the Ganges with misery and death. Tender and delicate women, whose veils had never been lifted before the public gaze, came forth from the inner chambers in which Eastern jealousy had kept watch over their beauty, threw themselves on the earth before the passers-by, and, with loud wailings, implored a handful of rice for their children. The Hoogley every day rolled down thousands of corpses close to the porticoes and gardens of the English conquerors. The very streets of Calcutta were blocked up by the dying and the dead. The lean and feeble survivors had not energy enough to bear the bodies of their kindred to the funeral pile or to the holy river, or even to scare away the jackals and vultures, who fed on human remains in the face of day. The extent of the mortality was never ascertained; but it was popularly reckoned by millions. This melancholy intelligence added to the excitement which already prevailed in England on Indian subjects. The proprietors of East India stock were uneasy about their dividends. All men of common humanity were touched by the calamities of our unhappy subjects; and indignation soon began to mingle itself with pity. It was rumoured that the Company's servants had created the famine by engrossing all the rice of the country; that they had sold grain for eight, ten, twelve times the price at which they had bought it; that one English functionary who, the year before, was not worth a hundred guineas, had, during that season of misery, remitted sixty thousand pounds to London. These charges we believe to have been unfounded. That servants of the Company had ventured, since Clive's departure, to deal in rice, is probable. That, if they dealt in rice, they must have gained by the scarcity, is certain. But there is no reason for thinking that they either produced or aggravated an evil which physical causes sufficiently explain. The outcry which was raised against them on this occasion was, we suspect, as absurd as the imputations which, in times of dearth at home, were once thrown by statesmen and judges, and are still thrown by two or three old women, on the corn factors. It was, however, so loud and so general that it appears to have imposed even on an intellect raised so high above vulgar prejudices as that of Adam Smith. What was still more extraordinary, these unhappy events greatly increased the unpopularity of Lord Clive. He had been some years in England when the famine took place. None of his measures had the smallest tendency to produce such a calamity. If the servants of the Company had traded in rice, they had done so in direct contravention of the rule which he had laid down, and, while in power, had resolutely enforced. But, in the eyes of his countrymen, he was, as we have said, the Nabob, the Anglo-Indian character personified; and, while he was building and planting in Surrey, he was held responsible for all the effects of a dry season in Bengal.

Parliament had hitherto bestowed very little attention on our

Eastern possessions. Since the death of George the Second, a rapid succession of weak administrations, each of which was in turn flattered and betrayed by the Court, had held the semblance of power. Intrigues in the palace, riots in the capital, and insurrectionary movements in the American colonies, had left the advisers of the crown little leisure to study Indian politics. Where they did interfere, their interference was feeble and irresolute. Lord Chatham, indeed, during the short period of his ascendency in the councils of George the Third, had meditated a bold and sweeping measure respecting the acquisitions of the Company. But his plans were rendered abortive by the strange malady which about that time began to overcloud his splendid genius.

At length, in 1772, it was generally felt that Parliament could no longer neglect the affairs of India. The Government was stronger than any which had held power since the breach between Mr. Pitt and the great Whig connexion in 1761. No pressing question of domestic or European policy required the attention of public men. There was a short and delusive lull between two tempests. The excitement produced by the Middlesex election was over; the discontents of America did not yet threaten civil war; the financial difficulties of the Company brought on a crisis; the ministers were forced to take up the subject; and the whole storm, which had long been gathering, now broke at once on the head of Clive.

His situation was indeed singularly unfortunate. He was hated throughout the country, hated at the India House, hated, above all, by those wealthy and powerful servants of the Company, whose rapacity and tyranny he had withstood. He had to bear the double odium of his bad and of his good actions, of every Indian abuse and of every Indian reform. The state of the political world was such that he could count on the support of no powerful connexion. The party to which he had belonged, that of George Grenville, had been hostile to the Government, and yet had never cordially united with the other sections of the Opposition, with the little band which still followed the fortunes of Lord Chatham, or with the large and respectable body of which Lord Rockingham was the acknowledged leader. George Grenville was now dead: his followers were scattered; and Clive, unconnected with any of the powerful factions which divided the Parliament, could reckon only on the votes of those members who were returned by himself. His enemies, particularly those who were the enemies of his virtues, were unscrupulous, ferocious, implacable. Their malevolence aimed at nothing less than the utter ruin of his fame and fortune. They wished to see him expelled from Parliament, to see his spurs chopped off, to see his estate confiscated; and it may be doubted whether even such a result as this would have quenched their thirst for revenge.

Clive's parliamentary tactics resembled his military tactics. Deserted, surrounded, outnumbered, and with every thing at stake, he did not even deign to stand on the defensive, but pushed boldly forward to the attack. At an early stage of the discussions on Indian affairs he rose, and in a long and elaborate speech vindicated himself from a large part of the accusations which had been brought against him. He is said to have produced a great impression on his audience. Lord Chatham who, now the ghost of his former self, loved to haunt the scene of his glory, was that night under the gallery of the House of Commons, and declared that he had never heard a finer speech. It was subsequently printed under Clive's direction, and, when the fullest allowance has been made for the assistance which he may have obtained from literary friends, proves him to have possessed, not merely strong sense and a manly spirit, but talents both for disquisition and declamation which assiduous culture might have improved into the highest excellence. He confined his defence on this occasion to the measures of his last administration, and succeeded so far that his enemies thenceforth thought it expedient to direct their attacks chiefly against the earlier part of his life.

The earlier part of his life unfortunately presented some assailable points to their hostility. A committee was chosen by ballot to inquire into the affairs of India; and by this committee the whole history of that great revolution which threw down Surajah Dowlah and raised Meer Jaffier was sifted with malignant care. Clive was subjected to the most unsparing examination and cross-examination, and afterwards bitterly complained that he, the Baron of Plassey, had been treated like a sheep-stealer. The boldness and ingenuousness of his replies would alone suffice to show how alien from his nature were the frauds to which, in the course of his Eastern negotiations, he had sometimes descended. He avowed the arts which he had employed to deceive Omichund, and resolutely said that he was not ashamed of them, and that, in the same circumstances, he would again act in the same manner. He admitted that he had received immense sums from Meer Jaffier; but he denied that, in doing so, he had violated any obligation of morality or honour. He laid claim, on the contrary, and not without some reason, to the praise of eminent disinterestedness. He described in vivid language the situation in which his victory had placed him; a great prince dependent on his pleasure; an opulent city afraid of being given up to plunder; wealthy bankers bidding against each other for his smiles; vaults piled with gold and jewels thrown open to him alone. "By God, Mr. Chairman," he exclaimed, "at this moment I stand astonished at my own moderation."

The inquiry was so extensive that the Houses rose before it had been completed. It was continued in the following session. When at length the committee had concluded its labours, enlightened and impartial men had little difficulty in making up their minds as to the result. It was clear that Clive had been guilty of some acts which it is impossible to vindicate without attacking the authority of all the most sacred laws which regulate the intercourse of individuals and of states. But it was equally clear that he had displayed great talents, and even great virtues; that he had rendered eminent services both to his country and to the people of India; and that it was in truth not for his dealings with Meer Jaffier nor for the fraud which he had practised on Omichund, but for his determined resistance to avarice and tyranny, that he was now called in question.

Ordinary criminal justice knows nothing of set-off. The greatest desert cannot be pleaded in answer to a charge of the slightest transgression. If a man has sold beer on Sunday morning, it is no defence that he has saved the life of a fellow-creature at the risk of his own. If he has harnessed a Newfoundland dog to his little child's carriage, it is no defence that he was wounded at Waterloo. But it is not in this way that we ought to deal with men who, raised far above ordinary restraints, and tried by far more than ordinary temptations, are entitled to a more than ordinary measure of indulgence. Such men should be judged by their contemporaries as they will be judged by posterity. Their bad actions ought not, indeed, to be called good; but their good and bad actions ought to be fairly weighed; and, if on the whole the good preponderate, the sentence ought to be one, not merely of acquittal, but of approbation. Not a single great ruler in history can be absolved by a judge who fixes his eye inexorably on one or two unjustifiable acts. Bruce the deliverer of Scotland, Maurice the deliverer of Germany, William the deliverer of Holland, his great descendant the deliverer of England, Murray the good regent, Cosmo the father of his country, Henry the Fourth of France, Peter the Great of Russia, how would the best of them pass such a scrutiny? History takes wider views; and the best tribunal for great political cases is the tribunal which anticipates the verdict of history.

Reasonable and moderate men of all parties felt this in Clive's case. They could not pronounce him blameless; but they were not disposed to abandon him to that low-minded and rancorous pack who had run him down and were eager to worry him to death. Lord North, though not very friendly to him, was not disposed to go to extremities against him. While the inquiry was still in progress, Clive, who had some years before been created a Knight of the Bath, was installed with great pomp in Henry the Seventh's Chapel. He was soon after appointed Lord-Lieutenant of Shropshire. When he kissed hands, George the Third, who had always been partial to him, admitted him to a private audience, talked to him half an hour on Indian politics, and was visibly affected when the persecuted general spoke of his services and of the way in which they had been requited.

At length the charges came in a definite form before the House of Commons. Burgoyne, chairman of the committee, a man of wit, fashion, and honour, an agreeable dramatic writer, an officer whose courage was never questioned and whose skill was at that time highly esteemed, appeared as the accuser. The members of the administration took different sides; for in that age all questions were open questions except such as were brought forward by the Government, or such as implied some censure on the Government. Thurlow, the Attorney-General, was among the assailants. Wedderburne, the Solicitor-General, strongly attached to Clive, defended his friend with extraordinary force of argument and language. It is a curious circumstance that, some years later, Thurlow was the most conspicuous champion of Warren Hastings, while Wedderburne was among the most unrelenting persecutors of that great though not faultless statesman. Clive spoke in his own defence at less length and with less art than in the preceding year, but with much energy and pathos. He recounted his great actions and his wrongs; and, after bidding his hearers remember that they were about to decide not only on his honour but on their own, he retired from the House.

The Commons resolved that acquisitions made by the arms of the State belong to the State alone, and that it is illegal in the servants of the State to appropriate such acquisitions to themselves. They resolved that this wholesome rule appeared to have been systematically violated by the English functionaries in Bengal. On a subsequent day they went a step farther, and resolved that Clive had, by means of the power which he possessed as commander of the British forces in India, obtained large sums from Meer Jaffier. Here the House stopped. They had voted the major and minor of Burgoyne's syllogism; but they shrank from drawing the logical conclusion. When it was moved that Lord Clive had abused his powers, and set an evil example to the servants of the public, the previous question was put and carried. At length, long after the sun had risen on an animated debate, Wedderburne moved that Lord Clive had at the same time rendered great and meritorious services to his country; and this motion passed without a division.

The result of this memorable inquiry appears to us, on the whole, honourable to the justice, moderation, and discernment of the Commons. They had indeed no great temptation to do wrong. They would have been very bad judges of an accusation brought against Jenkinson or against Wilkes. But the question respecting Clive was not a party question; and the House accordingly acted with the good sense and good feeling which may always be expected from an assembly of English gentlemen, not blinded by faction.

The equitable and temperate proceedings of the British Parliament were set off to the greatest advantage by a foil. The wretched government of Louis the Fifteenth had murdered, directly or indirectly, almost every Frenchman who had served his country with distinction in the East. Labourdonnais was flung into the Bastile, and, after years of suffering, left it only to die. Dupleix, stripped of his immense fortune, and broken-hearted by humiliating attendance in antechambers, sank into an obscure grave. Lally was dragged to the common place of execution with a gag between his lips. The Commons of England, on the other hand, treated their living captain with that discriminating justice which is seldom shown except to the dead. They laid down sound general principles; they delicately pointed out where he had deviated from those principles; and they tempered the gentle censure with liberal eulogy. The contrast struck Voltaire, always partial to England, and always eager to expose the abuses of the Parliaments of France. Indeed he seems, at this time, to have meditated a history of the conquest of Bengal. He mentioned his design to Dr. Moore when that amusing writer visited him at Ferney. Wedderburne took great interest in the matter, and pressed Clive to furnish materials. Had the plan been carried into execution, we have no doubt that Voltaire would have produced a book containing much lively and picturesque narrative, many just and humane sentiments poignantly expressed, many grotesque blunders, many sneers at the Mosaic chronology, much scandal about the Catholic missionaries, and much sublime theophilanthropy, stolen from the New Testament, and put into the mouths of virtuous and philosophical Brahmins.

Clive was now secure in the enjoyment of his fortune and his honours. He was surrounded by attached friends and relations; and he had not yet passed the season of vigorous bodily and mental exertion. But clouds had long been gathering over his mind, and now settled on it in thick darkness. From early youth he had been subject to fits of that strange melancholy "which rejoiceth exceedingly and is glad when it can find the grave." While still a writer at Madras, he had twice attempted to destroy himself. Business and prosperity had produced a salutary effect on his spirits. In India, while he was occupied by great affairs, in England, while wealth and rank had still the charm of novelty, he had borne up against his constitutional misery. But he had now nothing to do, and nothing to wish for. His active spirit in an inactive situation drooped and withered like a plant in an uncongenial air. The malignity with which his enemies had pursued him, the indignity with which he had been treated by the committee, the censure, lenient as it was, which the House of Commons had pronounced, the knowledge that he was regarded by a large portion of his countrymen as a cruel and perfidious tyrant, all concurred to irritate and depress him. In the mean time, his temper was tried by acute physical suffering. During his long residence in tropical climates, he had contracted several painful distempers. In order to obtain ease he called in the help of opium; and he was gradually enslaved by this treacherous ally. To the last, however, his genius occasionally flashed through the gloom. It was said that he would sometimes, after sitting silent and torpid for hours, rouse himself to the discussion of some great question, would display in full vigour all the talents of the soldier and the statesman, and would then sink back into his melancholy repose.

The disputes with America had now become so serious that an appeal to the sword seemed inevitable; and the ministers were desirous to avail themselves of the services of Clive. Had he still been what he was when he raised the siege of Patna, and annihilated the Dutch army and navy at the mouth of the Ganges, it is not improbable that the resistance of the Colonists would have been put down, and that the inevitable separation would have been deferred for a few years. But it was too late. His strong mind was fast sinking under many kinds of suffering. On the twenty-second of November 1774, he died by his own hand. He had just completed his forty-ninth year.

In the awful close of so much prosperity and glory, the vulgar saw only a confirmation of all their prejudices; and some men of real piety and genius so far forgot the maxims both of religion and of philosophy as confidently to ascribe the mournful event to the just vengeance of God, and to the horrors of an evil conscience. It is with very different feelings that we contemplate the spectacle of a great mind ruined by the weariness of satiety, by the pangs of wounded honour, by fatal diseases, and more fatal remedies.

Clive committed great faults; and we have not attempted to disguise them. But his faults, when weighed against his merits, and viewed in connexion with his temptations, do not appear to us to deprive him of his right to an honourable place in the estimation of posterity.

From his first visit to India dates the renown of the English arms in the East. Till he appeared, his countrymen were despised as mere pedlars, while the French were revered as a people formed for victory and command. His courage and capacity dissolved the charm. With the defence of Arcot commences that long series of Oriental triumphs which closes with the fall of Ghizni. Nor must we forget that he was only twenty-five years old when he approved himself ripe for military command. This is a rare if not a singular distinction. It is true that Alexander, Condé, and Charles the Twelfth, won great battles at a still earlier age; but those princes were surrounded by veteran generals of distinguished skill, to whose suggestions must be attributed the victories of the Granicus, of Rocroi, and of Narva. Clive, an inexperienced youth, had yet more experience than any of those who served under him. He had to form himself, to form his officers, and to form his army. The only man, as far as we recollect, who at an equally early age ever gave equal proof of talents for war, was Napoleon Bonaparte.

From Clive's second visit to India dates the political ascendency of the English in that country. His dexterity and resolution realised, in the course of a few months, more than all the gorgeous visions which had floated before the imagination of Dupleix. Such an extent of cultivated territory, such an amount of revenue, such a multitude of subjects, was never added to the dominion of Rome by the most successful proconsul. Nor were such wealthy spoils ever borne under arches of triumph, down the Sacred Way, and through the crowded Forum, to the threshold of Tarpeian Jove. The fame of those who subdued Antiochus and Tigranes grows dim when compared with the splendour of the exploits which the young English adventurer achieved at the head of an army not equal in numbers to one half of a Roman legion.

From Clive's third visit to India dates the purity of the administration of our Eastern empire. When he landed in Calcutta in 1765, Bengal was regarded as a place to which Englishmen were sent only to get rich, by any means, in the shortest possible time. He first made dauntless and unsparing war on that gigantic system of oppression, extortion, and corruption. In that war he manfully put to hazard his ease, his fame, and his splendid fortune. The same sense of justice which forbids us to conceal or extenuate the faults of his earlier days compels us to admit that those faults were nobly repaired. If the reproach of the Company and of its servants has been taken away, if in India the yoke of foreign masters, elsewhere the heaviest of all yokes, has been found lighter than that of any native dynasty, if to that gang of public robbers which formerly spread terror through the whole plain of Bengal has succeeded a body of functionaries not more highly distinguished by ability and diligence than by integrity, disinterestedness, and public spirit, if we now see such men as Munro, Elphinstone, and Metcalfe, after leading victorious armies, after making and deposing kings, return, proud of their honourable poverty, from a land which once held out to every greedy factor the hope of boundless wealth, the praise is in no small measure due to Clive. His name stands high on the roll of conquerors. But it is found in a better list, in the list of those who have done and suffered much for the happiness of mankind. To the warrior, history will assign a place in the same rank with Lucullus and Trajan. Nor will she deny to the reformer a share of that veneration with which France cherishes the memory of Turgot, and with which the latest generations of Hindoos will contemplate the statue of Lord William Bentinck.

WARREN HASTINGS

(OCTOBER 1841)

Memoirs of the Life of Warren Hastings, first Governor-General of Bengal. Compiled from Original Papers, by the Rev. G. R. GLEIG, M.A. 3 vols. 8vo. London: 1841.

THIS book seems to have been manufactured in pursuance of a contract, by which the representatives of Warren Hastings, on the one part, bound themselves to furnish papers, and Mr. Gleig, on the other part, bound himself to furnish praise. It is but just to say that the covenants on both sides have been most faithfully kept; and the result is before us in the form of three big bad volumes, full of undigested correspondence and undiscerning panegyric.

If it were worth while to examine this performance in detail, we could easily make a long article by merely pointing out inaccurate statements, inelegant expressions, and immoral doctrines. But it would be idle to waste criticism on a bookmaker; and, whatever credit Mr. Gleig may have justly earned by former works, it is as a bookmaker, and nothing more, that he now comes before us.

More eminent men than Mr. Gleig have written nearly as ill as he, when they have stooped to similar drudgery. It would be unjust to estimate Goldsmith by the History of Greece, or Scott by the Life of Napoleon. Mr. Gleig is neither a Goldsmith nor a Scott; but it would be unjust to deny that he is capable of something better than these Memoirs. It would also, we hope and believe, be unjust to charge any Christian minister with the guilt of deliberately maintaining some propositions which we find in this book. It is not too much to say that Mr. Gleig has written several passages, which bear the same relation to the Prince of Machiavelli that the Prince of Machiavelli bears to the Whole Duty of Man, and which would excite amazement in a den of robbers, or on board of a schooner of pirates. But we are willing to attribute these offences to haste, to thoughtlessness, and to that disease of the understanding which may be called the *Furor Biographicus*, and which is to writers of lives what the *goître* is to an Alpine shepherd, or dirt-eating to a Negro slave.

We are inclined to think that we shall best meet the wishes of our readers, if, instead of dwelling on the faults of this book, we attempt to give, in a way necessarily hasty and imperfect, our own view of the life and character of Mr. Hastings. Our feeling towards him is not exactly that of the House of Commons which impeached him in 1787; neither is it that of the House of Commons which uncovered and stood up to receive him in 1813. He had great qualities, and he rendered great services to the state. But to represent him as a man of stainless virtue is to make him ridiculous; and from regard for his memory, if from no other feeling, his friends would have done well to lend no countenance to such puerile adulation. We believe that, if he were now living, he would have sufficient judgment and sufficient greatness of mind to wish to be shown as he was. He must have known that there were dark spots on his fame. He might also have felt with pride that the splendour of his fame would bear many spots. He would have preferred, we are confident, even the severity of Mr. Mill to the puffing of Mr. Gleig. He would have wished posterity to have a likeness of him, though an unfavourable likeness, rather than a daub at once insipid and unnatural, resembling neither him nor any body else. "Paint me as I am," said Oliver Cromwell, while sitting to young Lely. "If you leave out the scars and wrinkles, I will not pay you a shilling." Even in such a trifle, the great Protector showed both his good sense and his magnanimity. He did not wish all that was characteristic in his countenance to be lost, in the vain attempt to give him the regular features and smooth blooming cheeks of the curl-pated minions of James the First. He was content that his face should go forth marked with all the blemishes which had been put on it by time, by war, by sleepless nights, by anxiety, perhaps by remorse; but with valour, policy, authority, and public care written in all its princely lines. If men truly great knew their own interest, it is thus that they would wish their minds to be portrayed.

Warren Hastings sprang from an ancient and illustrious race. It has been affirmed that his pedigree can be traced back to the great Danish sea-king, whose sails were long the terror of both coasts of the British channel, and who, after many fierce and doubtful struggles, yielded at last to the valour and genius of Alfred. But the undoubted splendour of the line of Hastings needs no illustration from fable. One branch of that line wore, in the fourteenth century, the coronet of Pembroke. From another branch sprang the renowned Chamberlain, the faithful adherent of the White Rose, whose fate has furnished so striking a theme both to poets and to historians. His family received from the Tudors the earldom of Huntingdon, which, after long dispossession, was regained in our time by a series of events scarcely paralleled in romance.

The lords of the manor of Daylesford, in Worcestershire, claimed to be considered as the heads of this distinguished family. The main stock, indeed, prospered less than some of the younger shoots. But the Daylesford family, though not ennobled, was wealthy and highly considered, till, about two hundred years ago, it was overwhelmed by the great ruin of the civil war. The Hastings of that time was a zealous cavalier. He raised money on his lands, sent his plate to the mint at Oxford, joined the royal army, and, after spending half his property in the cause of King Charles, was glad to ransom himself by making over most of the remaining half to Speaker Lenthal. The old seat at Daylesford still remained in the family; but it could no longer be kept up; and in the following generation it was sold to a merchant of London.

Before this transfer took place, the last Hastings of Daylesford had presented his second son to the rectory of the parish in which the ancient residence of the family stood. The living was of little value; and the situation of the poor clergyman, after the sale of the estate, was deplorable. He was constantly engaged in lawsuits about his tithes with the new lord of the manor, and was at length utterly ruined. His eldest son, Howard, a well-conducted young man, obtained a place in the Customs. The second son, Pynaston, an idle worthless boy, married before he was sixteen, lost his wife in two years, and died in the West Indies, leaving to the care of his unfortunate father a little orphan, destined to strange and memorable vicissitudes of fortune.

Warren, the son of Pynaston, was born on the sixth of December 1732. His mother died a few days later, and he was left dependent on his distressed grandfather. The child was early sent to the village school, where he learned his letters on the same bench with the sons of the peasantry. Nor did any thing in his garb or fare indicate that his life was to take a widely different course from that of the young rustics with whom he studied and played. But no cloud could overcast the dawn of so much genius and so much ambition. The very ploughmen observed, and long remembered, how kindly little Warren took to his book. The daily sight of the lands which his ancestors had possessed, and which had passed into the hands of strangers, filled his young brain with wild fancies and projects. He loved to hear stories of the wealth and greatness of his progenitors, of their splendid housekeeping, their loyalty, and their valour. On one bright summer day, the boy, then just seven years old, lay on the bank of the rivulet which flows through the old domain of his house to join the Isis. There, as three-score and ten years later he told the tale, rose in his mind a scheme which, through all the turns of his eventful career, was never abandoned. He would recover the estate which had belonged to his fathers. He would be Hastings of Daylesford. This purpose, formed in infancy and poverty, grew stronger as his intellect expanded and as his fortune rose. He pursued his plan with that calm but indomitable force of will which was the most striking peculiarity of his character. When, under a tropical sun, he ruled fifty millions of Asiatics, his hopes, amidst all the cares of war, finance, and legislation, still pointed to Daylesford. And when his long public life, so singularly chequered with good and evil, with glory and obloquy, had at length closed for ever, it was to Daylesford that he retired to die.

When he was eight years old, his uncle Howard determined to take charge of him, and to give him a liberal education. The boy went up to London, and was sent to a school at Newington, where he was well taught but ill fed. He always attributed the smallness of his stature to the hard and scanty fare of this seminary. At ten he was removed to Westminster school, then flourishing under the care of Dr. Nichols. Vinny Bourne, as his pupils affectionately called him, was one of the masters. Churchill, Colman, Lloyd, Cumberland, Cowper, were among the students. With Cowper, Hastings formed a friendship which neither the lapse of time, nor a wide dissimilarity of opinions and pursuits, could wholly dissolve. It does not appear that they ever met after they had grown to manhood. But forty years later, when the voices of many great orators were crying for vengeance on the oppressor of India, the shy and secluded poet could image to himself Hastings the Governor-General only as the Hastings with whom he had rowed on the Thames and played in the cloister, and refused to believe that so good-tempered a fellow could have done any thing very wrong. His own life had been spent in praying, musing, and rhyming among the water-liles of the Ouse. He had preserved in no common measure the innocence of childhood. His spirit had indeed been severely tried, but not by temptations which impelled him to any gross violation of the rules of social morality. He had never been attacked by combinations of powerful and deadly enemies. He had never been compelled to make a choice between innocence and greatness, between crime and ruin. Firmly as he held in theory the doctrine of human depravity, his habits were such that he was unable to conceive how far from the path of right even kind and noble natures may be hurried by the rage of conflict and the lust of dominion.

Hastings had another associate at Westminster of whom we shall have occasion to make frequent mention, Elijah Impey. We know little about their school days. But, we think, we may safely venture to guess that, whenever Hastings wished to play any trick more than usually naughty, he hired Impey with a tart or a ball to act as fag in the worst part of the prank.

Warren was distinguished among his comrades as an excellent swimmer, boatman, and scholar. At fourteen he was first in the examination for the foundation. His name in gilded letters on the walls of the dormitory still attests his victory over many older competitors. He stayed two years longer at the school, and was looking forward to a studentship at Christ Church, when an event happened which changed the whole course of his life. Howard Hastings died, bequeathing his nephew to the care of a friend and distant relation, named Chiswick. This gentleman, though he did not absolutely refuse the charge, was desirous to rid himself of it as soon as possible. Dr. Nichols made strong remonstrances against the cruelty of interrupting the studies of a youth who seemed likely to be one of the first scholars of the age. He even offered to bear the expense of sending his favourite pupil to Oxford. But Mr. Chiswick was inflexible. He thought the years which had already been wasted on hexameters and pentameters quite sufficient. He had it in his power to obtain for the lad a writership in the service of the East India Company. Whether the young adventurer, when once shipped off, made a fortune, or died of a liver complaint, he equally ceased to be a burden to any body. Warren was accordingly removed from Westminster school, and placed for a few months at a commercial academy, to study arithmetic and book-keeping. In January 1750, a few days after he had completed his seventeenth year, he sailed for Bengal, and arrived at his destination in the October following.

He was immediately placed at a desk in the Secretary's office at Calcutta, and laboured there during two years. Fort William was then a purely commercial settlement. In the south of India the encroaching policy of Dupleix had transformed the servants of the English company, against their will, into diplomatists and generals. The war of the succession was raging in the Carnatic; and the tide had been suddenly turned against the French by the genius of young Robert Clive. But in Bengal the European settlers, at peace with the natives and with each other, were wholly occupied with ledgers and bills of lading.

After two years passed in keeping accounts at Calcutta, Hastings was sent up the country to Cossimbazar, a town which lies on the Hoogly, about a mile from Moorshedabad, and which then bore to Moorshedabad a relation, if we may compare small things with great, such as the city of London bears to Westminster. Moorshedabad was the abode of the prince who, by an authority ostensibly derived from the Mogul, but really independent, ruled the three great provinces of Bengal, Orissa, and Bahar. At Moorshedabad were the court, the haram, and the public offices. Cossimbazar was a port and a place of trade, renowned for the quantity and excellence of the silks which were sold in its marts, and constantly receiving and sending forth fleets of richly laden barges. At this important point, the Company had established a small factory subordinate to that of Fort William. Here, during several years, Hastings was employed in making bargains for stuffs with native brokers. While he was thus engaged, Surajah Dowlah succeeded to the government, and declared war against the English. The defenceless settlement of Cossimbazar, lying close to the tyrant's capital, was instantly seized. Hastings was sent a prisoner to Moorshedabad, but, in consequence of the humane intervention of the servants of the Dutch Company, was treated with indulgence. Meanwhile the Nabob marched on Calcutta; the governor and the commandant fled; the town and citadel were taken, and most of the English prisoners perished in the Black Hole.

In these events originated the greatness of Warren Hastings. The fugitive governor and his companions had taken refuge on the dreary islet of Fulda, near the mouth of the Hoogly. They were naturally desirous to obtain full information respecting the proceedings of the Nabob; and no person seemed so likely to furnish it as Hastings, who was a prisoner at large in the immediate neighbourhood of the court. He thus became a diplomatic agent, and soon established a high character for ability and resolution. The treason which at a later period was fatal to Surajah Dowlah was already in progress; and Hastings was admitted to the deliberations of the conspirators. But the time for striking had not arrived. It was necessary to postpone the execution of the design; and Hastings, who was now in extreme peril, fled to Fulda.

Soon after his arrival at Fulda, the expedition from Madras, commanded by Clive, appeared in the Hoogly. Warren, young, intrepid, and excited probably by the example of the Commander of the Forces who, having like himself been a mercantile agent of the Company, had been turned by public calamities into a soldier, determined to serve in the ranks. During the early operations of the war he carried a musket. But the quick eye of Clive soon perceived that the head of the young volunteer would be more useful than his arm. When, after the battle of Plassey, Meer Jaffier was proclaimed Nabob of Bengal, Hastings was appointed to reside at the court of the new prince as agent for the Company.

He remained at Moorshedabad till the year 1761, when he became a member of Council, and was consequently forced to reside at Calcutta. This was during the interval between Clive's first and second administration, an interval which has left on the fame of the East India Company a stain, not wholly effaced by many years of just and humane government. Mr. Vansittart, the Governor, was at the head of a new and anomalous empire. On the one side was a band of English functionaries, daring, intelligent, eager to be rich. On the other side was a great native population, helpless, timid, accustomed to crouch under oppression. To keep the stronger race from preying on the weaker, was an undertaking which tasked to the utmost the talents and energy of Clive. Vansittart, with fair intentions, was a feeble and inefficient ruler. The master caste, as was natural, broke loose from all restraint; and then was seen what we believe to be the most frightful of all spectacles, the strength of civilisation without its mercy. To all other despotism there is a check, imperfect indeed, and liable to gross abuse, but still sufficient to preserve society from the last extreme of misery. A time comes when the evils of submission are obviously greater than those of resistance, when fear itself begets a sort of courage, when a convulsive burst of popular rage and despair warns tyrants not to presume too far on the patience of mankind. But against misgovernment such as then afflicted Bengal it was impossible to struggle. The superior intelligence and energy of the dominant class made their power irresistible. A war of Bengalees against Englishmen was like a war of sheep against wolves, of men against dæmons. The only protection which the conquered could find was in the moderation, the clemency, the enlarged policy of the conquerors. That protection, at a later period, they found. But at first English power came among them unaccompanied by English morality. There was an interval between the time at which they became our subjects, and the time at which we began to reflect that we were bound to discharge towards them the duties of rulers. During that interval, the business of a servant of the Company was simply to wring out of the natives a hundred or two hundred thousand pounds as speedily as possible, that he might return home before his constitution had suffered from the heat, to marry a peer's daughter, to buy rotten boroughs in Cornwall, and to give balls in St. James's Square. Of the conduct of Hastings at this time, little is known; but the little that is known, and the circumstance that little is known, must be considered as honourable to him. He could not protect the natives: all that he could do was to abstain from plundering and oppressing them; and this he appears to have done. It is certain that at this time he continued poor; and it is equally certain, that by cruelty and dishonesty he might easily have become rich. It is certain that he was never charged with having borne a share in the worst abuses which then prevailed; and it is almost equally certain that, if he had borne a share in those abuses, the able and bitter enemies who afterwards persecuted him would not have failed to discover and to proclaim his guilt. The keen, severe, and even malevolent scrutiny to which his whole public life was subjected, a scrutiny unparalleled, as we believe, in the history of mankind, is in one respect advantageous to his reputation. It brought many lamentable blemishes to light; but it entitles him to be considered pure from every blemish which has not been brought to light.

The truth is that the temptations to which so many English functionaries yielded in the time of Mr. Vansittart were not temptations addressed to the ruling passions of Warren Hastings. He was not squeamish in pecuniary transactions; but he was neither sordid nor rapacious. He was far too enlightened a man to look on a great empire merely as a buccaneer would look on a galleon. Had his heart been much worse than it was, his understanding would have preserved him from that extremity of baseness. He was an unscrupulous, perhaps an unprincipled statesman; but still he was a statesman, and not a freebooter.

In 1764 Hastings returned to England. He had realized only a very moderate fortune; and that moderate fortune was soon reduced to nothing, partly by his praiseworthy liberality, and partly by his mismanagement. Towards his relations he appears to have acted very generously. The greater part of his savings he left in Bengal, hoping probably to obtain the high usury of India. But high usury and bad security generally go together; and Hastings lost both interest and principal.

He remained four years in England. Of his life at this time very little is known. But it has been asserted, and is highly probable, that liberal studies and the society of men of letters occupied a great part of his time. It is to be remembered to his honour, that in days when the languages of the East were regarded by other servants of the Company merely as the means of communicating with weavers and money-changers, his enlarged and accomplished mind sought in Asiatic learning for new forms of intellectual enjoyment, and for new views of government and society. Perhaps, like most persons who have paid much attention to departments of knowledge which lie out of the common track, he was inclined to overrate the value of his favourite studies. He conceived that the cultivation of Persian literature might with advantage be made a part of the liberal education of an English gentleman; and he drew up a plan with that view. It is said that the University of Oxford, in which Oriental learning had never, since the revival of letters, been wholly neglected, was to be the seat of the institution which he contemplated. An endowment was expected from the munificence of the Company; and professors thoroughly competent to interpret Hafiz and Ferdusi were to be engaged in the East. Hastings called on Johnson, with the hope, as it should seem, of interesting in this project a man who enjoyed the highest literary reputation, and who was particularly connected with Oxford. The interview appears to have left on Johnson's mind a most favourable impression of the talents and attainments of his visiter. Long after, when Hastings was ruling the immense population of British India, the old philosopher wrote to him, and referred in the most courtly terms, though with great dignity, to their short but agreeable intercourse.

Hastings soon began to look again towards India. He had little to attach him to England; and his pecuniary embarrassments were great. He solicited his old masters the Directors for employment. They acceded to his request, with high compliments both to his abilities and to his integrity, and appointed him a Member of Council at Madras. It would be unjust not to mention that, though forced to borrow money for his outfit, he did not withdraw any portion of the sum which he had appropriated to the relief of his distressed relations. In the spring of 1769 he embarked on board of the Duke of Grafton, and commenced a voyage distinguished by incidents which might furnish matter for a novel.

Among the passengers in the Duke of Grafton was a German of the name of Imhoff. He called himself a baron; but he was in distressed circumstances, and was going out to Madras as a portrait-painter, in the hope of picking up some of the pagodas which were then lightly got and as lightly spent by the English in India. The baron was accompanied by his wife, a native, we have somewhere read, of Archangel. This young woman who, born under the Arctic circle, was destined to play the part of a Queen under the tropic of Cancer, had an agreeable person, a cultivated mind, and manners in the highest degree engaging. She despised her husband heartily, and, as the story which we have to tell sufficiently proves, not without reason. She was interested by the conversation and flattered by the attentions of Hastings. The situation was indeed perilous. No place is so propitious to the formation either of close friendships, or of deadly enmities as an Indiaman. There are very few people who do not find a voyage which lasts several months insupportably dull. Any thing is welcome which may break that long monotony, a sail, a shark, an albatross, a man overboard. Most passengers find some resource in eating twice as many meals as on land. But the great devices for killing the time are quarrelling and flirting. The facilities for both these exciting pursuits are great. The inmates of the ship are thrown together far more than in any country-seat or boarding-house. None can escape from the rest except by imprisoning himself in a cell in which he can hardly turn. All food, all exercise, is taken in company. Ceremony is to a great extent banished. It is every day in the power of a mischievous person to inflict innumerable annoyances; it is every day in the power of an amiable person to confer little services. It not seldom happens that serious distress and danger call forth in genuine beauty and deformity heroic virtues and abject vices which, in the ordinary intercourse of good society, might remain during many years unknown even to intimate associates. Under such circumstances met Warren Hastings and the Baroness Imhoff, two persons whose accomplishments would have attracted notice in any court of Europe. The gentleman had no domestic ties. The lady was tied to a husband for whom she had no regard, and who had no regard for his own honour. An attachment sprang up, which was soon strengthened by events such as could hardly have occurred on land. Hastings fell ill. The baroness nursed him with womanly tenderness, gave him his medicines with her own hand, and even sat up in his cabin while he slept. Long before the Duke of Grafton reached Madras, Hastings was in love. But his love was of a most characteristic description. Like his hatred, like his ambition, like all his passions, it was strong, but not impetuous. It was calm, deep, earnest, patient of delay, unconquerable by time. Imhoff was called into council by his wife and his wife's lover. It was arranged that the baroness should institute a suit for a divorce in the courts of Franconia, that the baron should afford every facility to the proceeding, and that, during the years which might elapse before the sentence should be pronounced, they should continue to live together. It was also agreed that Hastings should bestow some very substantial marks of gratitude on the complaisant husband, and should, when the marriage was dissolved, make the lady his wife, and adopt the children whom she had already born to Imhoff.

We are not inclined to judge either Hastings or the baroness severely. There was undoubtedly much to extenuate their fault. But we can by no means concur with the Reverend Mr. Gleig, who carries his partiality to so injudicious an extreme, as to describe the conduct of Imhoff, conduct the baseness of which is the best excuse for the lovers, as "wise and judicious."

At Madras, Hastings found the trade of the Company in a very disorganized state. His own tastes would have led him rather to political than to commercial pursuits: but he knew that the favour of his employers depended chiefly on their dividends, and that their dividends depended chiefly on the investment. He therefore, with great judgment, determined to apply his vigorous mind for a time to this department of business, which had been much neglected, since the servants of the Company had ceased to be clerks, and had become warriors and negotiators.

In a very few months he effected an important reform. The Directors notified to him their high approbation, and were so much pleased with his conduct that they determined to place him at the head of the government of Bengal. Early in 1772 he quitted Fort St. George for his new post. The Imhoffs, who were still man and wife, accompanied him, and lived at Calcutta "on the same wise and judicious plan,"—we quote the words of Mr. Gleig,—which they had already followed during more than two years.

When Hastings took his seat at the head of the council-board, Bengal was still governed according to the system which Clive had devised, a system which was, perhaps, skilfully contrived for the purpose of facilitating and concealing a great revolution, but which, when that revolution was complete and irrevocable, could produce nothing but inconvenience. There were two governments, the real and the ostensible. The supreme power belonged to the Company, and was in truth the most despotic power that can be conceived. The only restraint on the English masters of the country was that which their own justice and humanity imposed on them. There was no constitutional check on their will, and resistance to them was utterly hopeless.

But, though thus absolute in reality, the English had not yet assumed the style of sovereignty. They held their territories as vassals of the throne of Delhi; they raised their revenues as collectors appointed by the imperial commission; their public seal was inscribed with the imperial titles; and their mint struck only the imperial coin.

There was still a nabob of Bengal, who stood to the English rulers of his country in the same relation in which Augustulus stood to Odoacer, or the last Merovingians to Charles Martel and Pepin. He lived at Moorshedabad, surrounded by princely magnificence. He was approached with outward marks of reverence, and his name was used in public instruments. But in the government of the country he had less real share than the youngest writer or cadet in the Company's service.

The English council which represented the Company at Calcutta was constituted on a very different plan from that which has since been adopted. At present the Governor is, as to all executive measures, absolute. He can declare war, conclude peace, appoint public functionaries or remove them, in opposition to the unanimous sense of those who sit with him in council. They are, indeed, entitled to know all that is done, to discuss all that is done, to advise, to remonstrate, to send protests to England. But it is with the governor that the supreme power resides, and on him that the whole responsibility rests. This system, which was introduced by Mr. Pitt and Mr. Dundas in spite of the strenuous opposition of Mr. Burke, we conceive to be on the whole the best that was ever devised for the government of a country where no materials can be found for a representative constitution. In the time of Hastings the governor had only one vote in council, and, in case of an equal division, a casting vote. It therefore happened not unfrequently that he was overruled on the gravest questions; and it was possible that he might be wholly excluded, for years together, from the real direction of public affairs.

The English functionaries at Fort William had as yet paid little or no attention to the internal government of Bengal. The only branch of politics about which they much busied themselves was negotiation with the native princes. The police, the administration of justice, the details of the collection of revenue, they almost entirely neglected. We may remark that the phraseology of the Company's servants still bears the traces of this state of things. To this day they always use the word "political" as synonymous with "diplomatic." We could name a gentleman still living, who was described by the highest authority as an invaluable public servant, eminently fit to be at the head of the internal administration of a whole presidency, but unfortunately quite ignorant of all political business.

The internal government of Bengal the English rulers delegated to a great native minister, who was stationed at Moorshedabad. All military affairs, and, with the exception of what pertains to mere ceremonial, all foreign affairs, were withdrawn from his control; but the other departments of the administration were entirely confided to him. His own stipend amounted to near a hundred thousand pounds sterling a-year. The personal allowance of the nabobs, amounting to more than three hundred thousand pounds a-year, passed through the minister's hands, and was, to a great extent, at his disposal. The collection of the revenue, the administration of justice, the maintenance of order, were left to this high functionary; and for the exercise of his immense power he was responsible to none but the British masters of the country.

A situation so important, lucrative, and splendid, was naturally an object of ambition to the ablest and most powerful natives. Clive had found it difficult to decide between conflicting pretensions. Two candidates stood out prominently from the crowd, each of them the representative of a race and of a religion.

The one was Mahommed Reza Khan, a Mussulman of Persian extraction, able, active, religious after the fashion of his people, and highly esteemed by them. In England he might perhaps have been regarded as a corrupt and greedy politician. But, tried by the lower standard of Indian morality, he might be considered as a man of integrity and honour.

His competitor was a Hindoo Brahmin whose name has, by a terrible and melancholy event, been inseparably associated with that of Warren Hastings, the Maharajah Nuncomar. This man had played an important part in all the revolutions which, since the time of Surajah Dowlah, had taken place in Bengal. To the consideration which in that country belongs to high and pure caste, he added the weight which is derived from wealth, talents, and experience. Of his moral character it is difficult to give a notion to those who are acquainted with human nature only as it appears in our island. What the Italian is to the Englishman, what the Hindoo is to the Italian, what the Bengalee is to other Hindoos, that was Nuncomar to other Bengalees. The physical organization of the Bengalee is feeble even to effeminacy. He lives in a constant vapour bath. His pursuits are sedentary, his limbs delicate, his movements languid. During many ages he has been trampled upon by men of bolder and more hardy breeds. Courage, independence, veracity, are qualities to which his constitution and his situation are equally unfavourable. His mind bears a singular analogy to his body. It is weak even to helplessness, for purposes of manly resistance; but its suppleness and its tact move the children of sterner climates to admiration not unmingled with contempt. All those arts which are the natural defence of the weak are more familiar to this subtle race than to the Ionian of the time of Juvenal, or to the Jew of the dark ages. What the horns are to the buffalo, what the paw is to the tiger, what the sting is to the bee, what beauty, according to the old Greek song, is to woman, deceit is to the Bengalee. Large promises, smooth excuses, elaborate tissues of circumstantial falsehood, chicanery, perjury, forgery, are the weapons, offensive and defensive, of the people of the Lower Ganges. All those millions do not furnish one sepoy to the armies of the Company. But as usurers, as money-changers, as sharp legal practitioners, no class of human beings can bear a comparison with them. With all his softness, the Bengalee is by no means placable in his enmities or prone to pity. The pertinacity with which he adheres to his purposes yields only to the immediate pressure of fear. Nor does he lack a certain kind of courage which is often wanting in his masters. To inevitable evils he is sometimes found to oppose a passive fortitude, such as the Stoics attributed to their ideal sage. An European warrior who rushes on a battery of cannon with a loud hurrah will sometimes shriek under the surgeon's knife, and fall into an agony of despair at the sentence of death. But the Bengalee who would see his country overrun, his house laid in ashes, his children murdered or dishonoured, without having the spirit to strike one blow, has yet been known to endure torture with the firmness of Mucius, and to mount the scaffold with the steady step and even pulse of Algernon Sydney.

In Nuncomar, the national character was strongly and with exaggeration personified. The Company's servants had repeatedly detected him in the most criminal intrigues. On one occasion he brought a false charge against another Hindoo, and tried to substantiate it by producing forged documents. On another occasion it was discovered that, while professing the strongest attachment to the English, he was engaged in several conspiracies against them, and in particular that he was the medium of a correspondence between the court of Delhi and the French authorities in the Carnatic. For these and similar practices he had been long detained in confinement. But his talents and influence had not only procured his liberation, but had obtained for him a certain degree of consideration even among the British rulers of his country.

Clive was extremely unwilling to place a Mussulman at the head of the administration of Bengal. On the other hand, he could not bring himself to confer immense power on a man to whom every sort of villany had repeatedly been brought home. Therefore, though the nabob, over whom Nuncomar had by intrigue acquired great influence, begged that the artful Hindoo might be intrusted with the government, Clive, after some hesitation, decided honestly and wisely in favour of Mahommed Reza Khan, who had held his high office seven years when Hastings became Governor. An infant son of Meer Jaffier was now nabob; and the guardianship of the young prince's person had been confided to the minister.

Nuncomar, stimulated at once by cupidity and malice, had been constantly attempting to undermine his successful rival. This was not difficult. The revenues of Bengal, under the administration established by Clive, did not yield such a surplus as had been anticipated by the Company; for, at that time, the most absurd notions were entertained in England respecting the wealth of India. Palaces of porphyry, hung with the richest brocade, heaps of pearls and diamonds, vaults from which pagodas and gold mohurs were measured out by the bushel, filled the imagination even of men of business. Nobody seemed to be aware of what nevertheless was most undoubtedly the truth, that India was a poorer country than countries which in Europe are reckoned poor, than Ireland, for example, or than Portugal. It was confidently believed by lords of the treasury and members for the city that Bengal would not only defray its own charges, but would afford an increased dividend to the proprietors of India stock, and large relief to the English finances. These absurd expectations were disappointed; and the directors, naturally enough, chose to attribute the disappointment rather to the mismanagement of Mahommed Reza Khan than to their own ignorance of the country intrusted to their care. They were confirmed in their error by the agents of Nuncomar; for Nuncomar had agents even in Leadenhall Street. Soon after Hastings reached Calcutta, he received a letter addressed by the Court of Directors, not to the council generally, but to himself in particular. He was directed to remove Mahommed Reza Khan, to arrest him, together with all his family and all his partisans, and to institute a strict inquiry into the whole administration of the province. It was added that the Governor would do well to avail himself of the assistance of Nuncomar in the investigation. The vices of Nuncomar were acknowledged. But even from his vices, it was said, much advantage might at such a conjuncture be derived; and, though he could not safely be trusted, it might still be proper to encourage him by hopes of reward.

The Governor bore no good will to Nuncomar. Many years before, they had known each other at Moorshedabad; and then a quarrel had risen between them which all the authority of their superiors could hardly compose. Widely as they differed in most points, they resembled each other in this, that both were men of unforgiving natures. To Mahommed Reza Khan, on the other hand, Hastings had no feelings of hostility. Nevertheless he proceeded to execute the instructions of the Company with an alacrity which he never showed, except when instructions were in perfect conformity with his own views. He had, wisely as we think, determined to get rid of the system of double government in Bengal. The orders of the directors furnished him with the means of effecting his purpose, and dispensed him from the necessity of discussing the matter with his council. He took his measures with his usual vigour and dexterity. At midnight, the palace of Mahommed Reza Khan at Moorshedabad was surrounded by a battalion of sepoys. The minister was roused from his slumbers, and informed that he was a prisoner. With the Mussulman gravity, he bent his head and submitted himself to the will of God. He fell not alone. A chief named Schitab Roy had been intrusted with the government of Bahar. His valour and his attachment to the English had more than once been signally proved. On that memorable day on which the people of Patna saw from their walls the whole army of the Mogul scattered by the little band of Captain Knox, the voice of the British conquerors assigned the palm of gallantry to the brave Asiatic. "I never," said Knox, when he introduced Schitab Roy, covered with blood and dust, to the English functionaries assembled in the factory, "I never saw a native fight so before." Schitab Roy was involved in the ruin of Mahommed Reza Khan, was removed from office, and was placed under arrest. The members of the council received no intimation of these measures till the prisoners were on their road to Calcutta.

The inquiry into the conduct of the minister was postponed on different pretences. He was detained in an easy confinement during many months. In the mean time, the great revolution which Hastings had planned was carried into effect. The office of minister was abolished. The internal administration was transferred to the servants of the Company. A system, a very imperfect system, it is true, of civil and criminal justice, under English superintendence, was established. The nabob was no longer to have even an ostensible share in the government; but he was still to receive a considerable annual allowance, and to be surrounded with the state of sovereignty. As he was an infant, it was necessary to provide guardians for his person and property. His person was entrusted to a lady of his father's haram, known by the name of the Munny Begum. The office of treasurer of the household was bestowed on a son of Nuncomar, named Goordas. Nuncomar's services were wanted, yet he could not safely be trusted with power; and Hastings thought it a masterstroke of policy to reward the able and unprincipled parent by promoting the inoffensive child.

The revolution completed, the double government dissolved, the Company installed in the full sovereignty of Bengal, Hastings had no motive to treat the late ministers with rigour. Their trial had been put off on various pleas till the new organization was complete. They were then brought before a committee, over which the Governor presided. Schitab Roy was speedily acquitted with honour. A formal apology was made to him for the restraint to which he had been subjected. All the Eastern marks of respect were bestowed on him. He was clothed in a robe of state, presented with jewels and with a richly harnessed elephant, and sent back to his government at Patna. But his health had suffered from confinement; his high spirit had been cruelly wounded; and soon after his liberation he died of a broken heart.

The innocence of Mahommed Reza Khan was not so clearly established. But the Governor was not disposed to deal harshly. After a long hearing, in which Nuncomar appeared as the accuser, and displayed both the art and the inveterate rancour which distinguished him, Hastings pronounced that the charges had not been made out, and ordered the fallen minister to be set at liberty.

Nuncomar had purposed to destroy the Mussulman administration, and to rise on its ruin. Both his malevolence and his cupidity had been disappointed. Hastings had made him a tool, had used him for the purpose of accomplishing the transfer of the government from Moorshedabad to Calcutta, from native to European hands. The rival, the enemy, so long envied, so implacably persecuted, had been dismissed unhurt. The situation so long and ardently desired had been abolished. It was natural that the Governor should be from that time an object of the most intense hatred to the vindictive Brahmin. As yet, however, it was necessary to suppress such feelings. The time was coming when that long animosity was to end in a desperate and deadly struggle.

In the mean time, Hastings was compelled to turn his attention to foreign affairs. The object of his diplomacy was at this time simply to get money. The finances of his government were in an embarrassed state; and this embarrassment he was determined to relieve by some means, fair or foul. The principle which directed all his dealings with his neighbours is fully expressed by the old motto of one of the great predatory families of Teviotdale, "Thou shalt want ere I want." He seems to have laid it down, as a fundamental proposition which could not be disputed, that, when he had not as many lacs of rupees as the public service required, he was to take them from any body who had. One thing, indeed, is to be said in excuse for him. The pressure applied to him by his employers at home, was such as only the highest virtue could have withstood, such as left him no choice except to commit great wrongs, or to resign his high post and with that post all his hopes of fortune and distinction. The directors, it is true, never enjoined or applauded any crime. Far from it. Whoever examines their letters written at that time will find there many just and humane sentiments, many excellent precepts, in short, an admirable code of political ethics. But every exhortation is modified or nullified by a demand for money. "Govern leniently, and send more money; practise strict justice and moderation towards neighbouring powers, and send more money;" this is in truth the sum of almost all the instructions that Hastings ever received from home. Now these instructions, being interpreted, mean simply, "Be the father and the oppressor of the people; be just and unjust, moderate and rapacious." The directors dealt with India, as the church, in the good old times, dealt with a heretic. They delivered the victim over to the executioners, with an earnest request that all possible tenderness might be shown. We by no means accuse or suspect those who framed these despatches of hypocrisy. It is probable that, writing fifteen thousand miles from the place where their orders were to be carried into effect, they never perceived the gross inconsistency of which they were guilty. But the inconsistency was at once manifest to their lieutenant at Calcutta who, with an empty treasury, with an unpaid army, with his own salary often in arrear, with deficient crops, with government tenants daily running away, was called upon to remit home another half million without fail. Hastings saw that it was absolutely necessary for him to disregard either the moral discourses or the pecuniary requisitions of his employers. Being forced to disobey them in something, he had to consider what kind of disobedience they would most readily pardon; and he correctly judged that the safest course would be to neglect the sermons and to find the rupees.

A mind so fertile as his, and so little restrained by conscientious scruples, speedily discovered several modes of relieving the financial embarrassments of the government. The allowance of the Nabob of Bengal was reduced at a stroke from three hundred and twenty thousand pounds a-year to half that sum. The Company had bound itself to pay near three hundred thousand pounds a-year to the Great Mogul, as a mark of homage for the provinces which he had intrusted to their care; and they had ceded to him the districts of Corah and Allahabad. On the plea that the Mogul was not really independent, but merely a tool in the hands of others, Hastings determined to retract these concessions. He accordingly declared that the English would pay no more tribute, and sent troops to occupy Allahabad and Corah. The situation of these places was such, that there would be little advantage and great expense in retaining them. Hastings, who wanted money and not territory, determined to sell them. A purchaser was not wanting. The rich province of Oude had, in the general dissolution of the Mogul Empire, fallen to the share of the great Mussulman house by which it is still governed. About twenty years ago, this house, by the permission of the British government, assumed the royal title; but, in the time of Warren Hastings, such an assumption would have been considered by the Mahommedans of India as a monstrous impiety. The Prince of Oude, though he held the power, did not venture to use the style of sovereignty. To the appellation of Nabob or Viceroy, he added that of Vizier of the monarchy of Hindostan, just as in the last century the Electors of Saxony and Brandenburg, though independent of the Emperor, and often in arms against him, were proud to style themselves his grand Chamberlain and Grand Marshal. Sujah Dowlah, then Nabob Vizier, was on excellent terms with the English. He had a large treasure. Allahabad and Corah were so situated that they might be of use to him and could be of none to the Company. The buyer and seller soon came to an understanding; and the provinces which had been torn from the Mogul were made over to the government of Oude for about half a million sterling.

But there was another matter still more important to be settled by the Vizier and the Governor. The fate of a brave people was to be decided. It was decided in a manner which has left a lasting stain on the fame of Hastings and of England.

The people of Central Asia had always been to the inhabitants of

India what the warriors of the German forests were to the subjects of the decaying monarchy of Rome. The dark, slender, and timid Hindoo shrank from a conflict with the strong muscle and resolute spirit of the fair race, which dwelt beyond the passes. There is reason to believe that, at a period anterior to the dawn of regular history, the people who spoke the rich and flexible Sanscrit came from regions lying far beyond the Hyphasis and the Hystaspes, and imposed their yoke on the children of the soil. It is certain that, during the last ten centuries, a succession of invaders descended from the west on Hindostan; nor was the course of conquest ever turned back towards the setting sun, till that memorable campaign in which the cross of Saint George was planted on the walls of Ghizni.

The Emperors of Hindostan themselves came from the other side of the great mountain ridge; and it had always been their practice to recruit their army from the hardy and valiant race from which their own illustrious house sprang. Among the military adventurers who were allured to the Mogul standards from the neighbourhood of Cabul and Candahar, were conspicuous several gallant bands, known by the name of the Rohillas. Their services had been rewarded with large tracts of land, fiefs of the spear, if we may use an expression drawn from an analogous state of things, in that fertile plain through which the Ramgunga flows from the snowy heights of Kumaon to join the Ganges. In the general confusion which followed the death of Aurungzebe, the warlike colony became virtually independent. The Rohillas were distinguished from the other inhabitants of India by a peculiarly fair complexion. They were more honourably distinguished by courage in war, and by skill in the arts of peace. While anarchy raged from Lahore to Cape Comorin, their little territory enjoyed the blessings of repose under the guardianship of valour. Agriculture and commerce flourished among them; nor were they negligent of rhetoric and poetry. Many persons now living have heard aged men talk with regret of the golden days when the Afghan princes ruled in the vale of Rohilcund.

Sujah Dowlah had set his heart on adding this rich district to his own principality. Right, or show of right, he had absolutely none. His claim was in no respect better founded than that of Catherine to Poland, or that of the Bonaparte family to Spain. The Rohillas held their country by exactly the same title by which he held his, and had governed their country far better than his had ever been governed. Nor were they a people whom it was perfectly safe to attack. Their land was indeed an open plain, destitute of natural defences; but their veins were full of the high blood of Affghanistan. As soldiers, they had not the steadiness which is seldom found except in company with strict discipline; but their impetuous valour had been proved on many fields of battle. It was said that their chiefs, when united by common peril, could bring eighty thousand men into the field. Sujah Dowlah had himself seen them fight, and wisely shrank from a conflict with them. There was in India one army, and only one, against which even those proud Caucasian tribes could not stand. It had been abundantly proved that neither tenfold odds, nor the martial ardour of the boldest Asiatic nations, could avail aught against English science and resolution. Was it possible to induce the Governor of Bengal to let out to hire the irresistible energies of the imperial people, the skill against which the ablest chiefs of Hindostan were helpless as infants, the discipline which had so often triumphed over the frantic struggles of fanaticism and despair, the unconquerable British courage which is never so sedate and stubborn as towards the close of a doubtful and murderous day?

This was what the Nabob Vizier asked, and what Hastings granted. A bargain was soon struck. Each of the negotiators had what the other wanted. Hastings was in need of funds to carry on the government of Bengal, and to send remittances to London; and Sujah Dowlah had an ample revenue. Sujah Dowlah was bent on subjugating the Rohillas; and Hastings had at his disposal the only force by which the Rohillas could be subjugated. It was agreed that an English army should be lent to the Nabob Vizier, and that, for the loan, he should pay four hundred thousand pounds sterling, besides defraying all the charge of the troops while employed in his service.

"I really cannot see," says the Reverend Mr. Gleig, "upon what grounds, either of political or moral justice, this proposition deserves to be stigmatized as infamous." If we understand the meaning of words, it is infamous to commit a wicked action for hire, and it is wicked to engage in war without provocation. In this particular war, scarcely one aggravating circumstance was wanting. The object of the Rohilla war was this, to deprive a large population, who had never done us the least harm, of a good government, and to place them, against their will, under an execrably bad one. Nay, even this is not all. England now descended far below the level even of those petty German princes who, about the same time, sold us troops to fight the Americans. The hussar-mongers of Hesse and Anspach had at least the assurance that the expeditions on which their soldiers were to be employed would be conducted in

M—13*

conformity with the humane rules of civilised warfare. Was the Rohilla war likely to be so conducted? Did the Governor stipulate that it should be so conducted? He well knew what Indian warfare was. He well knew that the power which he covenanted to put into Sujah Dowlah's hands, would, in all probability, be atrociously abused; and he required no guarantee, no promise that it should not be so abused. He did not even reserve to himself the right of withdrawing his aid in case of abuse, however gross. Mr. Gleig repeats Major Scott's absurd plea, that Hastings was justified in letting out English troops to slaughter the Rohillas, because the Rohillas were not of Indian race, but a colony from a distant country. What were the English themselves? Was it for them to proclaim a crusade for the expulsion of all intruders from the countries watered by the Ganges? Did it lie in their mouths to contend that a foreign settler who establishes an empire in India is a *caput lupinum?* What would they have said if any other power had, on such a ground, attacked Madras or Calcutta, without the slightest provocation? Such a defence was wanting to make the infamy of the transaction complete. The atrocity of the crime, and the hypocrisy of the apology, are worthy of each other.

One of the three brigades of which the Bengal army consisted was sent under Colonel Champion to join Sujah Dowlah's forces. The Rohillas expostulated, entreated, offered a large ransom, but in vain. They then resolved to defend themselves to the last. A bloody battle was fought. "The enemy," says Colonel Champion, "gave proof of a good share of military knowledge; and it is impossible to describe a more obstinate firmness of resolution than they displayed." The dastardly sovereign of Oude fled from the field. The English were left unsupported; but their fire and their charge were irresistible. It was not, however, till the most distinguished chiefs had fallen, fighting bravely at the head of their troops, that the Rohilla ranks gave way. Then the Nabob Vizier and his rabble made their appearance, and hastened to plunder the camp of the valiant enemies, whom they had never dared to look in the face. The soldiers of the Company, trained in an exact discipline, kept unbroken order, while the tents were pillaged by these worthless allies. But many voices were heard to exclaim, "We have had all the fighting, and those rogues are to have all the profit."

Then the horrors of Indian war were let loose on the fair valleys and cities of Rohilcund. The whole country was in a blaze. More than a hundred thousand people fled from their homes to pestilential jungles, preferring famine, and fever, and the haunts of tigers, to the tyranny of him, to whom an English and a Christian government had, for shameful lucre, sold their substance, and their blood, and the honour of their wives and daughters. Colonel Champion remonstrated with the Nabob Vizier, and sent strong representations to Fort William; but the Governor had made no conditions as to the mode in which the war was to be carried on. He had troubled himself about nothing but his forty lacs; and, though he might disapprove of Sujah Dowlah's wanton barbarity, he did not think himself entitled to interfere, except by offering advice. This delicacy excites the admiration of the reverend biographer. "Mr. Hastings," he says, "could not himself dictate to the Nabob, nor permit the commander of the Company's troops to dictate how the war was to be carried on." No, to be sure. Mr. Hastings had only to put down by main force the brave struggles of innocent men fighting for their liberty. Their military resistance crushed, his duties ended; and he had then only to fold his arms and look on, while their villages were burned, their children butchered, and their women violated. Will Mr. Gleig seriously maintain this opinion? Is any rule more plain than this, that whoever voluntarily gives to another irresistible power over human beings is bound to take order that such power shall not be barbarously abused? But we beg pardon of our readers for arguing a point so clear.

We hasten to the end of this sad and disgraceful story. The war ceased. The finest population in India was subjected to a greedy, cowardly, cruel tyrant. Commerce and agriculture languished. The rich province which had tempted the cupidity of Sujah Dowlah became the most miserable part even of his miserable dominions. Yet is the injured nation not extinct. At long intervals gleams of its ancient spirit have flashed forth; and even at this day, valour, and self-respect, and a chivalrous feeling rare among Asiatics, and a bitter remembrance of the great crime of England, distinguish that noble Afghan race. To this day they are regarded as the best of all sepoys at the cold steel; and it was very recently remarked, by one who had enjoyed great opportunities of observation, that the only natives of India to whom the word "gentleman" can with perfect propriety be applied are to be found among the Rohillas.

Whatever we may think of the morality of Hastings, it cannot be denied that the financial results of his policy did honour to his talents. In less than two years after he assumed the government, he had, without imposing any additional burdens on the people subject to his authority, added about four hundred and fifty thousand pounds to the annual income of the Company, besides procuring about a million in ready money. He had also relieved the finances of Bengal from military expenditure, amounting to near a quarter of a million a year, and had thrown that charge on the Nabob of Oude. There can be no doubt that this was a result which, if it had been obtained by honest means, would have entitled him to the warmest gratitude of his country, and which, by whatever means obtained, proved that he possessed great talents for administration.

In the mean time, Parliament had been engaged in long and grave discussions on Asiatic affairs. The ministry of Lord North, in the session of 1773, introduced a measure which made a considerable change in the constitution of the Indian government. This law, known by the name of the Regulating Act, provided that the presidency of Bengal should exercise a control over the other possessions of the Company; that the chief of that presidency should be styled Governor-General; that he should be assisted by four Councillors; and that a supreme court of judicature, consisting of a chief justice and three inferior judges, should be established at Calcutta. This court was made independent of the Governor-General and Council, and was entrusted with a civil and criminal jurisdiction of immense and, at the same time, of undefined extent.

The Governor-General and Councillors were named in the act, and were to hold their situations for five years. Hastings was to be the first Governor-General. One of the four new Councillors, Mr. Barwell, an experienced servant of the Company, was then in India. The other three, General Clavering, Mr. Monson, and Mr. Francis, were sent out from England.

The ablest of the new Councillors was, beyond all doubt, Philip Francis. His acknowledged compositions prove that he possessed considerable eloquence and information. Several years passed in the public offices had formed him to habits of business. His enemies have never denied that he had a fearless and manly spirit; and his friends, we are afraid, must acknowledge that his estimate of himself was extravagantly high, that his temper was irritable, that his deportment was often rude and petulant, and that his hatred was of intense bitterness and long duration.

It is scarcely possible to mention this eminent man without adverting for a moment to the question which his name at once suggests to every mind. Was he the author of the Letters of Junius? Our own firm belief is that he was. The evidence is, we think, such as would support a verdict in a civil, nay, in a criminal proceeding. The handwriting of Junius is the very peculiar handwriting of Francis, slightly disguised. As to the position, pursuits, and connexions of Junius, the following are the most important facts which can be considered as clearly proved: first, that he was acquainted with the technical forms of the secretary of state's office; secondly, that he was intimately acquainted with the business of the war-office; thirdly, that he, during the year 1770, attended debates in the House of Lords, and took notes of speeches, particularly of the speeches of Lord Chatham; fourthly, that he bitterly resented the appointment of Mr. Chamier to the place of deputy secretary-at-war; fifthly, that he was bound by some strong tie to the first Lord Holland. Now, Francis passed some years in the secretary of state's office. He was subsequently chief clerk of the war-office. He repeatedly mentioned that he had himself, in 1770, heard speeches of Lord Chatham; and some of these speeches were actually printed from his notes. He resigned his clerkship at the war-office from resentment at the appointment of Mr. Chamier. It was by Lord Holland that he was first introduced into the public service. Now, here are five marks, all of which ought to be found in Junius. They are all five found in Francis. We do not believe that more than two of them can be found in any other person whatever. If this argument does not settle the question, there is an end of all reasoning on circumstantial evidence.

The internal evidence seems to us to point the same way. The style of Francis bears a strong resemblance to that of Junius; nor are we disposed to admit, what is generally taken for granted, that the acknowledged compositions of Francis are very decidedly inferior to the anonymous letters. The argument from inferiority, at all events, is one which may be urged with at least equal force against every claimant that has ever been mentioned, with the single exception of Burke: and it would be a waste of time to prove that Burke was not Junius. And what conclusion, after all, can be drawn from mere inferiority? Every writer must produce his best work; and the interval between his best work and his second best work may be very wide indeed. Nobody will say that the best letters of Junius are more decidedly superior to the acknowledged works of Francis than three or four of Corneille's tragedies to the rest, than three or four of Ben Jonson's comedies to the rest, than the Pilgrim's Progress to the other works of Bunyan, than Don Quixote to the other works of Cervantes. Nay, it is certain that the Man in the Mask, whoever he may have been, was a most unequal writer. To go no further than the letters which bear the signature of Junius; the letter to the king, and the letters to Horne Tooke, have little in common, except the asperity; and asperity was an ingredient seldom wanting either in the writings or in the speeches of Francis.

Indeed, one of the strongest reasons for believing that Francis was Junius is the moral resemblance between the two men. It is not difficult, from the letters which, under various signatures, are known to have been written by Junius, and from his dealings with Woodfall and others, to form a tolerably correct notion of his character. He was clearly a man not destitute of real patriotism and magnanimity, a man whose vices were not of a sordid kind. But he must also have been a man in the highest degree arrogant and insolent, a man prone to malevolence, and prone to the error of mistaking his malevolence for public virtue. "Doest thou well to be angry?" was the question asked in old time of the Hebrew prophet. And he answered, "I do well." This was evidently the temper of Junius; and to this cause we attribute the savage cruelty which disgraces several of his letters. No man is so merciless as he who, under a strong self-delusion, confounds his antipathies with his duties. It may be added that Junius, though allied with the democratic party by common enmities, was the very opposite of a democratic politician. While attacking individuals with a ferocity which perpetually violated all the laws of literary warfare, he regarded the most defective parts of old institutions with a respect amounting to pedantry, pleaded the cause of Old Sarum with fervour, and contemptuously told the capitalists of Manchester and Leeds that, if they wanted votes, they might buy land and become freeholders of Lancashire and Yorkshire. All this, we believe, might stand, with scarcely any change, for a character of Philip Francis.

It is not strange that the great anonymous writer should have been willing at that time to leave the country which had been so powerfully stirred by his eloquence. Every thing had gone against him. That party which he clearly preferred to every other, the party of George Grenville, had been scattered by the death of its chief; and Lord Suffolk had led the greater part of it over to the ministerial benches. The ferment produced by the Middlesex election had gone down. Every faction must have been alike an object of aversion to Junius. His opinions on domestic affairs separated him from the ministry; his opinions on colonial affairs from the opposition. Under such circumstances, he had thrown down his pen in misanthropical despair. His farewell letter to Woodfall bears date the nineteenth of January 1773. In that letter, he declared that he must be an idiot to write again; that he had meant well by the cause and the public; that both were given up; that there were not ten men who would act steadily together on any question. "But it is all alike," he added, "vile and contemptible. You have never flinched that I know of; and I shall always rejoice to hear of your prosperity." These were the last words of Junius. In a year from that time, Philip Francis was on his voyage to Bengal.

With the three new Councillors came out the judges of the Supreme Court. The chief justice was Sir Elijah Impey. He was an old acquaintance of Hastings; and it is probable that the Governor-General, if he had searched through all the inns of court, could not have found an equally serviceable tool. But the members of Council were by no means in an obsequious mood. Hastings greatly disliked the new form of government, and had no very high opinion of his coadjutors. They had heard of this, and were disposed to be suspicious and punctilious. When men are in such a frame of mind, any trifle is sufficient to give occasion for dispute. The members of Council expected a salute of twenty-one guns from the batteries of Fort William. Hastings allowed them only seventeen. They landed in ill-humour. The first civilities were exchanged with cold reserve. On the morrow commenced that long quarrel which, after distracting British India, was renewed in England, and in which all the most eminent statesmen and orators of the age took active part on one or the other side.

Hastings was supported by Barwell. They had not always been friends. But the arrival of the new members of Council from England naturally had the effect of uniting the old servants of the Company. Clavering, Monson, and Francis formed the majority. They instantly wrested the government out of the hands of Hastings; condemned, certainly not without justice, his late dealings with the Nabob Vizier; recalled the English agent from Oude, and sent thither a creature of their own; ordered the brigade which had conquered the unhappy Rohillas to return to the Company's territories; and instituted a severe inquiry into the conduct of the war. Next, in spite of the Governor-General's remonstrances, they proceeded to exercise, in the most indiscreet manner, their new authority over the subordinate presidencies; threw all the affairs of Bombay into confusion; and interfered, with an incredible union of rashness and feebleness, in the intestine disputes of the Mahratta government. At the same time, they fell on the internal administration of Bengal and attacked the whole fiscal and judicial system, a system which was undoubtedly defective, but which it was very improbable that gentlemen fresh from England would be competent to amend. The effect of their reforms was that all protection to life and property was withdrawn, and that gangs of robbers plundered and slaughtered with impunity in the very suburbs of Calcutta. Hastings continued to live in the Government-house, and to draw the salary of Governor-General. He continued even to take the lead at the council-board in the transaction of ordinary business; for his opponents could not but feel that he knew much of which they were ignorant, and that he decided, both surely and speedily, many questions which to them would have been hopelessly puzzling. But the higher powers of government and the most valuable patronage had been taken from him.

The natives soon found this out. They considered him as a fallen man; and they acted after their kind. Some of our readers may have seen, in India, a cloud of crows pecking a sick vulture to death, no bad type of what happens in that country, as often as fortune deserts one who has been great and dreaded. In an instant, all the sycophants who had lately been ready to lie for him, to forge for him, to pandar for him, to poison for him, hasten to purchase the favour of his victorious enemies by accusing him. An Indian government has only to let it be understood that it wishes a particular man to be ruined; and, in twenty-four hours, it will be furnished with grave charges, supported by depositions so full and circumstantial that any person unaccustomed to Asiatic mendacity would regard them as decisive. It is well if the signature of the destined victim is not counterfeited at the foot of some illegal compact, and if some treasonable paper is not slipped into a hiding-place in his house. Hastings was now regarded as helpless. The power to make or mar the fortune of every man in Bengal had passed, as it seemed, into the hands of the new councillors. Immediately charges against the Governor-General began to pour in. They were eagerly welcomed by the majority who, to do them justice, were men of too much honour knowingly to countenance false accusations, but who were not sufficiently acquainted with the East to be aware that, in that part of the world, a very little encouragement from power will call forth, in a week, more Oateses, and Bedloes, and Dangerfields, than Westminster Hall sees in a century.

It would have been strange indeed if, at such a juncture, Nuncomar had remained quiet. That bad man was stimulated at once by malignity, by avarice, and by ambition. Now was the time to be avenged on his old enemy, to wreak a grudge of seventeen years, to establish himself in the favour of the majority of the Council, to become the greatest native in Bengal. From the time of the arrival of the new Councillors, he had paid the most marked court to them, and had in consequence been excluded, with all indignity, from the Government-house. He now put into the hands of Francis, with great ceremony, a paper containing several charges of the most serious description. By this document Hastings was accused of putting offices up to sale, and of receiving bribes for suffering offenders to escape. In particular, it was alleged that Mohammed Reza Khan had been dismissed with impunity, in consideration of a great sum paid to the Governor-General.

Francis read the paper in Council. A violent altercation followed. Hastings complained in bitter terms of the way in which he was treated, spoke with contempt of Nuncomar and of Nuncomar's accusation, and denied the right of the council to sit in judgment on the governor. At the next meeting of the Board, another communication from Nuncomar was produced. He requested that he might be permitted to attend the council, and that he might be heard in support of his assertions. Another tempestuous debate took place. The Governor-General maintained that the council-room was not a proper place for such an investigation; that from persons who were heated by daily conflict with him he could not expect the fairness of judges; and that he could not, without betraying the dignity of his post, submit to be confronted with such a man as Nuncomar. The majority, however, resolved to go into the charges. Hastings rose, declared the sitting at an end, and left the room, followed by Barwell. The other members kept their seats, voted themselves a council, put Clavering in the chair, and ordered Nuncomar to be called in. Nuncomar not only adhered to the original charges, but, after the fashion of the East, produced a large supplement. He stated that Hastings had received a great sum for appointing Rajah Goordas treasurer of the Nabob's household, and for committing the care of his Highness's person to the Munny Begum. He put in a letter purporting to bear the seal of the Munny Begum, for the purpose of establishing the truth of his story. The seal, whether forged, as Hastings affirmed, or genuine, as we are rather inclined to believe, proved nothing. Nuncomar, as every body knows who knows India, had only to tell the Munny Begum that such a letter would give pleasure to the majority of the council, in order to procure her attestation. The majority, however, voted that the charge was made out; that Hastings had corruptly received between thirty and forty thousand poinds; and that he ought to be compelled to refund.

The general feeling among the English in Bengal was strongly in favour of the Governor-General. In talents for business, in knowledge of the country, in general courtesy of demeanour, he was decidedly superior to his persecutors. The servants of the Company were naturally disposed to side with the most distinguished member of their own body against a clerk from the war-office, who, profoundly ignorant of the native languages and the native character, took on himself to regulate every department of the administration. Hastings, however, in spite of the general sympathy of his countrymen, was in a most painful situation. There was still an appeal to higher authority in England. If that authority took part with his enemies, nothing was left to him but to throw up his office. He accordingly placed his resignation in the hands of his agent in London, Colonel Macleane. But Macleane was instructed not to produce the resignation, unless it should be fully ascertained that the feeling at the India House was adverse to the Governor-General.

The triumph of Nuncomar seemed to be complete. He held a daily levee, to which his countrymen resorted in crowds, and to which, on one occasion, the majority of the Council condescended to repair. His house was an office for the purpose of receiving charges against the Governor-General. It was said that, partly by threats, and partly by wheedling, the villanous Brahmin had induced many of the wealthiest men of the province to send in complaints. But he was playing a perilous game. It was not safe to drive to despair a man of such resource and of such determination as Hastings. Nuncomar, with all his acuteness, did not understand the nature of the institutions under which he lived. He saw that he had with him the majority of the body which made treaties, gave places, raised taxes. The separation between political and judicial functions was a thing of which he had no conception. It had probably never occurred to him that there was in Bengal an authority perfectly independent of the council, an authority which could protect one whom the council wished to destroy, and send to the gibbet one whom the council wished to protect. Yet such was the fact. The Supreme Court was, within the sphere of its own duties, altogether independent of the Government. Hastings, with his usual sagacity, had seen how much advantage he might derive from possessing himself of this stronghold; and he had acted accordingly. The Judges, especially the Chief Justice, were hostile to the majority of the council. The time had now come for putting this formidable machinery into action.

On a sudden, Calcutta was astounded by the news that Nuncomar had been taken up on a charge of felony, committed, and thrown into the common jail. The crime imputed to him was that six years before he had forged a bond. The ostensible prosecutor was a native. But it was then, and still is, the opinion of every body, idiots and biographers excepted, that Hastings was the real mover in the business.

The rage of the majority rose to the highest point. They protested against the proceedings of the Supreme Court, and sent several urgent messages to the Judges, demanding that Nuncomar should be admitted to bail. The Judges returned haughty and resolute answers. All that the Council could do was to heap honours and emoluments on the family of Nuncomar; and this they did. In the mean time the assizes commenced; a true bill was found; and Nuncomar was brought before Sir Elijah Impey and a jury composed of Englishmen. A great quantity of contradictory swearing, and the necessity of having every word of the evidence interpreted, protracted the trial to a most unusual length. At last a verdict of guilty was returned, and the Chief Justice pronounced sentence of death on the prisoner.

Mr. Gleig is so strangely ignorant as to imagine that the Judges had no further discretion in the case, and that the power of extending mercy to Nuncomar resided with the Council. He therefore throws on Francis and Francis's party the whole blame of what followed. We should have thought that a gentleman who has published five or six bulky volumes on Indian affairs might have taken the trouble to inform himself as to the fundamental principles of the Indian Government. The Supreme Court had, under the Regulating Act, the power to respite criminals till the pleasure of the Crown should be known. The Council had, at that time, no power to interfere.

That Impey ought to have respited Nuncomar we hold to be perfectly clear. Whether the whole proceeding was not illegal, is a question. But it is certain that, whatever may have been, according to technical rules of construction, the effect of the statute under which the trial took place, it was most unjust to hang a Hindoo for forgery. The law which made forgery capital in England was passed without the smallest reference to the state of society in India. It was unknown to the natives of India. It had never been put in execution among them, certainly not for want of delinquents. It was in the highest degree shocking to all their notions. They were not accustomed to the distinction which many circumstances, peculiar to our own state of society, have led us to make between forgery and other kinds of cheating. The counterfeiting of a seal was, in their estimation, a common act of swindling; nor had it ever crossed their minds that it was to be punished as severely as gang-robbery or assassination. A just judge would, beyond all doubt, have reserved the case for the consideration of the sovereign. But Impey would not hear of mercy or delay.

The excitement among all classes was great. Francis and Francis's few English adherents described the Governor-General and the Chief Justice as the worst of murderers. Clavering, it was said, swore that, even at the foot of the gallows, Nuncomar should be rescued. The bulk of the European society, though strongly attached to the Governor-General, could not but feel compassion for a man who, with all his crimes, had so long filled so large a space in their sight, who had been great and powerful before the British empire in India began to exist, and to whom, in the old times, governors and members of council, then mere commercial factors, had paid court for protection. The feeling of the Hindoos was infinitely stronger. They were, indeed, not a people to strike one blow for their countryman. But his sentence filled them with sorrow and dismay. Tried even by their low standard of morality, he was a bad man. But, bad as he was, he was the head of their race and religion, a Brahmin of the Brahmins. He had inherited the purest and highest caste. He had practised with the greatest punctuality all those ceremonies to which the superstitious Bengalees ascribe far more importance than to the correct discharge of the social duties. They felt, therefore, as a devout Catholic in the dark ages would have felt, at seeing a prelate of the highest dignity sent to the gallows by a secular tribunal. According to their old national laws, a Brahmin could not be put to death for any crime whatever. And the crime for which Nuncomar was about to die was regarded by them in much the same light in which the selling of an unsound horse, for a sound price, is regarded by a Yorkshire jockey.

The Mussulmans alone appear to have seen with exultation the fate of the powerful Hindoo, who had attempted to rise by means of the ruin of Mahommed Reza Khan. The Mahommedan historian of those times takes delight in aggravating the charge. He assures us that in Nuncomar's house a casket was found containing counterfeits of the seals of all the richest men of the province. We have never fallen in with any other authority for this story, which in itself is by no means improbable.

The day drew near; and Nuncomar prepared himself to die with that quiet fortitude with which the Bengalee, so effeminately timid in personal conflict, often encounters calamities for which there is no remedy. The sheriff, with the humanity which is seldom wanting in an English gentleman, visited the prisoner on the eve of the execution, and assured him that no indulgence, consistent with the law, should be refused to him. Nuncomar expressed his gratitude with great politeness and unaltered composure. Not a muscle of his face moved. Not a sigh broke from him. He put his finger to his forehead, and calmly said that fate would have its way, and that there was no resisting the pleasure of God. He sent his compliments to Francis, Clavering, and Monson, and charged them to protect Rajah Goordas who was about to become the head of the Brahmins of Bengal. The sheriff withdrew, greatly agitated by what had passed, and Nuncomar sat composedly down to write notes and examine accounts.

The next morning, before the sun was in his power, an immense concourse assembled round the place where the gallows had been set up. Grief and horror were on every face; yet to the last the multitude could hardly believe that the English really purposed to take the life of the great Brahmin. At length the mournful procession came through the crowd. Nuncomar sat up in his palanquin, and looked round him with unaltered serenity. He had just parted from those who were most nearly connected with him. Their cries and contortions had appalled the European ministers of justice, but had not produced the smallest effect on the iron stoicism of the prisoner. The only anxiety which he expressed was that men of his own priestly caste might be in attendance to take charge of his corpse. He again desired to be remembered to his friends in the Council, mounted the scaffold with firmness, and gave the signal to the executioner. The moment that the drop fell, a howl of sorrow and despair rose from the innumerable spectators. Hundreds turned away their faces from the polluting sight, fled with loud wailings towards the Hoogley, and plunged into its holy waters, as if to purify themselves from the guilt of having looked on such a crime. These feelings were not confined to Calcutta. The whole province was greatly excited; and the population of Dacca, in particular, gave strong signs of grief and dismay.

Of Impey's conduct it is impossible to speak too severely. We have already said that, in our opinion, he acted unjustly in refusing to respite Nuncomar. No rational man can doubt that he took this course in order to gratify the Governor-General. If we had ever had any doubts on that point, they would have been dispelled by a letter which Mr. Gleig has published. Hastings, three or four years later, described Impey as the man "to whose support he was at one time indebted for the safety of his fortune, honour, and reputation." These strong words can refer only to the case of Nuncomar; and they must mean that Impey hanged Nuncomar in order to support Hastings. It is, therefore, our deliberate opinion that Impey, sitting as a judge, put a man unjustly to death in order to serve a political purpose.

But we look on the conduct of Hastings in a somewhat different light. He was struggling for fortune, honour, liberty, all that makes life valuable. He was beset by rancorous and unprincipled enemies.

From his colleagues he could expect no justice. He cannot be blamed for wishing to crush his accusers. He was indeed bound to use only legitimate means for that end. But it was not strange that he should have thought any means legitimate which were pronounced legitimate by the sages of the law, by men whose peculiar duty it was to deal justly between adversaries, and whose education might be supposed to have peculiarly qualified them for the discharge of that duty. Nobody demands from a party the unbending equity of a judge. The reason that judges are appointed is, that even a good man cannot be trusted to decide a cause in which he is himself concerned. Not a day passes on which an honest prosecutor does not ask for what none but a dishonest tribunal would grant. It is too much to expect that any man, when his dearest interests are at stake, and his strongest passions excited, will, as against himself, be more just than the sworn dispensers of justice. To take an analogous case from the history of our own island: suppose that Lord Stafford, when in the Tower on suspicion of being concerned in the Popish plot, had been apprised that Titus Oates had done something which might, by a questionable construction, be brought under the head of felony. Should we severely blame Lord Stafford, in the supposed case, for causing a prosecution to be instituted, for furnishing funds, for using all his influence to intercept the mercy of the Crown? We think not. If a judge, indeed, from favour to the Catholic lords, were to strain the law in order to hang Oates, such a judge would richly deserve impeachment. But it does not appear to us that the Catholic lord, by bringing the case before the judge for decision, would materially overstep the limits of a just self-defence.

While, therefore, we have not the least doubt that this memorable execution is to be attributed to Hastings, we doubt whether it can with justice be reckoned among his crimes. That his conduct was dictated by a profound policy is evident. He was in a minority in Council. It was possible that he might long be in a minority. He knew the native character well. He knew in what abundance accusations are certain to flow in against the most innocent inhabitant of India who is under the frown of power. There was not in the whole black population of Bengal a place-holder, a place-hunter, a government tenant, who did not think that he might better himself by sending up a deposition against the Governor-General. Under these circumstances, the persecuted statesman resolved to teach the whole crew of accusers and witnesses that, though in a minority at the council board, he was still to be feared. The lesson which he gave them was indeed a lesson not to be forgotten. The head of the combination which had been formed against him, the richest, the most powerful, the most artful, of the Hindoos, distinguished by the favour of those who then held the government, fenced round by the superstitious reverence of millions, was hanged in broad day before many thousands of people. Every thing that could make the warning impressive, dignity in the sufferer, solemnity in the proceeding, was found in this case. The helpless rage and vain struggles of the Council made the triumph more signal. From that moment the conviction of every native was that it was safer to take the part of Hastings in a minority than that of Francis in a majority, and that he who was so venturous as to join in running down the Governor-General might chance, in the phrase of the Eastern poet, to find a tiger, while beating the jungle for a deer. The voices of a thousand informers were silenced in an instant. From that time, whatever difficulties Hastings might have to encounter, he was never molested by accusations from natives of India.

It is a remarkable circumstance that one of the letters of Hastings to Dr. Johnson bears date a very few hours after the death of Nuncomar. While the whole settlement was in commotion, while a mighty and ancient priesthood were weeping over the remains of their chief, the conqueror in that deadly grapple sat down, with characteristic self-possession, to write about the Tour to the Hebrides, Jones's Persian Grammar, and the history, traditions, arts, and natural productions of India.

In the mean time, intelligence of the Rohilla war, and of the first disputes between Hastings and his colleagues, had reached London. The directors took part with the majority, and sent out a letter filled with severe reflections on the conduct of Hastings. They condemned, in strong but just terms, the iniquity of undertaking offensive wars merely for the sake of pecuniary advantages. But they utterly forgot that, if Hastings had by illicit means obtained pecuniary advantages, he had done so, not for his own benefit, but in order to meet their demands. To enjoin honesty, and to insist on having what could not be honestly got, was then the constant practice of the Company. As Lady Macbeth says of her husband, they "would not play false, and yet would wrongly win."

The Regulating Act, by which Hastings had been appointed Governor-General for five years, empowered the Crown to remove him on an address from the Company. Lord North was desirous to procure such an address. The three members of Council who had been sent out from England were men of his own choice. General Clavering, in particular, was supported by a large parliamentary connexion, such as no cabinet could be inclined to disoblige. The wish of the minister was to displace Hastings, and to put Clavering at the head of the government. In the Court of Directors parties were very nearly balanced. Eleven voted against Hastings; ten for him. The Court of Proprietors was then convened. The great sale-room presented a singular appearance. Letters had been sent by the Secretary of the Treasury, exhorting all the supporters of government who held India stock to be in attendance. Lord Sandwich marshalled the friends of the administration with his usual dexterity and alertness. Fifty peers and privy-councillors, seldom seen so far eastward, were counted in the crowd. The debate lasted till midnight. The opponents of Hastings had a small superiority on the division; but a ballot was demanded; and the result was that the Governor-General triumphed by a majority of above a hundred votes over the combined efforts of the directors and the cabinet. The ministers were greatly exasperated by this defeat. Even Lord North lost his temper, no ordinary occurrence with him, and threatened to convoke parliament before Christmas, and to bring in a bill for depriving the Company of all political power, and for restricting it to its old business of trading in silks and teas.

Colonel Macleane, who through all this conflict had zealously supported the cause of Hastings, now thought that his employer was in imminent danger of being turned out, branded with parliamentary censure, perhaps prosecuted. The opinion of the crown lawyers had already been taken respecting some parts of the Governor-General's conduct. It seemed to be high time to think of securing an honourable retreat. Under these circumstances, Macleane thought himself justified in producing the resignation with which he had been intrusted. The instrument was not in very accurate form; but the directors were too eager to be scrupulous. They accepted the resignation, fixed on Mr. Wheler, one of their own body, to succeed Hastings, and sent out orders that General Clavering, as senior member of Council, should exercise the functions of Governor-General till Mr. Wheler should arrive.

But, while these things were passing in England, a great change had taken place in Bengal. Monson was no more. Only four members of the government were left. Clavering and Francis were on one side, Barwell and the Governor-General on the other; and the Governor-General had the casting vote. Hastings, who had been during two years destitute of all power and patronage, became at once absolute. He instantly proceeded to retaliate on his adversaries. Their measures were reversed: their creatures were displaced. A new valuation of the lands of Bengal, for the purposes of taxation, was ordered; and it was provided that the whole inquiry should be conducted by the Governor-General, and that all the letters relating to it should run in his name. He began, at the same time, to revolve vast plans of conquest and dominion, plans which he lived to see realised, though not by himself. His project was to form subsidiary alliances with the native princes, particularly with those of Oude and Berar, and thus to make Britain the paramount power in India. While he was meditating these great designs, arrived the intelligence that he had ceased to be Governor-General, that his resignation had been accepted, that Wheler was coming out immediately, and that, till Wheler arrived, the chair was to be filled by Clavering.

Had Hastings still been in a minority, he would probably have retired without a struggle; but he was now the real master of British India, and he was not disposed to quit his high place. He asserted that he had never given any instructions which could warrant the steps taken at home. What his instructions had been, he owned he had forgotten. If he had kept a copy of them he had mislaid it. But he was certain that he had repeatedly declared to the Directors that he would not resign. He could not see how the court, possessed of that declaration from himself, could receive his resignation from the doubtful hands of an agent. If the resignation were invalid, all the proceedings which were founded on that resignation were null, and Hastings was still Governor-General.

He afterwards affirmed that, though his agents had not acted in conformity with his instructions, he would nevertheless have held himself bound by their acts, if Clavering had not attempted to seize the supreme power by violence. Whether this assertion were or were not true, it cannot be doubted that the imprudence of Clavering gave Hastings an advantage. The General sent for the keys of the fort and of the treasury, took possession of the records, and held a council at which Francis attended. Hastings took the chair in another apartment, and Barwell sat with him. Each of the two parties had a plausible show of right. There was no authority entitled to their obedience within fifteen thousand miles. It seemed that there remained no way of settling the dispute except an appeal to arms; and from such an appeal Hastings, confident of his influence over his countrymen in India, was not inclined to shrink. He directed the officers of the garrison of Fort William and of all the neighbouring stations to obey no orders but his. At the same time, with admirable judgment, he offered to submit the case to the Supreme Court, and to abide by its decision. By making this proposition he risked nothing; yet it was a proposition which his opponents could hardly reject. Nobody could be treated as a criminal for obeying what the judges should solemnly pronounce to be the lawful government. The boldest man would shrink from taking arms in defence of what the judges should pronounce to be usurpation. Clavering and Francis, after some delay, unwillingly consented to abide by the award of the court. The court pronounced that the resignation was invalid, and that therefore Hastings was still Governor-General under the Regulating Act; and the defeated members of the Council, finding that the sense of the whole settlement was against them, acquiesced in the decision.

About this time arrived the news that, after a suit which had lasted several years, the Franconian courts had decreed a divorce between Imhoff and his wife. The Baron left Calcutta, carrying with him the means of buying an estate in Saxony. The lady became Mrs. Hastings. The event was celebrated by great festivities; and all the most conspicuous persons at Calcutta, without distinction of parties, were invited to the Government-house. Clavering, as the Mahommedan chronicler tells the story, was sick in mind and body, and excused himself from joining the splendid assembly. But Hastings whom, as it should seem, success in ambition and in love had put into high good-humour, would take no denial. He went himself to the General's house, and at length brought his vanquished rival in triumph to the gay circle which surrounded the bride. The exertion was too much for a frame broken by mortification as well as by disease. Clavering died a few days later.

Wheler, who came out expecting to be Governor-General, and was forced to content himself with a seat at the Council Board, generally voted with Francis. But the Governor-General, with Barwell's help and his own casting vote, was still the master. Some change took place at this time in the feeling both of the Court of Directors and of the Ministers of the Crown. All designs against Hastings were dropped; and, when his original term of five years expired, he was quietly reappointed. The truth is that the fearful dangers to which the public interests in every quarter were now exposed made both Lord North and the Company unwilling to part with a Governor whose talents, experience, and resolution, enmity itself was compelled to acknowledge.

The crisis was indeed formidable. That great and victorious empire, on the throne of which George the Third had taken his seat eighteen years before, with brighter hopes than had attended the accession of any of the long line of English sovereigns, had, by the most senseless misgovernment, been brought to the verge of ruin. In America millions of Englishmen were at war with the country from which their blood, their language, their religion, and their institutions were derived, and to which, but a short time before, they had been as strongly attached as the inhabitants of Norfolk and Leicestershire. The great powers of Europe, humbled to the dust by the vigour and genius which had guided the councils of George the Second, now rejoiced in the prospect of a signal revenge. The time was approaching when our island, while struggling to keep down the United States of America, and pressed with a still nearer danger by the too just discontents of Ireland, was to be assailed by France, Spain, and Holland, and to be threatened by the armed neutrality of the Baltic; when even our maritime supremacy was to be in jeopardy; when hostile fleets were to command the Straits of Calpe and the Mexican Sea; when the British flag was to be scarcely able to protect the British Channel. Great as were the faults of Hastings, it was happy for our country that at that conjuncture, the most terrible through which she has ever passed, he was the ruler of her Indian dominions.

An attack by sea on Bengal was little to be apprehended. The danger was that the European enemies of England might form an alliance with some native power, might furnish that power with troops, arms, and ammunition, and might thus assail our possessions on the side of the land. It was chiefly from the Mahrattas that Hastings anticipated danger. The original seat of that singular people was the wild range of hills which runs along the western coast of India. In the reign of Aurungzebe the inhabitants of those regions, led by the great Sevajee, began to descend on the possessions of their wealthier and less warlike neighbours. The energy, ferocity, and cunning of the Mahrattas, soon made them the most conspicuous among the new powers which were generated by the corruption of the decaying monarchy. At first they were only robbers. They soon rose to the dignity of conquerors. Half the provinces of the empire were turned into Mahratta principalities. Freebooters, sprung from low castes, and accustomed to menial employments, became mighty Rajahs. The Bonslas, at the head of a band of plunderers, occupied the vast region of Berar. The Guicowar, which is, being interpreted, the Herdsman, founded that dynasty which still reigns in Guzerat. The houses of Scindia and Holkar waxed great in Malwa. One adventurous captain made his nest on the impregnable rock of Gooti. Another became the lord of the thousand villages which are scattered among the green rice-fields of Tanjore.

That was the time, throughout India, of double government. The form and the power were every where separated. The Mussulman nabobs who had become sovereign princes, the Vizier in Oude, and the Nizam at Hyderabad, still called themselves the viceroys of the house of Tamerlane. In the same manner the Mahratta states, though really independent of each other, pretended to be members of one empire. They all acknowledged, by words and ceremonies, the supremacy of the heir of Sevajee, a *roi fainéant* who chewed bang and toyed with dancing girls in a state prison at Sattara, and of his Peshwa or mayor of the palace, a great hereditary magistrate, who kept a court with kingly state at Poonah, and whose authority was obeyed in the spacious provinces of Aurungabad and Bejapoor.

Some months before war was declared in Europe, the government of Bengal was alarmed by the news that a French adventurer, who passed for a man of quality, had arrived at Poonah. It was said that he had been received there with great distinction, that he had delivered to the Peshwa letters and presents from Louis the Sixteenth, and that a treaty, hostile to England, had been concluded between France and the Mahrattas.

Hastings immediately resolved to strike the first blow. The title of the Peshwa was not undisputed. A portion of the Mahratta nation was favourable to a pretender. The Governor-General determined to espouse this pretender's interest, to move an army across the peninsula of India, and to form a close alliance with the chief of the house of Bonsla, who ruled Berar, and who, in power and dignity, was inferior to none of the Mahratta princes.

The army had marched, and the negotiations with Berar were in progress, when a letter from the English consul at Cairo brought the news that war had been proclaimed both in London and Paris. All the measures which the crisis required were adopted by Hastings without a moment's delay. The French factories in Bengal were seized. Orders were sent to Madras that Pondicherry should instantly be occupied. Near Calcutta, works were thrown up which were thought to render the approach of a hostile force impossible. A maritime establishment was formed for the defence of the river. Nine new battalions of sepoys were raised, and a corps of native artillery was formed out of the hardy Lascars of the Bay of Bengal. Having made these arrangements, the Governor-General with calm confidence pronounced his presidency secure from all attack, unless the Mahrattas should march against it in conjunction with the French.

The expedition which Hastings had sent westward was not so speedily or completely successful as most of his undertakings. The commanding officer procrastinated. The authorities at Bombay blundered. But the Governor-General persevered. A new commander repaired the errors of his predecessor. Several brilliant actions spread the military renown of the English through regions where no European flag had ever been seen. It is probable that, if a new and more formidable danger had not compelled Hastings to change his whole policy, his plans respecting the Mahratta empire would have been carried into complete effect.

The authorities in England had wisely sent out to Bengal, as commander of the forces and member of the council, one of the most distinguished soldiers of that time. Sir Eyre Coote had, many years before, been conspicuous among the founders of the British empire in the East. At the council of war which preceded the battle of Plassey, he earnestly recommended, in opposition to the majority, that daring course which, after some hesitation, was adopted, and which was crowned with such splendid success. He subsequently commanded in the south of India against the brave and unfortunate Lally, gained the decisive battle of Wandewash over the French and their native allies, took Pondicherry, and made the English power supreme in the Carnatic. Since those great exploits near twenty years had elapsed. Coote had no longer the bodily activity which he had shown in earlier days; nor was the vigour of his mind altogether unimpaired. He was capricious and fretful, and required much coaxing to keep him in good-humour. It must, we fear, be added that the love of money had grown upon him, and that he thought more about his allowances, and less about his duties, than might have been expected from so eminent a member of so noble a profession. Still he was perhaps the ablest officer that was then to be found in the British army. Among the native soldiers his name was great and his influence unrivalled. Nor is he yet forgotten by them. Now and then a white-bearded old sepoy may still be found, who loves to talk of Porto Novo and Pollilore. It is but a short time since one of those aged men came to present a memorial to an English officer, who holds one of the highest employments in India. A print of Coote hung in the room. The veteran recognised at once that face and figure which he had not seen for more than half a century, and, forgetting his salam to the living, halted, drew himself up, lifted his hand, and with solemn reverence paid his military obeisance to the dead.

Coote, though he did not, like Barwell, vote constantly with the Governor-General, was by no means inclined to join in systematic opposition, and on most questions concurred with Hastings, who did his best, by assiduous courtship, and by readily granting the most exorbitant allowances, to gratify the strongest passions of the old soldier.

It seemed likely at this time that a general reconciliation would put an end to the quarrels which had, during some years, weakened and disgraced the government of Bengal. The dangers of the empire might well induce men of patriotic feeling,—and of patriotic feeling neither Hastings nor Francis was destitute,—to forget private enmities, and to cooperate heartily for the general good. Coote had never been concerned in faction. Wheler was thoroughly tired of it. Barwell had made an ample fortune, and, though he had promised that he would not leave Calcutta while his help was needed in Council, was most desirous to return to England, and exerted himself to promote an arrangement which would set him at liberty. A compact was made, by which Francis agreed to desist from opposition, and Hastings engaged that the friends of Francis should be admitted to a fair share of the honours and emoluments of the service. During a few months after this treaty there was apparent harmony at the council-board.

Harmony, indeed, was never more necessary; for at this moment internal calamities, more formidable than war itself, menaced Bengal. The authors of the Regulating Act of 1773 had established two independent powers, the one judicial, the other political; and, with a carelessness scandalously common in English legislation, had omitted to define the limits of either. The judges took advantage of the indistinctness, and attempted to draw to themselves supreme authority, not only within Calcutta, but through the whole of the great territory subject to the presidency of Fort William. There are few Englishmen who will not admit that the English law, in spite of modern improvements, is neither so cheap nor so speedy as might be wished. Still, it is a system which has grown up among us. In some points, it has been fashioned to suit our feelings; in others, it has gradually fashioned our feelings to suit itself. Even to its worst evils we are accustomed; and therefore, though we may complain of them, they do not strike us with the horror and dismay which would be produced by a new grievance of smaller severity. In India the case is widely different. English law, transplanted to that country, has all the vices from which we suffer here; it has them all in a far higher degree; and it has other vices, compared with which the worst vices from which we suffer are trifles. Dilatory here, it is far more dilatory in a land where the help of an interpreter is needed by every judge and by every advocate. Costly here, it is far more costly in a land into which the legal practitioners must be imported from an immense distance. All English labour in India, from the labour of the Governor-General and the Commander-in-Chief, down to that of a groom or a watchmaker, must be paid for at a higher rate than at home. No man will be banished, and banished to the torrid zone, for nothing. The rule holds good with respect to the legal profession. No English barrister will work, fifteen thousand miles from all his friends, with the thermometer at ninety-six in the shade, for the emoluments which will content him in Chambers that overlook the Thames. Accordingly, the fees at Calcutta are about three times as great as the fees of Westminster Hall; and this, though the people of India are, beyond all comparison, poorer than the people of England. Yet the delay and the expense, grievous as they are, form the smallest part of the evil which English law, imported without modifications into India, could not fail to produce. The strongest feelings of our nature, honour, religion, female modesty, rose up against the innovation. Arrest on mesne process was the first step in most civil proceedings; and to a native of rank arrest was not merely a restraint, but a foul personal indignity. Oaths were required in every stage of every suit; and the feeling of a quaker about an oath is hardly stronger than that of a respectable native. That the apartments of a woman of quality should be entered by strange men, or that her face should be seen by them, are, in the East, intolerable outrages, outrages which are more dreaded than death, and which can be expiated only by the shedding of blood. To these outrages the most distinguished families of Bengal, Bahar, and Orissa, were now exposed. Imagine what the state of our own country would be, if a jurisprudence were on a sudden introduced among us, which should be to us what our jurisprudence was to our Asiatic subjects. Imagine what the state of our country would be, if it were enacted that any man, by merely swearing that a debt was due to him, should acquire a right to insult the persons of men of the most honourable and sacred callings and of women of the most shrinking delicacy, to horsewhip a general officer, to put a bishop in the stocks, to treat ladies in the way which called forth the blow of Wat Tyler. Something like this was the effect of the attempt which the Supreme Court made to extend its jurisdiction over the whole of the Company's territory.

A reign of terror began, of terror heightened by mystery; for even that which was endured was less horrible than that which was anticipated. No man knew what was next to be expected from this strange tribunal. It came from beyond the black water, as the people of India, with mysterious horror, call the sea. It consisted of judges not one of whom was familiar with the usages of the millions over whom they claimed boundless authority. Its records were kept in unknown characters; its sentences were pronounced in unknown sounds. It had already collected round itself an army of the worst part of the native population, informers, and false witnesses, and common barrators, and agents of chicane, and, above all, a banditti of bailiffs' followers, compared with whom the retainers of the worst English spunging-houses, in the worst times, might be considered as upright and tender-hearted. Many natives, highly considered among their countrymen, were seized, hurried up to Calcutta, flung into the common jail, not for any crime even imputed, not for any debt that had been proved, but merely as a precaution till their cause should come to trial. There were instances in which men of the most venerable dignity, persecuted without a cause by extortioners, died of rage and shame in the gripe of the vile alguazils of Impey. The harams of noble Mahommedans, sanctuaries respected in the East by governments which respected nothing else, were burst open by gangs of bailiffs. The Mussulmans, braver and less accustomed to submission than the Hindoos, sometimes stood on their defence; and there were instances in which they shed their blood in the doorway, while defending, sword in hand, the sacred apartments of their women. Nay, it seemed as if even the faint-hearted Bengalee, who had crouched at the feet of Surajah Dowlah, who had been mute during the administration of Vansittart, would at length find courage in despair. No Mahratta invasion had ever spread through the province such dismay as this inroad of English lawyers. All the injustice of former oppressors, Asiatic and European, appeared as a blessing when compared with the justice of the Supreme Court.

Every class of the population, English and native, with the exception of the ravenous pettifoggers who fattened on the misery and terror of an immense community, cried out loudly against this fearful oppression. But the judges were immoveable. If a bailiff was resisted, they ordered the soldiers to be called out. If a servant of the Company, in conformity with the orders of the government, withstood the miserable catchpoles who, with Impey's writs in their hands, exceeded the insolence and rapacity of gang-robbers, he was flung into prison for a contempt. The lapse of sixty years, the virtue and wisdom of many eminent magistrates who have during that time administered justice in the Supreme Court, have not effaced from the minds of the people of Bengal the recollection of those evil days.

The members of the government were, on this subject, united as one man. Hastings had courted the judges; he had found them useful instruments. But he was not disposed to make them his own masters, or the masters of India. His mind was large; his knowledge of the native character most accurate. He saw that the system pursued by the Supreme Court was degrading to the government and ruinous to the people; and he resolved to oppose it manfully. The consequence was, that the friendship, if that be the proper word for such a connexion, which had existed between him and Impey, was for a time completely dissolved. The government placed itself firmly between the tyrannical tribunal and the people. The Chief Justice proceeded to the wildest excesses. The Governor-General and all the members of Council were served with writs, calling on them to appear before the King's justices, and to answer for their public acts. This was too much. Hastings, with just scorn, refused to obey the call, set at liberty the persons wrongfully detained by the Court, and took measures for resisting the outrageous proceedings of the sheriffs' officers, if necessary, by the sword. But he had in view another device which might prevent the necessity of an appeal to arms. He was seldom at a loss for an expedient; and he knew Impey well. The expedient, in this case, was a very simple one, neither more nor less than a bribe. Impey was, by act of Parliament, a judge, independent of the government of Bengal, and entitled to a salary of eight thousand a-year. Hastings proposed to make him also a judge in the Company's service, removable at the pleasure of the government of Bengal; and to give him, in that capacity, about eight thousand a-year more. It was understood that, in consideration of this new salary, Impey would desist from urging the high pretensions of his court. If he did urge these pretensions, the government could, at a moment's notice, eject him from the new place which had been created for him. The bargain was struck; Bengal was saved; an appeal to force was averted; and the Chief Justice was rich, quiet, and infamous.

Of Impey's conduct it is unnecessary to speak. It was of a piece with almost every part of his conduct that comes under the notice of history. No other such judge has dishonoured the English ermine, since Jefferies drank himself to death in the Tower. But we cannot agree with those who have blamed Hastings for this transaction. The case stood thus. The negligent manner in which the Regulating Act had been framed put it in the power of the Chief Justice to throw a great country into the most dreadful confusion. He was determined to use his power to the utmost, unless he was paid to be still; and Hastings consented to pay him. The necessity was to be deplored. It is also to be deplored that pirates should be able to exact ransom, by threatening to make their captives walk the plank. But to ransom a captive from pirates has always been held a humane and Christian act; and it would be absurd to charge the payer of the ransom with corrupting the virtue of the corsair. This, we seriously think, is a not unfair illustration of the relative position of Impey, Hastings, and the people of India. Whether it was right in Impey to demand or to accept a price for powers which, if they really belonged to him, he could not abdicate, which, if they did not belong to him, he ought never to have usurped, and which in neither case he could honestly sell, is one question. It is quite another question, whether Hastings was not right to give any sum, however large, to any man, however worthless, rather than either surrender millions of human beings to pillage, or rescue them by civil war.

Francis strongly opposed this arrangement. It may, indeed, be suspected that personal aversion to Impey was as strong a motive with Francis as regard for the welfare of the province. To a mind burning with resentment it might seem better to leave Bengal to the oppressors than to redeem it by enriching them. It is not improbable, on the other hand, that Hastings may have been the more willing to resort to an expedient agreeable to the Chief Justice, because that high functionary had already been so serviceable, and might, when existing dissensions were composed, be serviceable again.

But it was not on this point alone that Francis was now opposed to Hastings. The peace between them proved to be only a short and hollow truce, during which their mutual aversion was constantly becoming stronger. At length an explosion took place. Hastings publicly charged Francis with having deceived him, and with having induced Barwell to quit the service by insincere promises. Then came a dispute, such as frequently arises even between honourable men, when they may make important agreements by mere verbal communication. An impartial historian will probably be of opinion that they had misunderstood each other; but their minds were so much embittered that they imputed to each other nothing less than deliberate villany. "I do not," said Hastings, in a minute recorded on the Consultations of the Government, "I do not trust to Mr. Francis's promises of candour, convinced that he is incapable of it. I judge of his public conduct by his private, which I have found to be void of truth and honour." After the Council had risen, Francis put a challenge into the Governor-General's hand. It was instantly accepted. They met, and fired. Francis was shot through the body. He was carried to a neighbouring house, where it appeared that the wound, though severe, was not mortal. Hastings inquired repeatedly after his enemy's health, and proposed to call on him; but Francis coldly declined the visit. He had a proper sense, he said, of the Governor-General's politeness, but could not consent to any private interview. They could meet only at the Council-board.

In a very short time it was made signally manifest to how great a danger the Governor-General had, on this occasion, exposed his country. A crisis arrived with which he, and he alone, was competent to deal. It is not too much to say that, if he had been taken from the head of affairs, the years 1780 and 1781 would have been as fatal to our power in Asia as to our power in America.

The Mahrattas had been the chief objects of apprehension to Hastings. The measures which he had adopted for the purpose of breaking their power, had at first been frustrated by the errors of those whom he was compelled to employ; but his perseverance and ability seemed likely to be crowned with success, when a far more formidable danger showed itself in a distant quarter.

About thirty years before this time, a Mahommedan soldier had begun to distinguish himself in the wars of Southern India. His education had been neglected; his extraction was humble. His father had been a petty officer of revenue; his grandfather a wandering dervise. But though thus meanly descended, though ignorant even of the alphabet, the adventurer had no sooner been placed at the head of a body of troops than he approved himself a man born for conquest and command. Among the crowd of chiefs who were struggling for a share of India, none could compare with him in the qualities of the captain and the statesman. He became a general; he became a sovereign. Out of the fragments of old principalities, which had gone to pieces in the general wreck, he formed for himself a great, compact, and vigorous empire. That empire he ruled with the ability, severity, and vigilance of Louis the Eleventh. Licentious in his pleasures, implacable in his revenge, he had yet enlargement of mind enough to perceive how much the prosperity of subjects adds to the strength of governments. He was an oppressor; but he had at least the merit of protecting his people against all oppression except his own. He was now in extreme old age; but his intellect was as clear, and his spirit as high, as in the prime of manhood. Such was the great Hyder Ali, the founder of the Mahommedan kingdom of Mysore, and the most formidable enemy with whom the English conquerors of India have ever had to contend.

Had Hastings been governor of Madras, Hyder would have been either made a friend, or vigorously encountered as an enemy.

Unhappily the English authorities in the south provoked their powerful neighbour's hostility, without being prepared to repel it. On a sudden, an army of ninety thousand men, far superior in discipline and efficiency to any other native force that could be found in India, came pouring through those wild passes which, worn by mountain torrents, and dark with jungle, lead down from the table-land of Mysore to the plains of the Carnatic. This great army was accompanied by a hundred pieces of cannon; and its movements were guided by many French officers, trained in the best military schools of Europe.

Hyder was every where triumphant. The sepoys in many British garrisons flung down their arms. Some forts were surrendered by treachery, and some by despair. In a few days the whole open country north of the Coleroon had submitted. The English inhabitants of Madras could already see by night, from the top of Mount St. Thomas, the eastern sky reddened by a vast semicircle of blazing villages. The white villas, to which our countrymen retire after the daily labours of government and of trade, when the cool evening breeze springs up from the bay, were now left without inhabitants; for bands of the fierce horsemen of Mysore had already been seen prowling among the tulip-trees, and near the gay verandas. Even the town was not thought secure, and the British merchants and public functionaries made haste to crowd themselves behind the cannon of Fort St. George.

There were the means indeed of assembling an army which might have defended the presidency, and even driven the invader back to his mountains. Sir Hector Munro was at the head of one considerable force; Baillie was advancing with another. United, they might have presented a formidable front even to such an enemy as Hyder. But the English commanders, neglecting those fundamental rules of the military art of which the propriety is obvious even to men who have never received a military education, deferred their junction, and were separately attacked. Baillie's detachment was destroyed. Munro was forced to abandon his baggage, to fling his guns into the tanks, and to save himself by a retreat which might be called a flight. In three weeks from the commencement of the war, the British empire in southern India had been brought to the verge of ruin. Only a few fortified places remained to us. The glory of our arms had departed. It was known that a great French expedition might soon be expected on the coast of Coromandel. England, beset by enemies on every side, was in no condition to protect such remote dependencies.

Then it was that the fertile genius and serene courage of Hastings